Capitalism and the Emergence of
Civic Equality in Eighteenth-Century France

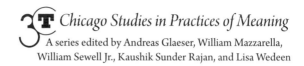

Chicago Studies in Practices of Meaning
A series edited by Andreas Glaeser, William Mazzarella,
William Sewell Jr., Kaushik Sunder Rajan, and Lisa Wedeen

Published in collaboration with the Chicago Center for Contemporary Theory
http://ccct.uchicago.edu

RECENT BOOKS IN THE SERIES

Routine Crisis: An Ethnography of Disillusion
by Sarah Muir

Justice Is an Option: A Democratic Theory of
Finance for the Twenty-First Century
by Robert Meister

Authoritarian Apprehensions: Ideology,
Judgment, and Mourning in Syria
by Lisa Wedeen

Deadline: Populism and the Press in Venezuela
by Robert Samet

Guerrilla Marketing: Counterinsurgency
and Capitalism in Colombia
by Alexander L. Fattal

What Nostalgia Was: War, Empire,
and the Time of a Deadly Emotion
by Thomas Dodman

The Mana of Mass Society
by William Mazzarella

The Sins of the Fathers: Germany, Memory, Method
by Jeffrey K. Olick

The Politics of Dialogic Imagination: Power
and Popular Culture in Early Modern Japan
by Katsuya Hirano

American Value: Migrants, Money, and
Meaning in El Salvador and the United States
by David Pedersen

Capitalism and the Emergence of Civic Equality in Eighteenth-Century France

WILLIAM H. SEWELL JR.

The University of Chicago Press CHICAGO AND LONDON

The University of Chicago Press, Chicago 60637
The University of Chicago Press, Ltd., London
© 2021 by The University of Chicago
Published 2021
Printed in the United States of America

30 29 28 27 26 25 24 23 22 21   1 2 3 4 5

ISBN-13: 978-0-226-77032-1 (cloth)
ISBN-13: 978-0-226-77046-8 (paper)
ISBN-13: 978-0-226-77063-5 (e-book)
DOI: https://doi.org/10.7208/chicago/9780226770635.001.0001

Library of Congress Cataloging-in-Publication Data

Names: Sewell, William H., Jr., 1940– author.
Title: Capitalism and the emergence of civic equality in
eighteenth-century France / William H. Sewell, Jr.
Other titles: Capitalism and the emergence of civic equality in
18th century France | Chicago studies in practices of meaning.
Description: Chicago : University of Chicago Press, 2021. |
Series: Chicago studies in practices of meaning | Includes
bibliographical references and index.
Identifiers: LCCN 2020035444 | ISBN 9780226770321 (cloth)
| ISBN 9780226770468 (paperback) | ISBN 9780226770635
(ebook)
Subjects: LCSH: Equality—France—History—18th century.
| Social change—Economic aspects—France—History—18th
century. | Capitalism—France—History—18th century.
Classification: LCC HN440.S6 S49 2021 | DDC 305.50944—
dc23
LC record available at https://lccn.loc.gov/2020035444

For Jan

Contents

III. Royal Administration and the Promise of Political Economy

The French Revolution and the Shock of Civic Equality

All men are born and remain free and equal in rights.
Public distinctions may be founded only upon common utility. . . .
Law is an expression of the general will. . . . It must be the same for all,
whether it protects or punishes. All citizens, being equal in its eyes, are
equally admissible to all dignities, places, and public employment
according to their capacity and with no other distinction than
that of their virtues and their talents.

It is perhaps difficult to recognize, in the early twenty-first century, how
remarkable these words of the Declaration of the Rights of Man and
Citizen were when proclaimed by the French National Assembly on
September 26, 1789. Much of today's world takes formal constitutional
guarantees of civic equality for granted. And besides, we have realized
that formal equality before the law like that proclaimed in the declaration has proved compatible with shocking levels of real inequality—of
wealth, political power, recognition, and well-being—among the citizens
of modern democracies. But in 1789, in France, the Declaration of the
Rights of Man and Citizen was a thoroughly radical document. The revolution it announced astounded the Euro-American world and eventually
transformed political possibilities all around the globe. To grasp why the
Revolution's embrace of civic equality was such a transformative act, the
reader must understand the state and society in which it took place.[1]

Old regime France was profoundly hierarchical in both its formal

---

1. I adopt the French convention of capitalizing the word *revolution* when it refers
specifically to the French Revolution. I see this usage as indicating that in the eyes of the
French, the Revolution of 1789 remains the paradigmatic revolution. I develop an argument for its paradigmatic status in Sewell (1996).

structures and its daily practices. Everyone knows that France was a monarchical country and had a rich and powerful nobility. But the pervasiveness of social hierarchy went far deeper than the existence of king and nobles. It was built into legal, cultural, and social structures from the top to the bottom of the social order. Navigating one's path through life—whether as a great lord, a prosperous merchant, a struggling peasant, or an impoverished laundress or day laborer—required recognizing and working within universally acknowledged differences of status, power, and honor. In order to accomplish their goals in life, French men and women of all social descriptions had both to defend whatever social distinction they could claim for themselves and to act deferentially toward their superiors—relying upon the patronage of superiors in order to get ahead or to avoid setbacks. Establishing a state and society based on civic equality was therefore an extremely radical undertaking. It not only redefined political rights but also both dissolved and reconstituted social relations of all descriptions.

It is extremely rare for reasonably well-functioning societies to transform themselves so fundamentally. It is of course true that the French Revolution arose out of a serious political crisis. But the crisis leading to the French Revolution was not caused by regime-destroying military defeats of the sort that touched off the Russian Revolution of 1917, the German Revolution of 1918, or the Chinese Revolution of the late 1930s and 1940s. The crisis in France was not military but fiscal—by 1786, the state debt had grown so big that bankruptcy seemed imminent.[2] The debt was a consequence of the repeated and very expensive wars of the past century, but the most recent of these, the American Revolutionary War, had been a victory for France, not a defeat. By the end of 1786, it became clear that France would need to overhaul its fiscal system thoroughly, presumably subjecting the nobility, hitherto exempt from most taxes, to a greatly increased fiscal burden. The fiscal crisis eventually induced the king to call a meeting of the long-silenced Estates General, a body made up of representatives of the three estates of the realm—the clergy, the nobility, and the commoners or Third Estate—to find a solution. But there was no state failure in the run-up to the French Revolution. The state continued to perform its bureaucratic and military functions up to the taking of the Bastille in July 1789, and Louis XVI retained much of his popularity and prestige for many months thereafter. Why, then, did the French take this astonishingly bold leap into civic equality, a leap that, as it happened, launched an extended period of political strife

---

2. Here I disagree with Skocpol (1979).

and of civil and international warfare that eventually engulfed the entire continent?

It is certainly obvious that the egalitarian character of the French Revolution was powerfully influenced by Enlightenment discourses of reason and natural rights, which had gained wide currency in France over the course of the eighteenth century (Edelstein 2014). But this recognition raises a prior question: Why did these discourses find such resonance in a society constructed on the hierarchical principles of aristocracy, corporate privilege, patronage, and deference? Why, when the French monarchical state fell into severe financial and political crisis, did replacing the existing mode of government with a regime of civic equality emerge as an acceptable, even attractive, option to members of the Estates General—including many representatives of the clergy and the nobility whose extensive legal privileges were annihilated by the new legal and political regime?

During most of the twentieth century, the answer to these questions seemed obvious to most historians: it was that the rise of capitalism in the eighteenth century had in fact sapped the power of the monarchical and aristocratic social order and brought the bourgeoisie to a position of ever greater wealth and self-confidence. The Enlightenment was an idealized expression of the interests of this rising class, and when the fiscal and political crisis of the monarchy occurred, the bourgeoisie seized power and reconstructed the state around the principles that their philosophical spokesmen had already developed. This was the position elaborated most famously by the great French scholars of the Revolution Georges Lefebvre (1947) and Albert Soboul ([1962] 1975).

But since the later 1960s, this Marxist or Marxisant explanation has been thoroughly undermined by historical scholarship. Above all, it turned out to be impossible to find any coherent "revolutionary bourgeoisie" that seized power in 1789. As Elizabeth Eisenstein pointed out, when Georges Lefebvre, the greatest of the Marxisant historians, identified the leaders of what he termed the "bourgeois revolution," he named the comte de Mirabeau, the Marquis de Lafayette, and the abbé Sieyès—two nobles and an ecclesiastic (Eisenstein 1965, 69–71; Lefebvre 1947). Very few of the deputies of the Third Estate, who initially spearheaded the Revolution, were merchants or manufacturers: most were lawyers or lower-level state or municipal officers, by no stretch of the imagination capitalist entrepreneurs (Cobban 1968, 54–67; Tackett 1996, 35–39). Although commercial and industrial wealth did rise impressively in the eighteenth century, the fortunes of merchants and manufacturers generally remained far inferior to those of the upper nobility. Nobles still retained financial as well as social and political superiority in France.[3] Many of the wealthiest bourgeois actually used their fortunes to buy their way into the nobility, electing to join the aristocracy rather than to challenge it (Bien 1989). Moreover, it has long been clear that many nobles, clerics, and officers of the royal state were ardent participants, as both producers and consumers, in Enlightenment intellectual projects.[4] The celebrated salons in which the philosophes shone were generally directed by nobles and primarily populated by nobles. It is therefore not obvious that the Enlightenment should be characterized as a "bourgeois" project. In short, it is no longer plausible to explain the Revolution's establishment of civic equality as the product of a triumphant capitalist bourgeoisie.

Since the collapse of this once predominant Marxisant interpretation, most historians have attempted to explain the centrality of civic equality in the Revolution by some combination of intellectual and political processes. Work on the history of political culture, in particular, has done much to clarify the origins and development of key revolutionary ideas, including the idea of civic equality. With rare exceptions, this work has simply assumed that the question of economic causes of the Revolution has been definitively answered—in the negative.[5] Yet this assumption seems doubtful. After all, we know that the French economy grew significantly in the eighteenth century, especially in commerce and manufacturing. It hardly seems plausible that several decades of sustained economic growth would have had no effect on the way the French understood their social and political situation. Indeed, the bourgeoning of political economy as a literary genre in the prerevolutionary decades makes it clear that the French were passionately concerned about economic issues during that time. In the four decades before the Revolution, there were more political economy books published in France than novels—this in the century of the emergence of the novel as a major literary form (Shovlin 2006, 2).[6]

3. Tackett (1996) estimates that average incomes of noble deputies in the Estates General of 1789 were eight times those of Third Estate deputies.

4. Noble-born Enlightenment thinkers include the mathematician and philosopher marquis de Condorcet, the political economist and royal official Turgot, the physiocrat marquis de Mirabeau, the encyclopedist chevalier de Joucourt, and the political philosopher Montesquieu, a baron. Enlightenment clerics were legion—for example, the abbés Morellet, Raynal, Condillac, Coyer, Sieyès, and Mably.

5. The key text in the turn to political culture was Furet (1978, 1981). See also Ozouf (1976, 1988, 1989), Furet (1988, 1992), Furet and Ozouf (1989), Baker (1990), and Hunt (1984, 1992).

6. One measure of the significance of eighteenth-century French political-economic discourse is its effect on the vocabulary of economics, even in English. *Laissez-faire*

Recent scholarship on the discourse of French political economy makes it clear that writers were deeply concerned about how economic development, particularly the booming Atlantic trade and new patterns of urban consumption, was transforming the society and the state. Some political economists worried above all that the traditional aristocratic and monarchical constitution destined France to lose out to its more "republican" rivals—that is, the Netherlands and England—in the new and strategically crucial world maritime economy (Cheney 2010). Meanwhile, certain political economists also feared that the vogue for dazzling consumer goods was feminizing the nobility and sapping its traditional martial virtues—although others praised commerce and luxury production for their contribution to economic growth and for softening and polishing French manners (Shovlin 2006; Kwass 2003, 2004). The physiocrats, the best organized and most systematic of the political-economic schools, focused above all on agriculture, which they saw as the only genuine source of economic productivity. But they were also fervent advocates of free markets, favoring the abolition of guild regulations, monopolies, and restrictions on the market for grain (Vardi 2012; Fox-Genovese 1976). Whatever their particular doctrines or opinions, eighteenth-century French political economists clearly thought that burgeoning commercial capitalism posed important challenges to the traditional social and political order (Meyssonnier 1989; Perrot 1991; Larrère 1992; Shovlin 2006; Cheney 2010). If contemporaries were so clearly concerned about the consequences of economic changes, it seems downright perverse for historians of the Revolution to assume that such changes can safely be ignored.

This book argues that the notion of civic equality enunciated by the philosophes and built into the new regime launched in 1789 arose and was disseminated in response to the French experience of capitalism, although by a quite different process than the class struggle of the bourgeoisie against the nobility claimed by Lefebvre. It is controversial to claim that French economic development in the eighteenth century should be thought of as capitalist. The eighteenth-century term for the economic changes of this era—in France and elsewhere—was *commerce*. The rise of commerce, it was generally agreed, was a defining feature of the age. This was, to be sure, a commercial capitalism, but it nonetheless deserves the title "capitalism" because of its sustained dynamism, which was pow-

---

and *entrepreneur* were borrowed from the French, as was the term *economist*, originally used to designate the eighteenth-century French economic thinkers also known as physiocrats.

ered by the widespread and ever-increasing production of commodities for sale on the market. This commercial eighteenth-century capitalism was quite distinct from the factory-based industrial capitalism analyzed by Marx in the mid-nineteenth century. Although what we would call "industrial" activity certainly increased substantially in eighteenth-century France, most of this industrial production was strongly marked by commercial features. With rare exceptions, industrial goods were produced by hand in small workshops or in workers' domiciles. Indeed, in the textile industry, by far the biggest and one of the fastest-growing industries in the eighteenth century, most production actually took place in the countryside, where poor rural dwellers, some of them part-time peasants, spun and weaved in their homes. Although the textile producers were generally quite poor and were exploited very effectively by the merchants who supplied them with raw materials and marketed the products, they were not actually wage workers. Instead, the relations between capital and labor in this rapidly growing industry were commercial in character, formally governed by the purchase and sale of goods and regulated by credit, not by wage contracts. In the eighteenth century, before the spread of the mechanized factory, "commerce" seemed to contemporaries an adequate term for the manufacture as well as the buying and selling of goods.

But how did eighteenth-century capitalist development make Enlightenment discourses of reason and natural rights seem plausible or encourage political actors to recast the French state in terms of civic equality? The arguments I offer about the effects of capitalist development rely on a Marxist conceptualization of capitalism and its effects but a very different form of Marxism than that embraced by Lefebvre or Soboul in the middle years of the twentieth century. Their Marxism appears to have been based essentially on the *Communist Manifesto* and the preface to the *Critique of Political Economy* rather than on *Capital* or the *Gründrisse*, and it seems to have remained entirely ignorant of writings of the Frankfurt School or of Georg Lukács. Lefebvre and Soboul understood capitalism as a mode of production based on a particular form of property and class relations, and they saw the social and political effects of capitalist development as mediated by class formation and class struggles. Their causal argument about the Revolution was that the development of capitalism produced an increasingly wealthy, powerful, and class-conscious bourgeoisie, which seized power from the declining aristocratic ruling class in the Revolution. Hence when historical research made it clear that this posited self-conscious revolutionary bourgeois class could not be found and that the aristocracy seems not to have been declining, the Marxisant historians were incapable of mounting a coherent challenge to those who denied altogether the relevance of capitalism to the French Revolution.

The Marxist arguments I use are largely derived from *Capital*, especially the first chapter of volume 1, entitled "The Commodity" (Marx [1867] 1977). Here I have been influenced by a reinterpretation of Marx's social theory by Moishe Postone, who argues that the definitive dynamic of capitalism is not the formation of bourgeois and proletarian classes but the spread of the commodity form. The generalization of the commodity form, according to Postone, gives rise to a uniquely abstract form of social relations, governed above all by a logic of exchange of equivalents in markets (1993).[7] In this book, I argue that eighteenth-century French commercial capitalist development fostered a vigorous growth of abstract commodity-based social relations and that the growing experience of such abstraction in daily life helped make the notion of civic equality both conceivable and attractive by the 1780s. This argument postulates a very different kind of causation than the classical Marxist scenario of Lefebvre and Soboul. It sees capitalist development influencing the Revolution not through a mechanism of class struggle but through a far more gradual and diffuse social and cultural process.[8]

Capitalism's tendency to form abstract social relations derives from the monetary logic of exchange. Every commodity—whether a bolt of cloth, a loaf of bread, a digitally recorded song, or an hour of labor—has intrinsic, incommensurable, and sensuous qualities that endow them with what Marx calls a "use value." But in the market, commodities appear also as "exchange values"—that is, as abstract equivalents measured by the quantity of money for which they can be exchanged and ultimately, according to Marx, by the quantity of "socially necessary labor time" they embody. Thus the commodity has both a concrete aspect (its use value) and an abstract aspect (its exchange value). The latter, because it is quantitative in character, is always commensurable with the exchange values of other commodities. Commodity exchange is, of course, a real social relation between those who produce or sell commodities and those who purchase and ultimately use them. But this is an attenuated and abstract social rela-

---

7. Postone's arguments (and mine) were significantly influenced by Lukács (1968).

8. I do not deny the existence of class tensions and class struggles in the French Revolution. For example, Markoff (1977) demonstrates that the issues raised in the *cahiers de doléances* of nobles, bourgeois, and peasants in 1789 were strikingly different from one another. He also demonstrates that it was peasant resistance and violence that forced the destruction of the rural feudal system between 1789 and 1793. What I deny is that the shift from a hierarchical society to one based on civic equality in 1789 can be explained by the political action of an organized bourgeois class.

tion; at its deepest level, according to Marx, it is the exchange of one form of socially necessary labor for another, but with this labor typically congealed in concrete products bought and sold in markets. The growth of capitalism hence means—by definition—an expansion of abstract social relations, social relations characterized by monetary equivalence, quantitative logics, and increasing anonymity.

Civic equality, as embodied in the French Declaration of the Rights of Man and Citizen, was abstract in an analogous sense. It declared men (although not, it should be emphasized, women) equal *in rights*. A person might be rich or poor, intelligent or stupid, learned or ignorant, a peasant, a merchant, an artisan, a banker, or a landowner. They were, hence, hardly rendered concretely equal by the declaration of rights. But abstractly, they were rendered *equivalent* by their equality before the law and their equal legal eligibility for distinctions, places, and public employment. It was no longer to be their permanent status as commoners, nobles, or clerics but their mutable and largely voluntary personal knowledge, initiative, and wealth that would determine their possibilities in social life. Like commodities in a market, they were concretely distinct entities but were rendered equivalent by their subjection to universally and impersonally applicable formal rules—the legal system granting equality before the law. It was, I am arguing, people's experience of the increasing independence, flexibility, and anonymity of market relations over the course of the eighteenth century and the relatively greater range of social actions governed by commodity logics that made civic equality, by 1789, seem a reasonable and comprehensible way of regulating social and political affairs. It was in this sense that commercial capitalism paved the way for the establishment of civic equality.[9]

France experienced economic growth of a recognizably capitalist character in the eighteenth century. However, this was not a period of what could be called the triumph of a capitalist social order. Rather, capitalist development (in international, colonial, and domestic trade; in manufacturing; in agriculture; in finance) is better conceptualized as taking place in the interstices of such preexisting institutional structures as the monarchical state; the royal court; the venerable hierarchy of the Three Estates (the clergy, the nobility, and the commoners); the jumble of assorted privileged jurisdictions; the church; the rural seigneuries; the corporately

---

9. About a decade into my research for this book, I found an article by Lucien Goldmann (1967) arguing for a link between the abstraction of what he called the "philosophy of the Enlightenment" and the abstract character of commodity exchange under capitalism. Hence my hypothesis of such a connection is by no means unique to me.

organized provinces, municipalities, and guilds; and so on. Pride of birth still took precedence over wealth or achievement in eighteenth-century society, and getting ahead in daily life was virtually impossible without deference to one's superiors and the pursuit of patronage—the typical social devices of a hierarchical society.

Yet in the interstices of this elaborate network of hierarchically constructed institutions, commercial capitalism took root and flourished. It was often possible either to get around guild regulations or to capture the guild and bend its regulations in favor of the wealthiest and most entrepreneurial masters. Much new manufacturing was established in the countryside, where guild regulations did not apply and where labor was cheap and pliable, or in a wide range of privileged spaces that were exempt from guild controls. New consumer products, like carriages, lacquered snuffboxes, wigs, flowered silk brocades, colorful Indian cottons, dressing and writing tables, clocks, crockery, watches, coffeepots and teapots, fans, umbrellas, and so forth found ever-expanding markets. New retail shops flourished. The commerce in books boomed, and more and more people learned to read them. Commercial forms of entertainment flourished. Many agriculturalists turned their efforts toward supplying cash crops to the big cities, especially Paris. The fiscal affairs of the state depended increasingly on wealthy financiers and the Paris stock market. In these and many other ways, the daily life of French men and women, while still dominated by privilege, hierarchy, honor, patronage, and deference, was interlaced with new market forms of social relations.

Capitalism, in the eighteenth century, did not pose itself overtly as an alternative to the existing social order but infiltrated and colored social relations both within the old institutions and in their interstices. Karl Marx, in the *Gründrisse*, remarked that "in all forms of society there is one specific kind of production which predominates over the rest, whose relations thus assign rank and influence to the others. It is a general illumination which bathes all the other colours and modifies their particularity" (Marx 1993, 106–7). I argue that what the eighteenth-century French called "commerce" was increasingly bathing all of society and its institutions in its particular light. Switching metaphors, we could use Raymond Williams's term and say that pervasive but interstitial capitalist development was creating a "structure of feeling," a powerful but difficult-to-define set of experiential pressures that inefficiently and haltingly brought into consciousness an awareness of new social forces and a recognition of novel possibilities for the organization of social life (Williams 1977). The philosophes and the political economists, among others, can be said to have given explicit articulation to this emerging structure of feeling. This sort of subtle and gradual yet pervasive and powerful historical process is, of course, difficult to grasp and describe. But I am convinced that a history of interstitial capitalist abstraction is necessary to make proper sense of the origins of the French Revolution. Empirically demonstrating the reality of these abstracting effects of capitalist development is not a straightforward task. It requires what I call *a concrete history of abstraction*—certainly an oxymoron, but not, I aim to demonstrate, a practical impossibility. The abstracting effects of capitalist development were, as I see it, highly diffuse, affecting all the social relations that were influenced in one way or another by the spread of commodity exchange—which is to say virtually all social relations, although to differing degrees and often in quite different fashions.

A Concrete History of Abstraction

The methodological problem of tracking the effects of highly diffuse processes that subtly steer diverse forms of social relations in a particular direction over a period of several decades has, to put it mildly, not been widely discussed in historiographical or social scientific literature. Both historians and social scientists generally prefer to look at clear and discrete causal relations—how the victory of a particular political faction changes government policies, how the introduction of a new technological process affects relations between workers and management, how a fall in death rates affects the structure of families, how the introduction of a powerful new concept spreads through various intellectual disciplines. The causal agent I invoke in this book—an increasing availability of relatively abstract commercial relations as a means of accomplishing social goals—may be experienced variously in different areas of social life. But by introducing a differently structured type of social relations and providing a wider range of options to social actors, it had a net tendency to loosen the bonds of hierarchy, privilege, and constituted authority. It increased the possibilities for independent thinking and novel forms of social action.

But in what sense can commercial relations be qualified as "abstract"? Commercial relations, like any social relations, are concrete in the sense of being real, specific, time bound, and material. Participants in commercial relations buy and sell specific products or services, whether bread, labor, theater tickets, or futures contracts. But by comparison with social relations based on hierarchy, status, patronage, and deference, market relations tend to be more anonymous and more voluntary. Many market transactions are utterly anonymous, as when a stranger enters a random shop and buys a loaf of bread or an investor buys a bond on the open market. To be sure, in eighteenth-century conditions, there were often thicker social relations between the buyer and seller. A customer was likely to patronize a specific neighborhood bakery and might well have a credit account there—if she was regarded by neighbors as being an honorable and creditworthy person. Similarly, a decision to invest was frequently dependent on a degree of trust between the investor and a borrower whose reputation the investor knew. But these relations remained, at base, voluntary in character and could be formed and abandoned at will, something that was certainly not true of one's position in the old regime social hierarchy. Moreover, transactions in markets are governed by price and do not depend on status differences. A bolt of cloth is sold to a noble at the same price as to a commoner. A noble's investment in a money-making scheme will be determined by his assessment of the likely return, not by whether the scheme is organized by a noble or a commoner. In all these respects, one could say that market relations are more abstract than status relations.

Commercial relations were also abstract in a different sense. The dominant fact governing commercial relations is the price of goods in a market. The prices of goods in a commercial society are determined less by the specific interaction between a buyer and a seller than by the demand and supply of the goods in a market that transcends the particular transaction. The price of bread in a bakery in Paris is determined by the relative abundance of the recent harvest, not only in the area surrounding Paris but in Europe as a whole. Because the eighteenth-century market for grain encompassed virtually all of Europe, prices in Paris varied in the same direction as those in Amsterdam, Madrid, Glasgow, or Milan. An abundant harvest in the Parisian basin would not result in low prices in Paris if harvests in England, the Rhineland, and Poland had been mediocre. Likewise, the price that a weaver or a merchant could get for a piece of cloth depended not only on the costs of production and transport of the cloth but on fluctuations in consumer taste that could make the cloth he put on the market significantly more or less valuable than it would have been in the previous year. The interest rates a purchaser of a house or a farm had to pay on a mortgage would vary not only according to the purchaser's reputation for probity and reliability but also based on fluctuations in rates that arise from financial dealings utterly beyond the control of lender and borrower alike. In all these respects, commercial social relations were abstract in a way that relations of patronage, privilege, and deference were not.

My history of abstraction in social life is a concrete history in the sense that it is based on the real, concretely experienced interactions between persons and between persons and things. But it endeavors to seek out the ways, both manifest and subtle, that the abstractions inherent in capitalist relations played out in the daily life and the strategies of action of concrete persons.

One could imagine various methods of pursuing the hypothesis that drives this book, many of which would imply considerable digging in eighteenth-century French archives. But because the process I have hypothesized is highly general, I have chosen instead to cast my net widely, surveying three very different aspects of eighteenth-century social life that I believe were significantly shaped by the expansion of commercial capitalist relations. Rather than attempting detailed archival research, I have instead relied primarily on the extremely rich historical research available for this period—supplemented by close readings of a significant number of printed works dating from the seventeenth and eighteenth centuries. Because of the historical importance and spectacular character of the French Revolution, the historical literature on prerevolutionary France is particularly rich. Indeed, no historical era has a more sophisticated and thorough historiography: almost everywhere one turns in the history of the French old regime, there are already multiple careful, solid, and frequently brilliant writings by generations of scholars. Although none of these works, as far as I have been able to discover, has pursued the hypothesis that guides my inquiry, many of them contain arguments and evidence that bear on my questions. This fact has had obvious advantages for a study like mine, which, rather than attempting to bring to light hitherto unknown facts, has instead attempted to develop a novel interpretive framework for facts that are, broadly speaking, already known. This book is, in short, what the French call an *essai de synthèse*— that is, an attempt to pull together already known facts and arguments about this fascinating historical era into a new synthetic account that subjects them to a novel interpretation. It is for the readers to decide whether I have succeeded at this task.

The Structure of the Argument

This book traces a diffuse but systemic sociocultural process: the ways eighteenth-century French commercial capitalism gave rise to more abstract social relations and more abstract ways of understanding the social and political world. It does so by developing accounts of three distinct aspects of eighteenth-century French social life: first, the development of commercially formed urban publics; second, the career strategies of upwardly mobile philosophes; and third, the adoption by the king's own ministerial elite of an administrative strategy based on a new political-economic understanding of the social world. In each case, I argue, the emergence of capitalist socioeconomic logics provides an explanation of social and cultural transformations that helped make possible the embrace of civic equality in 1789.

I begin with two chapters that provide necessary background for my more particular arguments. Chapter 1, entitled "Old Regime State and Society," sets forth the structure of the French social and political order in the late seventeenth and eighteenth centuries. It first traces the prevailing ideological conception of a God-given hierarchical society capped by an absolute monarch and then sets forth the highly complex and much more contradictory institutional forms of the actual old regime French state. Chapter 2, "The Eighteenth-Century Economy: Commerce and Capitalism," surveys the evidence of significant economic growth in France, particularly in the years from 1720 to the Revolution, and develops an argument about the specifically commercial form and dynamics of early French capitalism.

The remainder of the book is divided into three parts: "The Emergence of an Urban Public," "The Philosophes and the Career Open to Talent," and "Royal Administration and the Promise of Political Economy." Part 1, which consists of three chapters, investigates a crucial change in eighteenth-century urban society—the formation of a diverse set of urban publics generated by new or intensified commercial developments. Chapter 3, "The Commercial Public Sphere," begins with a reconsideration of Jürgen Habermas's pathbreaking *The Structural Transformation of the Public Sphere* (1989). Although this book has been much celebrated by historians, political theorists, and historical sociologists alike, I argue that most commentators have paid insufficient attention to Habermas's insistence on the capitalist origins of the public sphere that emerged in the eighteenth century. I attempt to rescue his argument that the public sphere was a specific product of early capitalist development and that it was deeply structured by capitalist social forms. The chapter goes on to analyze the dynamics of a broad range of commercial publics that emerged in the eighteenth century: reading publics, theater publics, shopping publics, and more.

Chapter 4, "The Empire of Fashion," takes a deep dive into one aspect of the commercial public sphere: the frenetic and economically consequential world of fashion. The chapter focuses on the silk fabric trade, with production based in Lyon but sales primarily in Paris, that dominated the high end of fashion throughout Europe in the eighteenth century. The chapter shows how the dynamics of fashion, most spectacularly but not exclusively in the silk trade, saturated the urban consuming public and underwrote one of the most dynamic spheres of the eighteenth-century French economy.

Chapter 5, "The Parisian Promenade," examines the rise of the urban promenade in eighteenth-century Paris. A novel cross-class strolling and leisure culture flourished in eighteenth-century Paris, stimulated both by the royal state's provision of public spaces for strolling and the private provision of attractive consumer destinations—such as cafés, shops, and entertainment venues—lining the promenade grounds. There arose in this context an ethic of situational civic equality, in which nobles, bourgeois, and artisans tacitly agreed to share the public space and the commercial attractions and to be stimulated and amused rather than intimidated or offended by the public's tremendous social diversity.

Part 2 of the book, "The Philosophes and the Career Open to Talent," examines the careers of four philosophes, using a close study of their experiences navigating a society structured simultaneously by rigid hierarchy and commercial possibility. I examine with particular care a question rarely emphasized by those who have written about the philosophes: how they managed to make enough money to survive and prosper as men of letters. Although a few nobles and wealthy bourgeois became philosophes, it is striking that many rose from humble origins to become the leading public intellectuals of their day. Many philosophes, that is, embodied spectacularly the experience of what was called "the career open to talent," a goal that became fundamental to the civic equality established by the French Revolution. Happily, two philosophes who were sons of obscure provincial artisans—the political economist abbé André Morellet and the political philosopher and novelist Jean-Jacques Rousseau—wrote detailed memoirs from which their financial histories can be reconstructed in some detail. Existing biographical work on Denis Diderot, another famous artisan's son, is sufficiently rich to assemble an account of his financial career as well.

Chapter 6, "The Philosophe Career and the Impossible Example of Voltaire," introduces the two principal modes of advancement pursued by impecunious men of letters: patronage by the great and commercial publishing. The philosophe career normally passed through salons. These weekly meetings, held in the homes of wealthy aristocrats or financiers, vied for the services of the brilliant young men whose conversation and wit would enhance their salon's prestige. The men of letters gained free meals and got acquainted with potential patrons. But while they sought financial support through elite patronage, aspiring men of letters simultaneously pursued commercial publication of their writings. They rarely made much money by writing, but it was the publication of books that established and sustained their literary and intellectual reputations—that, indeed, made them "philosophes." By publishing their thoughts, the philosophes showed themselves to be free and intellectually independent thinkers, which gained them prestige that also made more lucrative patronage available. In this sense, the philosophes' career embodied the contradictions of eighteenth-century French society at the same time that their thought pointed beyond such contradictions.

Chapter 6 also briefly relates the career of Voltaire, who did more than anyone else to establish the intellectual program of the philosophes. He provided an attractive moral and intellectual model for young men of letters, but one in many respects impossible to follow. Voltaire was born a rich bourgeois and became vastly richer, not through the sales of his books but by means of sagacious investments. He was much more openly disdainful of the political and religious authorities than were his many emulators, but he could afford this defiance because for most of his career he lived in splendor at a distance from Paris, its royal courts, and its police. The three other philosophes whose careers I examine in chapters 8, 9, and 10—Diderot, the abbé Morellet, and Rousseau, all of them sons of obscure artisans or shopkeepers—spent their careers living with some frugality in Paris and its vicinity and hence were vulnerable to arbitrary arrest and repression if their publications were too radical. Carefree defiance like Voltaire's was impossible for his would-be imitators, who had to make their way through varied and sometimes agonizing combinations of publication and patronage.

Part 3 of the book, "Royal Administration and the Promise of Political Economy," traces the story of the royal administration's attempts, in the second half of the eighteenth century, to resolve the crushing fiscal difficulties of the French state. Their task was complicated by their limited ability to tax the great wealth of the privileged nobility and clergy. Many administrators were attracted by a program of reforms based on the emerging discourse of political economy, which argued that removing barriers to enterprise would enhance national wealth—and hence increase tax revenue. Political economy conceptualized persons not as members of hierarchically ranked orders but as producers and consumers linked by exchange in markets—a notion with a strong bias toward civic equality. But reforming administrators were repeatedly frustrated by the tenacity of hierarchy and privilege in the monarchical regime. Only after 1789 could many of the reforms they had been advocating be put into practice.

Chapter 10, "Tocqueville's Challenge: Royal Administration and the Rise of Civic Equality," examines Alexis de Tocqueville's claim that the egalitarianism of the French Revolution derived, ironically, from the old regime monarchy's project of administrative centralization. The royal policy, he argued, established equality of conditions by reducing the nobility to the same political nullity already occupied by the bourgeoisie. I agree that the royal administration pursued policies with an equalizing tendency. But I argue that this did not arise, as Tocqueville claimed, from a universal "instinct that drives all governments to take charge of all affairs." Rather, the administrators, obsessed by the ever-mounting royal deficit, pursued greater equality of conditions because they believed that doing so would increase revenues by creating more taxable wealth.

Chapter 11, "Warfare, Taxes, and Administrative Centralization: The Double Bind of Royal Finance," examines the royal administration's efforts to finance the ever-spiraling cost of warfare in the later seventeenth and eighteenth centuries. The peasants were already so squeezed that raising their taxes would reduce agricultural production and lower the tax yield. Meanwhile, nobles, who possessed vast wealth, held privileges exempting them from taxation. The crown adopted various fiscal stratagems but eventually found itself in a double bind: over the long run, it had somehow to abolish fiscal privileges, but doing so threatened to drive the state into bankruptcy in the short run. Such was the royal administration's impossible dilemma.

Chapter 12, "Political Economy: A Solution to the Double Bind?," examines the development of French political economy, which flourished in the years after 1750. Political economists conceptualized persons not as inhabiting a hierarchy of statuses but as producers and consumers linked by commercial relations. In this sense, it modeled a civic equality in the economic sphere. Eliminating the constraints of caste, privilege, and government regulation, political economists argued, would free both producers and consumers to follow their economic interests and enhance the nation's wealth. These ideas won a following among royal administrators, who hoped such reforms could increase the wealth from which taxes were drawn, promising a possible escape from the fiscal double bind.

Chapter 13, "Navigating the Double Bind: Efforts at Reform," examines two reform ministries in the waning years of the old regime. Turgot, a "philosophe minister" who served from 1774 to 1776, instituted far-reaching reforms inspired by the new political economy, but the opposition of conservatives managed to drive him from office. He was followed by Necker, from 1776 to 1781, who reversed Turgot's reforms but undertook a far-reaching effort to reform the state's baroque financial institutions. Yet he, too, was eventually dismissed, and his reforms were reversed. The tale of these two initially promising ministries indicates the strength of resistance to reform in the old regime political system.

The conclusion, "The Revolution and the Advent of Civic Equality," brings the book's story to the French Revolution. It shows how the double bind of the old regime state blocked the possibility of reform even when, in 1786, it became clear that a devastating fiscal crisis loomed. The result was an unprecedented revolution that, in 1789, dismantled the existing hierarchical state and society and built a new regime on the basis of civic equality. The revolutionary regime proved unstable and was eventually rolled back by Napoleon's coup d'état in 1799 and a restoration of the monarchy in 1815. But even the restored monarchy made no attempt to restore the old regime's tangle of hierarchy and privilege. Civic equality not only endured but, over the course of the nineteenth century, became the organizing juridical principle in most of the Euro-American world.

Old Regime State and Society

I have stated that prerevolutionary French society was "hierarchical." In this chapter, I sketch out how this hierarchy worked, both in theory and in practice, in the century or so preceding the Revolution. The old regime state and society were highly complex—an avowedly "absolutist" monarchical state with an elaborate administrative and judicial apparatus that oversaw a society marked by entrenched privileges and much de facto local control of social, economic, and even political life. Meanwhile, France was a great power engaged in frequent international warfare that strained the country's productive capacity and resulted in a permanently rising royal debt. All this was leavened during the eighteenth century by an increasingly prosperous national economy that created new circuits of wealth based not on principles of hierarchy and privilege but on market exchange and commercial intermediation.

An Old Regime Theory of the Social Order

I begin with a classical statement of the old regime's hierarchical assumptions. Charles Loyseau was a jurist whose treatises, composed in the early seventeenth century, remained authoritative down to the end of the old regime. His three great treatises—on *seigneuries* (lordships), offices, and orders and dignities—were published in the first decade of the seventeenth century and republished repeatedly between then and 1701 (Loyseau 1608, 1610a, 1610b).[1] It is the *Traité des ordres et simples dignitez* (Treatise on Orders and Simple Dignities) that most directly addresses

---

1. These were published in collected form in 1640 and republished in 1641, 1660, 1666, 1678, and 1701.

the question of social hierarchy.[2] This treatise sets forth many of the political, legal, and metaphysical assumptions that were taken for granted as the basis of the old regime's social life.

The term *order* in the seventeenth or eighteenth century implied at once hierarchical rank and proper arrangement. Loyseau saw order as the fundamental principle of human society but also as a defining characteristic of the universe, one that flowed necessarily from God's design. He begins his treatise with this statement:

> It is necessary that there be order in all things, for their well-being and for their direction. . . . Inanimate creatures are all placed according to their high or low degree of perfection. . . . As for animate creatures, the celestial intelligences have their hierarchical orders, which are immutable. And in regard to men, who are ordered by God so that they may command the other animate creatures of this world here below, although their order is changeable and subject to vicissitude, on account of the particular liberty that God has given them for good and for evil, they nevertheless cannot exist without order. Because we cannot live together in equality of condition, it is necessary that some command and others obey. (13–14)

In a world otherwise governed by divinely ordered necessity, Loyseau tells us, mankind alone has been granted free will. But this freedom must be subjected to a worldly order in which "some command and others obey" because, as Loyseau assumes, without feeling a need to argue the point, "we cannot live together in equality of condition."

The worldly governor or sovereign is, of course, the king, "who is the living image of God." "August" and "full of majesty," like God himself, the king exercises a "lieutenancy of God on Earth" and an "absolute power over men" (27).[3] He serves as a link between heaven and earth and as a guarantor of order among humans. He is a semipriestly figure, a status that was signified by rituals performed at his coronation, where his body was anointed with holy oil from an ampul whose contents had been miraculously renewed ever since the coronation of Clovis, the first French king, in the fifth century. And immediately after he was crowned, the king took communion in both kinds—that is, both the wafer and the

---

2. My quotations are from Loyseau (1987). Hereafter, citations from this text will be given in parentheses. An English translation of the entire treatise is Loyseau (1994). For an analysis of the treatise, see Sewell (1974).

3. *Men* is the proper word. Virtually everything discussed in Loyseau's treatise refers to persons of the male gender.

wine—an act that otherwise was restricted to priests and that endowed the king with a kind of sacerdotal authority.[4]

The subjects ruled by the king, according to Loyseau, make up "a body with several heads . . . the three orders or Estates General of France: the clergy, the nobility, and the Third Estate." The clergy, the First Estate, is dedicated to the highest occupation, "the service of God"; the nobility, or Second Estate, is dedicated to "protecting the state by its arms"; and the Third Estate, the commoners, is dedicated to the lowly task of "nourishing and maintaining" the state "through peaceful occupations." Each of these three estates "is again subdivided into . . . subordinate orders, following the example of the celestial hierarchy," thus replicating at a lower level the system's hierarchical logic (14–15).

But what precisely is an "order"? According to Loyseau, *order* may be defined as a "dignity with aptitude for public power." Order is "a species of dignity, or honorable quality." It gives a person a stable "rank," which confers "a particular aptitude and capacity to attain either offices or *seigneuries* (lordships)." Thus, for example, a man can be a member of the order of priests without holding a benefice or a member of the order of nobles without possessing a seigneurie. But a man must be a member of the order of priests to exercise the office of *curé* (priest) of a parish or be a member of the noble order to become the seigneur of a village with the right to dispense justice. One's order determines his rank and formal capacities in society; it is, as Loyseau puts it, "the dignity and the quality which is the most stable and the most inseparable from a man." This is why, he adds, the French also call one's order one's "estate" (15). The order to which one belongs, it could be said, is one's state of being. "Forming the estate of a person and imprinting upon the individual a perpetual character," order is something more fundamental than the offices, powers, or occupations in which one may at any moment be engaged (16). The system of distinct orders was the foundation of the old regime's social hierarchy.

The most perfect orders, not surprisingly, were those of the Catholic Church, which form for Loyseau the ideal model for orders of all descriptions. Passing from a lower to a higher order within the church hierarchy required a period of training and a test of capabilities and was marked by a solemn ceremony. When a man rises to a new clerical order, he receives a distinctive mark—the stole for the deacon, the chasuble for the priest, the miter and staff for the bishop, and so on. These ranks are also strictly observed—and thus made visible—in sitting or marching on ceremonial

4. For a description of the coronation ceremony of Louis XIII, which was followed with only minor changes for Louis XIV, XV, and XVI, see Jackson (1984, 15–23).

occasions. Loyseau observes that like the orders of the church, nonclerical orders commonly have solemn ceremonies of initiation; this is true, for example, of orders of knighthood, of licentiates and doctorates for men of letters, and even of initiation into masterships in trades. Although Loyseau fails to mention the fact, these initiations nearly always contained religious elements and frequently included a special mass to consecrate those raised to a new dignity. Likewise, different orders proudly displayed specific marks of membership upon their persons, at least on ceremonial occasions: rings, gowns, hats, spurs, swords, coats of arms, and the like (16–17).

The great exception to the prevalence of initiation ceremonies was the nobility. Although in practical terms, the distinction between nobles and commoners was the most salient distinction in French society, the nobility doesn't quite fit Loyseau's general schema. "There are," Loyseau remarks, "no ceremonies to make princes and gentlemen." This is because the orders of the nobility are what he terms "*irregular orders*, since they come from *birth* and not from any particular grant" (16; italics added). Loyseau was clearly uncomfortable about the passing on of order by birth, which was, of course, the standard defining characteristic of nobles not only in France but elsewhere in Europe and was precisely the nobles' greatest source of pride. Loyseau's misgivings on this point were metaphysical. He remarks that although the qualities of plants and beasts are "retained infallibly from their generation" because "their vegetative or sensitive soul proceeds absolutely from a physical source," this is not true of humans: "The rational soul of men, which comes directly from God who creates it when he sends it into the human body, does not have any natural participation in the qualities of the generative semen of the body to which it is joined." Yet as a practical jurist, Loyseau accepts the fact that "those who have issued from good blood have been esteemed above others" and have "been constituted as a separate order and been given a degree of honor which sets them apart from the great majority of the people" (21). Here the seemingly pagan concept that traditionally imparted distinctions to the nobility fails to fit Loyseau's very Catholic philosophical scruples. As Loyseau resisted admitting, the social order of the old regime was in fact an amalgam of quite different principles of hierarchy, principles not reducible to his fundamentally theological schema. In fact, the principles of superiority of birth penetrated to the core of the religious field itself: In the eighteenth century, it was virtually impossible for a commoner to rise to the dignity of bishop. The pinnacle of the religious hierarchy was open only to nobles, and many of the resentments felt by commoners toward nobles were also felt by ordinary clerics toward the episcopate.

Although it was normal for nobility to be passed down in the blood from father to son, the king, "who is ordained by God to distribute the substantial honors of this world," has the quasi-miraculous power to transform commoners into nobles. This he may do "by means of a letter written expressly to this end." But also, and in fact much more frequently, he may appoint commoners to certain "offices and seigneuries that carry nobility with them." In either case, "this ennoblement purges the blood and the posterity of the ennobled of all stain of commonness, raising him to the same quality and dignity as if his race had always been noble." Yet as Loyseau notes, the ennobled are in fact "less esteemed than nobles by blood." Loyseau seems to share this opinion, declaring that the purging of the blood from the stain of commonness "is only effacing a mark that remains" and therefore "seems more a fiction than a truth." Here he cites a philosophical principle: the prince "cannot reduce being to non-being" (23). What Loyseau fails to mention in his treatise is that these ennobling offices were, with rare exceptions, sold to wealthy commoners as a means of raising funds for the royal treasury. Much of the disdain felt by the old nobility, generally known as the "sword nobles," toward these "robe nobles," who had gained nobility by purchasing state offices, arose from disapproval of the pecuniary means by which the nobility had been obtained, not from philosophical scruples about the king's power to purge the blood of commonness.

Whether of ancient lineage or newly minted, the noble order enjoyed very great advantages. They alone were eligible for most of the highest offices in the state, including those of the king's household. They made up the vast majority of the military officers and in principle had the exclusive right to hold fiefs and seigneuries. They also enjoyed great pecuniary privileges, especially exemption from the taille, the most onerous of all taxes, which meant that the nobles, generally the wealthiest of all the king's subjects, paid far lower tax rates than the simple peasants over whom they held their seigneurial jurisdictions. Nobles also had the exclusive right to hunt game, a privilege much resented by commoners. Moreover, "when they commit a crime, they are not punished as rigorously as the common people"—"they are never flogged or hanged, as common people are," but "have the privilege of being decapitated in cases of capital crimes" (24–25). The divide between nobles and commoners was indeed sharp. The very occupations that commoners were expected to perform were actually forbidden to nobles. Any noble who worked at "activities . . . performed for profit"—for example, as a merchant—could be stripped of his noble status on the grounds that he had "derogated" his nobility (28).

The Third Estate was essentially the residual order, one made up of persons lacking distinction. As Loyseau puts it, the Third Estate was "not properly an order" at all—because order is, by definition, "a species of dignity," and few members of the Third Estate were "in dignity." The Third Estate could be considered an order only to the extent that "order" signifies merely "a condition or occupation, or a distinct kind of person." Nevertheless, Loyseau remarks that the Third Estate counts for something in the state. It "enjoys much greater power and authority in our time than it did formerly, because nearly all of the officeholders of justice and finance belong to it, the nobility having scorned letters and embraced idleness." Here Loyseau, himself a member of the Third Estate and a highly lettered and influential legal theorist, insinuates a certain criticism, even a certain scorn, for the idle and sometimes unlettered nobility's claims to generalized superiority (27–28).

Loyseau divides the Third Estate into eight ranks: men of letters, financiers, legal professions, merchants, husbandmen, lower officers of the courts, artisans, and laborers. He makes clear that this ranking is his opinion, not something established by law. Thus he says, "For the honor which is due to knowledge, *I have put* men of letters in the first rank"; "*In my opinion*, financiers must rank after men of letters"; and "Husbandmen must, *in my opinion*, follow merchants" (29–30; italics added). Unlike the ranks among the nobility or the clergy, the superiority or inferiority of the various occupations of the Third Estate is not established by clear and enforceable legal distinctions. Yet Loyseau is certainly right that in this society, where questions of rank and precedence were so charged among the clergy and nobility at the summit of the social hierarchy, commoners took their somewhat vaguer claims to superiority very seriously. These claims could not be sorted out on any single dimension but had a rather ad hoc character. It might be said that this is what we should expect about distinctions within an order that, defined by its lack of dignity, was not truly an order at all.

Men of letters, Loyseau states, are "divided into four principal faculties or branches of knowledge: theology, jurisprudence . . . medicine, and the arts." These four lettered occupations were unique in the Third Estate because they each had clearly distinct internal ranks of bachelor, licentiate, and doctor, of which the latter two gave them access to offices as teachers or practitioners. These ranks were awarded in solemn ceremonies after years of study and the passing of examinations. In this respect, they were closely modeled on the orders of the church—not surprisingly, since the universities that awarded the degrees derived from clerical foundations. Financiers, by contrast, had no clear internal ranks or structures—they rated highly because they were wealthy and handled the king's business. Loyseau ranks next those legal professionals who wear "the long robe"—that is, judges, clerks of the court, notaries, and attorneys. Here we see again the arbitrariness of ranking within the Third Estate, since both judges and attorneys would seem already to have been ranked as men of letters—they had to have at least a licentiate in law. The legal professionals are followed by merchants, whose rank Loyseau justifies by their utility and their "usual opulence." Merchants are followed by "husbandmen," even though the peasants are generally regarded as "vile persons." Loyseau ranks them above both minor legal officers and artisans because "rural life is the ordinary occupation of the nobility," and "there is no life more innocent, no gain more in accord with nature than that of tilling the soil, which philosophers have preferred to all other vocations." Husbandmen are followed by legal officers "of the short robe, namely sergeants, trumpeters, appraisers, and vendors" (29–30).

After the minor legal officers, Loyseau places artisans, "those who exercise the mechanical arts . . . so named to distinguish them from the liberal arts." These trades, he notes, "were formerly practiced by serfs and slaves, and indeed we commonly call *mechanical* anything that is vile and abject." The mechanical arts were, however, highly differentiated, including a vast range of different urban trades whose practice, Loyseau notes, requires "considerable skill." Thus skilled artisans of all kinds stood above day laborers, whose work was deemed to be without skill and purely bodily in nature. Artisans, Loyseau assures us, "are properly mechanics and reputed to be vile persons," yet "there are certain trades in which manufacture and commerce are combined," which makes them more honorable—he mentions apothecaries, goldsmiths, jewelers, mercers, wholesalers, and drapers. Other trades "reside more in bodily strength than in the practice of commerce or in mental subtlety, and these are the most vile." In practice, it should be said, these differences in honor (or relative lack of dishonor) were hotly contested among the trades, all of which claimed distinction based on the subtlety and difficulty of their crafts. The mechanical arts, like the clergy and like the liberal arts practiced by the men of letters, had internal ranks—in this case, apprentices, journeymen, and masters. A tradesman had to pass through the stages of apprentice and journeyman to attain a mastership; passage to the rank of master required the making of a chef d'oeuvre (masterpiece) that demonstrated mastery of the necessary skills (33–34).

Although Loyseau does not make the point, it is clear that the artisan trades were patterned after the orders of the church. Passage from one stage to the next was marked by solemn ceremonies, often including a mass in the church where the guild maintained a chapel for the patron saint of the trade. Each trade, moreover, was strictly organized by a guild, led by syndics empowered to enforce quality standards on the goods fashioned by the trade. This secular guild was also doubled by a religious confraternity, which organized observances of the trade's saint's day and provided proper funerals for deceased masters. Thus if the mechanical arts were disdained as vile by members of the higher orders of society, the tradespeople responded by forming elaborate organizations patterned on the most perfect orders—those of the church. And they emphasized the importance of their skill or craft, something they insisted took intelligence and finesse and required extended training. By these means, they demonstrated that they too deserved a respected place in the old regime's social hierarchy. It is significant that an artisan's trade was colloquially known as his *état* (estate). This distinguished artisans from mere day laborers, who were regarded as *sans état* (without estate). The trade guilds were in fact distinct corporate bodies, recognized by royal and municipal governments and possessing written statutes ratified by the king. And they were the proud possessors of privileges, particularly the exclusive privilege of engaging in and governing the manufacture and sale of a specified range of goods within a city.[5]

Loyseau's *Treatise on Orders and Simple Dignities* was one man's attempt to set forth the main themes and the complexities of social hierarchy in old regime society. But his towering prestige as a jurist makes his treatise an eminently useful starting point for understanding this era's social assumptions. Read carefully, it reveals many of the principal categories, distinctions, and concepts governing old regime social life, such as the division of society into the three estates of clergy, nobility, and commoners; the theoretically absolute and God-given powers of the king; the tremendous resonance of the practices and social forms developed by the church; and the ubiquity of formal orders and distinctions into which persons were arrayed at all levels of the social hierarchy. But despite Loyseau's effort to reduce this complex of orders to a rational system, his treatise also reveals some of the key tensions of old regime society, such as the fundamentally contradictory principles of the priority of birth, of spiritual purity, and of the superiority of learning over ignorance—not to mention the matter of wealth, which Loyseau noted must be recognized in ranking of orders within the Third Estate but that he left discretely

5. On trade guilds, see Saint Léon (1909), Olivier-Martin (1938), Coornaert (1941), Sewell (1980, 16–39), Sonenscher (1989), Bossenga (1991), Truant (1996), Kaplan (2001), and Crowston (2001).

aside in discussing the nobility and clergy. Old regime society was, as Loyseau's treatise clearly indicates, complex, elaborate, and multiply hierarchical. But it was also shot through with tensions, exceptions, and contradictions. The next section of this chapter, which sketches out the practical organization of the state and society, should help illuminate some of these tensions.

Old Regime Society in Practice

By eighteenth-century standards, France was a huge, powerful, and bewilderingly diverse kingdom. It had roughly twenty-three million inhabitants at the beginning of the eighteenth century and about twenty-eight million on the eve of the Revolution. In Europe, only sprawling, backward, and distant Russia had as big a population. Spain had ten million people at the beginning of the century and fourteen million in 1800; Britain, including Scotland and Wales, grew over the same years from about seven million to ten and a half million; Italy and Germany were divided into a multitude of small states; the Netherlands, although wealthy and politically prominent, had only two million inhabitants. France was not only big but linguistically diverse. Although French was the country's general language of government and culture and was spoken by intellectual elites all over Europe, French country people spoke many dialects, including varieties of the *langue d'oïl* in the north and of the *langue d'oc* in the south (so named for how one said *oui*, or yes). There was also Breton (a Gaelic language) in the northeast, Basque in the southwest, German dialects in the east (Alsace and Lorraine), and Flemish dialects in the extreme north. In contrast to England, which had lived under a unified code of laws—the "common law"—since the reign of Henry II, the law in France varied from province to province. Indeed, the kingdom was divided by two quite distinct systems of law—a form of Roman law in the south and a variety of common law in the north, with the boundary roughly, but only roughly, corresponding to that between the *langue d'oïl* and the *langue d'oc*. Governing such a country was a challenge.

The French kingdom grew by accretion over the centuries, not reaching its eighteenth-century limits until the late seventeenth-century wars of Louis XIV. When provinces acceded to France, by conquest or dynastic inheritance, different privileges, governing institutions, and tax regimes were negotiated with the royal government. Indeed, certain territories subjected to the French king were ruled, officially, not as subunits of the French kingdom but under distinct juridical relations. The king of France ruled as the count of Provence, as the king of Navarre, and as the king of Béarn. The Mediterranean port city of Marseille was subject to the French king but was "a state apart," a kind of free city with distinct rights and privileges (Mousnier 1980, 249). Territories in the north and east acquired by treaty under Louis XIV, such as Artois, Flanders, Hainault, Franche-Comté, Alsace, and Lorraine, were known as *provinces réputées étrangères* (provinces regarded as foreign) and were granted extensive exceptions to laws applicable elsewhere in the kingdom. In Alsace, for example, Lutherans were allowed to practice their religion freely and were thus exempted from the revocation of the Edict of Nantes of 1685, which had made the practice of any religion but Roman Catholicism illegal and had driven thousands of French Calvinists—the Huguenots— into exile in the Netherlands, Switzerland, England, and Prussia.

Although the polity ruled by the French monarchs was, thus, dizzyingly diverse, the kings claimed a vast—indeed, an "absolute"—authority. A particularly clear and strident statement of the monarch's powers came in 1766, during a dramatic confrontation with the Parlement of Paris (not a deliberative body like the English Parliament but the kingdom's highest law court). There Louis XV stated his authority as follows: "To me alone belongs legislative power without subordination and undivided. . . . Public order in its entirety emanates from me, and . . . the rights and interests of the nation . . . are necessarily united with my rights and interests, and repose only in my hands" (Flammermont 1898, 555–57). This claim of absolute power was always more theoretical than real, but the king's real powers were impressive. Over the course of the seventeenth century, the French provinces, whatever their specific constitutional relationship with the king might be, were increasingly reduced to obedience by the royal government, especially following the suppression of the major rebellion known as the Fronde in the middle of the seventeenth century. Beginning in the 1660s, Louis XIV and his great minister Colbert increasingly concentrated power in the royal administration. From that point on, the king was represented in every province by an "intendant." These were *commissaires*—that is to say, revocable officials appointed by the royal council with theoretically extensive powers to carry out the king's policies. They oversaw provincial authorities; intervened in local disputes; kept the royal council minutely informed about local affairs, both political and economic; and, perhaps most importantly, administered tax collection. With the help of the intendants, the royal government made sure that taxes were paid fully and promptly, that the royal will was obeyed, and that any hint of rebellion was immediately repressed. What had been a fractious state before Louis XIV became, in most respects, an obedient and meticulously administered one from the 1660s forward.

The king also possessed great riches in his own right and the authority to disperse riches and favor to others. It was once again Louis XIV who made the most effective use of these royal resources, building the astounding palace and gardens at Versailles in the 1660s and attracting the greatest nobles in the kingdom to his court by awarding them honored places in the royal household, regaling them with elaborate ceremonies and entertainments, and doling out generous pensions and gifts. Residence at Versailles also put the great nobles in touch with financiers, who in return for the protection and access they gained from the nobles could cut them in on lucrative financial opportunities and provide daughters with immense dowries as marriage partners for those great nobles whose means fell short of their rank—a common affliction of the nobility. The Versailles project had the happy effect, from the point of view of the monarch, of turning the high nobility—previously those most potentially dangerous to the king—into his clients and dependents.

But if Louis XIV had effectively rendered the kingdom obedient, its administrative structure was dauntingly complex. By the eighteenth century, the greater part of the kingdom's provinces, known as the *pays d'élection*, had been stripped of their provincial estates and subjected to direct rule by the crown. These provinces covered a vast swath stretching from Normandy, Picardy, the Île de France, and Champagne in the north through Bordelais, Guyenne, Auvergne, and Rousillon in the south. But other provinces, known as the *pays d'état*, managed to retain their provincial estates, which meant that they had considerable but varying rights of self-government. Brittany in the extreme west of France had provincial estates, as did Flanders and Hainault in the far north and a band of provinces in the east and south, including Burgundy, Franche-Comté, Dauphiné, Provence, Languedoc, and Béarn. The pays d'élection and the pays d'état alike were overseen by intendants, but the intendants' powers were less extensive in the latter, where they frequently had to negotiate with officials of the estates to carry out the royal council's policies. One of the most important powers of provincial estates was the right to negotiate the province's direct taxes with the crown and to oversee their collection—functions otherwise carried out by the intendant and his staff. The direct taxes were those based on wealth, above all wealth derived from the land. The oldest and most important of these was the *taille*, to which surtaxes called the *capitation* and *dixième* were added in 1695 and 1710. The assessment and collection of the direct taxes was one of the most important and controversial tasks of the royal government.

Different provinces also faced different regimes of "indirect" taxes levied on consumption goods. These included levies on goods entering cities, duties imposed on internal trade, and government monopolies on salt and tobacco. All these taxes were collected by the General Farms, a consortium of financiers who undertook the collection of the levies on behalf of the royal government as tax farmers—at great profit to themselves as well as to the state. Since the Middle Ages, the royal government had gradually seized control of the tolls formerly exacted by powerful lords on merchandise passing through their lands, turning these into royal taxes. Louis XIV's famous minister Colbert understood that such internal levies harmfully restricted commerce, but he was only able to suppress tolls in the quarter or so of the country in the region in northern France centered on Paris known as the "Five Great Farms," a region that did, however, contain about half the kingdom's population. Goods entering this "customs union" had to pay tolls at its border, as well as, often enough, additional tolls paid into to the coffers of the royal government on their way to the border (Bosher 1964).

But the most lucrative businesses of the General Farms were the salt tax (and monopoly) and the tobacco monopoly. Residents of the Five Great Farms not only had to pay roughly ten times the market price for salt—a necessity for both the preservation and preparation of food in the era before refrigeration—but were actually obligated to buy fifty pounds of salt annually from the General Farms, which had a legal monopoly on the mineral. This hated salt tax, the *gabelle*, was very uneven in its incidence. Certain provinces with seacoasts capable of yielding salt, most prominently Brittany, were entirely exempted from the gabelle. Since Brittany had a long border with provinces in the Five Great Farms, smuggling was rampant there, and the General Farms had to provide a sizable police force, controlled directly by the farmers, to combat it. Meanwhile, most of the provinces in the southeast were subject only to what was called the *petite gabelle*, and those on the northeastern borders paid the *salines*. These were considerably less onerous exactions, ranging from about a quarter to a half the gabelle paid in the Five Great Farms; moreover, households in these provinces were not required to buy any particular amount of salt. Meanwhile, most of the provinces in the southwest had long since purchased immunity from the gabelle and paid only 10 to 20 percent of the price charged in the greater Parisian region. In the seventeenth century, when tobacco from the Chesapeake found its way to France, the General Farm was granted a monopoly on its sale, which extended to the entire country with the exception of certain of the *provinces réputées étrangères*—Flanders, Artois, Alsace, and Franche-Comté—whose citizens could procure tobacco wherever they wished. The result was a huge profit for the treasury and the General Farms, but also an intensification of smuggling along the "tobacco border," which required expanding the General Farms' police force (Kwass 2014).

This somewhat breathless summary of the old regime tax system demonstrates that France was by no means an administratively uniform country. But the administrative diversity went beyond the distinction between pays d'élections and pays d'état or between the *pays de grande gabelle* and the *pays de petite gabelle* or *pays de salines*. Thus, for example, neither the jurisdictions of the courts nor the boundaries of the kingdom's episcopal sees mapped directly onto those of the provinces. An intendant pursuing a royal policy in his *élection* (district) might well have to deal with two or more courts following different bodies of law; in some cases, one court might follow common law and another Roman law. There were also many specialized courts whose jurisdictions overlapped with the ordinary ones: a waters and forests court, financial courts, admiralty courts, monetary courts, commercial courts, and tax courts. French cities normally possessed royal charters granting all kinds of rights and privileges that distinguished them and their denizens from inhabitants of the surrounding countryside and subjected them to different legal regimes. Within cities, guilds had exclusive rights to manufacture and/or sell items of a certain description and to enforce these rights on their membership and against interlopers. Within any geographical unit, whether city, province, parish, or bailiwick (*baillage*), certain persons or members of certain corporate bodies—for example, nobles or royal officers or ecclesiastical congregations or universities—would be exempt from various regulations, taxes, or fees that applied to the general run of citizens.

If there is any concept that could be said to encompass most of the dizzying complexity of the French polity, it would be "privilege." In our day, privilege has come to mean simply the possession of some advantage over others. One might say, for example, that a person is privileged by her wealth or her superior education. Privilege, in our usage, also tends to imply an unfair or unsavory advantage: privilege is a kind of sin against our assumption of the fundamental equality of citizens. But in old regime France, privilege had a much more specific meaning and lacked pejorative connotation. A privilege was, literally, a private law (the term is derived from the Latin *privus* and *lex* or *legem*)—that is, a law, regulation, right, or exemption that applied only to a particular person or (more commonly) a category of persons. Privilege, in short, represented almost precisely the opposite of the principle of civic equality or equality before the law.

Privilege was a fundamental category of the old regime social order. A privilege was a kind of property, something that belonged to a person, usually because of that person's membership in a corporate body, order, or estate. Privileges were a ubiquitous characteristic of old regime society.[6] Thus, for example, the fact that a person was a noble entailed the possession of numerous privileges, some relatively trivial, others highly consequential. Nobles had the relatively trivial but highly honorific right to wear their swords in public and to sit in the front pews in church and also possessed the highly lucrative exemption from paying the taille. In addition, nobles and only nobles were eligible for certain high offices, such as judgeships in a *parlement* (the highest appellate courts) or positions as *maîtres des requêtes* ("masters of requests"), an office required for ascension to a high royal office.

It was not only nobles who enjoyed privileges, however. The clergy, both secular clergymen and members of religious orders, had the honorific right to march first in public processions and were exempt from the taille. An assembly of the kingdom's clergy was expected to make an annually negotiated "free gift" to the royal fisc, but this gift was less than what would have been assessed had they been subject to the taille. Many commoners also possessed privileges, including various tax exemptions. Likewise, the members of trade guilds—for example, the shoemakers of Nantes or the coopers of Orleans—had the exclusive right to make and sell their wares in their city. Cities also possessed privileges, including exemptions from certain taxes. The right of the provincial estates of Languedoc or Brittany to negotiate and collect its taxes, the right of the denizens of the province of Dauphiné to pay only the petite gabelle, and the Alsatians' right to practice Lutheranism freely were also privileges. In short, the old regime state could be described as a highly diverse collection of privileged bodies held together by their common subjection to and dependence upon the king.

The existence of so much administrative diversity and of so many and such varied privileges belonging to so many different persons, territorial units, or corporate bodies certainly relativized the king's theoretically absolute authority. Although the privileges were in principle granted by the monarch, he was by no means in a position to simply cancel them if they

6. A Google Ngram search indicates that the term *privilege* first appeared in French printed texts in the later sixteenth century, rose in frequency until it accounted for around one word in every thousand by the 1680s (roughly once every three to five pages in all French-language books in the Google library!), and fell precipitously only after 1789, when legal privileges were abolished by the National Assembly, sinking to less than one word in every ten thousand by 1800 and fluctuating between one and five in every hundred thousand ever since. In short, the prevalence of the term *privilege* in French linguistic usage corresponds quite precisely with the period generally regarded as the "old regime."

became inconvenient or undermined the efficacy of his rule. If privileges were said to derive from royal favor or will, the king's legitimacy also derived from his status as the guarantor of these highly valued privileges. He could and did trim around the edges, but he was always aware that any wholesale revocation of privileges would risk revolt and disorder. His authority, however absolute in theory, was hedged by others' privileges in practice.

Nor was this the only real limit on the king's theoretically absolute power. Another was the deep indebtedness of the crown ever since the sixteenth century. The debt was a consequence of the series of increasingly expensive European wars, in which France, as the greatest European landed power, was a predominant participant. Hence the king's power was perennially limited by a shortage of funds. Over the course of the sixteenth and seventeenth centuries, the royal government greatly increased taxes. But by the late seventeenth century, taxes on the peasants had risen so high that increasing them further would have been counterproductive, impoverishing the agriculture on which the taxes were based. This of course meant that the royal state was constantly in debt and therefore dependent on financiers—most prominently but not only to those who made up the General Farms. It also meant that there were severe pecuniary limits on initiatives the king might wish to undertake.

The chronic shortage of funds for the state was what induced the French monarchs, all the way back to François I in the sixteenth century, to resort to the sale of state offices to wealthy subjects—most commonly financiers or merchants enriched by trade. The venality of offices, as it is usually called, was practiced in many European states in this period, but nowhere so systematically as in France. Offices of all sorts were sold off, thereby bringing precious cash to the royal treasury. The purchaser, in return for the payment, gained the prestige associated with state office, the flow of emoluments that were attached to the position, and usually the right to pass the office on to his heirs. The offices sold ranged widely, from those of city constables or measurers in market halls to *maîtres des requêtes* (masters of requests, an office required of all high judicial and administrative officials) and positions in the parlements. The purchase of an office conferred privileges, often including exemption from the taille and other taxes. In the case of the highest offices, the purchaser also gained personal nobility, which could be passed on to his heirs if he held the office long enough. Indeed, during the final two centuries of the old regime, it was above all by purchasing offices that commoners gained access to the noble order for themselves and their progeny (Mousnier 1980, 2:335–36).

The sale of offices limited the extent of the king's control over his officers for the obvious reason that he could not dismiss them at will. Because many if not most of the offices were in the legal system, this meant that the law courts had a significant independence from royal fiat. The term *venal office* might make the reader think that judges engaged in personal venality, essentially selling justice to the highest bidder. This was not the case in France, where the largely hereditary judicial corps produced by the sale of offices was intensely proud of its learning and seriousness; it provided the predictability and strict adherence to legal reasoning characteristic of good legal institutions. The parlements, which heard appeals from lower tribunals and therefore determined the interpretation of laws, were staffed almost exclusively by nobles, sometimes members of the ancient or sword nobility but more frequently hailing from the *noblesse de robe* (robe nobility), whose ancestors had gained nobility by purchasing an ennobling office. The parlements also had the duty to register and publish the king's laws and decrees to render them valid within their jurisdictions. Traditionally, a parlement had the right to remonstrate to the king before consenting to register laws if it regarded them as flawed or not in keeping with the kingdom's unwritten constitution. Louis XIV, king from 1643 to 1715, suppressed the parlements' right of remonstrance when he came of age in 1661, but the right was restored after his death and was used widely in the eighteenth century. The parlements, staffed by prestigious and learned noble judges who owned their offices, assured that the French judicial system retained a considerable autonomy from the dictates of the king and his ministers (Doyle 1974; Égret 1970; Stone 1986; Swann 1995).

In short, the French monarchs were absolute in theory and, by the standards of the day, very powerful in fact. But their powers were hedged in by many restraints. Some restraints, like the existence of manifold privileges, the state's lack of administrative unity, or the effective independence of the judiciary, were built into what was spoken of as the "constitution" of the state. Others, like the escalating cost of warfare and the consequent state indebtedness, were inherent in the European international system of the era; the debts of the English monarchs were even greater than those of the French. There were also significant practical problems involved in governing a state of such scale and complexity.

Louis XIV and Colbert created an effective administrative apparatus, based partly in Versailles and partly in Paris. Throughout Louis XIV's long reign, from the time he attained his majority in 1661 to his death in 1715, the king himself was not only the head of state but also the chief administrator, who spent countless hours hearing reports from the provinces and from various administrative bureaus. He carefully discussed options with his ministers and made most of the major policy decisions himself. Later monarchs lacked his extraordinary intelligence and discipline, not to mention his taste for hard administrative work. Under the regency of the Duke of Orleans (1715–23), the long rule of Louis XV (1723–74), and the ill-fated reign of Louis XVI (1774–92), day-to-day decision-making and even major policy-making tended to pass to the ministers, above all to the controller general of finances, who in effect became the chief minister. But the basic administrative structure created by Louis XIV and Colbert survived up to the Revolution. Positions in the higher levels of this apparatus—the controller general of finances, the secretaries of state, the intendants of finance and intendants of commerce, the heads of bureaus, and the provincial intendants—were staffed almost exclusively by robe nobles, often sons of state officials. By the eighteenth century, the upper reaches of the administration were filled by a proud caste of highly competent nobles dedicated to the service of the monarchical state. These royal administrators, however, were *commissaires*, which meant that unlike judicial officers, they served only at the king's pleasure (Goubert 1969).

Considering the size and complexity of the state it was administering, however, the scale of this central government apparatus was quite modest. Pierre Goubert estimates the size of the various councils of the central government, including the many secretaries and clerks (*commis*) who worked at the command of the high administrators, at not much more than two thousand in the eighteenth century (1969, 48–49). The thirty or so intendants, representing the central government in the provinces, for example, were expected to administer sizable regions with populations up to a million souls with something on the order of eight to ten employees. Add to this the fact that all correspondence and records had to be written by hand and that communications were slow. In 1765, it took fifteen and a half days for a passenger or a letter from Toulouse to reach Paris by fast coach and eight days from Nantes. Even after one of the royal administration's most effective efforts at infrastructural improvements, it still took seven and a half days from Toulouse and four and a half from Nantes in 1780 (Arbellot 1973, 790). A truly urgent matter in the district of Toulouse that had to be resolved by a decision of the royal council would require a wait of well over a month for a response from Versailles in 1765 and nearly a month in 1780. Hence many decisions had to be taken by the intendant on his own initiative. In order to know his territory and enforce his authority, the intendant had to spend many days touring his jurisdiction on horseback. And carrying out royal policy at the local level meant relying on the collaboration of local officials in scores or hundreds of villages, some of them illiterate and many of doubtful competence or loyalty. In cities, the problems of communications were far less daunting, but the urban officials were jealous of their cities' privileges and autonomy and often resisted the central government's wishes. The intendants, as the historical literature of the past few decades has demonstrated, were far from the omnipotent emissaries of central authority that they were sometimes imagined to be. In order to accomplish anything of note, they had to find ways of cooperating and negotiating with local powers (Emmanuelli 1981; Beik 1988; Smedley-Weil 1995). In short, however well-organized, efficient, and loyal the old regime administrative apparatus may have been, it was very far from capable of dominating the daily life of French society.

Indeed, old regime state and society look quite different when viewed from the periphery rather than the center. The vast majority of the population lived in the countryside. In 1750, only a little over 9 percent of the French population inhabited cities with populations over ten thousand (de Vries 1984, 39). Agriculture was by far France's predominant economic activity. The income of the nobility, certainly the dominant class of old regime society, was overwhelmingly derived from agriculture, and agriculture also accounted for the lion's share of the state's taxes. The rural community was the fundamental unit of French society.[7] In most of the country, the peasantry lived in tightly packed villages surrounded by cultivated fields, although in parts of western France—Brittany, the Vendée, and portions of Normandy—many peasants lived on isolated farms or in minuscule dispersed hamlets. Patterns of land tenure varied enormously. In the Parisian basin, there were many large consolidated holdings leased out to substantial tenant farmers, who employed gangs of landless or virtually landless laborers. Elsewhere, many cultivators were essentially peasant proprietors, although they generally owed various feudal dues to a noble seigneur, and in other areas, the majority of peasants were sharecroppers. Virtually everywhere there was marked stratification within the mass of peasantry, ranging from farmers sufficiently prosperous to have a team of horses or oxen of their own (commonly known as *laboureurs* or plowmen) down to microproprietors who possessed only a small scrap of land and made most of their income as agricultural wageworkers or country spinners or weavers. In all but the smallest villages, there were a few artisans—blacksmiths, harness makers, shoemakers, carpenters, and so on—most of whom also worked a small plot of land.

7. Research on rural society during the old regime was a specialty of French historiography between World War I and the 1970s (Bloch 1952; Lefebvre 1924; Labrousse 1944; Goubert 1960; Saint-Jacob 1960; Bois 1960; Le Roy Ladurie 1966).

The parish church was at the center of the peasant community, not only for religious observances but also as the place of assembly for the common business of the village. The peasant community had to manage matters concerning the common fields—grazing rights, times of planting and harvest, and the many disputes and issues that arose from the work of cultivation. It was also the village community as a whole that was responsible for collecting and apportioning the taille, a matter that generated plenty of disputes. In most villages, the *curé*, the village priest, was a central figure. As a literate and a more or less educated person, he was consulted in affairs both secular and sacred and called on to intervene, often by means of written requests, with higher authorities—as well acting to resolve intravillage disputes. In most villages, he provided some elementary education to at least the more ambitious boys, hardly ever to girls. The local seigneur, if he was resident in the village—or seigneurs, since there were often more than one per village—could also serve as a link to the larger world. But the seigneur, as a noble, was less accessible to the ordinary peasants than the priest, with whom they interacted regularly and who commonly was the son of a peasant himself.

This sketch of the village community, probably not too far from the truth for most of the great plain stretching from the Loire Valley to Paris and on to the English Channel and the border with Flanders, would have to be altered in various ways in some other regions. In Provence and Languedoc in southern France, the villages were larger and more diverse and might well contain a wider range of artisans, a few merchants, and a notary or a medical doctor. Here the wealthy peasants, called *ménagers* (from *ménage*, or household) usually lived in the countryside in their farm compounds (the *mas*), and many of the farm laborers (known as *travailleurs* or laborers) lived in the village and walked out to the farms to work (Agulhon 1970, 309–38). In the Vendée, just south of Brittany along the Atlantic coast, most peasants lived isolated behind the hedges of their farms, and the rural towns were filled with poor weavers. In this region of absentee seigneurs, it was above all the clergy and the church that held together the rural community (Tilly 1964, 82–145).

By far the most important crops were grains: above all rye and wheat, but also, in some regions, barley, oats, and buckwheat. In a few poor mountainous regions, chestnut consumption outstripped that of grains. But bread was the staple of the diet in nearly all regions of France and the grain harvest the most important single determinant of the health of the economy. Much of the population, both rural and urban, was poor enough that a rise in bread prices could mean serious hunger. During the harvest season, many town workers left their looms, needles, hammers, and shears behind and flowed into the countryside to take advantage of high wages paid during the annual emergency of the harvest. The greater Paris Basin was the breadbasket of France; this agricultural region is still dominated by wheat growing today. But grains of one description or another were grown almost everywhere. There were regions with other agricultural specialties, some of them very prosperous: wines in the Rhone and Loire Valleys, the Bordelais, and Burgundy; dairying in Normandy and cattle and sheep raising in the West and in the mountains; and market gardening in the vicinity of the larger cities. In the eighteenth century, the countryside in many regions of France was increasingly dotted with rural textile workers, both spinners and weavers, some working on their own account but most of them dependent on raw materials and credit from urban entrepreneurs. Most of these rural textile workers wove in their own homes, initially working on wool and flax, but with many moving into cotton later in the century. Nearly all engaged in varying amounts of agriculture on the side and abandoned their looms at harvest time to collect the good wages on offer from big farmers.

Although France was overwhelmingly rural, it also had a prosperous and well-established urban sector. French cities were, socially and legally, sharply distinct from the countryside. In the early Middle Ages—in, for example, the seventh, eighth, or ninth centuries—there were few settlements that would qualify as cities. When urban settlements began to form, their residents built walls and moats to protect themselves from raids by warlike nobles, adopted their own governing institutions, established industrial and commercial enterprises that made the cities prosperous, and declared themselves free—unlike the serfs who inhabited the countryside. Traditionally, the city was defined by its walls and its privileges or liberties, of which the most important was its right of self-government. The kings granted the cities charters that protected their liberties and privileges, essentially in exchange for wartime levies that gave the monarchs increasing independence from their noble vassals. One of the key privileges many cities gained was exemption from the royal taille. In France, as elsewhere in medieval Europe, the cities were islands of freedom in a sea of serfdom: as a German proverb put it, "The town air makes one free." Between the thirteenth and sixteenth centuries, when most French peasants became legally free, they nevertheless remained subject to seigneurial justice and to various feudal dues and regulations. Townsmen, by contrast, were subject to their own municipal governments and stood essentially outside feudal relations. The city, in short, was not simply a place where a sizable population lived densely packed together but a juridically, economically, and socially distinct entity.

Cities varied enormously in scale, wealth, and internal organization. Paris was unique: both a chartered city and the ancient capital of the realm, it was, by the standards of the time, immense. It had a population of something like one hundred thousand as early as 1300, rose to two hundred thousand by 1600, had passed five hundred thousand by 1700, and had at least six hundred thousand in 1789, on the eve of the Revolution. In 1789, Lyon was the only other city with a population over one hundred thousand; Marseille, Rouen, Bordeaux, and Nantes had between seventy thousand and one hundred thousand. Another thirteen had populations above thirty thousand, and eighty to ninety counted between ten thousand and thirty thousand.[8] In addition to these, there were smaller settlements that had walls and charters and counted juridically and socially as cities.[9]

Although the affairs of the cities were increasingly monitored by the royal government in the seventeenth and eighteenth centuries, their privileges and their right to self-government lasted to the very end of the old regime. They raised their own taxes for municipal purposes; maintained their streets, walls, and public buildings; paid for their own police forces; cared for their own poor; and frequently contributed to the upkeep of a secondary school (a *collège*) or in some cases a university. It was city governments that guaranteed the city's privileges and oversaw the regulations of the trade guilds. As Pierre Goubert remarks, urban society was in fact much more hierarchical than rural society (1969, 171). It was above all in the cities that the complex hierarchies so lovingly described by Loyseau were manifested. In villages, there was the immense superiority of the (often absent) lord over the peasants and the distinct prestige of the curé. But among the peasants, differences in wealth or kinship rather than formal status distinguished one from another. It was in cities that corps of every description proliferated. Cities had not only parish priests but cathedral chapters, convents, and houses of Jesuits, Oratorians, Paulists, Augustinians, and other clerical orders, each with identifiable garb; sometimes universities with their privileges and their distinctions between doctors, masters, and bachelors; parlements and lower courts with their judges, barristers, bailiffs, and the like; in some cases provincial estates with their manifold officers; the municipal govern-

8. The eighteenth-century figures, which must be considered estimates, are from Lepetit (1988, 450–52). The earlier figures for Paris are from De Vries (1984, 275).

9. The extensive historical literature on French cities in this period includes (Chartier et al. 1981). For an excellent brief overview, see Goubert (1969, 165–87). Monographs on individual cities include Goubert (1960), Deyon (1967), Couturier (1969), Garden (1970), and Perrot (1975).

ments whose *échevins* or consuls were owed deference; and guilds of all
sorts with their own internal hierarchies. Nobles above a certain rank or
level of wealth generally had an urban house as well as a rural dwelling
and demanded deference in the city. These differences in honor and privilege were often visible in people's garb: specific types of hats and robes
of varying cut, length, and color. In cities, as Goubert puts it, the various
corps or orders "appear with an exceptional clarity . . . almost perfectly
defined and conscious of being so" (172).

Cities had distinct profiles and orientations. Aix-en-Provence, Dijon,
Rennes, or Toulouse were seats of provincial estates and parlements and
had high proportions of nobles, jurists, lawyers, and officials. Port cities
like Marseille, Bordeaux, Nantes, or Saint-Malo were dominated by merchants, sailors, and fishermen. All cities had artisans and shopkeepers:
bakers, butchers, and grocers who provided food; carpenters, masons,
joiners, roofers, glaziers, and locksmiths who provided housing; tailors,
shoemakers, hatters, seamstresses, milliners, and haberdashers who made
and sold clothing; and so forth. Some cities had substantial numbers of
artisans who produced goods for national or international markets—like
the silk workers of Lyon, the thread makers of Lille, or the woolen workers of Sedan. All cities, in different degrees, were centers of commerce
and industry and had sizable populations engaged in what we would call
services: merchants, carters, bankers, porters, brokers, coachmen, and
notaries. Everywhere there were hordes of domestic servants of both
sexes. There were also day laborers, prostitutes, and beggars.

France was a fundamentally rural and agricultural country during the
old regime. But France's cities were formidable containers of wealth,
power, intelligence, and sophistication. France was governed from its
cities, and much wealth production, even in the countryside, was ultimately controlled by urban people and the commercial networks centered there. In Goubert's words, "The importance of cities did not derive
from the number of their inhabitants. . . . They concentrated [France's]
wealth, talents, all that was brilliant, all that counted, all that held power,
force, and culture. The urban minority dominated" (1969, 165). The cities,
for all their archaic qualities, ruled France's commercial and intellectual
life and governed the country as a whole. Cities paradoxically combined
the dynamism of the market and the solvent of the cash nexus with the
archaisms of a society defined by privilege and hierarchy.

This sketch of the structure and functioning of French society has emphasized the perennial features of old regime life rather than the rhythms
of change over time. But there were important changes in this era. In the
realm of politics, the later sixteenth century saw France wracked by ever-

renewed wars of religion, with internal peace restored only upon the ascension of Henri IV (1589–1610), a former Protestant who converted to
Catholicism when he became king. The reign of his successor, Louis XIII
(1610–43), was dominated by international warfare, especially the Thirty
Years' War (1618–48), and consequently by sharply rising taxes, which
caused much internal unrest. Louis XIV (1643–1715) was only four years
old when he acceded to the throne, and his mother, Queen Anne, acted
as regent until 1654, when Louis reached the age of majority. During the
early years of this regency, France was wracked by an immense revolt
known as the Fronde—finally brought to an end in 1653, thanks largely to
the firm actions of Cardinal Mazarin, the regent's chief minister.

Upon the death of Mazarin in 1661, Louis XIV declared that he would
reign personally rather than through ministers. His will continued
to dominate the affairs of the kingdom right up to his death in 1715—
although not without crucial assistance from ministers, of whom the
most important was Jean-Baptiste Colbert. Louis and Colbert undertook systematic reforms that greatly strengthened the king's power, ra-
tionalized government institutions, and provided domestic peace. But
from 1665 on, Louis XIV's reign was a period of intense international
warfare, which brought much glory to the monarch but also, by the end
of the long reign, left the country economically exhausted and deeply in
debt. Because Louis XIV's heir, Louis XV, was only five years old when
his great-grandfather died, Philippe, the Duke of Orleans, served as regent until 1723. Subsequently, Louis XV, who lacked the work ethic and
seriousness of his predecessor, ruled through a succession of ministers.
His reign, like that of Louis XIV, was punctuated by expensive wars, including the disastrous Seven Years' War of 1756–63 that saw England
displacing France as the leading European power. But the administration set up by Louis XIV continued to function effectively to the very
end of the old regime. During Louis XV's reign, a succession of ministers instituted some important reforms and oversaw a period of significant economic prosperity. Louis XVI, the grandson of Louis XV, was
more popular than his grandfather but no more competent. During his
reign, the French gained revenge against their British enemies by joining the American Revolutionary War on the side of the insurgents, but
the cumulated debts generated by successive wars gave rise to a severe financial crisis that eventually produced the Revolution. The eighteenth-
century monarchs were of much weaker character than Louis XIV; most
of their ministers worked within the structures that he and Colbert had
established. But the French continued to enjoy a state that provided
fundamental stability, predictability, and reasonably efficient govern-

ment right up to the Revolution. Moreover, the France that succumbed to an astounding revolution in 1789 was significantly more prosperous than the country had been at the death of Louis XIV. As we shall see in the final chapters of this book, it was not general economic or political weakness that brought the old regime to an end but a fiscal crisis of the state.

The Eighteenth-Century Economy

COMMERCE AND CAPITALISM

If eighteenth-century France remained a bureaucratic absolute monarchy dominated by nobles and structured by hierarchy and privilege, the eighteenth century was also a period of striking economic growth. The expanding French economy was still "preindustrial" in character: the industrial revolution, with its large-scale factories, was only in its early stages at the end of the eighteenth century, even in England, where it first emerged, and a mere handful of enterprises in France could be counted as factories. Capital was invested mainly in circulating rather than fixed capital, and relations between workers and entrepreneurs even in manufacturing were commonly mediated by credit rather than wages. But this French economy was characterized by the product innovation, rapidly changing consumer demand, entrepreneurial investment, and sustained rise in per-capita incomes that characterize the capitalist epoch. France's capitalism in the eighteenth century was commercial in character, but as I will try to demonstrate, it was genuine capitalism.

The economic history of the old regime can be divided into three distinct periods. In France and elsewhere in Europe, what is sometimes called the "long sixteenth century," from roughly 1480 to 1620, was a time of vigorous economic and population growth. The seventeenth century, by contrast, was an era of hardship, of what has been called, with perhaps some exaggeration, "the general crisis of the seventeenth century" (Hobsbawm 1954). Crisis there certainly was, but it was not quite general. During the seventeenth century, the fates of different areas of Europe diverged sharply. Germany, Italy, and Spain experienced declines in wealth and population while England and the Netherlands had sustained growth in both. The experience of France was intermediate: the population and economy were essentially stagnant during the seventeenth century—which, in France and elsewhere, was a period of cold and damp weather and occasional disastrous harvests that led to localized famines and epidemics. The era of Louis XIV's greatest glory was one of much suffering for the French people.

By contrast, the eighteenth century, which is the main focus of this book, was a period of warmer weather, better harvests, and significant economic and population growth—in France and in Europe generally. In retrospect, eighteenth-century economic growth may be seen to mark the spread over much of Europe of the early capitalist development that was already evident in the Netherlands in the late sixteenth century and that had spread to England in the seventeenth. It is well known that the eighteenth century was on the whole a period of optimism in Europe, an optimism manifested most obviously in the forward-looking modes of thought generally signified by the term *Enlightenment*. This optimism was surely a response, in part, to the century's long economic upswing.

It is, however, impossible to be precise about the extent of economic growth in eighteenth-century France. Ever since the 1950s, economists have done their best to make informed growth estimates, but these are all based on incomplete and often shaky data. Figures for the overall population, more reliable than those for economic output, show a rise from approximately twenty-three million at the beginning of the century to twenty-eight million in 1790, an increase of about 22 percent (Dupâquier 1988). Guillaume Daudin, author of the most thorough recent evaluation of eighteenth-century economic growth data, estimates the per-capita increase in French real physical product over the century at about 0.6 percent per year.[1] This translates to about a 60 percent rise in per-capita physical product between 1700 and 1789. Although much less impressive than the growth rates achieved in the nineteenth or twentieth centuries, this was quite remarkable by comparison with the past. In periods of sustained economic growth before the eighteenth century (for example, in the sixteenth or thirteenth century), rises in production tended to be outstripped by population growth, meaning that per-capita incomes actually tended to fall as production rose. The simultaneous and sustained rise of population and incomes over the course of a century was a sign that a new economic dynamic was afoot in eighteenth-century France.

The rates of growth varied considerably by sector. It is generally agreed

1. The term *real* means figures have been adjusted for inflation, which was about 50 percent between 1700 and 1790. These figures are for the "physical product," which means that they exclude services. Since services, particularly commercial services, certainly increased as a proportion of the national product over the eighteenth century, the actual per-capita product presumably rose somewhat faster than this (Daudin 1911, 19). Daudin's calculations are based largely on Marczewski (1961), Bourguignon and Lévy-Leboyer (1985), and Toutain (1961, 1987).

that per-capita agricultural output in France rose slightly, if at all, over the century—the actual figures are uncertain. However, it is clear that after the hard winter of 1709–10, which resulted in local famines, food was never again so scarce in France as to cause death rates to rise substantially. This is a contrast to the seventeenth century, when surges in famine-related deaths occurred on several occasions. Daudin suggests that the absence of famine argues for some increase in per-capita product, by perhaps 10 to 15 percent over the century. It is virtually certain that labor productivity in agriculture rose more rapidly than total output over the course of the century. The population living in towns or cities of five thousand or more seems to have risen from around 17 to around 20 percent of the total population from 1700 to 1790, which would mean that the rural population declined from about 83 to about 80 percent of the total (Daudin 2011, 21–22).[2] Moreover, as we shall see, over the course of the century, a significantly rising portion of the rural population was employed in industry rather than in agriculture. It follows that the agricultural labor force must, at most, have grown only slightly and may even have declined over the course of the century. Yet it was producing between 20 percent and 35 percent more in real terms in 1790 than it had in 1700—around 20 percent if we make the conservative assumption that agricultural product grew at the same rate as the population and around 35 percent if, as Daudin suggests, it may have grown by 15 percent. In summary, although agricultural production grew only slowly, there were signs of progress in the agricultural sector.

Increases in agricultural productivity were not the result of major technological breakthroughs, which came only in the later nineteenth century with chemical fertilizers and mechanical harvesting and threshing. Rather, agriculture improved gradually with more systematic or more widespread application of methods that had, in some cases, been available since the High Middle Ages—improved crop rotations, increased irrigation, more frequent plowing, greater regional specialization, and intensified use of human and animal waste for fertilizer (especially on farms near large cities). George Grantham has calculated that agricultural productivity in the later eighteenth century was sufficiently high for the subsistence needs in wheat and rye of the entire population to be supplied by no more than 40 percent of the adult male population. Something like 60 percent of the population, that is, was free for employment in other pursuits. Of this non-staple-producing 60 percent, some 20 percent lived

---

2. In the rest of this chapter, citations to Daudin will be presented with the page numbers only in parentheses.

in towns with populations over five thousand, but roughly 40 percent remained in the countryside or in smaller towns. A sizable proportion of this rural population was engaged in the production of cash crops other than wheat or rye: fruit and vegetable farming, livestock raising and dairying, wine growing, or production of industrial crops like flax, wool, or hemp. And an increasing proportion of country residents became industrial producers, particularly of textiles. Nearly all these rural people, however, worked in the grain-producing sector during harvest time, as did plenty of urban workers, when the crushing need for labor made harvest work more lucrative than most urban trades (Grantham 1993).

In short, French agriculture during the eighteenth century progressed, but slowly and unevenly. Agricultural yields per hectare on large farms in the Parisian basin, where large farms were plentiful, were probably as high as in the much-lauded English capitalist agriculture at the same time (Allen and O'Grada 1988; Hoffman 1991). Yields in French Flanders, where very intensive farming with complex crop rotations was common, were higher yet. Those in the west and the south, however, were considerably lower (Grantham 1993, 486). Right through the nineteenth century, French agriculture remained labor intensive, dominated, except in the Parisian basin, by small farms operated by peasant proprietors or share-croppers. Much of the progress in agriculture in the eighteenth century and into the early nineteenth seems to have been a consequence of greater specialization, a process pushed forward above all by improved market access—which, as Adam Smith and all economists since tell us, gives rise to increased division of labor and hence greater efficiency.[3] This market-driven specialization was enhanced above all in the vicinity of urban areas, where demand was high, money circulated freely, and better roads meant lower transportation costs, both for carts carrying food to the cities and for carts returning with loads of urban manure. In the unique case of Paris, which was gigantic by the standards of the time, the effects were felt much farther away—for example, much of the meat consumed in Paris came from livestock pastured in Brittany and the Vendée in the west of France.

If progress in agriculture was slow, industry grew much more rapidly. Rates of growth of industry varied greatly by sector: not much above 1 percent a year in woolens (the largest single industry), but nearer 2 percent in iron or linen and silk, and probably 3 percent to 4 percent in cotton

---

3. This is the conclusion of George Grantham (1989, 1991, 1993, 1997), whose accounts of eighteenth-century agriculture I find most convincing.

and coal. Urban trades producing for local markets probably grew more slowly, although consumption figures for clothing indicate a substantial increase. Daudin estimates the overall annual rate of increase of industrial production at between 1.5 percent and 1.9 percent, which would correspond to roughly a tripling or quadrupling of overall industrial production between 1700 and 1789.[4] This was a rate of increase at least as rapid in per-capita terms as that of Great Britain in the same years, although any French advantage probably resulted from starting at a lower level of industrial development in 1700 (Crouzet 1966a; Crafts 1985). In any case, French industrial development in the eighteenth century was vigorous.

Since the industrial revolution of the nineteenth century, we strongly associate industry with cities. But in eighteenth-century France, the most rapid growth of manufacturing activity and the manufacturing workforce was in the countryside. There was plenty of manufacturing located in cities, but it primarily served the local urban population and was carried out within the traditional structures of the guilds: of clothing workers, building workers, butchers and bakers, and manufacturers of many varieties of consumer goods—and of producer goods like barrels, baskets, cauldrons, tools, and wagons. These industrial activities and their practitioners undoubtedly increased over the course of the century as cities' populations grew—but urban growth was relatively slow in eighteenth-century France. There were also artisans producing for local consumption in many villages. A few French industries experienced the development of protofactories in these years—for example, in royal arsenals, cotton spinning and printing, papermaking, metallurgy, and glassmaking. But these establishments generally had fairly simple machinery, and their overall weight in industrial production was small (35–41).

Much industrial growth in the eighteenth century was in rural production intended for wider national and even international markets— what has come to be called "protoindustry" (Mendels 1972; Deyon and Mendels 1979; Kriedte, Medick, and Schlumbohm 1981). Most protoindustrial development in France was in the textile industry, which was also by far the biggest eighteenth-century industry in France and elsewhere. Over the eighteenth century, hundreds of thousands of poor rural residents took up spinning and weaving at the behest of urban textile entrepreneurs. Indeed, a number of textile cities that had once housed many weavers—for example, Caen, Lille, and Valenciennes—saw their

---

4. Daudin (2011, 23–24) uses figures provided by Markovich (1976a, 1976b), Léon (1970), Marczewski (1961), Toutain (1987), and Bourgain and Lévy-Leboyer (1985).

weaver populations decline, in spite of the fact that the cloth industries in their regions were prospering. Protoindustrialization took advantage of surplus labor in the countryside, where men and women, some of whom already had at least rudimentary textile skills, were willing to work for considerably lower remuneration than urban workers—in part because they could gain subsistence from their garden plots and could temporarily turn from their textile work to take advantage of high wages during harvest time. Urban merchants continued to handle the commercial side of the textile trade and sent their agents into the countryside to furnish the spinners and weavers with raw materials and to collect the finished goods. The preparation of the raw fibers for spinning and the finishing and dyeing of cloth was usually done in town by skilled workers. Protoindustrialization, practiced in many regions of France in the eighteenth century—and well into the nineteenth—significantly increased the labor supply and cut labor costs, thus enabling a profitable expansion of the textile industry. The substantial increase in industrial production in eighteenth-century France was based above all on these rural industrial producers (41–57).

Daudin argues persuasively that the key catalyst of economic growth in the eighteenth century, even for the growth of agricultural and industrial production, was commercial intermediation (95). Commerce took many forms under the old regime. Goods were bought and sold at face-to-face village or town markets, at regional fairs, in artisans' or grocers' shops, and by wandering peddlers (Margairaz 1988; Fontaine 1996). But such local marketplaces featuring face-to-face encounters between local buyers and sellers were the least dynamic form of commercial exchange. Commerce quickened economic growth most powerfully when it introduced new products or cheaper or better versions of previously existing products. Such goods were usually produced on a larger scale and were sold well outside the immediate region. It was therefore merchants with translocal connections whose intermediation was most consequential for economic growth.

The primary problems that such merchants faced concerned credit, in its dual meanings of deferred payment and trustworthiness. The two meanings were closely intertwined in practice, since obtaining the goods one wished to sell or use in production commonly entailed obtaining credit from the producer or wholesaler, and to get such credit, one had to be "creditable"—that is, be an honest and honorable merchant known for delivering goods and paying bills on time. In the conditions of the eighteenth century, bills were seldom settled in hard cash, since metallic currency was in short supply. The typical device was the letter of credit, a promissory note made out by one merchant to another but that could be signed over to a third party at a negotiated discount. Thus a wholesale cloth merchant who had received an order of woolens on credit from a manufacturer could use a letter of credit from a tailor or retailer who had bought cloth from him to repay the manufacturer when the money was due. Letters of credit, often bearing several successive signatures, circulated as a de facto form of money, at once a means of payment and a store of value. But the value varied according to the reputation of the merchant who originated the letter, who was, in the last analysis, responsible for the payment.

Most translocal trade was carried out through correspondence, in letters carried by the semipublic postal service or by private operators. But merchants tended to spend time on the road, both seeking out reliable suppliers and buyers and renewing contact with past trading partners. Face-to-face contact and the establishment of solid relationships were essential in a credit-based economy in which decisions had to be made on the basis of incomplete information—necessarily incomplete because relevant information took anything from several days to several weeks to reach the merchant from distant correspondents. Some of the bigger merchants would employ traveling agents (*commis*) to act on their behalf, but once again the element of trust was crucial. An agent acting at several days' distance from the principal had to be trusted to make decisions without immediate guidance. In short, the skills of merchants consisted not only in solid bookkeeping, shrewd negotiating, a sense of evolving consumer taste, and an eye for bargains but also in sustaining relationships with a wide range of sellers, buyers, agents, and transporters—not to mention competitors in their field of enterprise, who might well be collaborators on future projects and whose goodwill and opinion was of considerable value. A wise merchant paid close attention to sustaining or accumulating human capital and social capital of this sort if he wished to accumulate financial capital and personal wealth. This complex network of commercial relations undergirded the rising production and circulation of goods in the eighteenth century.[5]

One very clear example of the contribution made by mercantile intermediaries is the case of rural protoindustrial development. Textile manufacture was the most important industrial complex in eighteenth-century

---

5. Daudin (2011, 143–66) has an illuminating discussion of the components of commercial activities in the eighteenth century.

France. The key figures in the textile industry were city-based entrepreneurs, variously called *marchands* or *fabricants*, who typically oversaw all steps of the manufacturing process and marketed the cloth to wholesalers or retailers when it was completed. They purchased the raw fibers, sometimes locally, sometimes from considerable distances, as in the case of Spanish wool, East Indian or West Indian cotton, or Italian silk. They then had the fibers prepared for spinning (typically in urban workshops) and put the fibers out to spinners (usually women), either in the city or in the surrounding countryside. The spun yarn was then distributed by merchants to weavers (usually men), again either in the city or in the countryside. The merchants collected the completed pieces of cloth and had them (variously) dyed, bleached, pressed, or otherwise "finished" to make them ready for sale.

The organization of textile production varied by region and from one type of cloth to another. But the role played by these entrepreneurs everywhere was essentially commercial in character. Their physical capital was relatively limited—a shop and warehouse, perhaps dyeing vats or wool-combing or wool-shearing gear. Their investment was overwhelmingly in circulating capital, primarily raw materials and unfinished or finished cloth. Much of the finished cloth might be outside the merchant's physical possession, consigned to wholesalers or retailers. In this respect, the cloth entrepreneurs were merchants like any others. But they also used commercial techniques to organize the production process. Very few of the workers who made textiles were employed for a wage—principally some of those who prepared fibers or worked in dyeing and finishing. The spinners and weavers who constituted the vast majority of the textile labor force were, legally speaking, independent entrepreneurs themselves, most of whom bought raw materials from the fabricants/marchands and sold them the finished yarns or cloths they produced. However, given the poverty of the spinners and weavers and the relative wealth of the merchants, these were essentially debt/credit relations. The raw materials, sometimes even the looms and wheels used to work them up, were provided on credit, with interest on the loan deducted from the payment for the finished product. This commercially organized production process was utterly dominated by the wealthy fabricants/marchands, who, over the course of the eighteenth century, expanded these production networks farther and farther into the countryside, reducing their production costs by seeking out poor and underemployed rural people as spinners and weavers. This was clearly an objectively exploitative relationship, but from the macroeconomic point of view, it also absorbed underutilized rural labor into a commercial capitalist productive process, thereby making a major contribution to increasing France's overall wealth over the course of the century.[6]

Protoindustrial textile production was one clear example of how commercial intermediation, by reorganizing the productive capacity of rural regions, served as a stimulus to economic growth. But the most spectacular and profitable commercial operations went on at a grander scale. The fastest-growing sector of the French economy in the eighteenth century was international trade, which expanded roughly fourfold, about three times as fast as the economy as a whole (192).[7] In fact, French international trade grew considerably more rapidly than that of England in the eighteenth century. On the eve of the Revolution, France, not England, was Europe's top international trading nation in terms of sheer volume (Daudin 2011, 198–99; Crouzet 1996b).

Some of this international trade crossed land borders, but the bulk of it was maritime, since waterborne trade was generally faster and cheaper, even for commerce with European countries. But the most profitable and fastest-growing international trade was with Asia, the Americas, and Africa (203–6). The transoceanic trading operations of the French port cities were dominated by merchants with considerable capital resources, who typically split their investments between several voyages simultaneously—not to mention their holdings in more stable investments like land and state debt. It was important to distribute risks in this fashion, since many hazards loomed—for example, shipwrecks, warfare, piracy, or the miscalculation of conditions in distant markets. But for those rich enough to hedge their bets by making investments in multiple simultaneous ventures, profits were generous—significantly above the norm for other available investments.[8] The vast bulk of eighteenth-century French ocean-borne trade passed through the three great Atlantic ports, Bordeaux, Nantes, and Rouen-Le Havre, and the Mediterranean port of Marseille. Of these, Bordeaux was the most dynamic in the eighteenth century, in part because (in addition to wines) it specialized in the colonial and African slave trades, which boomed in these years. Bordeaux's population doubled from about fifty thousand in 1700 to about one hundred thousand at the beginning of the Revolution, by which time

6. There was tremendous variation in the organization of textile production in different regions, for different fibers, and for different products (Dornic 1955; Kaplow 1964; Guignet 1979; Engrand 1979; Dayon 1979; Reddy 1984; Liu 1994; Johnson 1995; Terrier 1996; Gayot 1998). The silk industry, which remained essentially urban, is discussed in chapter 4.

7. This estimate is based primarily on figures derived from Arnaud (1791).

8. On maritime mercantile strategies, see Carrière (1973) and Butel (1974).

it was the most important reexporter of such island-produced goods as sugar, coffee, cotton, and indigo to the rest of Europe (Daudin 2011, 322–23; Crouzet 1996b; Lepetit 1988, 450).

Not only was this transoceanic trade fast growing and highly profitable, but it also had a transformative effect on French and European consumption patterns. Chinese and Japanese porcelains, Chinese tea, and light and colorful printed Indian cottons (known as calicoes in England and as *indiennes* in France) found voracious markets among consumers all across Europe after being introduced by the Dutch East India Company in the early seventeenth century. By the eighteenth century, the British and the French were also importing vast quantities of such Asian goods. Exotic stimulants—coffee, chocolate, and tobacco, all cultivated in the Americas—eventually won masses of European consumers. Tea, coffee, and chocolate were generally consumed with sugar, a product long known in Europe but produced in rapidly expanding quantities in Brazil and the West Indies, on plantations using African slave labor. Sugar became the most important single driver of transoceanic trade in the eighteenth century. Cotton, a fiber already known in Europe but whose popularity soared after the introduction of Indian calicoes, also was cultivated in the West Indies and in the southern colonies on the American mainland in the eighteenth century, to be woven up in Europe. On the eve of the Revolution, the French colony of Saint-Domingue—present-day Haiti—was the leading exporter of sugar, cotton, and coffee to Europe, most of it passing through Bordeaux, and much of it reexported at a substantial profit to other European countries.

These "exotic" commodities reshaped the consumption landscape of France and of other European countries. Coffeehouses—in France, the famous cafés—proliferated and changed the very textures of urban life. It was in the eighteenth century that café au lait became the standard breakfast of urban French men and women of all classes and the café a favorite place of recreation (C. Jones and Spang 1999). Disrupted and inspired by the craze for light, colorful, and relatively inexpensive Indian calicoes, the fashion industry became France's most dynamic industry in the eighteenth century. The silk industry of Lyon developed its own version of bright floral patterns inspired by calicoes but with a luxurious sheen that cotton could never attain.[9] And by the 1780s, France had the biggest cotton-printing industry in Europe, churning out copies of both the Indian designs and new designs of its own (Chapman and Chassagne 1981, 8). Umbrellas and fans, commodities originally in-

9. See chapter 4.

troduced from China and Japan, became must-have fashion accessories (Fairchilds 1993). The popularity of coffee, tea, and chocolate gave rise to a much-enhanced demand for the earthenware and porcelain tableware in which they were served: cups; saucers; and tea, coffee, and chocolate pots, some of them fashioned after Asian models but others based on neoclassical European designs (*Thé* 2015). Crucially, all these new consumption goods penetrated much further down the social hierarchy in the course of the eighteenth century than had the luxury items of previous centuries. Stimulated significantly by new "exotic" goods, consumer demand for ever-new products became a major driver of commerce and industry alike in the eighteenth century.

Eighteenth-Century Capitalism?

The eighteenth-century French economy, in short, was expanding impressively—at least by the standards of previous centuries. But should this expanding economy be characterized as capitalist? This is a complex and contested issue. Most economic historians would probably regard the question as purely terminological. For them, the issue is whether or not a society is experiencing "economic growth," defined as a sustained increase in income per capita. This, however, is a purely empirical standard: it says nothing about the socioeconomic dynamics that enable incomes to rise in a sustained fashion.

It was Karl Marx whose writings most powerfully posed the question of capitalism's dynamics. For Marx, the emergence of capitalism constituted a sharp break from previous types of economic and social life. Under capitalism, economic life takes the form of the production and exchange of commodities with the exclusive goal of pecuniary profit. This imposes a pervasive abstraction on economic life: the value of things comes increasingly to lie only in their exchange value—that is, what price they can fetch in the market.[10] Of course, market exchange had been in existence in Europe and other regions of the world for centuries. And where markets of any sort exist, people prefer to buy cheap and sell dear. But before the emergence of capitalism, most goods were not offered on the market at all. They were used by their producers rather than offered up for sale

---

10. The first chapter of Marx's *Capital* is entitled "The Commodity" and demonstrates, as he puts it, that although "a commodity appears at first sight an extremely obvious, trivial thing . . . its analysis brings out that it is a very strange thing, abounding in metaphysical subtleties and theological niceties" (1977, 163). The chapter stretches for sixty-two dense pages.

or were exchanged as gifts or extracted without payment from their producers by force or by custom—as in the rural feudal economy of the European Middle Ages. Moreover, the value of many goods was thought to reside in their utility or beauty or in their meaning to those who made, acquired, or used them, not in the price they could fetch in the market. Viewed from a long-term or worldwide perspective, a fully commodified economy appears exceptional and even uncanny (Sewell 2008, 2014b).

For Marx, the transition to capitalism required the universalization of commodity production. This, crucially, entailed that human labor be made into a commodity to be exchanged in the market like any other. When labor became commodified, a fundamental element of human sensuous experience was shaped by and abstracted into its monetary value. Labor, in this sense, became alienated from what Marx, in his 1840 manuscripts, called its "human essence" (1978). Rather than an expression of the worker's being or of God's decree, labor became just another commodity whose activities and products belonged to the person who bought it. Marx reasoned that it was only when humans became "doubly free"—that is, both juridically free and therefore able to make a contract to sell their labor at will and "free" of property in the means of production and therefore forced to seek employment—that they became fully exploitable proletarians. Once workers must sell their labor power in exchange for a wage in order to subsist, their labor becomes a commodity, subject like any other commodity to the play of market forces (Marx [1867] 1977, 272–73).

But human labor is a commodity of a unique sort, because, unlike a tool, a machine, or a raw material, it is a commodity that, if effectively employed, can regularly produce more value than its cost to the employer. Like the value of any commodity, the value of labor, according to Marx, is determined by its cost of production. The cost of production of the laborer is the cost of the food, clothing, housing, recreation, and so forth that makes it possible for him or her to show up at work and perform a day's labor regularly and raise children who will become the wage workers of the future. This cost will, on average, determine the level of the laborer's wage. But the worker is a peculiarly *elastic* means of production; the worker can be induced—by fear, discipline, pride, or enticements of various sorts—to work intensely and enhance the value of the goods produced by considerably more than the value of the wage he or she is paid. Other commodities used as means of production lack this peculiar elasticity: they are capable, on average, of producing only a value equivalent to the price the entrepreneur pays for them. The unpaid *surplus value* that only labor can create is, according to Marx, the secret of the sustained profitability of capitalism and hence its ability to expand indefinitely. It is the regular daily harvesting of this surplus value created by the laborer and the plowing of the resultant profits back into production in order to produce yet more surplus value that, Marx claims, impart to the capitalist economy its peculiar dynamism.

Marx further points out that there are two distinct means by which the capitalist may harvest surplus value from his labor force. The first crude but effective method is simply prolonging the working day or speeding up the pace of production. If the worker can produce a value equivalent to his wage in eight hours, the employer can increase the time of labor to ten hours and take the added 25 percent of value produced as profit. (The same result could be reached by maintaining an eight-hour day and increasing the speed of work by 25 percent.) This produces what Marx calls "absolute surplus value." But there is also the more sophisticated route of what he calls "relative surplus value." In this case, the employer reorganizes production, typically but not only by introducing new technology, in order to increase labor productivity—that is, enabling the worker to produce more value in each hour of labor. This also increases the surplus value extracted in a day of labor but has the advantage of not wearing down the worker (Marx [1867] 1977, 643–54).

Although capitalist employers use both of these methods, it is increasing relative surplus value that imparts to capitalism its peculiarly sustained dynamism. When an entrepreneur institutes a new technological or organizational scheme that increases the productivity of the firm's laborers, the firm will be able to produce items at a lower unit cost than its competitors. It therefore could simply continue to sell the items at the industry's going price and make significantly enhanced profits. But the wiser strategy is to undercut the competition by lowering the price of the product to a level that still produces a good profit per unit but significantly undersells the competition, thereby increasing the innovating firm's volume of sales and its overall profit. This situation of enhanced profits, however, is bound to be temporary: some competitors will be driven out of business, but others will copy the innovation in order to compete effectively, with the result that profits will eventually be driven down to more or less the level they had reached before the initial innovation. This, in turn, provides an incentive for further cost-cutting innovations, setting the cycle in motion once again. The consequence for the larger economy of the pursuit of *relative* surplus value will be a long-term tendency toward expansion of production and increasing efficiency—in other words, toward indefinitely sustained economic growth, what in Marxian terms might be called the endless accumulation of capital. Marx's dynamic of relative surplus value, in short, is a key distinguishing feature of capitalism. If, as I suggest, we accept Marx's general framework, the question of whether the eighteenth-century French economy was capitalist hinges on the extent to which it enabled the production of surplus value and in particular whether it was characterized by the upward-spiraling dynamic of relative surplus value.

In *Capital*, Marx developed this theory of capitalist dynamics by studying the leading industry of the nineteenth century's most dynamic capitalist country—that is, the English cotton industry. This was an industry characterized by large, highly mechanized factories driven by steam power and employing vast numbers of fully proletarianized workers. Such a situation made visible to Marx's keen eye the exploitation of labor that fueled the rapid accumulation of capital so evident in the English cotton industry. It also enabled him to grasp the peculiar dynamics of absolute and relative surplus value, both prominent in this industry. But Marx's focus on English cotton production also led him to make what I regard as an incorrect inference about the origins of capitalism. He reasoned that a capitalist dynamic could only arise in a situation where there the two poles of capitalist exploitation he found in nineteenth-century England were already in place—that is, where a sizable collection of doubly free laborers and capital-rich potential employers could find one another in the market and enter into a capitalist labor contract. This assumption led Marx into what I regard as an ultimately futile search for a moment of "primitive accumulation," some historical event that suddenly produced potential workers who were both juridically free and desperately needy and wealthy potential capitalists eager to employ them (Marx [1867] 1977, 879–940).

I suggest that we put aside Marx's assumption that without the existence of doubly free laborers there can be no production of absolute and relative surplus value, and hence no capitalism. Rather, we should regard the fully proletarian condition that Marx analyzed in volume one of *Capital* as a gradually produced *outcome* rather than as a *prerequisite* of early capitalist development. To demonstrate that something worthy of the name *capitalism* existed in eighteenth-century France, we need to show not that a large, fully proletarianized labor force had come into existence but rather that surplus value was somehow being extracted from whatever labor was employed and that the extent of surplus value extraction increased over the course of the century. In particular, we must show that a recognizable version of the dynamic of relative surplus value was operative in a significant proportion of eighteenth-century French economic life.

Capitalist dynamics were least evident in eighteenth-century agriculture, the most important economic activity in France. The overall growth rate in agriculture was modest, at best, in the eighteenth century. Indeed, it seems certain that something approaching half of all agricultural production in eighteenth-century France must have been directly consumed by the agriculturalists themselves—by the peasant and sharecropper families who occupied the soil. Such peasant cultivators would put on the market only the surplus, if any, beyond the consumption needs of the family. This conservative peasant agriculture, geared to the subsistence needs of the family, remained essentially outside the circuits of capital. Self-sufficient peasant agriculture remained an impediment to capitalist development in France not only in the eighteenth century but right through the nineteenth century and well into the twentieth. It does, however, appear that even this most sluggish sector of the eighteenth-century French economy was evolving in a more capitalist direction. Agriculturalists who lived near cities increasingly produced for the market in response to rising urban demand. We have seen that in the Paris region, virtually landless laborers worked on large estates that produced primarily for the urban market. Such large farms were fundamentally capitalist, and their labor forces certainly produced plenty of absolute surplus value. Given the farms' dependence on competitive production for the market and their relatively high productivity, the dynamics of relative surplus value must also have been in play there. The small farmers near the cities who grew cash crops for urban consumers were certainly dependent on the market, often employed wage labor, and, like many small businessmen, could be regarded as self-exploiting petty capitalists. It is also possible that as the eighteenth century progressed, even many farm families that produced most of their own food sent more of their high-value wheat and rye to the market, ate starches with less market value, and used the proceeds of grain sales to purchase a rising volume of manufactured consumer goods. Such families could hardly be characterized as engaging in capitalist agriculture, but their lives were increasingly caught up in the commodity relations that accompanied capitalist development.

Capitalist relations of production were much more common in eighteenth-century French industry. Few production sites remotely resembled nineteenth-century English cotton factories. The cotton-spinning mills or paper mills or iron foundries that existed in France by the 1780s were generally far smaller and less technically advanced than Marx's nineteenth-century cotton factories. Although typically staffed by wage laborers subject to the dynamics of both absolute and relative surplus value, the weight of such establishments in the overall economy was slight. Far more economically significant were the hundreds of thousands of textile workers in the woolen, cotton, silk, and linen industries, the vast majority of whom, as we have seen, were juridically independent but indebted petty contractors, not wage earners. One suspects that they were exploited as effectively as wage laborers would have been, but via the putter-out's manipulation of prices and interest rates rather than by low wages and long working days.

From the Marxian perspective outlined in this chapter, the exploitation suffered by putting-out textile workers would seem, on the whole, to have been forms of absolute surplus value extraction. Weavers and spinners were forced by unequal debt relations to perform extra labor in order to compensate for the underpayment or high rates of interest imposed on them by the putting-out merchants. This form of surplus extraction certainly should qualify as capitalist in character. The exploitation produced by putting-out definitely contributed to the forward thrust of capitalism in eighteenth-century France. Although no exact figures are available, it is clear that the sheer number of putting-out workers rose substantially over the century, both absolutely and relative to the overall population. Men and women previously only casually employed or engaged in marginally productive farming now made their living by producing textile commodities for sale. Although juridically self-employed, they were an expanding portion of a commodity-producing and market-dependent labor force, whose productive work contributed directly to the growing profits of the textile entrepreneurs. The expansion of this textile labor force created few of Marx's doubly free wage workers, but through its massive production of absolute surplus value, it was nevertheless a major component of the expansion of capitalist relations in eighteenth-century France.[11]

Putting-out textile manufacture could also promote the technical progress characteristic of relative surplus value. For example, in the area around Rouen, cotton weavers initially used linen or wool rather than cotton for their warp yarns because the spinners were unable to produce sufficiently strong cotton yarns. But under market pressure from the putters-out, spinners developed greater skill and were eventually able to make acceptably strong cotton warp threads, resulting in cheaper, superior, and more competitive goods. A parallel improvement in skills took place in the vast and scattered French woolen industry. The woolen merchants forced or induced their spinners and weavers to upgrade their skills and thereby the quality of the woolen cloths. As a consequence, although the

---

11. Capitalist relations also advanced in the large and prosperous silk industry centered in the Lyon. In this case of strictly urban putting out, the particular dynamics were different, but the capitalist character of the enterprises was absolutely clear. See chapter 4.

number of pieces of cloth produced increased only a little in the eighteenth century, the value of the cloth produced doubled (Markovich 1976b, 494–95). The cotton and woolen industries both experienced significant increases in productivity of labor in the eighteenth century. In short, dynamics of relative as well as absolute surplus value production were in evidence in these industries even though both had labor forces composed predominantly of juridically independent but chronically indebted rural artisans, not wage workers.

Urban Manufacturing

If rural manufacturing was booming, it has often been observed that stifling guild regulations slowed the development of urban manufacturing in France. Guilds retarded the adoption of capitalist manufacturing by monopolizing markets in their cities, limiting access to masterships, and regulating methods of producing goods. It was partly for this reason that urban population growth in France was so restricted. However, manufacturing nevertheless thrived in many regions and many branches of industry and in some cases thrived in urban settings, in spite of the guilds. Several studies of eighteenth-century French urban manufactures indicate that in newer industries or industries with rapidly expanding demand, guilds could be sidestepped or could themselves enact regulations that accommodated changes in techniques or design. As we will see in some detail in chapter 4, in the silk industry of Lyon—France's biggest and wealthiest industrial complex in the eighteenth century— the guild organization was completely taken over by the silk merchants and shaped to eminently capitalist ends. On a smaller scale, the guild of the rapidly expanding linen thread industry of Lille placed no limits on the number of thread-twisting mills a single master could operate. The consequence was a more than threefold increase in mills, and presumably in output, between 1720 and 1789 (Bossenga 1991, 153–55). By contrast, Lille's woolen weavers maintained their restrictive control of woolen cloth production, but this largely resulted in the migration of production to the guild-free nearby industrial villages of Roubaix and Tourcoing, where production thrived.

Michael Sonenscher has shown that in Paris, the manufacture and decoration of lacquered coaches, which became extraordinarily popular among the wealthy, effectively sidestepped regulations purportedly governing the various trades employed in this booming industry—including joiners, metalworkers, painters, gilders, sculptors, turners, engravers, and goldsmiths. The Martin brothers, inventors of a lacquer that they claimed could produce goods superior to the much-in-demand Chinese and Japanese lacquer wares, specialized in coachbuilding and were granted the distinction of *vernisseur du roi* (royal varnisher), a title that freed them from normal guild regulations. They took advantage of this privilege to set up highly specialized luxury coach manufactures but simultaneously entered much more modest but highly profitable trades such as producing lacquered papier-mâché snuffboxes that would normally have been monopolized by the guild of *tabletiers* (Sonenscher 1989, 210–43). The coachbuilding trade was far from unique. The highly skilled luxury trades of Paris were, as Sonenscher points out, "one of the most substantial components of the eighteenth-century urban economy" (1989, 212). Indeed, these trades remained numerous and prosperous well into the nineteenth century in Paris (Harvey 2003, 153–57). In the eighteenth century, they proved devilishly difficult to control by means of guild regulations, in part because designs, materials, and techniques were constantly changing to capture the fancy of customers, changing so rapidly that guild regulations could not keep up.

These volatile high-end luxury trades, driven by constant design changes and fickle consumer tastes, were supplemented by more modest consumer goods industries producing what Cissie Fairchilds dubbed "populuxe goods"—that is, cheap versions of items that prosperous consumers had made fashionable. Many modest artisans and servants in eighteenth-century Paris owned new types of furniture, crockery, and such items as gold watches, fans, and umbrellas that had become fashionable among their betters. Fairchilds shows how knock-off versions of products supposedly monopolized by guilds, such as umbrellas and fans, were manufactured either in workers' homes or in the Faubourg Saint-Antoine—immediately east of Paris, where Parisian guilds had no powers—and were sold by peddlers or street sellers (Fairchilds 1993). Similarly, Steven Kaplan has discovered that the Parisian guilds had little success in suppressing the countless so-called false workers who made cheap versions of furniture and other goods in their domiciles in Paris and especially in the Faubourg Saint-Antoine (Kaplan 1988).

Where demand was high and tastes fickle, the guilds could fight only a rearguard battle. Urban trades producing for new and expanding markets usually found ways to modify or get around guild regulations. It was mainly trades producing for the more restricted markets of their own cities—for example, bakers, butchers, or the building trades—that continued to observe strict guild restrictions. Even these restrictions were loosened in the wake of the reforming Controller General Turgot's attempted abolition of guilds in 1776, which led not to their disappearance but to a substantial weakening of their powers (Kaplan 2001). The persistence of guilds certainly constrained urban industries, but it did so unevenly and incompletely.

Moreover, many French manufacturers obtained what Jeff Horn has felicitously dubbed "the privilege of liberty," assorted exemptions that allowed them to ignore both royal and guild regulations. Colbert, the architect of a regime of strict regulations governing the woolen textile industry, established a regime of "royal manufactures," enterprises that were exempted from many of the usual guild and regulatory constraints and sometimes given subsidies by the state. These were generally created to encourage technical or product innovation (Minard 1998; Deyon and Guignet 1980). The installation of English-style cotton manufactures in Normandy in the 1780s, often founded by entrepreneurs who had migrated from England, was typically supported by making these enterprises royal manufactures (Horn 2015, 87–89). This was actually a longstanding policy. As early as 1646, a royal manufacture was established in the newly captured city of Sedan, near the border of the Spanish Netherlands, to enable the French to make fine woolen cloths of the type that were, at this time, typically made in Holland and England. By the middle of the eighteenth century, the royal manufacture in Sedan had become the leading producer of fine woolens in France (Gayot 1998).

The royal manufactures were only one example of "privileges of liberty." In the territorial hodgepodge that was old regime France, there were many enclaves in which the seigneurs, not the royal state, held the right of high justice. These seigneurs, who might be princes, nobles, bishops, abbots, or abbesses, held powers of "police" over the territory and consequently could free enterprises from tax requirements or from oversight by guilds or state inspectors (Horn 2012, 2015). The Faubourg Saint-Antoine, an eastern suburb of Paris that was under the jurisdiction of the Abbey of Saint-Antoine-des-Champs, was a major site of manufacturing in the Paris region and a perpetual thorn in the side of the Parisian guilds. The Faubourg Saint-Antoine specialized particularly in the furniture industry but also sheltered the production of many other goods otherwise regulated in principle by the guilds. It was the site of some substantial establishments, including the famous Revillon wallpaper factory, which produced another new and very stylish consumer good. There were comparable enclaves in most large cities, notably including the ecclesiastical enclaves Saint-Seurin and Saint-André just outside Bordeaux, which were also hives of enterprise (Horn 2015, 26–35). The Saint-Sever neighborhood directly across the Seine River from Rouen became a sort of enterprise zone. The enclave hosted seven royal manufactures but also bristled with other industrial activities. It had some twenty protofactories devoted to cotton spinning, as well as cotton dyeing and bleaching works, ceramics workshops, glassmakers, and chemical manufactures. It was a magnet for British manufacturers and skilled workers eager to set up enterprises in the Rouen area, just a few miles down the Seine River from the English Channel. The experience of Saint-Sever indicated clearly the potential advantages of the privilege of liberty in the context of the French polity (Horn 2015, 85–89).

The experience of urban trades that thrived in spite of guild restrictions and entrepreneurs who managed to take advantage of "privileges of liberty" indicates that capitalism was alive and well in urban as well as rural areas in eighteenth-century France. It is certainly true that guilds constrained such developments where they could and that other aspects of French economic arrangements weighed on the possibility of more rapid industrial growth—for example, perverse internal barriers to trade and a taxation system that grotesquely favored idle landowners over industrious farmers, merchants, and manufacturers. Old regime France was hardly a paradise for capitalism, but inventive entrepreneurs, both large and small, found ways to prosper.

Colonial Capitalism

We have seen that overseas trade had the highest profit rates in eighteenth-century France. This trade dealt largely in exotic agricultural commodities produced by slave labor in the French Caribbean and Indian Ocean colonies. Slave-based agriculture was also, in my opinion, an essentially capitalist undertaking. This is a contentious position, particularly among Marxian scholars, many of whom have held that slavery was more feudal than capitalist. The colonial plantations produced veritable mountains of commodities for the European market, primarily sugar but also coffee, cacao, indigo, and cotton. All were cash crops, intended for European consumption, and were produced overwhelmingly by slave labor. Plantations required a heavy investment of capital—production of sugar, in particular, required sizable agricultural holdings and elaborate and expensive boilers and machinery. The plantation labor force was made up not of wage workers but of slaves, exported by the thousands from Africa. Slaves who were owned by the planter were a component—indeed, usually by far the biggest component—of the planter's *capital*; they were, from a technically economic point of view, analogous to cattle or horses, as the term *chattel slavery*, common in the American South, implies. But they were, of course, chattel of a peculiar kind, with the familiar sort of elasticity that was also characteristic of other exploited humans, such as wage workers or rural weavers. Slaves' work in the fields was systematically organized by overseers to extract a maximum quantity of labor. Discipline was severe and corporal punishment an ever-present threat. Indeed, the high death rate of slaves in the Caribbean and Indian Ocean colonies suggests that slaves were often driven well beyond the economic optimum. The strong preference for male over female slaves and the acceptance of high death rates may have reflected a calculation that it was cheaper to replace this human capital with new purchases than to support its reproduction in the colony.

This colonial slavery had little in common with feudal relations. Caribbean and Indian Ocean slaves produced commodities for a market and were themselves fully commodified, available for sale on the market, and entirely at the disposal of their owners. Marx's doubly free proletarianized laborers were merely constrained to sell their labor power as a commodity; they remained juridically free, including, crucially, free to seek employment elsewhere. If fully proletarianized workers were an indubitable sign of capitalism, then the slave plantation was an intensified version of capitalist enterprise based on a grotesque form of absolute surplus value production unconstrained by the niceties of European labor relations. In short, the slave-based plantations of the French colonies, which, as we have seen, were the engine of the most profitable and rapidly expanding branch of eighteenth-century French commerce, were capitalist— indeed, in some respects, hypercapitalist—institutions.[12]

The colonies were also prime sites of a distinctly capitalist form of exploitation not theorized by Marx: what Jason W. Moore has called the "commodity frontier." Beginning in the sixteenth century, Europeans used their increasing domination of the seas as a means of gaining cheap commodities from distant regions. The earth and what then seemed its inexhaustible fruits were increasingly plundered for material gain. The commodities extracted from these new frontiers included food (e.g., Baltic grain, North Atlantic cod, North Sea herring, and Caribbean sugar), industrial raw materials (Swedish iron and Norwegian, Baltic, and North American timber and pitch), labor (African slaves), land (for new plan-

---

12. The pioneering work on slavery and capitalism in the Caribbean on the British colonies was Mintz (1985, 19–73). See also Williams (1984) and Austen (2017). Blackbourn (1997) is an impressive general treatment. Recent work on slavery in the French Caribbean includes (Dubois 2004; D. Garrigus 2001; J. Garrigus 2006; Cheney 2017).

tations and for timber extraction, mines, and colonial settlements), and means of circulation (gold and silver). These commodity frontiers were exploited (and frequently exhausted) at an unprecedented rate. The influx of cheap commodities provided important windfall profits in the countries that established commodity frontiers. It lowered the cost of living (and hence wages) in the metropole, lowered costs of capital goods (especially raw materials), accelerated the circulation of value, and strongly stimulated commercial development. Exploitation of such commodity frontiers helped power the breakthrough to capitalism in the Netherlands in the late sixteenth and seventeenth centuries and was copied by the British and the French in the later seventeenth and eighteenth centuries. It is no coincidence that, as we have seen, the most rapidly expanding component of eighteenth-century French economic advance was Atlantic maritime trade. The exploitation of commodity frontiers, nowhere more brutally than in the Caribbean colonies, was a crucial feature of old regime French capitalism.[13]

In short, the application of what I take to be appropriate Marxian criteria for the existence of capitalism—the production of absolute and relative surplus value and the exploitation of commodity frontiers—reveals that there was plenty of capitalism in eighteenth-century France and its overseas appendages. To be sure, France was not a fully capitalist economy. Most peasant cultivators, who made up the largest segment of the French population, were only minimally affected by capitalist economic dynamics. The greatest accumulations of wealth, those of the landed nobility, were based on inherited rents and on state offices and emoluments—but the royal state, on which they increasingly depended, was itself ever more dominated by financial worries that could be solved only by sustained economic growth, something that capitalist development alone promised. Many urban workers and employers were in industries controlled by highly constraining guild regulations—but French cities were also command posts of the expanding capitalist economy and centers of the production and consumption of new forms of consumer goods. The expanding capitalist sectors of the economy were big and dynamic enough to assure sustained growth in the overall economy and to influence the thought and the conduct even of those whose occupations

13. Indeed, according to Moore (2010a, 2010b), the proliferation of exploitative commodity frontiers has been an essential ingredient of all capitalism before or since. Think, for example, of coal, oil, the clear-cutting of forests, imperialist and postimperialist land grabs, and the use of the earth's environment as an inexhaustible source of materials and a gigantic sink.

placed them outside the most clearly capitalist sectors. This was a capitalism dominated not by coal, steam, and factories, like the nineteenth-century economies spawned by the industrial revolution, but by expanding markets and a rising commercial culture both within France and across the high seas. If industry was both the keyword and the driver of the nineteenth-century economy, commerce was the keyword and driver in the eighteenth century.

I

The Emergence of an Urban Public

* 3 *

The Commercial Public Sphere

In the introduction to this book, I proposed that the embrace of civic equality by the French revolutionaries was a consequence of the advance of capitalism during the eighteenth century. In chapter 2, I attempted to demonstrate not only that France experienced significant economic growth but that this economic growth was powered by a nascent capitalist dynamic. But how, precisely, did this economic dynamic, taking place as it did in a profoundly hierarchical society, give rise to the notion of civic equality? How could capitalist development affect people's social experiences, expectations, feelings, and thoughts enough to make it seem not only possible but desirable in 1789 to reorder the French state and society in terms of civic equality?

I have suggested that a fundamental feature of capitalism is its construction of relatively abstract social relations. In precapitalist societies, a person's form of life was strongly determined by her or his location in a fixed and hierarchical social world. Whom you would marry, what your occupation would be, how you should behave, and where you would stand in the eyes of others—such basic facts of social life were largely determined by one's birth into a given family with a given rank. Capitalist social relations, based on the relatively anonymous exchange of commodities, opened new possibilities. Increasingly a person's options depended on their ability to maneuver in a world governed by buying and selling, including, of course, selling one's own labor or the products of one's labor or hiring the labor of others. By taking advantage of the possibilities of commodity exchange, a person could, potentially, accumulate assets—including skills, knowledge, and modes of behavior—and use those assets to construct a life significantly different from the one into which he or she was born. This life construction was possible not only as a producer but also as a consumer. As new goods became available on the market, one could change one's consumption styles—for example, purchase different clothing, engage in different forms of leisure activity, gain exposure to commercially available media—thus forming a new social profile with different expectations and possibilities. In a capitalist world, one's life trajectory was relatively uncertain, potentially more hazardous than in a precapitalist world but also open to a wider range of possibilities. The stirrings of capitalism both opened the potential for a certain individuation and self-development and generated new forms of voluntary social relations in the context of which persons could develop new styles of life. A fundamental tendency of capitalist society—a somewhat utopian tendency that is rarely realized in practice—is for a person's social position to be determined by his or her actions rather than inherited standing. My claim is that this potential of capitalist society provides an underlying basis for the emergent legal and moral norm of civic equality.

The proliferation of commercial relations not only affected personal trajectories, both real and imagined; it also brought into prominence a particular form of social relations: what were known as "publics." The word *public* is of course very old. It has now, and had in the eighteenth century, a range of meanings. It could be used as an adjective, signifying something available to or pertaining to all, as in a public bath, a public promenade, a public market, or public knowledge, or something pertaining to the state, as in public law or public power. *Public* could also be used as a noun, to signify the totality of the people of a state, an audience of a performance or an exhibition, or the clientele of a merchant, an author, a playwright, or a publication. A public was an actually existing yet anonymous collectivity whose open-ended membership was made up of purchasers of goods, participants in promenades or fairs, audiences at performances, readers of books, viewers at exhibitions, and so forth. The commercial availability of things and of experiences, whether books or clothing or cafés or theatrical performances, created corresponding publics. Such real but anonymous publics created a kind of actually existing civic equality, creating a thin and temporary but real commonality that implied no deeper social engagement or equality of condition outside the context of the particular public. Publics were predominately an urban affair, since it was particularly in cities that commercially available goods and experiences multiplied in the eighteenth century. This made the possibilities of life in cities quite different from previous urban life, even though, as we have seen, most French cities grew only slowly over the course of the century. Increasingly, one's experience of urban social life depended not only on one's rank and connections but also on the publics that commercial developments made available. The place of such publics was, of course, particularly salient in Paris, which was much bigger and more anonymous than other French cities.

The rise of urban publics was reflected in eighteenth-century word usage and can be traced by means of Google Ngrams, which count the usage of words in books. Over the course of the eighteenth century, the noun *le public* became more common in books published in French. Its usage slightly more than doubled between 1750 and 1756 and then rose sharply again in the early 1770s, reaching a peak in 1790–91. This later surge, of course, corresponds to the terminal political crisis of the old regime and the advent of the Revolution, in which claims on behalf of a now politically defined public rose sharply. Increasingly, this general public was regarded as having opinions—indeed, opinions that ought to have great weight in political affairs (Baker 1990, 167–99). Thus the Google Ngram for *opinion publique* rises from virtually nothing in 1750 to a plateau between 1757 and 1770 and then rises at a sharply accelerating rate from the late 1770s to a lofty peak during the Revolution in 1791.

The publics created by the intensified urban commerce of the eighteenth century were integral to the emergence of the political public invoked so prominently in the run-up to the French Revolution. The goal

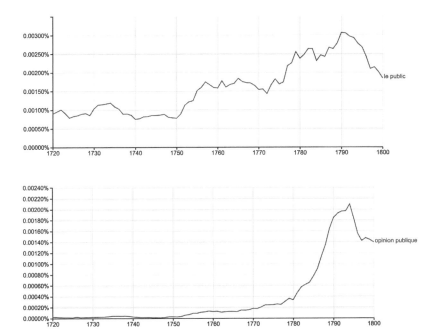

FIGURES 1 & 2. Google Ngrams for *le publique* and *opinion publique*.

of this chapter, and of part 1 of the book, is to offer concrete examples of how the expanding reach of capitalist social relations in eighteenth-century France created social practices and social spaces in which new forms of life and such new aspirational ideals as "the public," "public opinion," and civic equality were worked out. I argue that the emergence of such networks and spaces, in what I am calling a "commercial public sphere," eventually helped make civic equality thinkable and desirable as a means of reordering the state and society when France entered into a deep political crisis in the late 1780s.

Jürgen Habermas and the Public Sphere

My thinking about the public has been influenced by Jürgen Habermas's brilliant and justly celebrated book, *The Structural Transformation of the Public Sphere* (1962, 1989).[1] The object of Habermas's inquiry was the emergence and subsequent transformations of what he called a "bourgeois public sphere," by which he meant a set of institutions and practices that enabled "private persons" to band together to put "reason to use," thereby, eventually, forming what came to be known as public opinion (xviii). Habermas's use of the adjective *bourgeois* (*Bürgerlich*) to characterize the public sphere had a double sense in German. *Bürgerlich* is derived from the noun *Bürger*, which is, on the one hand, a synonym of the French *bourgeois* (a property-owning nonnoble townsman) but is also the German term for *citizen*. The adjective *Bürgerlich*, hence, means both "bourgeois" and "civic" or "civil."[2] Habermas's emergent "bourgeois public sphere" had, by definition, a civic rather than a purely private character and mission. But Habermas also emphasized that the emergent public sphere was "bourgeois" in a double sociological sense: it was, he argues, a product of emergent capitalism, and it was composed primarily of bourgeois persons.

Habermas's concept of the public sphere was widely taken up by historians of eighteenth-century France when his book, published in German in 1962, was, belatedly, translated into French and English.[3] But historians have generally embraced Habermas's notion in a way that left his Marxism and his discussion of the economic foundations of the public sphere in the shadows, if not out of the picture altogether. Most have treated

---

1. In this section of the chapter, citations to pages in Habermas (1989) will be in parentheses in the text.
2. Translator's note (Habermas 1989, xv).
3. A French translation is Habermas (1978).

the public sphere as a purely cultural or political-cultural phenomenon. Rarely have they appended the adjective *bourgeois* to the noun *public sphere* or considered seriously the links that Habermas suggests between capitalist development and the public sphere's morphology (Baker 1990; Chartier 1991; Maza 1993; Goodman 1994; Gordon 1994). I aim to spotlight this aspect of Habermas's argument, which has been an inspiration for my reflection on capitalism and the emergence of civic equality. I make no attempt here to reproduce the full range of Habermas's arguments. Rather, I specifically examine his frequently overlooked thoughts about connections between the public sphere and capitalism.

From a sociological point of view, Habermas's public sphere is elusive. It is a category of social life constituted, in Habermas's phrase, "by private people putting reason to use"—and, I would add, by doing so in public—so that their speech acts are available for the critical examination of their co-reasoners (xviii). It therefore refers not to a delimitable population or to any specific institution or collection of institutions but to a set of intellectual interchanges—to acts of conversation, reading, writing, and thought. It also implies the existence of a set of locations or sites in which these interchanges took place. Some of the sites, like coffeehouses or the aristocratic parlors where salons met, can be specifically pinpointed in time and space. Others, like newspapers, novels, or letters are spatially mobile media that created a wider and more anonymous public. But the public sphere is also a "location" in a social imaginary. As a sphere of reasoned argument, it is in some sense present wherever such argument takes place. Its boundaries are necessarily blurry, since the only explicit and legitimate criterion for exclusion is an absence of rational argument. Although it is true that in the eighteenth century rationality was thought to be highly correlated with education and some modicum of wealth, the bounds of rationality could only be determined in the debate itself. The public sphere therefore tended to exclude the poor in practice, but it could never do so absolutely or explicitly. It therefore cannot be defined in strictly class terms.

Habermas points out that the public sphere, which he sees emerging in the late seventeenth century in England and in the eighteenth century in France and Germany, was a product of early capitalism and of the bourgeois merchants who were capitalism's agents. He notes the capitalist origins of the media and institutions that enabled the public sphere's emergence, beginning with the seemingly simple medium known as the letter. Regular letter writing grew out of what Habermas calls "early capitalist long-distance trade. . . . With the expansion of trade, merchants' market-oriented calculations required more frequent and more exact information about distant events." Hence it was "the merchants who organized the first mail routes" (15). What merchants were seeking was information relevant to their calculations about commodity exchange, but the institution of the regular mail and the assumption that its contents were to be kept private were adapted to other ends as well. The seemingly humble letter assumed a particularly prominent place in the emerging public sphere. The eighteenth century, Habermas tells us, "became the century of the letter." The letter was particularly important because it was a literary form in which "the individual unfolded himself in his subjectivity" (48).[4] The letter, in spite of its mundane commercial origin, became a prime instrument for the cultivation of the private subjectivity that was, according to Habermas, a necessary condition for the emergence of the public sphere. The centrality of letters to eighteenth-century public culture is clear. This seemingly private literary genre also became a public form. Letters were written—for example, by Voltaire or Goethe—with the intention that they be shared with others or published. Epistolary novels— from Richardson's *Clarissa* and *Pamela*, to Montesquieu's *Les lettres persanes*, to Laclos's *Les liaisons dangereuses*, to Rousseau's *Julie ou la nouvelle Héloïse*—were among the most influential literary efforts of the century. Philosophical works such as Diderot's *Lettre sur les aveugles* or Rousseau's *Lettre à M. d'Alembert* were written in the ostensible form of letters.

News grew out of the same commercial network. Merchants' letters included news—about currency exchange rates, weather, harvests, rebellions, or threats of war—that is, about anything that might affect the prices of commodities. This traffic in commercially relevant news was soon organized and commodified in the form of newsletters or primitive newspapers that were printed and sold. By the eighteenth century, once again, these newspapers began to carry not only commercially useful news but essays, cultural commentary, and, of course, advertising. The newspaper became a major public-sphere medium, and news became a prime topic of public-sphere discussions.

Commercial printing long predated the eighteenth century. But in the eighteenth century, as Habermas points out, the number of books sold became so substantial that it became possible for authors to live by their pens—with commercial publishers rather than patrons as their paymasters (38). As we shall see in part 2 of this book, living by one's pen was at best a struggle for eighteenth-century authors (Darnton 1982, 1–40; Turnovsky 2010). But the proliferation of commercially available books

---

4. It was not, in fact, exclusively "his subjectivity." For letter writing in the development of eighteenth-century French women's subjectivity, see Goodman (2009).

at that time established a new relation between authors and their readers, affording authors a new autonomous authority. Meanwhile, the theater, fine arts, and music also became increasingly liberated from royal, clerical, or aristocratic patrons. Habermas points out that beginning in the 1720s, commercial public concerts began to be held in various German cities. From this time forward, music lovers could listen to "music as such" rather than as an accompaniment to religious or royal ceremony or noble ostentation (39–40). Meanwhile, rising public interest in the various arts led to the emergence of the art critic, who, naturally, published his criticism in the commercial newspapers or magazines. Culture, the core interest of the early public sphere, became a commercial affair (41). Finally, one must mention the coffeehouses or cafés at which, beginning in the late seventeenth century, men gathered to trade information about the markets, read newspapers, argue about the theater or the latest opera, and otherwise debate the interests of the emerging public sphere. Cafés were commercial establishments that were dependent on the booming world trade, specifically trade in the new colonial commodities coffee, tea, chocolate, and sugar. They were in every respect a product of mercantile capitalist development. It goes without saying but should be said explicitly that all these activities—letter writing; the production and reading of newspapers, periodicals, and books; the development of a market for art, music, and literature; the emergence of coffeehouses—were utterly dependent on the emergence of a sizable class of literate and prosperous urban dwellers. In its origins, the public sphere was, emphatically, a "bourgeois public sphere."

However, there is some question about the extent to which Habermas's public sphere as it developed in the eighteenth century was bourgeois in a sociological sense. First, most of the "bourgeois" who participated in the public sphere were not what Marxists have typically meant by "the bourgeoisie"—that is, owners of the means of production. Speaking particularly about the German case, Habermas mentions that the rise of bureaucratic states coincided with the rise of a new "stratum of bourgeois people . . . which occupied a central position within the 'public'" (23). He mentions state officials, doctors, pastors, professors, and scholars. In France as well, the "bourgeois" who participated in the public sphere were rarely those most directly involved in capitalist production and exchange. Instead, they were assorted public officials, men of letters, members of the "liberal professions," or financiers whose business was tied closely to the state. Moreover, there were plenty of aristocrats who participated actively in the public sphere. Habermas notes, for example, that "the early institutions of the bourgeois public sphere originally were closely bound up with aristocratic society as it became dissociated from the court" (43). Here he is presumably thinking of the salons, a preexisting aristocratic institution, which, in eighteenth-century France, absorbed bourgeois men of letters and became a major center of public-sphere activity (Lilti 2005; Goodman 1994). Indeed, Habermas remarks that "in many ways the nobility in its salons was more receptive to the enlightened mode of thought of bourgeois intellectuals than was the bourgeoisie itself" (68). One might ask, If this is so, why should one claim that this is a bourgeois mode of thought at all?

In the end, I think it is more confusing than clarifying to append the adjective *bourgeois* to the *public sphere*. The terms *bourgeois* and *bourgeoisie* are notoriously sociologically ambiguous—referring at times to capitalists, at times to well-to-do nonnobles of all descriptions, at times to a vast range of social positions between the aristocracy and the working poor, and at times to those with a certain social outlook or ideology (Maza 2003). I suggest the "commercial public sphere" as a more appropriate label. It is difficult to argue that the public sphere of eighteenth-century France was structured by the class interests of the bourgeoisie, however defined. Nevertheless, I believe that logics of commodity relations, arising out of commercial exchange, structured the public sphere's architecture and assumptions in a subtle but distinctive fashion. Let me suggest three passages where I see Habermas arguing for the structuring role of commodity relations in the emergence of the public sphere.

First, Habermas argues that the independence of moral judgment characteristic of the public sphere derived initially from the autonomy inherent in commodity ownership: "In a certain fashion commodity owners could view themselves as autonomous. To the degree that they were emancipated from governmental directives and controls, they made decisions freely in accord with standards of profitability. In this regard, they owed obedience to no one and were subject only to the anonymous laws functioning in accord with an economic rationality immanent, so it appeared, in the market. These laws were backed up by the ideological guarantee of a notion that market exchange was just, and they were altogether supposed to enable justice to triumph over force" (46). Merchants' experience of the anonymous market for commodities, Habermas suggests, gave rise to a sense of moral autonomy and immanent justice in human interchange, a sense that was transferred from commodity exchange to the exchange of ideas and opinions in the public sphere.

A second passage strongly implies an analogy between commodities in markets and individual persons in the public sphere. Habermas notes that the proceedings of public sphere forums such as coffeehouses, salons, and

Tischgesellschaften "preserved a kind of social intercourse that, far from presupposing the equality of status, disregarded status altogether. [This] tendency replaced the celebration of rank with a tact befitting equals. The parity on whose basis alone the authority of the better argument could assert itself against that of social hierarchy and in the end can carry the day meant, in the thought of the day, the parity of 'common humanity'" (36). It is hard not to hear in this passage a strong analogy with Marx's discussion of commodity exchange in the first chapter of volume 1 of *Capital*. There commodities meet as equivalent exchange values in the market, in spite of the fact that as use values, they are in fact incommensurate ([1867] 1977, 125–28). The implied suggestion, as I read Habermas's passage, is that the notion of parity among participants in public sphere discussion in spite of their differences of status may be based or modeled, ultimately, upon the parity of commodities in market exchange. Another way of putting this point would be to say that the habit of abstracting the exchange value of commodities from their use values, or from the peculiar characteristics of the merchants who brought them to market or those of the customers who purchased them, was generalized from the sphere of commodity exchange to the emerging sphere of public discussion. In both cases, exchange was understood to take place in a context of consensually willed situational parity between exchangers.

A third passage, rather than working at the level of analogies between public-sphere relations and the social relations inherent in the commodity form, argues that there were specific market-based mediations that sustained the ethic of inclusiveness in the public sphere. The existence of the various publics that proliferated in eighteenth-century cities— and gave rise to the generalized public that could be called *le public*— established an assumed parity among all potential participants in cultural discussions. As Habermas put the point,

The same process that converted culture into a commodity (and in this fashion constituted it as a culture that could become an object of discussion to begin with) established the public as in principle inclusive. However exclusive the public might be in any given instance, it could never close itself off entirely and become consolidated as a clique; for it always understood and found itself immersed within a more inclusive public of all private people, persons who—insofar as they were propertied and educated—as readers, listeners, and spectators could avail themselves via the market of the objects that were subject to discussion. The issues discussed became "general" not merely in their significance, but also in their accessibility. (37)

Habermas, then, sees commercial capitalism as undergirding the public sphere in more than one way. Capitalism was, to be sure, crucial because it brought into existence the commercialized material matrix of coffeehouses, concerts, theatrical performances, books, newspapers, and postal services that provided the public sphere with both sites of discussion and subjects to be discussed. Capitalism also caused the proliferation of certain socioeconomic categories of persons who made up the majority of the participants in the public sphere. The most obvious are, of course, the capitalists—the merchants, bankers, brokers, or manufacturers. But the proliferation of lawyers, medical practitioners, and men of letters in the cities of Northwestern Europe was itself largely a secondary product of capitalist development. And finally, the rise of this category of the so-called liberal professions, as well as the multiplication of state employees, also resulted from the rise of the bureaucratic, mercantilist state in the late seventeenth and eighteenth centuries—which in turn was a response to and an intended lever for the development of capitalism. As state power came to depend ever more on monetary revenues, bureaucracies grew steadily: to oversee the extraction of revenue, to govern the economic activities on which revenue extraction was based, and to oversee the rational expenditure of such revenues. And finally, those who could gain access to cultural matters via commercial print media or via performances or expositions open to the public all became potential participants in the public sphere.

But Habermas, in the passages I have quoted at length, also implies that capitalist commodity exchange provided the architecture of social forms that was built into the social and intellectual exchanges constituting the early public sphere. The logic of the commodity form was one of abstract parity of exchange values in spite of the incommensurable differences among use values. This logic, Habermas implies, underlay the peculiar form of equality, or parity, that characterized public sphere interchanges. The public sphere did not assume, nor did it necessarily argue on behalf of, any ideal of increasing equality of means or of status in the larger society. As Habermas put it, the public sphere did not presuppose equality of status; rather, it "disregarded status altogether." I think what he means is that upon entering the public sphere, one hung one's status at the door, as it were. There was a price of admission: sufficient education and intelligence to be able to engage in rational discussion, and this implied a certain level of material means. But whether one was a nobleman of ancient lineage like the Marquis de Condorcet, or a fabulously wealthy financier like Helvétius, or the son of a cutler like Denis Diderot, what mattered within the confines of the public sphere was the quality of one's arguments. In this sense, there was a parity in intellectual exchange between persons whose particular social qualities were in no way commensurate.

I think this quality of public-sphere forums may help explain a paradox of the eighteenth-century French public sphere that Habermas pointed out: the very considerable attraction of this seemingly "bourgeois" institution to nobles. It might seem peculiar that nobles, who were at the top of the old regime pecking order, would wish to engage as equals in discussion with persons from a lower social stratum. Why would this possibility be attractive? Why wouldn't they prefer to mix exclusively with their own kind and receive the elaborate deference of their social inferiors? Let me suggest a possible answer. In the social interactions that sustained courtly society, nobles were constantly jockeying for social superiority and recognition. The nobility was not a solidary group of equals but was made up of a finely differentiated hierarchy of distinctions. To engage in courtly interactions was to put one's standing constantly at risk, to be wary of snubs and slights to one's dignity, and to be ready to dish out snubs and slights of one's own. To position oneself as a noble was to insert oneself into an unending cascade of disdain, in which one had to endure the disdain that rained down from above and could only compensate by showering one's disdain upon those below. This kind of social interaction could be wearying and unedifying. It seems likely that some of the more sensitive or intellectually ambitious nobles found the parity of interactions in the public sphere exhilarating and liberating precisely because they were freed from the duty of enacting hierarchical distinction and could engage in more or less spontaneous discussion with others in common pursuit of the best arguments. As we shall see in part 2 of this book, salons in which nobles played a predominant role but in which self-made intellectuals from mediocre backgrounds could shine, constituted the pinnacle of the Parisian public sphere.

The artificial equality of the public sphere must have been as intoxicating to nobles as it was to commoners. In the specific circumstances of the profoundly hierarchical societies of the European old regime, the anonymous character of market relations, once abstracted from the hustle and bustle of the market place, could serve as a kind of generalized model for utopian ideals of all sorts. After another two and a half centuries of experience, we have come—quite properly—to equate capitalism and markets with inequality, self-seeking, and multiple forms of oppression. But in the rosy dawn of commercial and industrial expansion, markets could be seen very differently: as dissolving or suspending existing forms of domination and as providing a matrix of relations based on free and equal consent. Thus the very commodity relations that during the nineteenth and twentieth centuries were to undermine the liberal bourgeois public sphere provided, in the eighteenth century, its DNA, the essential modeling principles on which it was originally constructed.

Habermas, in short, suggests both concrete and more abstract ways that capitalism enabled the emergence of the public sphere. The concrete institutions without which the public sphere would not exist—the letter, the newspaper, the café, the printing industry, and commercial forms of theater, art, and music—were products of early capitalism. It was the commercial availability of these institutions that assured the continued openness in principle of the public sphere's objects of discussion to anyone capable of gaining access to them. Capitalist development also produced an expanding and highly differentiated population of "bourgeois" persons. They were crucial participants who joined with nobles in the discussions and social gatherings or forums that constituted the public sphere. And finally, the abstraction inherent in commodity exchange provided the largely unconscious model for the intellectual exchanges and social relations that constituted the public sphere's essential form. Habermas clearly has much to offer my inquiry.

Habermas's brilliant and suggestive work certainly suggests a relation between emerging capitalism and the thinkability of civic equality. The object of his study is the historical emergence of a sphere of rational public debate, of which a constitutive element was a notion of civic equality. But the object of my inquiry is different than Habermas's. He is a political philosopher whose life's work has been the development of a general theory of democratic legitimacy; his book is an early contribution to that project. I am a historian attempting to show how emerging commercial capitalism in eighteenth-century France generated the thinkability of civic equality. His account of eighteenth-century developments is extraordinarily astute and full of theoretical insights useful to my project. But empirically, it is thin.

Habermas provides particularly interesting historical detail about the German case but less about England and even less about France. However, the French case figures importantly in Habermas's account. France was, after all, at the center of the European Enlightenment. It produced the most radical developments in eighteenth-century political thought and a profound political revolution in 1789. But Habermas made virtually no use of French-language sources. Much of his substantive discussion of France is based on Arnold Hauser's *The Social History of Art* (1951) and Elinor Barber's *The Bourgeoisie in 18th Century France* (1955) and most quotations from eighteenth-century French authors are from English translations. As a consequence, Habermas's judgments about France, while often astute, are scattered and not well contextualized. My discussion in the remainder of this chapter and in several that follow will attempt to put some flesh and skin on Habermas's skeletal account and sometimes reconstruct the skeleton itself, tracing out aspects of the French case of which Habermas seems to have been unaware.

I also develop a different and broader conception of the public sphere, one signaled in my chapter title, "The Commercial Public Sphere." Habermas is interested in the network of intellectual interchanges that gave rise to the regulative ideals of a democratic public sphere. But he has relatively little to say about the wider urban sphere of sociable consumption behavior—the world of shopping, theatergoing, art exhibits, public commensality, fashion display, promenades, and commercial entertainment—that provided the buzzing backdrop and the condition of possibility for the reading, writing, and serious conversation examined in *The Structural Transformation of the Public Sphere*. Part 1 of my book is an attempt to explore—incompletely, to be sure—the newly developing eighteenth-century French urban commercial world that constituted this relatively anonymous and less hierarchical public realm. In doing so, my focus is less on Habermas's question of how capitalist social relations enabled the emergence of a rational sphere of public debate than on sketching the outlines of emerging forms of public sociability that encompassed rational debate but also included less elevated matters such as entertainment, fashion, and vying for social recognition. This everyday urban social experience, I will argue, helped make civic equality thinkable and attractive.

The Printed Word

I begin with the trade in printed words, which was one of the era's great commercial ventures. The rise of commercial publishing in Europe and in France dates back to the early sixteenth century and was well established by the dawn of the eighteenth (Eisenstein 1979, 1983). By 1700, the Parisian printers' guild dominated French publishing, having virtually wiped out serious competition, mainly from Lyon and Rouen, during seventeenth-century trade wars (Birn 1970–71; Darnton 2015, 511). In eighteenth-century France, the production and reading of books increased sharply. Literacy rates, lower than in Protestant countries like the Netherlands, Prussia, and England, nevertheless rose over the eighteenth century. Male literacy was 29 percent in 1686–90 and 47 percent in 1786–90; female literacy was lower and far more stagnant, rising only from 24 to 27 percent over the same century. There was a tripling or quadrupling of French book production between 1700 and the 1780s (Chartier 1991, 69, 91). Studies of probate inventories indicate that it was common for relatively wealthy people to own books but that some domestic servants or master artisans were book owners as well. The most detailed study, based on inventories in nine cities in the west of France, shows the modal number of books owned rose sharply for all categories of the population between the late seventeenth century and 1789. Over these years, the mode for medical and legal professionals in these cities rose from a single volume to 20–100, that of members of the clergy from 20–50 to 100–300, and that of nobles and high officials from 1–20 to over 300.[5]

Meanwhile, the readership of books greatly surpassed the ownership of books. Because books were expensive, friends frequently loaned volumes to one another. Men of letters had access to libraries that were selectively open to the public, although only for limited hours each week. Sixteen French provincial cities had at least one public library, and there were eighteen in Paris (Chartier and Roche 1984, 411–12). There were also *cabinets littéraires* attached to book shops and private clubs with reading rooms. Many booksellers lent out books that could be taken home to read and made periodicals available to read in the shop or in the street in front of the shop—forms of access that catered to people with limited means (Chartier and Roche 1984, 414–16).

Unlike the thriving book business in England, the Netherlands, Switzerland, and the German states, the French publishing industry was subject to systematic censorship (Birn 1970–71; Hesse 1991, 5–22). All books published in France had to be submitted to the royal censor, and printed matter "tending to attack religion, to disturb minds, to attack our authority, and to trouble the order and tranquility of our States" were to be denied publication (Chartier 1991, 47). This rather vague set of criteria was put into practice selectively by the director of the book trade, since strict enforcement would have paralyzed the activity of publishers—what did it mean, after all, for a book "to disturb minds" or to "trouble tranquility"?

Chrétien-Guillaume de Lamoignon de Malesherbes was named director of the book trade in 1750, at a crucial moment in the publishing history of France when the philosophes' works were capturing the public's attention. (For example, Montesquieu's *The Spirit of the Laws* had been published in 1748, the first volume of Diderot and d'Alembert's *Encyclopédie* appeared in 1751, and Rousseau's *Discourse on the Origins of In-*

5. The cities studied were Rouen, Caen, Saint-Malo, Le Mans, Anjou, Renne, Nantes, Quimper, and Brest (Quéniart 1978, figures 29, 34, and 38 at end of book). Figures also cited by Chartier and Roche (1984, 405).

equality in 1754.) Malesherbes, a friend and supporter of the philosophes, used a light hand in censorship—as did his successors. He was convinced that the philosophes' work redounded to the public good. As he put it in 1775, "A tribunal has arisen independent of all powers and that all powers respect, that appreciates all talents, that pronounces on all people of merit. And in an enlightened century, in a century in which each citizen can speak to the entire nation by way of print, those who have a talent for instructing men and a gift for moving them—in a word, men of letters—are, amid the public dispersed, what the orators of Rome and Athens were in the middle of the public assembled."[6] Censorship, he argued, should be applied very selectively, outlawing only obscene books or those questioning the king's authority or challenging the foundation of religion (Chartier 1991, 46). Only books that challenged no orthodoxies could be given an outright privilege for publication, but the censor could also grant a "tacit privilege" to books in cases "in which one did not dare authorize a book publicly but nevertheless felt that it would not be possible to prohibit it." Such books could be published but were officially placed on a list "of works printed in foreign lands whose distribution is permitted in France" (Malesherbes 1979, 212). Their title pages alleged falsely that they were published, for example, in London or Amsterdam but listed a Parisian publisher at whose shop they were available. This dodge was widely used in the second half of the eighteenth century, when these "tacit" privileges were nearly as common as full privileges (Chartier 1991, 50–51). Tacit privileges were necessary, Malesherbes averred, because "a man who had never read any books other than those" with an explicit privilege "would be nearly a century behind his contemporaries" (Malesherbes 1979, 241).

But counting only books published with explicit or tacit approval would radically underestimate the number and misstate the nature of the books sold to French readers. According to Robert Darnton, "probably the majority of all new publications" written in French and sold in the 1770s and 1780s were printed in neighboring countries—especially Switzerland and Holland but also the Austrian Netherlands, the German states, the papal enclave of Avignon, and England (Darnton 2015, 510; 1995a; 1995b; see also Burrows 2018). They were smuggled into France and were widely available at booksellers—even in Paris under the eyes of the censors. Smuggling raised the books' prices, but the pirate publishers made up for this by decreasing the space between lines, shrinking margins, and using cheaper fonts. Pirated books were commonly shipped un-

6. Malesherbes (1775), quoted by Ozouf (1987, 424).

bound in bundles of sheets packed into bales and loaded onto wagons, to be bound by the bookseller or the buyer (Darnton 2015, 516).

Darnton has suggested that the majority of these pirated editions were what contemporaries termed "philosophical" books, although recent research by Simon Burrows shows that such books probably constituted a much smaller proportion of the total, about 15 percent (Burrows 2018, 124). Modern readers might be surprised to learn the titles of some of the books classified as "philosophical" in eighteenth-century France. Darnton's list of best sellers of the Société Typographique de Neuchatel, one of the most important suppliers of "philosophical" books, includes some works recognizable as philosophy, such as Helvétius's *De l'homme*, the complete works of Rousseau, and Voltaire's *Lettres philosophiques*. But equally prominent are scandalous accounts of life at the royal court, such as Pidansat de Mairobert's *Anecdotes sur Mme la comtesse du Barry* (King Louis XV's mistress), Moufle d'Angerville's *Vie privée de Louis XV*, or Voltaire's scabrous verse *La Pucelle d'Orléans*. There were also such books as the abbé Raynal's politically explosive *Histoire philosophique et politique des établissemens et du commerce des Européens dans les deux Indes* and Pidansat de Mairobert and Moufle d'Angerville's *Journal historique de la révolution opérée dans la constitution de la monarchie française par M. de Maupeou*. "Philosophical" books constituted a diverse but supposedly corrosive array that not only criticized official religious and political doctrines but ridiculed the morals of the monarch and court. Even apart from the popularity of these ubiquitous pirated "philosophical" books, readers' tastes shifted drastically over the course of the century. Religious books, which had accounted for half of the explicitly or tacitly permitted titles at the end of the seventeenth century, had declined to a third by the 1720s, a quarter by the 1750s, and a tenth in the 1780s. These were replaced by secular books—the arts and sciences and belles lettres, including novels (Chartier 1991, 70–71). The French reader on the eve of the Revolution had distinctly secular tastes.

Books were not the only reading matter available to the public. There were also periodicals, often published outside France where they could avoid censorship. The only newspaper legally published in France—the official weekly *Gazette de France*—was composed of dry diplomatic and political reports from the various capitals of Europe with occasional reports on doings at the French court in Versailles. To gain knowledge of French political affairs, the reader had to rely on French-language periodicals published in other countries—for example, the *Gazette de Leyde* (published in the Dutch city of Leiden) or the *Courrier d'Avignon*, which reported on political disputes such as the battles between the monarch and the parlements and intrigue at court (Popkin 1987; Joynes 1987). These were supplemented by a far more incendiary clandestine pamphlet press. More common yet were periodical publications of an apolitical sort that included extensive reviews of books, theatrical performances, and art exhibitions and that published poems, stories, historical essays, travelogues, reports about natural history, and letters by important literary figures. Many of these periodicals were available at bookstores and could be read on the premises for a few pennies. Roger Chartier speaks of "the hunger for reading matter that tormented even the humblest of city dwellers"—a hunger that could be satisfied by such practices (1991, 70).

Provincial newspapers and magazines, published in most of France's big cities, became increasingly common after midcentury (Sgard 1983, 125–45). Provincial periodicals that centered on art, culture, history, natural history, and the like were short-lived, typically lasting only a year or two. The most durable business model for the provincial press was the weekly advertising paper known as the *affiches*. The first of these publications was launched in Paris in 1745, followed by Lyon in 1750 and some sixty others between 1757 and the Revolution. According to Colin Jones, these little newspapers of four to eight pages had some twenty thousand subscribers, which he plausibly assumes means fifty to one hundred thousand readers (1996).[7] Most of their copy was advertisements for goods, for land and houses, and for a multitude of services. There were also announcements of cultural events such as concerts, theatrical performances, the publication of books, and public lectures; there were obituaries, lists of grain prices, arrival and departure dates of ships, announcements of winning lottery numbers, accounts of meetings of local academies, lost and found notices, poetry, and occasional news items; finally, there were articles on local history, science, agronomy, medicine, philosophy, and so on.[8] But the fundamental purpose of these ubiquitous newssheets was commerce: as the *Affiches de Lyon* put it, the goal was to publicize "everything that concerns trade and that bears the traits of utility" (C. Jones 1996, 19–20).

7. I have consulted collections of a sampling of these newspapers in the Bibliothèque National de France, a sampling that essentially confirms Jones's account: *Annonces, affiches, et avis divers, pour la Ville de Bordeaux* (1765–78); *Annonces, affiches, et avis divers de la Haute et Basse Normandie* (Rouen 1768–70); *Affiches, annonces, etc. de Toulouse, et du Haut-Languedoc* (1781–84); *Annonces, affiches et avis divers de Troyes, Capitale de la Champagne* (1782); and *Affiches, annonces, et avis divers* (Paris 1773).

8. An exhaustive study (Tulchin 2019) of the *Affiches de Bordeaux* shows that Enlightenment authors such as Voltaire, d'Alembert, Montesquieu, Rousseau, and Helvétius were discussed in its pages, often in laudatory terms.

Jones sees these affiches as based on a principle of inclusiveness. Whoever wished to buy or sell something, or simply to inform the community of readers about events or useful information, could contribute copy. These papers, he argues, were authentic voices of a burgeoning urban commercial society that was "horizontally disposed: grounded in human sociability and exchange" (1994, 14, 19). The affiches "revolved around the consumer, assumed a unitary economic subject, and predicated a hierarchy of wealth and taste, not birth or privilege. . . . Those who took a subscription to the Affiches were buying into a world of consumption, not corporative status." In this forum, citizens were encouraged to interact freely, anonymously, and on a basis of equality, "saturated in Enlightenment values of openness and transparency" (1996, 14, 19). From my perspective, the affiches could be said to have articulated and actively promoted an anonymous market-based civil egalitarian sensibility that thrived in the interstices of a still hierarchical urban society. They reflected and helped spread Enlightenment values over the course of the eighteenth century—values whose generalization among the literate classes of provincial French society was an essential condition of possibility for the Revolution's promulgation of civic equality.

The affiches were but one part in a thriving market for printed matter that exploded in the late eighteenth century—for books, periodicals, newspapers, and more transitory materials, such as brief topical poems praising or ridiculing public persons, handbills, or published legal briefs, of which the latter, as Sarah Maza has demonstrated, had increasingly powerful effects on public sentiments (Maza 1993). The urban world of eighteenth-century France was awash in commercially available printed matter. Reading these various offerings bound French men and women into the new commercially mediated literary public sphere.

Theater

Theater occupied a central place in the eighteenth-century French public sphere. Louis XIV, famously enthralled by theatrical spectacles of all kinds, played a major role as a patron of theater in both Versailles and Paris. In 1669, he established the Académie Royale de Musique, under the direction of Jean-Baptiste Lully, which had the exclusive right to perform operas and ballets in Paris. The Comédie-Française, which performed both comedies and tragedies, was founded in 1680 and had the exclusive right to perform French-language plays in Paris. There was also a Comédie-Italienne that performed commedia dell'arte and popular farces in Italian. French-language popular farces also played at Paris's two annual fairs.

The Comédie-Française, the kingdom's most prestigious theater company, had a peculiar constitution. It was a privileged royal company, overseen by the first gentleman of the royal bedchamber, but it was also a commercial enterprise. The day-to-day management and the choice of plays were in the hands of the company of actors. It was the collective body of both male and female players that heard readings of new dramatic manuscripts and decided whether to accept or reject them. The actors also chose the stage sets and designers, allocated the play's roles, and shared whatever profits their performances yielded, with one-ninth of the revenues allotted to the play's author (Rougemont 1988, 242; Brown 2005, 112–13).[9] The choice of plays was of course strongly affected by the actors' sense of their likely profitability; in this way, the Comédie-Française was definitively a commercial establishment. The company's actors made a very good living, yet they were simultaneously regarded as outcasts, officially denied communion and religious burial by the French Catholic Church—although these official rules were often ignored in practice (de Rougemont 1988, 205–9).

In the eighteenth century, Paris—and for that matter, all of urban France—was theater mad. The Comédie-Française and the Comédie-Italienne put on performances seven nights a week, except during a royally mandated three-week break at Easter. From the middle of the eighteenth century, the Comédie-Italienne began to produce a new and highly popular French-language genre, the *opéra comique*, that combined spoken parts with song, like musical comedies in our day. The traditional opera performed on Tuesdays, Thursdays, and Fridays in the summer and fall, adding Sunday performances in the winter and spring. And theaters at the Saint-Laurent fair, which ran from July through September, and the Saint-Germain fair, which ran from February to April, presented comic burlesques every night (Ravel 1999, 19–20). These were joined by several boulevard theaters that sprang up in the later eighteenth century.[10] In eighteenth-century Paris, theatrical performances were the talk of the salons and the cafés; famous actors and successful playwrights, particularly those associated with the Comédie-Française, became popular celebrities.[11] Opulent theatergoers rented boxes at the Comédie-Française, while the "parterre," the ground-floor area facing the stage, was

9. Jean-François Marmontel (1992, 150–56) gives a lively firsthand account of the experience of an author presenting his play to the company of actors.

10. The boulevard theaters will be discussed in chapter 5.

11. Marmontel (1992, 172), previously an unknown and impecunious writer, relates that as a consequence of a successful tragedy at the Comédie-Française, "in a day, almost in a moment, I found myself rich and famous."

occupied by less opulent men who stood for the performance and were notably vocal and sometimes downright disruptive in their comments on the offerings. It was the occupants of the parterre whose pronouncements and enthusiasms tended to dominate opinions about plays (Ravel 1999). Cafés sprang up around theatrical venues, where patrons would gather before and after performances to take refreshments and to discuss the plays and the players.

The repertoire of the Comédie-Française included both tragedies and comedies. The great seventeenth-century classics by Corneille, Racine, and Molière were staged regularly all through the eighteenth century. But eighteenth-century authors also wrote many plays that were presented on the Comédie's stage: Crébillon, Marivaux, Voltaire, Beaumarchais, and dozens of others. As the century wore on, ever more writers authored plays and presented them to the Comédie-Française, but the company turned down an increasing proportion, continuing to produce older plays that reliably drew an audience. Frustrated authors eventually began to publish plays rejected by the Comédie-Française, appealing directly to the "public opinion" embodied in the reading public over the heads of the players (Brown 2005, 95–96, 175). There was a growing market for published plays among eighteenth-century France's avid readers— all the more so because amateur theatricals were a common leisure activity.

Paris and the Comédie-Française were the pinnacles of the French theatrical world in the eighteenth century, but this era also saw a rapid expansion of theater in the provinces, especially after 1750. From only ten provincial cities with dedicated theater spaces in 1730, the number rose to sixty-six by 1789, and some of the new theater buildings, most spectacularly that in Bordeaux, which opened in 1780, rivaled the Comédie-Française itself (Clay 2013, 17, 50–52). Unlike the Comédie-Française or the Opéra, provincial theaters were solely profit-making private business ventures, not monarchical projects, although some gained financial support from municipal governments. Most provincial theaters were joint stock companies whose shares were sold to the public. Local elites, both noble and bourgeois, often subscribed to theater companies to enhance their reputations (Clay 2013, 27, 33). Theaters became important centers of public recreation and civic pride in eighteenth-century provincial cities, alongside new public gardens, academies, libraries, cafés, and other accoutrements of public life. Provincial theaters were managed not by a collective of actors but by directors, who made a contract with the theater-owning companies, assembled a troupe of salaried actors, and hoped to make a profit. Directors, recruited from the ranks of actors or music directors, usually had relatively short reigns. Provincial actors, too, were highly mobile and in each season negotiated fixed salaries with the directors. Women earned as much as men; some of the most successful provincial directors were women (Clay 2013, 102–13, 139). This was definitely, in the language of the time, a career open to talent.

The provincial theaters generally presented not only spoken dramas but also operas, *opéras comiques*, and ballets; only in Paris were there separate theaters for these different genres. Plays presented in the provinces were taken from the repertoire of the Parisian companies (Clay 2013, 115–17). The great stars of the Parisian stage could make good money by arranging tours of provincial cities, where they assured full houses (Clay 2013, 135). Indeed, the Comédie-Française, at the top of the theatrical hierarchy, established itself as the final arbiter of disputes about contracts between provincial actors and directors. The theater world of eighteenth-century France thus had a hierarchical unity of prestige and authority in spite of its organizational dimorphism (Clay 2013, 145–46).

Music

If Germans were, as Habermas avers, listening to "music as such" in commercial public concerts as early as the 1720s, the French music scene was long dominated instead by what Habermas calls "noble ostentation" (1989, 39–40). The most important musical institution in France was the Académie Royale de Musique, more commonly known as the Opéra. This, as we have seen, was a royal institution with a monopoly on the staging of operas and ballets in Paris, which were presented five days a week. The opera enticed the most distinguished noble men and women, who came to see and be seen (Johnson 1996, 9).[12] Spectators did not pay rapt attention to the music. They talked during the performances and visited one another's boxes. Meanwhile, the men who crowded onto the parterre made noisy wisecracks or sang along with the chorus (26–27). Performances were as much spectacle as music, often featuring showy special effects, like chariots bearing singers descending from the ceiling or real water flowing through tricked up brooks and fountains (23). There was as much ballet as singing in many of the operas, and pure ballet performances were nearly four times as common as operas in the years 1740–56 (20). In short, the music was more a divertissement than the main attraction. The mid-eighteenth-century opera was above all, in

---

12. In the rest of this section, page citations to this book will be in parentheses in the text.

the words of James Johnson, "a pageant of nobility on display" (34). Far from being "music as such," music at the opera was understood by mid-eighteenth-century observers as imitative of sounds in nature—singing birds, babbling brooks, battles, thunderstorms, and the like—or as strictly subordinated to the words of the libretto (36–38). The opera composer Rameau, who innovated by using complex musical accompaniments, dissonances, and key changes, was criticized on the grounds that he had "sacrificed the librettist to his own musical pride." Rousseau, himself an opera composer, criticized Rameau because he "made his accompaniments so confused, so overcharged, so incessant that the head can hardly tolerate the continuous din of the instruments" (45–46). The libretto, not the music, was the focus of operatic drama.

The Opéra did not have a monopoly on the Parisian musical scene. Beginning in 1725, concerts of sacred music (*concerts spirituels*) were made available to spectators who could afford the expensive subscriptions. Initially restricted to religious holidays and the Lenten season, when the Opéra was closed, they were extended in 1727 to all the days when the Opéra was not playing. In spite of their religious title, the concerts spirituels often included secular works as well, and the behavior of the audiences was as worldly as that at the Opéra. In the 1770s, the concerts spirituels were joined by several private concert societies that sponsored musical events for their wealthy and distinguished subscribers. Concerts were also commonly presented throughout the century in the houses of nobles and wealthy commoners as a feature of salons. The music was sometimes of the highest quality—the young Mozart played at a number of salons—but primarily served as an accompaniment to worldly sociability. Indeed, Mozart was disgusted by the inattentiveness of the salon audiences (71–72).

However, the arrival of Christoph Willibald von Gluck in Paris in 1774 shook the musical firmament. A German whose operas had triumphed in Vienna, Gluck took Paris by storm. His operas depicted human feelings in a newly direct and powerful way, minimizing ballet, simplifying staging, and intensifying the emotional core of the story. The quick reception of Gluck can be explained in part by the cult of sensibility that had begun to suffuse French cultural life—think of Rousseau's sentimental novel *Julie ou la nouvelle Héloïse*, the widely read English novels of Richardson, or the paintings of Greuze, all immensely popular at the time. For a few years, literary circles were engulfed in a war of the Gluckistes against the Piccinnistes—the latter supporting the Italian composer Piccinni, who resisted Gluck's innovations. The question of music thus became an important topic in the public sphere (81–86).

If the literati were divided about the new music, the public clearly embraced Gluck. Henceforth opera-goers did not wish to be distracted by stagecraft and elaborate ballets or the curious doings of gods, kings, and emperors that were the typical themes of previous operas. Although Gluck's stories came from ancient Greek mythology, the passions they emphasized were far from remote. His versions of *Orfée et Euridice* or of *Iphigénie en Tauride* dramatize above all the emotional anguish of loving families caught in tragic circumstances. The predominant emotions were, as Johnson remarks, "strikingly domestic" (66). Gluck's operas did not qualify as "music as such," since their popularity was a function of the audiences' emotional identification with his characters. As Gluck himself explained, "I have striven to restrict music to its true office . . . by following the situations of the story, without interrupting the action or stifling it with a useless superfluity of ornaments" (87). His operas, as Johnson puts it, "forged a new way of listening" that "facilitated aesthetic responses of a depth and intensity inconceivable to earlier generations of listeners" (82). After Gluck's revolution, attendance at operas soared and performances were no longer primarily an occasion for elite socialization: opera-goers, aristocrats and bourgeois alike, stopped chattering and began to listen in rapt silence. Music, by the eve of the Revolution, had become an intensely serious object of public aesthetic experience.

Fine Arts

The relationship of art to the public in eighteenth-century Paris was quite distinct from that of books, theater, or music. Artists were not economically dependent on a broad public as were writers, playwrights, actors, composers, or musicians. A moderately prosperous person could afford to stand in the parterre at the theater or the opera and could accumulate a modest library or subscribe to a periodical or two. But the market for paintings was limited to the truly wealthy and to the state and church; to thrive as an artist meant pleasing these constituencies, not a wide range of consumers. A broad public did, however, view and comment upon the latest productions of even the most important Parisian painters. This was a consequence of salon expositions mounted by the Royal Academy of Painting and Sculpture.

Beginning in 1737 and then in every odd-numbered year right up to the Revolution, the academy commandeered the immense *Salon carré* of the Louvre and covered its walls with paintings from floor to ceiling. These salons were free and were immensely popular with persons of all classes. Consequently, the spectators of this impossibly expensive genre were more socially diverse than those attending theater and opera and perhaps more diverse than the total body of urban readers. Estimates of salon attendance varied from twenty thousand to one hundred thousand per year (Crow 1985, 258). Pidansat de Mairobert's satirical account, written in 1777, was probably not far from the truth:

> You emerge through a stairwell . . . which is always choked despite its considerable width. . . . You cannot catch your breath before being plunged into an abyss of heat and a whirlpool of dust. . . . Here the Savoyard odd-job man rubs shoulders with the great noble . . . ; the fishwife trades her perfumes with those of a lady of quality . . . the rough artisan, guided only by natural feeling, comes out with a just observation, at which an inept wit nearly bursts out laughing only because of the comical accent in which it was expressed; while an artist hiding in the crowd unravels the meaning of it all and turns it to his profit. (Crow 1985, 4)

Given the popularity of the salon exhibitions, there were many commentaries upon the art on display—in pamphlets, in periodicals, and in fleeting and clandestine *libelles*. Early on, many lamented the decline of grand history painting characteristic of the academy's work under Louis XIV. But under Louis XV, the monarchy was no longer commissioning many works. The great bulk of demand was for more decorative Rococo art favored by wealthy aristocrats who increasingly abandoned Versailles and built new grand houses in need of decoration on the booming western edge of Paris. It was the more sensuous and frivolous art of Watteau, Boucher, and Fragonard that better suited their taste (Crow 1985, 11). Later in the century, however, the larger cultural shifts toward realism, philosophy, sentimentality, and a cult of patriotism taking place in the discourses of the public sphere influenced artists. Hence the artistic stars of the 1770s and 1780s were the realist Chardin, the painter of sentimental bourgeois scenes Greuze, and the severely patriotic Jacques-Louis David (Crow 1985). This evolution of taste ran roughly parallel to the contemporary musical craze for Gluck. The public was not important as buyers of artworks, but public commentary on art and general discourses clearly affected the interests and opinions of many of the artists and thus changed the nature of the art they produced.

The Café

The café was a key institution of eighteenth-century urban sociability. The first Parisian cafés seem to have been established in the later seventeenth century; by the middle of the eighteenth century, they were ubiquitous features of the urban environment.[13] High-end cafés featured mirrored walls, crystal chandeliers, and marble-topped tables, but many cafés were far more modest. Cafés served coffee, of course—which, although initially a beverage of the wealthy, soon became a virtual necessity for Parisians of all classes. It was in the later eighteenth century that a bowl of café au lait, taken either at home or in a café, emerged as the normal breakfast of Parisian workers and artisans (C. Jones and Spang 1999). But cafés, whose proprietors were members of the guild of the *limonadiers*, also served sugared drinks like lemonade, alcoholic beverages (with the exception of wine, whose sale was monopolized by another guild), hot chocolate, pastries, biscuits, and other light refreshments (Nemeitz 1727, 42–45).

The café promoted anonymity and a kind of everyday civic equality—tables and refreshments were available indiscriminately to anyone with the cash and the inclination. It is notorious that Parisian cafés became locations of quasi-public conversations and debates, often between customers who were unacquainted with each other. It was a common practice for customers to read aloud from newspapers, recite poems, retail the latest gossip, or offer opinions on cultural questions such as the merits of a recent book, theatrical performance, or opera (Rigogne 2018). As early as 1727, a guide to Paris intended for young noble visitors suggested that the voyager "go from time to time to cafés . . . to listen to the conversation of the news-mongers (*nouvellistes*)" who haunted them. "These men sometimes reason upside down and backwards (*à tort et à travers*), but they are often very clever. One is not obliged to join in the conversation or to combat opinions that one doesn't share" (Nemeitz 1727, 42–43). One satirist who called the café "the rendez-vous of those who wish to meet up, the center of chatter, the news bureau," claimed that one of his invented characters, "Manzir," spends his entire day in a café where "two pastries serve as his dinner and supper" and where he "judges the latest theatrical pieces" and "assigns a rank to all authors" (Caraccioli 1768, 30–31).

Parisian cafés were diverse. While some were prized for their conversations and lively debates between anonymous patrons, others were known for the quality of the chess played there. Some were haunted by

---

13. Rigogne (2013) argues that most of the published history of the Parisian café is more legend than history. The archives of the limonadier's guild were lost in the burning of the Hotel de Ville at the end of the Paris Commune in 1871, so systematic documentation about cafés is lacking. The most commonly cited but not very reliable accounts are Franklin (1893) and Bologne (1993).

the wealthy, others catered to the poor. Cafés, then as now, were common meeting places for friends or business associates. They were also a place to warm up during a stroll in the cold season or a refuge from unheated apartments. Although most of the customers were men, women patronized cafés with the same ease and anonymity. To the astonishment of a visiting English lady, "women are admitted into them just like men." And women did not seem at all embarrassed to be there. A woman "who seemed to belong to good society" entered and "asked for coffee, read the paper, paid and left, without any of the twenty people who were there showing any surprise at her behavior. Three other women came next; they asked for chocolate, and while one read the paper the other two played dominoes, like several of the other customers."[14] There were also many cafés—for example, those that set up tables under the trees on the boulevards—that had the usual casual anonymity but lacked declamations and conversations between tables, where pleasure and diversion took priority. The café, by the later eighteenth century, had become a ubiquitous, but also a multifarious, public cultural and commercial form.

The Restaurant

Establishments known as "restaurants" appeared in Paris in the 1760s. Like cafés, they were commercial establishments founded on principles of anonymity and de facto civic equality. Anyone could enter if they could pay. But if the café was already familiar, the restaurant was a decidedly odd newcomer.[15] "Restaurant," after all, is a curious name for an eating establishment. The name initially made sense only because the restaurant was invented as a particular kind of quasi-medical institution where weak or sickly diners were served a variety of restorative broths. Early restaurants differed from other places in Paris where one could be served a meal. The most common type of pre-restaurant eatery was the *table d'hôte* (host's table), where diners sat family-style around a large table and served themselves from a common platter or dish; the prices were not announced until the end of the meal, at which time diners either paid up or had the amount added to their account. The restaurant offered a more anonymous and individuated experience. Diners could order meals at any time; they sat at their own separate tables, ordered single servings from a fixed price menu, paid cash, and did not engage in conversation with those at other tables. This arrangement shocked a fic-

14. Cradock (1911, 27, 318–19), quoted by Rigogne (2018, 484).
15. The surprising early history of the restaurant has been exhumed by Spang (2000).

tionalized Peruvian observer in a novel published in 1801: "On arriving in the dining room, I remarked with astonishment numerous tables placed one beside another, which made me think that we were waiting for a large group, or were perhaps going to dine at a table d'hôte. But my surprise was at its greatest when I saw people enter without greeting each other and without seeming to know each other, seat themselves without looking at each other, and eat separately without speaking to each other, or even offering to share the food" (Rosny 1801, quoted in Spang 2000, 64).

Diners at the restaurant clearly entered into a very different and far more abstract form of social relations than those who dined at the table d'hôte. Indeed, in the beginning, even the food served was abstract: the restorative broths were thought to extract the essence of nutrition from such gross foodstuffs as meats and vegetables. The diner ingested the nutrient without ever having to chew. A good Marxist might say that restaurant diners seemed to be getting their value direct and liquid without having to pass through the messy stage of use value. Eating at the restaurant was an occasion when people quite clearly *experienced* abstract social relations based on the commodity form. One might suggest that the growing popularity of the restaurant format had much to do with its provision of a form of feeding powerfully abstracted from ordinary social relations. A visit to the restaurant in the years before the Revolution was, perhaps, something of a brief trip to the utopia—or the dystopia—immanent in contemporary forms of market exchange.

Shopping

In the last quarter of the seventeenth century, Paris became the universally recognized center of fashion in the European world (DeJean 2005). The splendor of Louis XIV's court at Versailles captured the imagination of kings and aristocrats all over Europe and set off a tide of emulation, architectural, behavioral, and sartorial. It was in Paris, where most of the court nobles maintained opulent residences, that the Versailles elite did its shopping. The city's shopkeepers responded to and stimulated this demand by sprucing up their shops and greatly expanding the range of items on sale. But the Parisian retail boom of the eighteenth century reached far beyond the great court nobles. If court nobles remained an essential customer base, there were plenty of other prosperous people in the capital who were enticed by the goods on display in the shops. Moreover, opulent visitors flocked to Paris from the provinces and from other European countries to stock up on the fashionable goods available only there. Between the late seventeenth century and 1789, shopkeepers and their avid customers created a novel retail landscape that should be understood as a fundamental component of the city's commercial public sphere.[16]

This shopping landscape must be understood as a fundamental feature of the emerging public sphere. The shops were open to all who had sufficient purchasing power, and their displays and ever-diversifying stocks of goods both catered to and shaped the tastes and habits of the expanding shopping public. Retail shops had of course existed in Europe for as long as there had been towns—urban people had to be supplied with food, clothing, and other goods. But the sort of retail establishments that emerged in the late seventeenth and eighteenth centuries were not simply supplying the necessities of urban life; they were self-consciously creating new needs and a new model of polite society signified by novel patterns of consumption available to an expanding clientele.

The most spectacular purveyors of the new patterns of consumption were the Parisian mercers (*merciers*), members of a guild whose members were, as Diderot put it in the *Encyclopédie*, "sellers of everything, makers of nothing" (1765, 369). The array of goods sold by different mercers could vary considerably: some might concentrate on fabrics, others on art objects, yet others on furnishings for the home (Sargentson 1996). By midcentury, the most prestigious mercers had shops on the rue du Faubourg Saint-Honoré, which stretched westward on the right bank of the Seine River from the center of Paris through a new and rapidly developing wealthy quarter of the city. Beginning in the mid-eighteenth century, many of these shops were outfitted with glazed front windows so that strollers passing on the street could be enticed by the goods on display (Sargentson 1996, 130). The most successful mercers in the furniture and furnishing branch of the trade specialized in custom design, becoming the creators and the arbiters of the latest home furnishing styles. They would offer specific designs and configurations of furnishings and coordinate the work subcontracted to joiners, tapestry makers, bronze workers, mirror makers, clockmakers, and producers of earthenware and porcelain (Sargentson 1996, 46–56). They also sold Chinese and Japanese porcelains, typically mounted in gilt bronze or silver to make new objects. They disassembled East Asian lacquerware and mounted it onto European items, such as writing desks, inkstands, chests, or candelabras (Sargentson 1996, 62–82). The products sold in shops of tapestry makers (*tapissiers*) overlapped substantially with those of the mercers. Although they might sell rugs and tapestries, they were purveyors of furniture and furnishings of all descriptions.

16. An indispensable work on the Parisian retail landscape is Coquery (2011).

The nobility dominated the high end of Paris's shopping landscape, but nearly all levels of the city's population were touched by the expanding market for consumer goods. One of the most important features of the new consumption regime was the rampant development of "semi-luxury" (*demi-luxe*) goods, which resembled luxurious items but used cheaper materials and sold for much lower prices. Examples included cloth that mixed silk with cotton, earthenware rather than porcelain, costume jewelry, and silver plate or pinchbeck rather than gold (Coquery 2011, 273–77). Eighteenth-century Parisian artisans famously developed ever-new and ingenious examples of such wares, which found an expanding market among Parisians and visitors to the city alike. Such "populuxe" goods were surprisingly abundant even in the inventories after the death of members of the Parisian popular classes. Domestic servants, master artisans, and manual workers owned books, bookcases, new furniture items like writing desks, canes, fans, snuffboxes, umbrellas, watches, coffeepots and teapots, crockery, and decorative sculpture, not to mention stylish garments (Fairchilds 1993).[17] As Fairchilds's research makes clear, the common people of Paris were enthusiastic participants in the new shopping landscape of their city.

The development of semiluxury can be seen clearly in the eighteenth-century Parisian jewelry trade. Far from attempting to pass off inferior goods as the real thing, jewelers touted the elegance of the semiluxury goods and the ingenuity of the artisans who fashioned them. An entry in the *Almanach général des marchands* observes, "In Paris pearls are made that imitate natural pearls so well, and are so inexpensive, that most women do without the real ones" (Coquery 2011, 275). This policy of offering both the fine and the mediocre meant that prices of many products spanned a very wide gamut—from goods of great luxury for the wealthy to affordable goods for the humble. Silver watches sold by one Parisian jeweler between 1773 and 1783 spanned a range from 12 to 72 livres. Gold watches began at 54 livres and rose as high as 720 livres (Coquery 2011, 299–300). It was this wide range that made it possible for Fairchilds's artisans or domestic servants to own watches. Fairchilds notes that many of the populuxe goods purchased by ordinary Parisians were produced in the suburbs of the city, particularly in the Faubourg Saint-Antoine, where Parisian guild regulations did not apply, and were sold by clandestine peddlers rather than in shops. Thus umbrellas, initially an Asian import that was copied and perfected in France, were legally a monopoly of the guild of *peigneurs-tablettiers* (makers of combs and small wooden ob-

17. See also Roche (1994, 2000).

jects) but were widely purchased by poorer customers from clandestine nonguild producers.[18] There were also plenty of well-stocked secondhand markets where inexpensive goods of all types could be found.

This proliferation of cheap versions of the stylish new goods resulted in a hierarchically structured market. But with the development and widespread availability of semiluxury or populuxe items, there was no definitive line between the tastes and styles of the wealthy elite and the ordinary people. The folding steel-framed umbrellas carried by nobles could not easily be distinguished from the cheap ones carried by master artisans or domestic servants on their days of leisure; the apprentice who had bought a secondhand suit originally sold to a secondhand dealer by a nobleman upgrading his wardrobe was not easily distinguishable from the latter when strolling in the Jardin des Tuileries or on the boulevards. The proliferating eighteenth-century consumer culture made it possible for people of quite modest means to participate, at least vicariously, in the polite society that had been developed by their social superiors.

This new world of retail used the printed matter that proliferated in the eighteenth century. Among the simplest examples were business cards and headings printed at the top of bills. Le Petit Dunquerque, a famous jewelry and metalwares shop, had a particularly elaborate business card, with an engraving of the fort of Dunquerque surrounded by ships and a foreground featuring the shop's wares (Sargentson 1996, 122). Shopkeepers also printed more detailed lists informing potential customers about goods available in their shops. Coquery reproduces the list of a mercer-jeweler from 1755 with over one hundred entries, including "garnet necklaces, fine and false . . . pearl necklaces . . . amber necklaces . . . necklaces to cure children's toothaches . . . all kinds of jet items for mourning . . . diamond sleeve buttons, coat buttons of diamond and mother of pearl . . . buttons of pinchbeck, buttons of copper for the troops . . . black buckles, buckles with diamonds, false gold and steel, for shoes or garters . . . dice for gambling, in bone and ivory . . . silk purses for the pocket . . . toothpicks . . . lanterns of ebony and wood . . . curtain cords of all colors . . . silk handkerchiefs . . . and generally all sorts of merchandise of mercery, jewelry, and hardware, all at fair prices" (2011, 379–80). Shopkeepers also placed notices in the affiches, the little commercial newspapers discussed earlier in this chapter, especially when a new shipment of goods arrived.

Especially in the second half of the eighteenth century, assorted pub-

18. It was the French in the eighteenth century who developed the folding steel-ribbed umbrella, which quickly became a de rigeur fashion accessory (Fairchilds 1993, 237–39).

lications devoted to retail began to appear. There were numerous guides to Paris aimed at visitors from the provinces or abroad. These included advice about Parisian customs, lodging, transportation, galleries, the opera and theaters, and pleasant promenades, as well as information about where visitors would find shops worthy of their interest (Coquery 2011, 59–78). More systematic information about the shopping landscape was purveyed in almanacs devoted to Paris. This was a major genre of literary production in the eighteenth century: 1,276 different titles were published between 1700 and 1789, with combined print runs of some fifty thousand each year. Almanacs covering the entire range of commercial operations appeared annually from the 1760s on, listing establishments alphabetically by trade (Coquery 2011, 79–197).[19]

It is easier to trace the goods or the shops that populated the eighteenth-century consumer landscape than the experience of the shoppers. But there are glimpses in the memoirs of the Baronne d'Oberkirch, a noblewoman from Alsace who made three extensive visits to Paris in the 1780s and frequently remarked on her shopping experiences (Oberkirch 1970).[20] Between house calls, visits to art galleries, and trips to the opera and theater, Madame d'Oberkirch made numerous Parisian shopping expeditions. One morning in 1782, she and a friend "spent several hours at Le Petit-Dunkerque. . . . Nothing is as pretty and brilliant as at this boutique, filled with jewelry and golden trinkets. . . . They sell at fixed prices . . . there are so many buyers that a guard is employed" to maintain order. "We chose a stylish toy, a sort of little windmill to mount on a clock" (233). She also chronicled a visit to a furniture maker (*ébéniste*). "He made marvelous furniture. He showed us all the styles. I spent over two hours there" (266). Another day she made "a woman's visit" to the shop of Rose Bertin, a milliner (*marchande de modes*) who catered to the highest nobility and was regarded by Marie Antoinette as her "minister of fashions." She found Bertin "a singular person, puffed up with her own importance, who acted as if she were the equal of princesses" (196). In 1784 she made another visit to mademoiselle Bertin in the company of the Duchesse de Bourbon. Bertin "*deigned* to receive us herself and *consented* to make a bonnet" for the duchess, but only "on the *condition* that she would not lend it to anyone else" (611). Mme d'Oberkirch was rather

19. Coquery (2011, 331–36) uses almanacs to construct maps of the location of retail establishments.

20. Subsequent citations to this work will consist only of page numbers in parentheses in the text.

pleased to learn, in 1787, that Bertin had suffered a bankruptcy, although she remarked that "her bankruptcy is not at all plebian; it's a bankruptcy of a great lady, two million!" (653).[21]

During her visit in 1784, Mme d'Oberkirch went with her daughter to the shop of one Mademoiselle Martin, who sold the finest rouge in Europe, to stock up on her own supply and to purchase gifts for others. These purchases were expensive, however: "the smallest pot costs a Louis"— that is to say, ten livres (598). She visited another furniture maker on the rue du Faubourg Saint-Honoré, where a huge crowd had gathered to gawk at "an admirably fashioned buffet destined to be taken to England to the home of the Duke of Northumberland" (417.) There was also a return visit to le Petit Dunquerque, where she and her husband found "ravishing novelties and elegant *petit riens* (little trifles)." Her husband bought a pair of bracelets for his mother for sixty livres (422). Next they visited a *tabletier* (a maker of small objects of wood, ivory, horn, etc., such as chess pieces, decorated boxes, and combs) and then a *tapissier* "for our provisions." A few days later: "Still more purchases. When we leave Paris we require wagons" (490–91).

Of course, only wealthy visitors or residents of Paris would have made so many purchases or visited so many fine shops. But these shops were in principle open to all customers, and it was perfectly possible to look at a wide range of goods without buying anything. We should note the overflowing crowds encountered in le Petit Dunquerque and the people packed in the street gawking at the Duke of Northumberland's fabulous buffet. The shopping streets were public thoroughfares, and the shops (although perhaps not that of Rose Bertin) were open to any respectable-looking potential customer, many of whom only browsed. Indeed, there is no indication whether Mme d'Oberkirch purchased any of the "marvelous" items of furniture she viewed during her two hours at the ébéniste's shop in 1782. It could be entertaining simply to stroll the busy streets and peer into the shops. The same was true of the stalls in the Halles (the municipal food market) or the passages where secondhand dealers could display their distinctly less gaudy wares. The shopping landscape was in this sense a public space—the goods and the shops were privately owned, but they were necessarily open to the curious potential customer. Indeed, the prosperity of the shops was often dependent on sales to anonymous shoppers lured in from the street or attracted by entries in almanacs as on regular customers.

21. On Rose Bertin, see Crowston (2013, 246–82).

Commerce and the Public Sphere

The institutions discussed in this chapter by no means exhaust the growing range of social relations encompassed by the expanding eighteenth-century public sphere. One could, for example, add considerations of provincial academies, agricultural societies, and masonic lodges, all of which hosted sociability, contributed significantly to public opinion, and were, in varying degrees, influenced in their activities by the burgeoning commercial relations that surrounded and penetrated them. Nor do my brief sketches do more than mark some of the contours of the emerging commercial society that structured social life and social experience in the eighteenth century. The next two chapters, however, will explore aspects of the nexus of commercial capitalism and social experience in greater depth. Chapter 4 considers the production and consumption of fashion goods, one of the distinctive dynamics of eighteenth-century society. And chapter 5 looks at the reshaping of public space through the lens of the urban promenade—a practice in which fashion and sociability combined to produce a novel experience of a limited but potent form of civic equality.

* 4 *

The Empire of Fashion

In the last quarter of the seventeenth century, France—and more particularly Paris—became the recognized arbiter of fashion in the European world, a position it sustained throughout the eighteenth century and beyond.[1] As Louis-Antoine Caraccioli wrote, "There is no court in Europe where French fabrics are not à la mode. They flatter the vanity of the great, the frivolity of women; they shine on days of gala. A dress that has not been made in Lyon, a diamond that hasn't been mounted in Paris, a fan that was not made there, are insipid in the eyes of foreigners. They are embraced only when they are seen as samples of French genius" (1777, 156). This French preeminence in fashion was a crucial feature of the French economy. As a contemporary Italian observer astutely noted, "This very word 'fashion' is an enormous and long-lasting treasure for France, and is considered by the French as a . . . highly-precious capital." The "empire of fashion," he also remarked, was for France what Potosi, the seemingly inexhaustible Peruvian silver mine, had once been for Spain.[2] In fact, fashion has been a more enduring treasure for the French than Potosi was for the Spanish. Luxury goods have been a leading sector of the French economy ever since the glory days of Versailles, and Paris has remained the world capital of fashion up to the present.

The business of fashion was intimately connected to the social and cultural transformations of French urban life, and especially Parisian life, in the eighteenth century. Fashionable clothing and accessories were meant to be paraded in public—in relatively restrictive gatherings like salons but also at the theater and opera, at cafés, at fairs, and in public promenades.

---

1. A somewhat longer version of this chapter, entitled "The Empire of Fashion and the Rise of Capitalism in Eighteenth-Century France," was published in *Past and Present* 206 (2010): 83–120. Reprinted by permission of the Past and Present Society.

2. Zanon (1764, 3:263–64; 1763, 2:123–24), quoted by Carlo Poni (1997, 44).

And if aristocrats occupied the pinnacle of fashion, the various components of the fashion industry—the producers and sellers of textiles; tailors and dressmakers; milliners, hatmakers, and wigmakers; makers of fans, umbrellas, gloves, and shoes; jewelers and watchmakers—were constantly looking to expand their markets to any likely customer. The fashion public that developed in the eighteenth century was immense, various, and growing.

Until recently, economic historians working in the eighteenth century generally showed much less interest in fashionable or "luxury" goods than in the economic and technical transformations seen as leading to the industrial revolution. They tended to view luxury industries, which were overwhelmingly based on craft skills, as technologically stagnant and irrelevant to the great issues of industrial take-off. But this view of fashionable goods is anachronistic when applied to the eighteenth-century economy: it is colored by a knowledge of the great technological transformation only beginning at the century's end. During the past few decades, an outpouring of work, most of it focused on England, has challenged this once-dominant view. Research into the production, design, and sale of fashionable consumer goods has demonstrated that the eighteenth-century English economy's dynamism, even its technical dynamism, depended to a surprising degree on burgeoning markets for fashionable goods—including woolen and cotton textiles, pottery, and small metal wares such as buttons, buckles, candlesticks, and cutlery (MacKendrick, Brewer, and Plum 1982; Brewer and Porter 1993; Berg 2002, 2004; Chapman and Chassagne 1981; Lemire 1991; Styles 2007).

Research on production and consumption of French consumer goods is less abundant than that on England, but it too has unearthed the existence of a burgeoning eighteenth-century consumer marketplace, one that extended far down the urban social scale (Roche 1994, 2000; Fairchilds 1993; Pardailhé-Galabrun 1991; Ferrières 2004; Kwass 2006). Contemporaries were quite aware of these changes. The remarkable output of books and pamphlets on political economy published in France in the eighteenth century was dominated by a fierce debate about the new luxury consumption, which some bemoaned as a sign of decadence and effeminacy and others praised as productive of comfort, politeness, and wealth (Shovlin 2006; Kwass 2003, 2004). The complex of manufacture, marketing, and consumption of fashionable goods that emerged between the late seventeenth and the late eighteenth centuries was crucial to the rise and triumph of capitalism in France. New logics of production and consumption of fashionable goods put in place an indefinitely reproducible and expandable recipe for enhanced capital accumulation, one that restructured enterprise, social relations, and consciousness. Although here I examine only the French case, there is reason to believe that the dynamic manifested in France was quite general in the eighteenth-century Atlantic world.[3]

My analysis of the economics of fashion departs from Marx's—in the sense of taking Marx as its starting point but also in the sense of moving beyond that starting point. As explained in chapter 2, Marx understood capital accumulation as arising out of the exploitation of labor through the production of surplus value. The laborer produces greater value than his or her own cost of (re)production, yet the capitalist, following the economic laws that govern all commodity exchange, pays the laborer a wage equal only to her or his cost of production. This difference between the wage paid and the value the laborer produces is the capitalist's perennial source of profit. Under capitalism, the extraction of surplus value takes place through formally voluntary market transactions—the wage labor contract—to which the laborer submits because he or she has been stripped of ownership of the means of production and is compelled to work for wages to survive. Labor is, as a consequence, *subsumed* under capital; that is to say, it is harnessed by the capitalist to the production of surplus value (Marx [1867] 1977, 645–48, 1019–38). In the eighteenth century, most subsumption of labor was what Marx called "formal" rather than "real." The putting-out system did not fundamentally transform the pre-existing labor process or means of production, but it subjected the organization, financing, and marketing of industrial production to the capitalist's control. I believe that Marx, whose notion of real subsumption was based on nineteenth-century English factory industry, seriously underestimated the transformative power of this *formal* subsumption of labor under capital. It was by mercantile means—through mechanisms of purchase and sale, lubricated by credit—that the subsumption of labor under capital progressed most spectacularly in eighteenth-century France.

This was particularly true of textiles, by far France's largest industrial sector. The advance of capitalist textile production took place in close symbiosis with a changing market for consumer products. Indeed, it is not always easy, in the eighteenth century, to separate the dynamics of production from those of consumption. The subsumption of *desire* under capital, one might say, was tightly intertwined with the subsumption of *labor* under capital. The most successful capitalists in the textile industry thrived by providing goods that had high consumer appeal, especially in Paris, the era's ultimate urban marketplace. New bright and

3. In addition to the works on Britain cited earlier, see Breen (1986, 2004).

elaborately patterned silk brocades and printed cottons were particularly desirable and tended to displace linen and woolens. French silks and cottons owed much of their appeal to the craze for colorful Indian cotton textiles that the Dutch, British, and French East India Companies made increasingly available in the second half of the seventeenth century. Initially, the new French textiles were domestic substitutes for these exotic luxuries, but the French producers quickly moved beyond mere imitation to create their own distinctive designs.[4] Their ingenuity helped create the volatile fashion-driven Parisian market, in which design sense, the continual production of novelty, and the ability to adapt quickly to the market's whims were essential to success. We cannot understand the dynamics of the eighteenth-century textile industry if we treat the manufacture and the consumption of textiles as two separate processes, joined only contingently by a market in cloth. The evolution of consumer taste reached back into the mode of producing cloth, and the merchants who directed production also did their utmost to shape the tastes of the consuming public.

Indeed, the value of the product in these industries was created not only in production but by securing an added fashion value in the market. A fashionable bolt of cloth that contained one hundred hours of labor had a higher value than a bolt of ordinary cloth containing the same number of hours of labor. This implies that enhancing consumer desire without increasing the labor expended on the product was an indirect means of increasing the productivity of labor; it enabled a given quantity of labor to produce more value without increasing labor input. It is therefore arguable that enhancing consumer desire creates a kind of surplus value.[5] Moreover, profit created through more effective design or better marketing, no less than that created through technological change, can set off a competitive spiral that places upward pressure on productivity—particularly quality enhancement and improvements in design and marketing—in the industry as a whole. In fashion goods industries, surplus value is produced both in the process of production and in the process of desire enhancement.

---

4. Maxine Berg (2002, 2004, 2005) has demonstrated that creative substitution for Asian luxuries was important for industrial growth in eighteenth-century Britain as well.

5. Here I clearly depart from an orthodox Marxian analysis, which would define the value of a product as equivalent to the necessary labor time incorporated into its production and would insist that surplus value can only be produced in the wage-labor relationship.

The Silk Industry of Lyon

This claim can be made more plausible by examining the eighteenth-century Lyonnais silk industry, which produced the most desirable silks in Europe and was the most innovative French textile industry in design, marketing, and technology (Poni 1997; Thornton 1965; Miller 1998; Sargentson 1996, 1998; Garden 1970; Godart [1899] 1976). In terms of value of product, it was easily the most important industrial complex in eighteenth-century France. The reason for the Lyonnais fabrics' desirability hinged on the subtlety and novelty of their floral-patterned designs, or *façonnées*. As early as the beginning of the eighteenth century, the Lyonnais industry produced a powerfully expansive nexus of design, production, marketing, and consumer desire—what, in the title of this chapter, I call the empire of fashion. Because this nexus has proved to be indefinitely expansible across a wide range of consumer products, it deserves to be recognized as an important instance of the endless accumulation of capital. As Carlo Poni has argued before me, it contributed a permanent source of dynamism to the emerging social form of capitalism.[6] It powered the French fashion industry, which from the late seventeenth century to the present has been the most reliably profitable and internationally competitive sector of the French capitalist economy. Meanwhile, by the mid-eighteenth century, its logics were spreading outward into the production and marketing of a much wider band of consumer goods, a spread that has continued ever since. The subsumption of desire under capital by means of distinctive design and astute marketing has had a long and distinguished career in the subsequent history of capitalism.

The preeminence of Lyonnais silks dates to the final decade or so of the seventeenth century, when they displaced Italian silks as the most prestigious fabrics in court society at Versailles—a maelstrom of sartorial competition that, by then, had spilled over into Paris and that, crucially, set the clothing fashions for polite society all over Europe. The Lyonnais producers were acutely aware of the importance of court patronage. According to a tract written in 1731, consumption of silks at court, "which is only of the most beautiful, the most perfect, and the newest" fabrics, was the "principal object of this commerce. . . . The court by its decisions about taste and about styles authorizes novelties that without its author-

6. As Poni put it, the Lyonnais industry "was a protagonist of the 'great transformation' proposed by Karl Polanyi, even if its role in the 'modern world system' as a promoter of profound social changes has as yet gone unrecognized" (1997, 41–42).

ity would never have gained favor." The approval of the court was important not only because courtiers themselves made substantial purchases but because consumption there was imitated by foreign courts and "by Paris, which in its turn is imitated by the provinces." This imitation, the tract went on, extended "all the way down to the smallest petite bourgeoisie." By, for example, scrupulously wearing black crêpe to observe the periods of mourning prescribed for the court, the bourgeoisie acted as if it "had the honor of being related to the crowned heads and the princes to whose memories the court pays tribute" (Sargentson 1996, 103–4). The implications of these observations are fascinating on more than one count. For the silk producer, of course, imitation meant expanded markets; by gaining the favor of the mighty at court, the silk producers not only won lucrative custom there but also gained sales with lesser nobles and French commoners as well as in foreign courts. Yet there was also something disconcerting about this scrupulous imitation of the highest nobility by the most mediocre bourgeois; the imitation seemed to be making a claim for a kind of honor that the bourgeois had no right to aspire to. The spread of fashion, as this text intimates, had potentially equalizing and therefore unsettling social and moral implications.

Court patronage and the widespread imitation of the court's styles meant hefty profits for the Lyonnais. The desirability of the Lyonnais fabrics arose from the subtlety and novelty of their floral-patterned designs (Thornton 1965). The previously dominant Italian silk textiles—Genoese velvets, Venetian damasks, Bolognese crêpes, or Florentine satins—tended to be monochromatic and relatively heavy. The Lyonnais fabrics were light, had a superior sheen and brighter colors, and most importantly, featured ever-varying, often multicolored floral motifs that gave them immediate visual distinction. The superiority of the Lyonnais in design was so complete that by the early eighteenth century, the other centers had all begun to produce copies of Lyonnais cloths. But the Lyonnais producers, in response, began to introduce new designs every year. This systematic annual product differentiation through design relegated foreign imitators to a permanent second place (Thornton 1965, 18–20). As one Lyonnais silk merchant put it, because it took foreigners a year to copy designs and put them into production, "we need only replace [one year's designs] by others, so that the old ones will have lost the merit of novelty. While the foreigner is busy copying ours, we will mount new ones" (Amoldi 1761, 82). Thus when English producers dutifully copied the latest Lyonnais designs, they had to worry that "a New Fashion should come from France, and render [theirs] despicable." The Lyonnais would take the "first of the market," leaving to others "the Fag-End."[7] This Lyonnais domination of the very lucrative high end of the European (and transatlantic) silk market, it should be pointed out, lasted right through the eighteenth century and through most of the nineteenth as well (Cottereau 1997).

One effect of the continually changing designs was that the durability of the Lyonnais fabrics tended to decline over the course of the eighteenth century. If dresses went out of fashion after a few years, there was no reason to make fabrics that would last for forty. One commentator remarked that Lyonnais silks "have little body, that they wear out in a short time, but one wants them for hardly more than a season."[8] The Lyonnais also produced both higher and lower quality goods intended for different market segments (Sargentson 1996, 97; Poni 1997, 105). Hence it is hardly surprising that silk goods began to be purchased by classes far below court society. Already in 1700, nearly 10 percent of garments owned by wage workers and domestic servants in Paris who had sufficient goods to be inventoried after their death were made of silk; by the 1780s, despite the much greater availability of cheaper printed cotton cloth, the proportion of silk among all garments in these occupational categories increased still further. And since the sheer number of garments owned by wage workers and domestics seems to have more than doubled over this period, the overall consumption of silks by these groups must have at least tripled.[9]

The ability of the Lyonnais to establish and maintain their advantage in design required close coordination between the world of fashion in Paris and the production of silks in Lyon. This was not a trivial problem, given that Lyon was some 350 kilometers to the south, a distance that, in the middle of the eighteenth century, required five or six days of travel by coach and three days for rapid postal delivery (Miller 1998, 149). The crucial link between the two cities was the professional designer, whose prominence within the industry had no parallel elsewhere. By the later eighteenth century, there were perhaps as many as two hundred designers in the Lyonnais industry, some working freelance, others employed directly by a firm, some in partnership with a merchant manufacturer (a

7. See *The Case of the Silk-Weavers* (1713, 42). Miller (1998, 159) and Sargentson (1998, 105) estimate that the value of a fabric declined by about a quarter the season after it first hit the market.

8. Poni (1997, 62), quoting Pinto (1771).

9. See the tables on pages 127 and 138 of Roche (1994). Roche notes that the number of garments possessed by male workers and domestic servants rose by 150 to 200 percent between 1700 and 1789 (136). He gives no comparable figure for women but implies that their consumption rose similarly.

marchand de soie)—the capitalist entrepreneurs who dominated the industry (Thornton 1965, 18). In addition to a rudimentary apprenticeship in weaving, designers studied drawing and flower painting. Once a designer found employment with a merchant manufacturer, he would spend several months every year in Paris. According to a designer and merchant manufacturer who wrote a small treatise on silk design in 1764, the designer should avail himself of the many artistic resources of Paris and its region, including the Versailles gardens, the Gobelins tapestry works, the Sèvres porcelain works, the displays of shells and butterflies at the Jardin des Plantes, menageries, museums, art galleries, theaters, and churches. The designer would also visit the shops of the most exclusive mercers to examine up-to-date furnishings and accessories for the fashionable household. Indeed, it was in the specialized silk shops of Paris "that the most marvelous of Lyon's productions over the years are piled up every day" (L'Hilberderie 1774, 86). Paradoxically, it was only by going to Paris, the leading center of sales, that a Lyonnais could get access to the full range of designs being produced in his own city.

On the basis of this Parisian experience, which imparted the knowledge of what designs were selling well, a sense of general fashion trends, and considerable artistic stimulation, the designer would send reports back to Lyon and prepare a set of new designs. Most new designs would be variations on those currently in vogue in Paris. But some were more adventurous efforts to anticipate or to set fashion trends. Back in Lyon, designs would be copied onto graph paper and the designer would work in cooperation with a weaver to transfer them from paper to loom before they were put out to the weavers who would produce them in substantial quantities (Poni 1997, 64–68; Miller 1998, 145–46; Thornton 1965, 18–20). As the key link between Lyonnais production and the Parisian market, designers were highly sought after and well paid; on the tax rolls of 1758–59, their assessments were similar to all but the upper level of the silk merchants, and many eventually became partners in silk firms (Miller 1998, 146).

The silk merchants themselves made occasional voyages to Paris. They also sent samples of their cloth to mercers and wholesalers and maintained regular relations with mercers and *commissionaires* (agents who relayed orders from customers), hawked new cloth to retailers, and sent samples of successful new silk designs and other relevant news to Lyon. Finally, the Parisian mercers, whose shops, as we have noted, were the great emporiums of fashionable life in Paris and the chief purveyors of fashionable goods to Versailles as well, corresponded regularly with their Lyonnais suppliers and made suggestions or specifications about designs and colors (Sargentson 1996, 97–112; Miller 1998, 149–52, 157). The mercers also produced dolls dressed in their latest wares that they sent to correspondents in all the European capitals, thereby stimulating international demand for the latest Lyonnais fabrics (DeJean 2005, 63–67).

In short, the relationship between silk production in Lyon and the evolving fashions in Paris was complexly reciprocal. The Lyonnais made a considerable investment in the production of new designs that continued to set the pace in the Parisian luxury market and through it the European luxury market more generally. But as the constant movement of letters, sketches, orders, samples, and personnel back and forth between the two cities makes clear, the Lyonnais producers were also constantly scouring the Parisian art and fashion scene to get new ideas for their products. They were also, of course, in constant competition with one another, making small modifications of other successful Lyonnais producers' designs and constantly attempting to steal a march on their rivals. They maintained substantial archives of their past designs, to which they could return some years later or which they could modify by recombining, simplifying, elaborating, enlarging, or diminishing elements, by varying colors, adding stripes, and so on (Sargentson 1996, 109; Miller 1998, 162–64). A substantial part of the very considerable profits that the Lyonnais silk industry produced in the eighteenth century arose from silk merchants' unique ability at once to influence and to learn from the evolving taste of the Parisian luxury market. Their decisive advantage was in what we would today call information—that is, their stocks of designs, the talents of their designers, the well-managed flow of news about Parisian market conditions, and the extraordinary nimbleness with which they responded to new information.

This exquisitely responsive reciprocal relationship between Parisian taste and Lyonnais production would not have been possible without a highly skilled and effectively managed labor force. Known aptly as "La Grande Fabrique," the Lyonnais silk industry was, by the standards of the day, a huge industrial and commercial complex: it employed about 14,000 adult men and perhaps as many as 20,000 women and children in the 1780s, in a city with a total population of about 150,000 (Garden 1970, 34, 39, 317–18.) This was nearly a quarter of the entire population of the city and probably accounted for some 40 percent of the active labor force. These men, women, and children worked at the behest of perhaps 350 to 450 merchants (Godart [1899] 1976, 26). It was the merchants who organized the industry and reaped the profits. The merchants bought the extremely valuable raw materials, mainly from Italy but also from Southern France; determined the colors, designs, and quantities of the cloths to be woven; and put out the raw materials to be woven up by, or under the supervision of, master weavers. This industry was a particularly sophisticated example of the formal subsumption of labor under capital. The master weavers were located exclusively in Lyon or the immediately adjacent suburbs, not in the surrounding countryside. This urban location made it easier for the merchants to maintain some degree of surveillance over them—an important matter given the high value of the silk yarns consigned to the weavers. The pilfering of even a small proportion of the yarns could cut sharply into the merchants' profits.

Master weavers generally worked in their own homes, where they would have one to three looms—at any given time, one loom might be employed by the master weaver, another by a journeyman or apprentice, while on a third, a new warp was being mounted. The master weavers were not wage laborers but subcontractors who possessed their own small capital (principally their looms) and hired and supervised their own journeymen. They would negotiate a *prix de façon* (literally a price for fabrication) with the merchant for each job, and when the job was completed, the merchant would weigh, measure, and inspect the cloth—making deductions from the payment if there were flaws. The master weaver would then pay his journeyman and any other assistants, retaining the rest as his share. He, too, although on a minuscule scale, was formally something of a capitalist. In order to collect the full prix de façon, the master had every reason to work very carefully and according to the specifications given to him by the merchant and to supervise carefully the work of his journeymen or apprentices. By this mechanism, the merchant exercised strong, if indirect, quality control over the labor process (Godart [1899] 1976; Amoldi 1761, 76).

Division of labor was quite advanced. There were two distinct categories of weavers who worked on different sorts of looms: those who made plain silks and those who produced patterned cloths. As of 1768, there were about equal numbers of weavers in these two categories (Miller 1998, 146; Garden 1970, 280). Both types of weavers required assistants. Specialized workers, commonly the wives of the weavers, prepared the warp for the weaver and mounted it on the loom. In the case of patterned cloth weaving, the weaver was assisted by a *tireuse* (a puller), whose job it was to pull, in order, the series of cords affixed to specific warp threads in order to lift them up—and to call out to the weaver which color weft yarn should be passed through the shed to form the desired multicolored design (Hafter 1995). Finally, the complex design had to be read into the harness that selectively lifted the warp threads. This was done by a highly skilled (usually female) *liseuse de dessins* (reader of designs; Godart [1899]

1976, 66–74). These jobs had to be performed every time the weaver switched from one design to another (Thornton 1965, 23).

It should be noted that this elaborate and sophisticated means of preparing the loom and carrying out the weaving task, made possible by a meticulously organized "reading" of the design onto the loom, provided the context out of which the Jacquard loom, patented in 1801, eventually arose. The Jacquard loom automated the reading of the design by means of perforated paper cards, analogous to the perforated cards used in early computers. It was the end point of technical changes over the course of the eighteenth century: indeed, perforated cards had been used in programming designs on looms as early as 1770 (Poni 1997, 66–67). These changes had improved the efficiency of the Lyonnais industry well before Jacquard took out his patent, further increasing its advantage over its competitors. The achievement of Jacquard's breakthrough in the Lyonnais silk industry at the very end of the century confirmed the capitalistic rationalization and technological dynamism already proceeding earlier (Ballot [1923] 1976, 334-83; Thornton 1965, 44).

This advanced division of labor was undertaken and supervised not by the merchant but by the master weaver. The division of labor significantly increased the productivity of labor, lowering labor costs per unit produced. But the master weaver, who was in direct competition with hundreds of others for commissions from the merchants, was probably unable to claim more than a small fraction of the incremental value created by the division of labor. The merchant simply paid the weaver, his subcontractor, enough to keep the weaver's family unit going. The merchant regularly collected surplus value from the exploited master weavers and, indirectly, from the family members he exploited in his turn. This double exploitation accounted for much of the silk merchants' very substantial profits.

But surplus value was also produced by enhancing the quality (or at least the desirability) and therefore the value of the product without increasing the cost of labor. Without the skills of the weavers and their families, the high quality and continual novelty of design that gave the silks of Lyon their special value in national and international markets would have been impossible to sustain. It was the weavers' community that developed the relevant skills and passed them on to the next generation. The technical training of weavers took place in the master weaver's workshop, where he taught the tricks of the trade to apprentices and supervised the work of journeymen who had already completed their apprenticeships and expected to become masters in their turn. Training costs were assumed by the apprentice, who had to work for his room and board without pay for

five years (Godart [1899] 1976, 118–24). The skills of the women who prepared the warps and read the designs onto the looms were presumably
passed on within the family and between female friends. Hence the merchants were able to profit from the skills of the silk workers, both the weavers and their auxiliaries, without having to pay the cost of training them.[10]
Gaining the benefits of training (in improved quality and therefore enhanced product value) without having to shoulder the costs of training
was another way for the silk merchants of Lyon to harvest surplus value.

That this exploitation of the master weavers by the merchants did not
go unchallenged is evident in the history of the silk weaving guild, a composite body made up not only of master weavers but also of silk merchants. At the beginning of the eighteenth century, many master weavers worked on their own account, either independently of the merchants
or, more likely, as a supplement to weaving yarn put out to them by merchants. But as the century wore on, the merchants, who dominated the
guild, mounted an offensive against the weavers' rights. As early as 1711,
they imposed a charge of three hundred livres on the master weavers who
wove on their own, and in 1731, they actually made it illegal to work both
on one's own account and as a putting-out worker (Godart [1899] 1976,
89–92; Garden 1970, 572–75). The merchants' opposition to the independent master weavers seems to have been motivated by the fact that the
latter commonly based their work on copied designs—just as weavers in
England or Italy were doing at this time. The merchants, who had paid
for the production of the designs, charged that the independent masters
were disloyally undercutting their profits. Once the silk industry became
design intensive—became an integral element in an emerging empire of
fashion—the relations between the social categories that had made up
the industry were profoundly transformed. The subsumption of desire
under capital acted back on the subsumption of labor under capital, rendering the interests of the merchants and independent masters newly incompatible (Poni 1997, 48–49).

After much futile contestation against the merchants over the course
of the century, the weavers launched a new offensive against the masters in 1786. As Maurice Garden commented in his massive study of
eighteenth-century Lyon, the master weavers had long struggled to regain
the possibility of an "independence as workers who were also merchants."

---

10. One presumes, however, that some of the costs of upgrading skills—when new
types of designs were introduced, for example—must have been borne by the silk merchants, whose designers had to work with weavers to be sure that the designs were actually feasible and to be sure that the weavers were producing them properly.

But by 1786, their goals—indeed, their mental map of the industry—had changed. Belatedly recognizing their common dependence on the merchants, the weavers organized a strike movement to obtain an agreed minimum price for work put out to them, "fixed in advance, for all possible cloths, to which the merchant would be obliged to conform." This ultimately unsuccessful strike movement marked the end of an ideal of obtaining a "mediocre happiness" as independent masters. The weavers now recognized that their only hope was to force the merchants to grant them "more decent conditions of life" as dependent workers (Garden 1970, 580).[11] This history of struggles bears witness to the consolidation of an increasingly evident exploitative relationship between the merchants and the master weavers over the course of the eighteenth century and hence to the maturation of thoroughly capitalist relations in silk manufacture.

It is not easy to determine the extent and rhythms of growth of this thriving but fractious industry over the course of the eighteenth century. I have found no figures for the number of bolts of cloth produced, let alone estimates of the value of production. There are scattered figures for the number of silk looms in Lyon and some estimates of the changing size of the labor force. There were just over 5,000 silk looms in Lyon in 1720, 8,331 in 1739, and 14,777 in 1788 (Godart [1899] 1976, 26). The number of master weavers rose from 3,299 in 1739 to 7,000 in 1786. And the number of silk workers (masters and journeymen combined) who married in Lyon rose from 452 in 1728–30 to 570 in 1749–51 and to 977 in 1786–88 (Garden 1970, 282). The figures for the size of the labor force both indicate a little more than a doubling from the 1730s to the 1780s. The figures for looms, which go back further, indicate almost a tripling since 1720 (Godart [1899] 1976, 26). This growth, however, was far from even: rapid growth between 1720 and the 1750s, a falloff during the Seven Years' War (1756–63), another rise between the mid-1760s and the mid-1770s, and a decline during the American Revolutionary War. Between the mid-1770s and the mid-1780s, there was a major boom, followed by a sharp contraction in the later 1780s.[12]

11. In the 1830s, the Lyonnais silk workers, toiling in an industry organized much as it had been in the 1780s, were in the vanguard of the newly emerging movement. Indeed, it was the Lyonnais silk workers' insurrection of 1831 that inspired the young Karl Marx to develop his theory of workers' revolution. On Lyonnais workers in the 1830s, see Rude (1944) and Bezucha (1974).

12. These fluctuations can be discerned best in Godart's (1976, 26) figures for the number of looms, but his figures for the number of masters in the industry show the same rough pattern. None of the series are detailed enough to indicate year-to-year or season-to-season fluctuations, which one would expect to be substantial in the typically volatile fashion sector. See also Leroudier (1911).

In spite of the fluctuations, the overall trend in the eighteenth century was clearly upward. From the beginning of the century to the 1780s, it would appear that production probably at least tripled.

This growth in the silk industry was of course an index of the accumulation of capital by the silk merchants. A major source of the merchants' profits was their intensified exploitation of the master weavers. But they also secured enhanced profits from the design and marketing efforts carried out by themselves, their designers, and the Parisian mercers who promoted their wares among the fashionable clientele of the rue Faubourg Saint-Honoré. By capturing and repeatedly inciting the desires of the wealthy (and even the not-so-wealthy) for social distinction and refinement, the Lyonnais merchants increased the value of their merchandise. This could not be done without incurring costs. Designers, who had scarce skills, probably captured a good share of the value they added to Lyonnais silks. But the attractiveness and the novelty of the designs enhanced the value of the silk weavers' and their families' labor without requiring merchants to pay more for that labor. Whatever portion of this enhancement of value that was not captured by the designers was profit for the merchants.

This ability of designers and merchants (aided by the mercers) to enhance the value of their goods by harnessing the desire of consumers, and to do so in a way that was sustained and renewable, is what I call the subsumption of desire under capital. The question of harnessing desire to the ends of capital has, in various ways, been noted in studies of twentieth-century consumer capitalism, with its huge advertising budgets, but has not figured much in accounts of capitalism's origins (Lears 1994; Cohen 2003; Zukin 1991).[13] The case of the Lyonnais silk industry shows that the importance of desire creation goes back very far into capitalism's history. As early as the dawning years of the eighteenth century, it was the fashion-driven desire for novelty that made possible the rise to dominance of this great Lyonnais mercantile-industrial complex. It does not seem to be the Lyonnais themselves who initially set into motion the fashion dynamic from which they profited so handsomely. Rather, the initiative came from the royal court at Versailles, where Louis XIV's own fashion leadership and the extraordinary concentration of wealthy nobles seeking social distinction and access to power set into motion a fierce sartorial competition among courtiers—and, notably, among their wives and daughters as well (DeJean 2005). The suppliers of luxury goods, of course, were primarily located not in Versailles but in Paris. By the beginning of the eighteenth

13. Important exceptions are Forty (1986) and Berg (2005).

century, the Parisian mercers began to set up mirror-lined, elaborately decorated shops that carried the latest fabrics, fashion accessories, and furnishings (Sargentson 1996, 18–20). It seems to have been around the beginning of the eighteenth century that the practice of annual changes in design became regularized and that the Lyonnais were acclaimed as the most fashionable producers in the Paris market and hence in Europe as a whole (Poni 1997, 41–42, 69–70). The emergence of the practices of densely mediated coordination between Lyon and Paris and between production and consumption seems to have coincided with the spread of the taste for continual novelty outward from the court proper—initially to foreign courts and to nobles and wealthy commoners who lived in Paris, but eventually to the rest of France, to well-to-do commoners elsewhere in Europe, and to less opulent classes. The expansion of the market and the quickened pace of innovation in design went hand in hand.

The fashion market, with its characteristic demand for novelty and steady expansion geographically outward and socially downward, had a dynamic of its own, one the Lyonnais silk merchants and other luxury producers could tap into but had not initiated and could not control. This market for fashionable goods was of course shaped by many clever merchants and manufacturers who produced and displayed all sorts of novel goods, and it would have been impossible without the hard labor of many thousands of skillful workers. But to understand the rise of the Lyonnais silk industry and many other consumer goods industries in the eighteenth century, we must grasp the peculiar and novel role of consumers themselves in the social construction of fashion in this era.

What was new in the late seventeenth and eighteenth centuries was the pronounced taste for novelty itself and the gradual democratization of status competition through consumption. In earlier times and in other places in the world, clothes that marked status in one generation could be passed down to the next without having declined in status value.[14] But in the new European, Paris-centered fashion system, old clothing and accessories lost value quickly: fashion-conscious consumers wanted new, up-to-the-minute styles. Hence they had to replenish their wardrobes much more quickly and pass out-of-date clothing along to poorer consumers, through gifts to their servants and through a thriving secondhand market, thus ushering these classes into the lower levels of the fashion system.[15] This eighteenth-century fashion system overwhelmed

14. The importance of intergenerational gifts of clothing in wills in the fourteenth through sixteenth centuries is made clear in Howell (2010, 171–91).
15. On the second-hand market, see Roche (1994, 344–63).

an older sartorial system, indexed by now moribund sumptuary laws, which had specified the distinct garments to be worn by people of different social categories. By the mid-eighteenth century, it was becoming ever more difficult to read position in the social hierarchy from public bodily adornment. The unceasing novelty and volatility of the emerging sartorial regime also meant that consumers had to put far more effort into assembling their wardrobes. They accumulated more clothes from which to choose and had to be ever alert about their outfits' appropriateness for the occasion. They became informed shoppers, who spent many hours critically observing and discussing the outfits of others at public and private events, reading the emerging fashion press, discriminating between the trendsetters and the hapless, and making visits to shops where new goods were displayed. Increasingly, it was women who became the great specialists in fashionable consumption (J. Jones 2004, 115–16, 141–48; DeJean 2005, 35–69).

The consumer was of course important to producers and marketers of silk and other novel goods as the buyer who enabled them to realize the value of the capital they had invested. But it is important to recognize that the capitalist gained an additional increment of profit from the unpaid, volunteer labor expended by the fashionable consumer whose increasingly assiduous efforts were the condition of possibility for the dynamism of the fashion system. Consumer labor, no less than the labor of the producers, created value. Aesthetically knowledgeable consumers displayed the new goods on their persons in public—on promenades, in salons, at parties, in cafés, when shopping—thereby arousing the curiosity and envy of other potential consumers. Elegantly turned-out consumers served, in effect, as voluntary living advertisements for fashion goods and thus as spurs to further consumption by those who noticed and envied them. By keeping informed about style, by conversing about new fabrics or designs with acquaintances, by educating their children in the ways of fashion, they reproduced the restless desires that are fashion's defining psychological characteristic—indeed, a defining feature of capitalist culture in general (Berman 1982). The dedicated pursuit of fashion also drew in ever-wider social circles. Servants, educated in the taste of their masters, were a particularly potent vector for the diffusion of fashion into the lower orders (Roche 1994, 78, 106, 144, 173).

In short, merchants like the Lyonnais silk producers gained enhanced profits by what can properly be termed the subsumption of consumer desire under capital—by inducing consumers to engage in unpaid labor that increased the value of their goods. The unpaid labor was freely performed by the consumers, who were pursuing goals of their own, such as status enhancement, career advancement, pursuit of aesthetic value, or pure diversion. But theirs was real labor, sustained and time-consuming human effort, with its share of tedium, routine, and anxiety. It was, moreover, imposed on those who undertook it by powerful social pressures. The labor of consumers was thus in a formal sense *exploited* by the silk merchants—that is, harnessed to the goal of making profits, as one can speak of the exploitation of a mine or a field.[16] In order to benefit from unpaid consumer labor, the silk merchants and their allies the mercers had to prime the pump of fashion by coming up with new designs that would keep their customers' desires, purchases, and unpaid desire-generating labor flowing. But the assiduous labor of consumers, performed voluntarily in civil society rather than in workshops or counting houses, was essential to the peculiar dynamism of the silk industry—and to French fashion industries in general. The "empire of fashion" was built not only on the unpaid surplus labor of direct producers but on the unpaid labor of consumers as well.

Other Textiles

Silk was, of course, a somewhat special case. It was by far the most expensive of textiles, a luxury commodity long in demand at the royal court. No other textile trade was so tightly organized by the merchant manufacturers from top to bottom, and rarely was there such continuous and dynamic feedback between design, marketing, and manufacture. Yet the general outlines of the argument about the silk industry apply to the cotton and woolen industries as well. These were handicraft industries organized on a putting-out basis, coordinated by mercantile techniques, and they expanded their output in the eighteenth century. In both cases, there was an enhancement of manufacturing skills and consequently in quality of product over the course of the century, but it was primarily the merchant manufacturers who profited from this increased productivity, not the direct producers. The manufacturers gained from the burgeoning fashion market, did their best to enhance their position within it, and profited from the consumers' ardent but unpaid labor.

Cotton was by far the most dynamic of the textile industries in eighteenth-century Europe. In the early part of the century, production of cotton cloth in Europe was only beginning; by the century's end, mech-

16. By using this term, I intend no moral claims about harsh or inhumane treatment of the "exploited." Indeed, whatever pains may have been imposed by consumer labor were probably exceeded by the concomitant pleasures.

anized production on a hitherto unimaginable scale had been attained in Britain and was spreading to France. Cotton textiles, which used a fiber produced mainly outside Europe, were originally exotic imports from India that became wildly popular, initially in elite circles. Imported Indian cottons (known simply as *indiennes*) were light, much less expensive than silks, and were printed or painted in bright floral patterns. In France, indiennes were initially employed above all for informal daywear, what the French called *déshabillé*, or "undress," particularly in the form of dressing gowns to be worn indoors. But over the course of the century, these déshabillé fashions were increasingly worn in public, and many other fashionable uses of cotton were devised. It was soon in demand for curtains and upholstery, for shirts and undergarments, for waistcoats and dresses. By the 1780s, white muslin cotton dresses, in the bucolic style made famous by Marie Antoinette, became the height of fashion (Weber 2006).

Because cotton was less expensive than silk or wool, the demand for it was particularly democratic.[17] The market for cottons spanned the gamut, from highly fashionable and moderately expensive printed cloths to rough and cheap fustians worn by the poor. Daniel Roche's figures on the consumption of clothing in Paris show that cotton progressed dramatically in the wardrobes of all social categories over the course of the eighteenth century. The expansion of cotton consumption cut sharply into consumption of linen at all social levels, as cotton shirts and undergarments triumphed. But among the poorest categories—domestic servants and wage earners—cotton also massively displaced woolens, which had made up about three-fifths of their wardrobes in 1700 but amounted to only between a quarter and a third in 1789 (see table 1). Cotton was used for shirts, kerchiefs, and undergarments; for colorful and stylish dressing gowns, waistcoats, dresses, and upholstery; and for workaday breeches, trousers, smocks, skirts, and aprons for the poorer classes. Hence the cotton industry was extremely varied, with its products ranging from fine muslins to heavy fustians and from plain or simple checked or striped fabrics to elaborate domestically produced indiennes.

In the case of cotton, demand outstripped supply from the first introduction of Indian textiles in the mid-seventeenth century to the very end of the eighteenth. Alarmed by the popularity of indiennes, interests representing the silk, linen, and woolen producers convinced the government at the end of the seventeenth century to outlaw the importation of

17. The research of Lemire (1991) and Styles (2007) makes this clear in the British case.

TABLE 1. Fabrics in wardrobes of Parisians of different classes, 1700 and 1789 (percentages)

	Nobles			Professionals			Artisans and shopkeepers			Domestics			Wage earners		
	1700	1789	Change	1700	1789	Change	1700	1789	Change	1700	1789	Change	1700	1789	Change
Silk	17	38	+21	17	31	+14	13	21	+8	9	12	+3	9	15	+6
Woolen	8	18	+10	22	23	+1	23	23	0	60	26	−34	58	33	−25
Linen	46	17	−29	37	13	−24	42	12	−30	16	8	−8	14	12	−2
Cotton	7	25	+18	3	20	+17	8	39	+31	7	40	+33	7	38	+31
Misc.	22	2	−20	21	13	−8	14	5	−9	8	14	+6	12	2	−10

Adapted from Roche (1994, 127, 138).

printed cloth from India or the production of printed cotton, linen, or woolen cloths in France; it even criminalized the wearing of such fabrics (Gottman 2016, 54; Chassagne 1980, 10). These prohibitions were widely evaded; indeed, indiennes were worn openly in courtly circles at the very time when it was officially illegal to do so. Clandestine cotton-printing operations went on continuously, and the smuggling of indiennes was a big business until the prohibitions were suppressed in 1759—after a vigorous campaign on the part of laissez-faire political economists.[18] Thereafter the production of indiennes in France grew vertiginously. The cotton printers, who were the large-scale producers and the leading capitalists in this industry, used the superior imported Indian cloth when they could find it but increasingly used domestically produced fabrics as well.

Raw cotton, unlike silk, was a relatively cheap commodity. In the silk industry, the merchant manufacturers imported most of their yarn from Italy and maintained strict control over its use by the weavers. The cotton trade, by contrast, was wide open, with many independent spinners and weavers scattered all over the countryside in many different areas of France. The merchants' control over the producers was usually purely mercantile: high-quality cloth, fine or tightly woven, and with an even texture and few broken threads, fetched a higher price. The subsumption of labor under capital in cotton manufacture was strictly formal. Indeed, some of the direct producers of cotton yarns and cotton cloth were, strictly speaking, independent petty commodity producers not formally ensnared in putting-out relations. But because they were deeply dependent on the merchants as purchasers of their goods, they were forced by the pressures of the market to improve the quality and therefore the value of their products. Given the abundant supply of underemployed rural men and women

18. On the smuggling of indiennes, see Kwass (2014) and Gottman (2016).

who could become cotton weavers and spinners, the benefits of this increase in skill and quality accrued mainly to the merchants.[19]

Progress in the production of plain cotton cloth was, however, primarily extensive rather than intensive: cotton production grew rapidly by spreading out into many rural regions and attracting more and more workers in each region. Intensive development occurred mainly at the final stage—printing, which required a greater capital outlay, market savvy, and investment in design. In this design-intensive branch of the cotton textile industry, the French were actually outproducing the British as late as 1785.[20] Serge Chassagne (1991, 102–3) has located the records of some fifty sizable cotton-printing enterprises, scattered over much of the national territory, founded between 1759 and 1789. A printing establishment like that of Christoffe-Philippe Oberkampf, founded in Jouy, a village near Paris, in 1760, immediately after cotton printing became legal in France, eventually employed several hundred workers, meticulously monitored by clerks and foremen. Oberkampf employed chemists to perfect his dyes and contracted with noted Parisian artists to design his prints, but most of the fabrication was done by hand (Chapman and Chassagne 1981, 170–82). Oberkampf's firm accumulated capital at a rapid pace and benefited massively from the production of surplus value—through improvements in skills that he did not remunerate in full, through cost-saving divisions of labor, and through technological innovation. Yet the financial structure of the enterprise was more commercial than industrial, since less than 10 percent of the firm's assets consisted of fixed capital (Chapman and Chassagne 1981, 138). And it was Oberkampf's shrewd ability at what he called "the creation of new taste" that assured the success of his firm. Although he began by making uncannily accurate copies of Indian designs, by the 1780s he was printing large cameo designs in Rococo style from copper plates, depicting outdoor or hunting scenes, or celebrating popular events of the day with titles such as "American Independence" and "the Marriage of Figaro" (Chapman and Chassagne 1981, 147–78). Like the Lyonnais silk merchants, Oberkampf took full advantage of the dynamic Parisian consumer market and its seemingly endless supply of volunteer labor, which engaged, effectively, in advertising his goods via competitive display. On the eve of the French Revolution, the consumer-driven cotton-printing industry remained outstandingly lucrative.

19. On the organization of the cotton industry, see Chassagne (1979, 1980, 1991), Reddy (1984, 22–47), Gullickson (1986), and Liu (1994).

20. In that year, the French produced 16 million meters of printed cotton cloth as opposed to the 12.4 million by the British (Chapman and Chassagne 1981, 8).

Woolen cloth had been manufactured in France for centuries. Given its already solid implantation, the woolen industry grew much more slowly than its new and exotic rival the cotton industry in the eighteenth century. The woolen industry was also closely regulated by the state. Royal inspectors of manufactures drew up production figures in all of France's provinces; for this reason, we actually have much more exact knowledge about the production of woolens in the eighteenth century than about other textiles. The number of pieces of woolen cloth produced in France rose modestly, by 41 percent, from 1716–18 to 1786–88. However, the total volume of cloth, measured by surface area, increased more rapidly, by 76 percent, and the total value more rapidly still, roughly doubling over these seventy years.[21] There was much less innovation in design in woolens than in the silk and cotton industries, although there were innovations in dyeing that significantly increased the range of available colors. The kind of "creation of taste" engaged in by the Lyonnais silk manufacturers or by Oberkampf was outside the range of possibility of eighteenth-century woolen producers. Yet they were attentive to fashion and changing demand. The striking fact about the woolen industry is the decline or stagnation of low-quality production and the more-than-offsetting rise of production of finer woolen goods. French woolen producers succeeded in the eighteenth century, in both French and foreign markets, by moving upmarket.

One indication of why they did so can be inferred from Daniel Roche's statistics about the fabrics used in clothing inventoried in eighteenth-century Parisian wardrobes. There was a general displacement of linen by cottons and a substantial rise in the consumption of silks among all classes. But the pattern for woolens varied sharply by class, with the proportion of woolen clothing rising among nobles and remaining constant among shopkeepers, officeholders, and professionals, while woolen cloth was massively displaced by cotton among domestic servants and wage earners (see table 1). These figures suggest that competition from cheap cotton goods devastated the low end of the woolen trade but that the manufacturers were agile enough to more than overcome these losses by specializing in the highest-quality goods, which retained or expanded their market position. This indicates that the successful entrepreneurs in the woolen industry made savvy adjustments to changes in the market—

---

21. Markovich (1976b, 494–95) found that the value of woolen production rose by 163 percent, but about 60 percent of this increase is probably due to inflation in the value of the livre. I take the inflation figure from Crouzet (1996a).

that they were quite aware of changes in fashion and were able to supply goods that remained highly desirable to the wealthy classes.

The woolen industry was notably dispersed: there were major centers in Flanders (Lille-Roubaix-Tourcoing), Picardy (Amiens), Normandy (Elbeuf), Champagne (Reims and Sedan), Maine (Le Mans), Languedoc (Lodève and Montauban), and minor centers spread all over the country (Markovich 1976b; Reddy 1984; Engrand 1979; Deyon 1979; Kaplow 1964; Gayot 1998; Dornic 1955; Thompson 1982; Johnson 1995). The exact organization of production varied, although putting-out was virtually universal. Spinning putting-out networks generally spread far out into the countryside; weaving, particularly of the finer varieties of cloth, was commonly done by urban workers or by weavers inhabiting the suburbs or very near countryside. The initial washing and carding and the finishing operations (dyeing, bleaching, tentering, shearing, sizing, and pressing) were usually done in town, under the supervision of merchant manufacturers, some of whom had large factory-like buildings for the purpose. In nearly all woolen centers, the merchants managed to impose ever-higher standards of skill on their weavers and spinners without having to increase their remuneration.

Gérard Gayot's splendid study of the woolen industry in Sedan shows how the top end of the French woolen industry prospered in the eighteenth century. Sedan, which specialized in the highest-quality broadcloths, was the most dynamic center of woolen production. The number of cloths produced roughly doubled from the 1720s to the 1780s, and the value of the product nearly quadrupled. This general rise was accompanied by a growing concentration of capital: the value of cloth turned out by the average firm rose about tenfold over these six decades (Gayot 1998, 313–14). This decrease in the number of firms and big increase in their size was the result of continuous competition, but while the manufacturers were assiduous about monitoring costs, competition was about quality as much as cost.

The Sedan industry produced for the top of the market, initially dominated by demand for black cloth for suits and coats and the ubiquitous black robes of the clergy and judicial officers. But over the course of the eighteenth century, more colored dyes were used, both for civilian dress and for the army, each of whose units had its own colors (Gayot 1998, 33). As the century wore on, the royal inspectors often clashed with manufacturers who felt constrained by the inspectors' inflexibility. As one manufacturer put it, "The tastes of consumers vary at every moment, either as a result of society, or because clever competitors have changed them by means of fortunate inventions." The proper goal of the manufacturers should therefore be "to follow or to anticipate the taste of consumers" (Gayot 1998, 78, 82).

Roche's figures for Parisian consumption show that linen was largely displaced by cotton over the eighteenth century (see table 1). But because there are fewer good studies of the linen industry than of silk, cotton, and wool, it is far more difficult to generalize about eighteenth-century developments. We do know that in Normandy, which had been a major linen-producing center in the seventeenth century, former linen spinners and weavers moved massively into cotton in the eighteenth (Chassagne 1979). By contrast, output nearly doubled in the northern region of high-quality linen production surrounding Valenciennes, Cambrais, and Saint-Quentin (Guignet 1979, 34).[22] The organization of production in this region was less controlled by urban merchants than most production of wool or even cotton. Linen cloth was generally collected by independent brokers and sold to merchants, who then contracted with others to bleach it; the merchants were concerned primarily with final marketing rather than with overseeing manufacture (Guignet 1979). Linen production tended to move upmarket in the eighteenth century, but this seems to have resulted as much from the displacement of linen by cotton in areas of low-quality production as from efforts to upgrade quality in the higher-quality regions.

Fashion beyond Textiles

The textile industries were particularly big and important, but they were not the only ones affected by the broader capitalist economic dynamic I have delineated in this chapter. Paris was the home of many eighteenth-century trades that thrived in the nexus between fashionable consumption and innovations in production. We get glimpses of this sector in Carolyn Sargentson's (1996, 21–23, 46–56) discussion of the role of mercers in designing products and coordinating the work of the artisans who produced stylish rococo furniture and furnishings; in Clare Crowston's (2001) study of dressmakers; in Michael Sonenscher's (1989, 210–43) work on the Martin brothers' coach making; in Steven Kaplan's study of the "faux ouvriers" (1988, 353–78) of the Faubourg Saint-Antoine; or in Michael Kwass's study of the production and consumption of wigs

---

22. On the geographical location of linen manufacture, see Béaur, Minard, and Laclau (1997, 74), Guignet (1977, 1979), and Terrier (1996).

(2006). As we have seen, the "luxury" trades not only catered to wealthy clients but found ways to make "populuxe" goods available to a broad consuming public (Fairchilds 1993).

There were also many luxury producers, who, like the Lyonnais silk manufacturers, were located outside Paris but produced primarily for the Parisian market. The royal manufactory of mirrors at Saint-Gobin was one of the industrial wonders of eighteenth-century Europe. It was long the sole supplier of the decorative mirrors that distinguished the most stylish boutiques and cafés in Paris—commercial spaces that, as we have seen, helped define new modes of consumption and sociability in the eighteenth century (Hamon and Perrin 1993; DeJean 2005, 120–77). Various porcelain and pottery works, of which the royal manufactory at Sèvres was the most famous, produced both imitations of Chinese crockery and original rococo and neoclassical designs. Supplying paper for the bourgeoning book trade and for newspapers gave rise to large-scale and mechanized papermaking establishments (Rosenband 2000).

As this incomplete listing makes clear, the range of products, services, and forms of production involved in the sphere of fashionable consumption in eighteenth-century France was extremely diverse. There were large manufactories with an advanced division of labor, as in porcelain manufacture, papermaking, or cotton printing or as at Saint-Gobin; there were trades still organized in traditional guilds, such as goldsmiths or bookbinders; there were dispersed domestic manufactures organized in putting-out networks, such as the production of textiles, watches, or cutlery; there were manufactures that brought together in novel ways the labor of various distinct skilled trades, as in carriage making or luxury furniture and furnishings; there were new retail establishments like cafés, restaurants, and the shops of *modistes*, mercers, and wigmakers; there was clandestine production of knock-off furniture, umbrellas, fans, and canes that were hawked in the streets to modest consumers who could not afford the guild-produced equivalents; and across the Atlantic, there were slaves who produced sugar, coffee, indigo, and tobacco for consumption in the metropole. One is impressed by the sheer diversity and flexibility of forms of production and distribution that developed in this society still formally structured by hierarchies of estates and orders and by guild privileges. Where consumer desires could be stimulated, there seemed always to be entrepreneurs and workers able to find means of both satisfying and further stimulating those desires. This was a commercially organized capitalism founded on flexibility and multiple means of producing and supplying desirable goods, not on any single dominant formula.

Fashionable consumption played a constitutive role in the development of French capitalism not only in the eighteenth century but over the long term. The central role of France (and above all Paris) in setting European style has paid handsome dividends to French capitalists, from the wealthy cotton printers, Sédanais drapers, Parisian mercers, and Lyonnais silk merchants to Coco Chanel, Yves Saint-Laurent, and Louis Vuitton. Probably no other national economy has been so dominated by luxury production for so long. But if there is something particularly French about the story I have told in this chapter, it is by no means an exclusively French story. Scholars are fully aware of the importance of advertising, design, and branding—that is, of enhancing the value of products by desire creation—in contemporary capitalism. This chapter shows that the value enhancement of this sort is not an innovation of the twentieth century but goes very far back into capitalism's history. The development of fashion, with its built-in obsolescence of products, its outward geographical and downward social expansion, and its powerful harnessing of the energies—the labor—of consumers for the creation of value, was already underway in late seventeenth-century Versailles and Paris but also, it seems clear, by the early eighteenth century in England and probably by the early seventeenth in the Netherlands (MacKendrick, Brewer, and Plum 1982; de Vries 2008).

In the nineteenth century, industrialization added a new dynamic to capitalist development, one centered on the production of goods that were what might be called "mere commodities"—goods like coal, steel, steam engines, and cheap cotton and woolen cloth that were not differentiated aesthetically—where the emphasis was not on desire enhancement through quality and design but on cutting costs and multiplying output through technological development. This is the capitalism analyzed so brilliantly by Karl Marx. But it is important to see this new form of capitalism as growing out of and supplementing but never displacing the design-intensive consumer capitalism that flourished in the eighteenth century. We should remember that the starting point of the industrial revolution, the breakthrough to immensely profitable capitalist production of "mere commodities," was the British cotton industry, whose remarkable eighteenth-century expansion was driven precisely by the demand for bright, colorful, and stylish calicoes, and that Matthew Boulton, best known to economic history as James Watt's partner in the production of the steam engine, was already famous as the manufacturer of fashionable metal buttons, buckles, and metal statuary when he made Watt's acquaintance (Robinson 1963).

The volunteer consumer labor that imparted a peculiar dynamic to these industries was supplied by both men and women, although consumption was increasingly gendered as female as the eighteenth century wore on (J. Jones 2004). Thus elite women, who almost never participated directly in the production and marketing of goods, were nevertheless crucial agents in the growth of capitalism in the eighteenth century through their massive participation in the development of a fashion public. Their social and cultural world was transformed by capitalism in this era, perhaps as much as that of cotton weavers or silk merchants. The dynamics of capitalism in this era are incomprehensible apart from the dynamics of fashion—and fashion is, of course, a system of symbolic distinctions, one complexly imbricated in other cultural systems. The ever-changing symbolic distinctions of the fashion world reached back into the marketing and the production of goods, changing the incentives and organizational possibilities facing direct producers, entrepreneurs, and suppliers. Likewise, the output of industries producing fashionable goods changed the range of symbolic distinctions and cultural strategies available to marketers and consumers. It is arguable that by inducing both nobles and wealthy commoners to engage in massive and very visible consumption of fashionable goods, eighteenth-century consumer capitalism helped shift conceptions of social difference from the criterion of birth to that of wealth, from a qualitative to a quantitative distinction between persons. In this way, then, the new forms of consumption were—perhaps paradoxically—conducive to notions of equality of the sort specified in the Declaration of the Rights of Man and Citizen in 1789.

✳ 5 ✳

The Parisian Promenade

In the eighteenth century, Paris was not only the center of commerce in fashionable goods but also a great center for the display of fashion—in the private spaces of dinners, balls, and salons, of course, but also in public, at theaters, at the opera, at fairs, and in the increasingly common practice of the public promenade.[1] In the seventeenth and eighteenth centuries, well-to-do Parisians did not stroll in the streets as of the city they do today.[2] The streets were generally overcrowded, narrow, unpaved, and without sidewalks, with a central gutter that served as a sewer for the waste of the surrounding population. On rainy days, streets were nearly impassable. To make matters worse, carriages plied the streets at dangerous speeds, splashing pedestrians with muck and threatening to run them down. In these circumstances, polite persons avoided walking in the streets if at all possible.[3] But over the course of the later seventeenth and eighteenth centuries, various sites were made available for promenades, at least for what were called "persons of quality." The practice of the promenade burgeoned over the course of the eighteenth century and became considerably more democratic. It was a prime site of public display and public entertainment.

The most prestigious of the promenade sites in the late seventeenth century were the Cours-la-Reine and the Jardin des Tuileries. The Cours-la-Reine was established in 1628 at the initiative of Marie de Medici, the

---

1. A longer version of this article was originally published as "Connecting Capitalism to the French Revolution: The Parisian Promenade and the Origins of Civic Equality in Eighteenth-Century France" in *Critical Historical Studies* 1, no. 1 (2014): 5–46.

2. The essential work on the old regime Parisian promenade is Turcot (2007).

3. This is a theme that appears in nearly all writing about eighteenth-century streets. See Turcot (2007, 11, 318–19, 403), Doppet (1788, 98), Peyssonnel (2007, 54–55), Nemeitz (1727, 54–55).

widow of Henri IV and the mother and sometime regent of Louis XIII. It was a long and narrow garden along the Seine River just to the west of the Jardin des Tuileries. A little less than two kilometers in length and only thirty-eight meters in width, enclosed by iron fences with royal guards at the gates, it quickly became the most prestigious Parisian site for promenades in carriages—*the* place in which to see and be seen. Although bourgeois outfitted with proper carriages and clothing could gain access to the Cours when the royal family was not in residence in Paris, this was essentially an aristocratic promenade. Toward the end of the seventeenth century, a visiting Englishman estimated that the Cours sometimes accommodated as many as six or seven hundred carriages at a time (Turcot 2007, 73–78). The promenade in the Cours was highly ritualized. According to the satirist La Bruyère, "Everyone passes in review before one another: carriages, horses, liveries, coats of arms, nothing escapes the eyes of the promeneur" ([1687] 1916, 72).

Strolling and Fashion in the Jardin des Tuileries

The Jardin des Tuileries, where the promenade was on foot rather than in carriages, was initially constructed during the sixteenth century as the private garden of the royal Tuileries Palace; it was considerably enlarged and improved in the seventeenth century by André le Nôtre, the designer of the Versailles gardens. Since the middle of the seventeenth century, it had been made available to a limited Parisian public whenever the king was not in residence in Paris—which was most of the time in the case of Louis XIV, who disliked the city and its residents. By the time Louis abandoned the Tuileries Palace for good to establish his court at Versailles, around 1680, the garden attached to the palace had already become a major site of elite sociability. One simply had to go and stroll in the Jardin. The garden was laid out much as it is at present, except that the Tuileries Palace then stood at its eastern end, where the Arc du Carrousel is now located. It was planted with rows of trees and had a circular pond and a long graveled central *allée* lined by benches, so it offered both sun and shade. Swiss guards were placed at the gates of the garden and instructed to refuse entry to servants and to persons of the lower orders. But—and this is a key to the evolution of the promenade—anyone who was well dressed and well mannered was allowed to enter, whether noble or common. And strollers were required by the regulations to leave their entourage of coachmen and lackeys behind at the gate. Once inside the garden, one was expected to obey strict rules of etiquette. It was, however, considered quite acceptable to take up a conversation with strangers—and plenty of strangers there were, since polite visitors from the provinces or abroad made it a special point to visit the famous Jardin (Turcot 2007, 209–60).

The Jardin des Tuileries was the ideal place to catch up on manners and fashions. Joachim-Christophe Nemeitz, the author of a guide to Paris intended for visitors from abroad, wrote in 1727 that foreigners should certainly visit the Jardin: "It is in the promenade at the Tuileries that one has the best opportunity for entering into relations with the beau monde" of the city. When the air begins to cool at the end of a summer day, "there are so many people of every age, sex, and condition that it is sometimes difficult, especially in the central allée, to make one's way through the crowd. There one sees the most carefully chosen outfits, the latest fashions; there one banters, talks seriously, and amuses oneself. . . . There one comes across the grandest personages of both sexes, often even princes and princesses of the royal family. . . . One passes by them as closely as possible in order to see them the better" (Nemeitz 1727, 87).[4]

The role of the Jardin in the display of the latest fashions was sustained later in the century, if we are to believe a vignette penned by the satirist Louis-Antoine Caraccioli: "There *Cloris* parades the crispness of a new dress the likes of which no one has seen before, and which draws around her a multitude of onlookers; it's there also that the elegant *Farfolet* [Caraccioli peppers his anecdotes with strangely named personages] in a taffeta suit the color of a rose, a jacket bedecked with blond threads, and a lorgnette in his hand, looks around while he is being looked at, and applauds himself for sharing with the divine *Cloris* the triumph of the festival. People press together, push one another aside to get a view of them" (1768, 303). The promenade, as this scene suggests, was a prime occasion for displaying one's new purchases and for informing oneself about the latest in styles. On promenade, well-dressed strollers became walking advertisements for the city's mercers, tailors, milliners, and dressmakers (not to mention opticians in the case of Farfolet's lorgnette), thereby stoking the passion for consumption that fueled the fashion industry. As this anecdote makes clear, the promenade and the fashion industry fed off one another in the late seventeenth and eighteenth centuries.

It follows that strolling in the Jardin could also serve as a lesson in taste and sophistication for any persons of mediocre birth who were decently enough attired to gain entry. The publicly performed rituals of politeness and taste could teach such a person much about how to behave politely— indeed, about how to pass oneself off, at least in this anonymous space,

---

4. Lemaire (1698, 97) made a similar point: "It is in this Royal Garden that one learns fashions, especially for suits."

as a person of quality. Here is another vignette from a promenade, this one penned by the political economist the Marquis de Mirabeau in 1756, twelve years before Caraccioli's: "In Paris," Mirabeau observed, "everyone has become a Monsieur. On Sunday a man in a black silk suit and a well-powdered wig came up to me, and as I fell all over myself offering him compliments, he introduced himself as the first assistant of my saddler or my blacksmith."[5] His anecdote makes the point clearly: by the 1750s, models of politeness and knowledge of fashion had become so widespread that an aristocratic stroller could no longer be sure whom he was observing or to whom he was talking.

This problem seems to have been exacerbated by the 1780s, if we are to believe the text of yet another urban stroller, Charles de Peyssonnel, published in 1785. One day he and a friend decided to take a ferry across the Seine and came upon a man sitting behind the counter in a bedraggled stall on the quai who was wearing an extremely stylish wig and a magnificent pearl-gray suit with heavy gold trimmings. This was the official collector of the two-penny tax that boatsmen had to pay for each passenger they carried across the river. Peyssonnel and his friend had a good laugh about this man who "attempted to elevate his lowly office by the luxury and elegance of his outfit." But the incident inspired Peyssonnel to reflect on the pervasive mismatches between rank and costume in the Paris of his day. The great, he notes, have given up wearing clothing laced with precious metals because lowly men like the toll collector have taken them up. They attempt instead to distinguish themselves by the tastefulness rather than the extravagance of their fabric choices and by using less ostentatious trimmings—for example, silk embroidery and fur. "They use gold and silver," he pointedly claims, "only for their servants' liveries" (2007, 98). Meanwhile, preening minor ecclesiastics walk the streets in elegant vestments of prune and violet, some of them festooned with gold buttons and braid. Soon, Peyssonnel suggests, "it will be possible to distinguish clerics from worldly gentlemen only by their scullcaps. Honest women dress like classy prostitutes while prostitutes dress modestly, like honest women" (99–100). Peyssonnel says that the rage for going out into town in dressing gowns (in *deshabillé*, or "undress," as it was called) "has masked all conditions; it is no longer possible to recognize anyone. The highest personage of the state travels the streets dressed like the lowest of citizens. One imagines oneself dealing with an attorney's clerk and it's a

5. Mirabeau (1756, 152). In the eighteenth century, the term *monsieur*, which has since become a universal term of address for men, was reserved for a person of some distinction, as its derivation "mon sieur" or "my lord" would suggest.

prince of the empire; one avoids a man who appears to be a recruiter of soldiers and it's one of our greatest magistrates" (102).[6]

Peyssonnel was a satirist, to be sure, so he undoubtedly exaggerated the extent to which clothing styles had ceased to correspond with rank. Mirabeau, likewise, probably invented his encounter with his saddler's assistant as a ploy in his wider polemic against luxury—but that he believed it would convince his readers argues for the story's verisimilitude. Moreover, corroborating testimony comes from an observer who was neither a satirist nor a polemicist—Madame d'Oberkirch, the Alsatian noblewoman we met in chapter 4. Reporting on a promenade in the Jardin des Tuileries in 1784, a year before the publication of Peyssonnel's work, she noted another change in fashion that obscured the distinction between ranks. Nobles, who in France had the exclusive right to carry arms, were ceasing to do so: "Gentlemen began to go about without arms and to wear swords only when dressed formally. The small fry [lesser nobles] soon imitated them; fashion has acted more strongly than authority ever could have. Had an order been given to cease the wearing of swords, no one would have consented. Some young anglomaniac [fashionable Frenchman who aped English styles] imagined this escapade; his friends did as he did and it has become the rage to do without. . . . Hence an ancient custom of the French nobility has been cast into the weeds! Fashion often leads to inanities." Madame d'Oberkirch also corroborates Peyssonnel's observation about the prostitutes plying the Jardin: "It is said that there were several kept women in the Tuileries. They are harder to recognize at first sight than I had thought and dress decently to make themselves appear to be respectable bourgeoises" (1970, 411–12).

Although there were complaints as early as the 1670s that well-to-do bourgeois women, and even some shop girls, were wearing dresses that copied those of noble ladies (Crowston 2001, 48–49), the correlation between dress and rank was then much tighter than it became in the later eighteenth century. Here it is indicative that Nemeitz, writing in the 1720s, suggested that if foreign visitors procured suits decorated with gold braid, they would have no difficulty gaining entry into court ceremonials at Versailles. With such a suit, "one can pass for a military officer, and in France officers are highly esteemed and welcomed everywhere." Here Nemeitz quotes a text by the abbé Bellegard from the end of the seventeenth century that went as follows: "A suit bedecked with gold opens

---

6. The "recruteur," who strolled about cities signing up desperate or drunken young men for long terms in the military, was a particularly loathed figure in eighteenth-century France.

the door into places where one would never be suffered when wearing less elegant clothing. Merit is not engraved on the forehead. A fool with a brilliant exterior will walk right over a man of parts who has nothing to offer but a great deal of knowledge" (1727, 32). This advice for fooling the Swiss guards at Versailles, written in the 1690s, still seemed valid to Nemeitz in the 1720s.

Such advice would presumably not have been uttered in the 1780s, when clothing so often gave false or ambiguous cues. In this respect, the eighteenth century marked a sea-change. In the mid-seventeenth century, one could normally identify a person's occupation or rank by observing their clothing—noble ladies wore headdresses and commoners kerchiefs, lawyers wore black robes, saddler's assistants wore leather aprons, and nobles wore silken finery with gold threads. But by the later eighteenth century, clothing was no longer a trustworthy clue; one could never be sure quite whom one was encountering. It is not that people no longer understood the formal significance of gold trimming or shabby dressing gowns in signaling social status. Rather, late eighteenth-century Parisian men and women of all classes ceased to feel that dressing according to the old codes was mandatory or even desirable—those of mediocre status above all because they sought to participate in a polite world constructed by their betters, persons of distinction because the resulting confusion of signs freed them from constricting rules and opened up a space of wider experimentation. By these circuitous paths, Parisians seem to have arrived at a certain vestimentary anonymity.

One key to this process of transformation was the fact that the empire of fashion had moved steadily down the social pyramid over the course of the eighteenth century. In 1700, fashion was the concern only of a thin layer of wealthy people, most of them nobles. But as we have seen in chapter 5, over the course of the century, all classes of the population began to seek out more up-to-date clothing and accessories. Daniel Roche's comparison of the estates left by Parisians who died in 1700 and 1789 shows that the total number of garments owned by both men and women had sharply increased among all classes of the population, roughly tripling in each category over these eighty years. The proportion of these more abundant garments that were made of silk, the ultimate luxury textile, also rose in all classes of the population. Garments made of colorful and stylish printed cottons skyrocketed for all classes (Roche 1994, 117–38). These findings are especially striking because it is well known that the wages of servants and laborers barely kept up with inflation in the eighteenth century (Weir 1991). Ordinary Parisian men and women clearly decided to spend a higher portion of their often meager incomes on fash-

ionable clothing late in the 1780s than they had in 1700. And as we have
seen, what was true of fashionable clothing was also true of assorted fashion accessories, such as gold watches and chains, umbrellas, fans, canes,
and stylish wigs and hats (Fairchilds 1993). The evidence seems unequiv-
ocal that the Parisian "little people," not to mention the bourgeoisie, came
to place a high value on the accoutrements of a polite public appearance.
By wearing fashionable clothing and bedecking themselves with fashionable accessories, they were declaring their membership in a larger polite
society that, in principle, was open to all who could demonstrate that
they belonged.

When fashion seeped downward in the social structure, its rules and
conventions became more volatile and consequently less confining. As
fashion turnover accelerated and as the market became socially broader,
the meticulous rules that had governed fashion at court came to seem too
restrictive. Once again Madame d'Oberkirch provides relevant testimony.
Invited to a theatrical performance at the court, she wrote, "I had to have
myself coiffed and put on my grand clothing to go to Versailles. . . . Getting dressed this way takes an eternity, and the road from Paris to Versailles is very tiring, when one worries above all about turning one's skirt
and its flounces into a rag" (1970, 264). If the rules of fashion at Versailles
were strict and the clothing uniformly uncomfortable, the more diverse
Parisian market allowed much greater room for experiment, ease, and individual initiative—here Farfolet's lorgnette and rose-colored suit serve
as perfect examples.

The fashion churning of the capital was a dynamic that linked adventurous or ambitious consumers to clever merchants and manufacturers—
the latter looking to increase profits by offering novel goods. Some of the
novelties broke quite sharply with the court's taste for heavy silk brocades
and extensive use of silver and gold threads and trimmings—this was
true of lighter and brighter satins, or of cotton indiennes, or of the dressing gowns into which they were often fashioned, or of the white muslin
dresses that became all the rage in the 1780s when Rousseau and more
"natural" modes of living became stylish and the queen herself played
at being a dairymaid (J. Jones 1994). As wealthy aristocrats' clothes circulated downward to servants through gifts and to bourgeois and artisans through the extensive secondhand clothing market, a man's servant
or a shopkeeper on his day off might be clad in a more traditionally distinguished outfit than a nobleman. Hence the phenomena Peyssonnel
remarks on—the lowly but brilliantly bedecked ferry collector and the
great magistrate out walking in his tattered dressing gown.

Stylish clothing was widely available in the secondhand market, where a multitude of *frippiers* offered secondhand garments for sale at cut-rate prices. André Doppet, the author of a guide to Paris for visitors, warned provincials and foreigners that the frippiers were likely to cheat them but at the same time made clear their value to the newly arrived. "A poor devil arrives in Paris from the provinces wearing his heavy woolen suit. This was his Sunday best when he lived in his village, but in the capital he looks like a grandfather. Hence he runs to the frippier, where morning coats of every color, garnished with stylish buttons, are on display. . . . He haggles over the price and pays a fourth of what the frippier asks" (1788, 24). Doppet nevertheless warns that "one is always pillaged in these shops." But prices were probably reasonably fair for those who knew their fashions and the routines of bargaining; after all, the Parisian secondhand market was extensive and had a multitude of sellers. Well-to-do men and women, who felt the need to buy new clothing constantly to keep up with the latest fashions, helped finance their new purchases by consigning their somewhat démodé garments to the frippiers, whence they found their way to less prosperous Parisians—not only to Doppet's hapless provincials but to tens of thousands of well-established Parisians of modest means who wished to appear fashionable—for example, Mirabeau's saddler's assistant. Nor was the possibility of upgrading one's appearance limited to buying secondhand clothing on the cheap. Doppet points out that there were also carriages for hire: "Anyone who wishes to appear to be a gentleman finds a carriage at so much per day, or per month. And besides the horses, he can even rent lackeys who may be dressed according to his fancy" (1788, 90). A person with a modicum of means might find it useful to splurge on a rented carriage and lackeys in order to make the right impression with a person of great power or wealth who might help him find a more distinguished place in the world. Here we see clearly how new forms of commercial development could simultaneously reinforce and undermine the predominant system of hierarchy and patronage.

One important consequence of loosening the link between appearance and status is that the public of strollers who used the Jardin des Tuileries in the later eighteenth century was far more socially diverse than it had been in 1700. Over the course of the century, the policy of restricting entry into the garden to well-dressed persons succeeded not in enforcing social exclusiveness but rather in promoting anonymous social mixing as those lower in the social hierarchy—encouraged, of course, by ever-resourceful merchants, including the frippiers—emulated their betters and enthusiastically joined the public of fashionable strollers. The entry of nonelites was also made easier by the fact that, to judge from the advice to travelers included in guide books, the once strict etiquette of the Jardin had relaxed considerably over the course of the century (Turcot 2007, 312). Moreover, the Jardin des Tuileries, although still frequently hailed as the most perfect of promenades, in fact declined in relative popularity. It lost ground especially to more socially indeterminate and freer spaces: to the Champs-Élysées, the shady, more informal, and socially unrestricted promenade immediately to the west of the Jardin, and to what were known as "the boulevards" (Turcot 2007, 209–71; Federici 2008).

The Rise of the Boulevards

The boulevards were the wide thoroughfare built atop the earthen remains of the former sixteenth-century city walls on the northern edge of the city. They stretched in a northerly arc from the Porte Saint-Antoine (the present-day Place de la Bastille) in the east almost to the far end of the Jardin des Tuileries in the west (to what is now the Place de la Madeleine). This was a vast promenade nearly four kilometers long— twice as long as the Cours-la-Reine. Between 1670 and 1690, these thoroughfares were planted with rows of trees. Between 1704 and 1762, the original boulevard was doubled by a boulevard on the city's southern periphery, which extended into what were then more rural precincts (Beguillet 1779, 64). The northern boulevards remained far more widely used than those in the south right through the eighteenth century and were far more commercially developed. The boulevards, which were connected to the city's network of streets, were open to all classes indiscriminately. They were sufficiently wide to afford separate lanes for wheeled and pedestrian traffic and by the early eighteenth century became a favorite haunt for both elite carriage riders and strollers of all categories— combining, as it were, the advantages of the Cours-la-Reine with those of the Jardin des Tuileries. Over the course of the century, the pedestrian ways were provided with stone benches and with chairs that could be rented, just as in the Jardin des Tuileries.

But whereas only a few sellers of drinks and pastries were authorized to engage in commerce in the Jardin des Tuileries, the northern boulevards were quickly colonized by commercial entrepreneurs of all sorts. By the middle years of the century, they were lined by stylish cafés that set up tables among the trees. This commercial development was especially prominent on the portion of the boulevard near the temple (the former grounds of the Knights Templars on the northeastern edge of the city proper and the current Place de la République), where the boulevards were particularly wide. As a guide for travelers to Paris put it in 1787, "It is the Boulevard du Temple that unites the most numerous forms of utility and pleasure: it is bounded . . . by very brilliant cafés, where one is sure to find all sorts of refreshments. These cafés, each the envy of the others, regale their customers with music. . . . Pastries, food, gambling, and entertainment, everything is available there" (Prévost de Saint-Lucien 1787, 35). The cafés, with their pleasant shaded tables, their musical entertainment, their ambient gaiety, and their varieties of refreshments— including coffee and alcoholic beverages as well as pastries and sweets— made the Jardin des Tuileries, let alone the Cours-la-Reine, seem stiff and dull by comparison. On the boulevard, the wealthy aristocrat could combine a pleasant carriage ride, a stroll, and a relaxing visit to a café. Meanwhile, more modest Parisians could walk to the boulevard from their neighborhoods to enjoy the promenade, have refreshments at a café, and take in the spectacle.

The "brilliant" cafés under the trees were far from the only commercial attractions on the boulevards. By the middle of the eighteenth century, the Boulevard du Temple had attracted a veritable swarm of commercial venues. Madame d'Oberkirch, who, as we have seen, was a curious explorer of the city and an intrepid shopper, designated the Boulevard du Temple the "beau boulevard" because of its theatrical performances, its wax museum, its displays of paintings, and its stylish shops, including, as we have seen, a boutique that, according to Madame d'Oberkirch, sold the most sought-after rouge in Europe (1970, 454, 598). But the Boulevard du Temple was also a center for a dazzling array of popular entertainments (Isherwood 1986). The entertainment venues are well described in eighteenth-century guides to Paris, which provide all kinds of rich information about Parisian social life (Doppet 1788; Dulaure 1787; Prévost de Saint-Lucien 1787; Thiéry 1784–87; Nougaret 1773). There were various theatrical troops: the Ambigu Comique, where child actors performed pantomimes; the Théâtre des Associés, which offered pared-down versions of tragedies like Racine's *Phèdre* and Voltaire's *Zaïre* for six sous; the Variétés Amusantes, which specialized in low comedy, as did the Délassements Comiques; and the Grands Danseurs de Corde, which featured tightrope walkers, tumblers, dancers, and acrobats but also skits that the author of one guidebook called "a hodgepodge of dialogues, that one can name neither comedy nor farce" (Doppet 1788, 86). In addition to the shows they performed indoors, these companies gave abridged performances (called *parades*) on small outdoor stages open to the street in order to lure customers inside. Besides these more strictly theatrical companies, there were magicians, scientific demonstrations, menageries of exotic animals, two wax museums, jugglers, displays of mechanical automatons, gambling houses, and, of course, the musicians who played outside the cafés. Just beyond the boulevard in the Faubourg du Temple, there was a pavilion where trained horses danced the minuet or engaged in mock battles—with tightrope walkers and strongmen on the side (Thiéry 1784–87, 421). On the Boulevard Saint-Martin, just to the west of the Boulevard du Temple, there was a "Wuxhall" patterned after its name-sake in London, which featured an elaborate garden and a dance floor. In short, every imaginable form of entertainment was available for purchase along the boulevards.

This range of attractions, together with the endless parade of elegant carriages and of strollers of every social type and rank, made the boule-vards the most popular of recreational destinations for Parisians of all classes in the second half of the century. It is particularly notable that even the rich and well-born elite largely abandoned the socially exclusive but highly ritualized precincts of the Cours-la-Reine in the early eigh-teenth century (Turcot 2007, 76–77). The long northern boulevards en-abled carriage riders to travel twice as far as on the Cours before turning around. But more importantly, there were interesting places to stop along the boulevards. One could take in a theatrical performance, witness a sci-entific experiment or a horse show, or sit under the trees at a café. "Sunday and Thursday afternoons," according to one guidebook, "are the rendez-vous of the prettiest women in Paris; two long files of carriages, one more brilliant than the other, form an ever-novel spectacle. . . . Everything is *di-vine*" (Dulaure 1787, 1:86). A drawing by Gabriel de Saint-Aubin, included here as figure 3, illustrates the elite presence on the boulevards perfectly: magnificently dressed young men and women stroll beneath the trees or share a table at a café. But the blissful rich are not the only figures pres-ent: at the extreme left of the drawing, a stooped and ragged older man holds out his hat in hopes of alms, and at the rear of the scene, one can just make out a female street entertainer grasping a hurdy-gurdy under her arm and a woman wearing a modest cap holding a child to her chest.

In sharp contrast with the Cours-la-Reine, and in contrast even with the Jardin des Tuileries, where ordinary Parisians could venture only when properly decked out, all classes of the population were to be found on the boulevard, from urchins, apprentices, and seamstresses to counts and duchesses. This is much more evident in another drawing of Saint-Aubin's, reproduced as figure 4. In the center of this image is a young couple hurrying across the busy carriage lanes of the boulevard, heading, perhaps, to the café beneath the trees on the left, where we see a *garçon de café* holding a platter aloft, a well-dressed group seated at a table at the front left and others at tables farther back. Again a man is holding out his hat and begging at the far left of the image. But whereas the image in

FIGURE 3. *Promenade sur les Boulevards*, drawing by Gabriel de Saint-Aubin, ca. 1760, photographed by T. Gorbokeneva. © The State Hermitage Museum, Saint Petersburg, reprinted with permission.

figure 3 breathes such equipoise, refinement, and luxury that it could almost have been a scene in a private aristocratic garden—were it not for the disconcerting figure of the beggar—the image in figure 4 is immediately recognizable as the boulevards.[7] We see the two files of carriages, complete with coachmen and postillions; an urchin running behind the carriage at the right, perhaps hoping to hitch a ride; a little dog running along the edge of the carriage-way; and a receding line of buildings de-

7. On these drawings, see Bailey et al. (2007, 194–95, 204–5).

fining the left border of the scene. Here, far from equipoise, everything
is hubbub and motion, and neither the couple crossing the carriage-way
nor the people seated at the tables are so elegantly attired as those in figure 3. This drawing perfectly captures the social mixing that was inherent
in the boulevard experience.

The promenade on the boulevards was a gathering of all sorts of people, from all classes of the population, strolling, riding carriages, or enjoying themselves more or less indiscriminately at the commercial establishments. This social promiscuity certainly made the boulevards far livelier
than the Cours—or, for that matter, the Jardin des Tuileries. As Madame
d'Oberkirch put it, the Boulevard du Temple "had a gaity, an animation
that was a pleasure to see. We stopped at all these open-air spectacles"
(1970, 454). The Cours, in particular, where one saw only other aristocratic carriage riders and their equipages, and where one could not get out
of the carriage for a drink or a stroll, came to seem utterly tedious. Parisian
aristocrats preferred the variety and liveliness of the mixed-class promenade of the boulevards, whose commercial entertainments also made
the relative formality of the Jardin des Tuileries seem pale. Indeed, some
wealthy nobles showed their inclination for the boulevards by building
luxurious *hôtels particuliers* (urban houses) along them in the last decade
before the Revolution (Turcot 2007, 186–206). Here again, the testimony
of Madame d'Oberkirch is vivid. In 1784, she was visiting Paris at the re-

FIGURE 4. *Le Boulevard*, drawing by Gabriel de Saint-Aubin, ca. 1760. Image
courtesy of Fondation Custodia, Collection Frits Lugt, Paris.

quest of the princesse de Condé. Their day included shopping at a boutique that sold exquisitely painted fans, a visit to the shop of Rose Bertin, stopping for dinner, and then taking in a pantomime theater performance in the Palais-Royal. After that, they repaired to an all-night theater on the boulevard: "That night we were very amused by certain drunken soldiers who claimed a girl was a bottle and insisted on taking off her bonnet. The Princess very much enjoyed herself at such festivities; she tormented me about going on to Porcheron [a yet more plebian destination a little north of the boulevards] but she gave up this plan for fear of being recognized and provoking the discontent of the house of Condé" (Oberkirch 1970, 611–12). As this vignette makes clear, nobles, even royals, were enchanted with the variety, liveliness, unpredictability, and nonstop gaiety on display at the boulevards.

The Palais-Royal

By 1784, the Palais-Royal, which had been the penultimate destination of Madame d'Oberkirch and the princesse de Condé, had begun to rival the popularity of the boulevards. The official residence of the junior Orléans branch of the Bourbon family, it was located near the center of Paris, just to the north of the Louvre. It had a large garden, about a third the size of the Jardin des Tuileries, which had long been open to the general public for promenades. The buildings bordering the garden housed a number of famous cafés and shops. In 1781, the new Duc d'Orléans, who was short of funds despite his immense fortune, decided to line the outer margin of the garden with apartment buildings, which housed some eighty shops on their ground floors. The shops benefited from a covered arcade that ran along the edge of the entire garden and was exceptionally well lit in the evenings. The rent from the apartments and the shops was intended to furnish the duke with a fresh income stream. The shops were quickly rented out, and the refurbished Jardin became a very stylish and popular site of promenades when it was opened to the public again in 1784 (Lever 1996, 187–89, 224–27).

As at the boulevards, the promenade at the Palais-Royal was much enhanced by the fascinating commercial offerings. One of the boulevard's theatrical companies moved to the arcades of the Palais-Royal, and two new companies opened—one called *les Ombres Chinoises*, which presented shadow plays, and another called *les Petits Comédiens*, which presented operas sung by off-stage singers and acted out in pantomime by child actors. It was the latter that Madame d'Oberkirch and the princesse de Condé visited in 1784. There were scientific demonstrations, and one of the boulevard's wax museums opened a branch in the Palais-Royal. New cafés joined the long-established ones. A large bathhouse offered steam baths, ascending and descending showers, hot and cold tubs, and so on. Given the favorable location of the Palais-Royal between the city center and the stylish western neighborhoods, there were also shops selling luxury goods (Prévost de Saint-Lucien 1787, 112–16). Finally, sellers of books and all sorts of printed matter were particularly attracted to the Palais-Royal because it was possible to freely sell texts that might be forbidden elsewhere. The Palais-Royal, as the property of a royal prince, enjoyed the "privilege of liberty." It was off-limits to the Parisian police authorities and therefore an exceptionally free space.

The renovated Palais-Royal made for a very attractive spectacle in the 1780s. Louis-Sébastien Mercier wrote that it is "unique on the face of the Globe. . . . Everything can be found there. Put a young man of twenty with an income of five thousand livres [in the Palais-Royal] and he will never be able to leave this fairyland." Mercier, like many contemporaries, was both charmed by the beauty, liveliness, and luxury of the scene at the Palais-Royal and critical of the vices it displayed. "It is," he says, "the temple of voluptuousness, whose sparkling vices have banished even the ghost of modesty" (1994, 930–31). The Palais-Royal was indeed renowned for its strolling prostitutes and also for its financiers eager to cut a deal. According to Mercier, "The speculators, who are the counterparts of the pretty prostitutes, go to the garden three times daily, and speak only of money and of political prostitution. . . . They set up banking operations in the cafés" (936). But all descriptions and classes of people were attracted to the Palais-Royal by the numerous shops, the cafés, and the sheer pleasure of watching the endlessly varied parade. In Caraccioli's *Lettres d'un Indien*, his hero, Zator, a visiting Indian nobleman, remarks of the Palais-Royal, "Nothing could be more pleasant than a comfortable lunch in this brilliant garden; one takes refreshments while having the pleasure of seeing all ages and all nations pass in review" (1789, 4–5). Filled with shoppers, foreign tourists, strollers, and café-goers during the day, the Palais-Royal was especially lively after dark, when, with its shops and cafés still open for business and its arcades and gardens lit by hundreds of lanterns until eleven o'clock, part of the crowd "breathes the pure air of the grand esplanade, while a multitude of groups, seated at little tables, dine on the frozen treats that the hot season renders so necessary and agreeable" while taking in the spectacle of this "nocturnal open-air ball" (Grimm [1784] 1879, 555).

The promenade at the Palais-Royal combined certain features of the promenades at the Jardin des Tuileries and the boulevards. Like the Tuileries, the Palais-Royal was adjacent to the wealthy neighborhoods of the city and was certainly a center of fashion—a place that attracted foreigners or provincials eager to see the latest in dresses, suits, hats, wigs, jewelry, and accessories arrayed on the bodies of stylish Parisians. But it was also open to the city, with no Swiss guards controlling access, and hence no requirement to "pass" as a member of polite society. It was also like the boulevards in its mixture of pleasurable strolling and commercial attractions. There were no menageries or horse shows (the rents were too high for such space-intensive enterprises) but plenty of cafés and inexpensive theaters. The Palais-Royal also had bookstores where one could buy the latest newspapers and pamphlets and cafés known for their nouvellistes, who passed on the latest scandals and discussed the political news—and where customers would hold ad hoc debates and discussions. The Palais-Royal combined Jürgen Habermas's public sphere of reasoned discussion with a commercial public sphere of nonstop shopping and public display.

The Palais-Royal would also seem to mark a convenient terminus for a chapter of a book on the relationship of commercial capitalism to the origins of the French Revolution. In the summer of 1789, when press censorship was lifted and the Estates General was beginning to meet, the cafés and book stalls at the Palais-Royal became the central news bureau and meeting place for those who followed the astounding politics of the time. The Marquis de Ferrières wrote in his memoirs that a constant crowd was drawn to the Palais-Royal by "a curiosity to hear and to know everything, a need to communicate with others": "One presented himself armed with a constitution that he believed must be the object of the Estates General's work; another declaimed emphatically from a text appropriate to the circumstances; a third railed against the ministers, against the nobles, against the priests; while a fourth, perched on a tabletop, discussed the great question of deliberations over the vote by head. . . . Each had his listeners."[8] Arthur Young, the well-known English writer on agricultural questions, was in Paris in the summer of 1789 and remarked something very similar. In his journal of June 9, 1789, he wrote, "The coffee houses in the Palais-Royal present . . . singular and astonishing spectacles; they are not only crowded within, but other expectant crowds are at the doors and windows, listening . . . to certain orators, who from chairs or tables harangue each his little audience. The eagerness with which they are heard, and the thunder of applause they receive for every sentiment of more than common hardiness or violence against the present government, cannot be easily imagined" (1792, 104). The freedom from harassment by the

---

8. Quoted in Lever (1996, 283).

police afforded by the Palais-Royal's privileged legal status, the easy avail-ability of pamphlets at the bookshops, the central Parisian location and its accessibility to strollers of all kinds, and the long tradition of discussing political news in the cafés all made the Palais-Royal the effective head-quarters of revolutionary politics in Paris in the pivotal summer of 1789.

But from the perspective of the argument in this chapter, the politi-cal centrality of the Palais-Royal in the Parisian revolution is largely be-side the point. It is true that the Palais-Royal could not have served this function had it not emerged as a well-known place of anonymous public assembly. Yet it was not the only site of public promenades where politi-cal speech was taken up in the spring and summer of 1789. Caraccioli's fictional Zator, who was fascinated by the reforms apparently in the off-ing in that year, reports ironically on political harangues in the normally far more sedate Jardin des Tuileries: "A man enraged against the century, against Paris, against the court, against himself, exhaled furor . . . every-one clapped their hands, often without having heard what he was saying. I pushed through the crowd, and I heard that Europe, such as it now is, has no common sense, that it must be refounded. . . . Every day there are little dramas of this sort that entertain the idle and capture the interest of the politically inclined" (1789, 248–50). One suspects that at this moment of generalized political fever, such discourses could also be heard wher-ever people congregated in Paris: on the boulevards, on the Pont-Neuf, at markets, and at busy street corners all over the city. The Palais-Royal, with its multiple advantages, was merely the central political node of what had become, by the summer of 1789, a highly politicized city.

Civic Equality in Public Spaces

I am interested in the political consequences of the evolving Parisian promenade that are subtler, more general, more lasting, and deeper than the sudden outbreak of political speech and political sociability in the Palais-Royal and elsewhere in Paris in the spring and summer of 1789. The evolution of the promenade in eighteenth-century Paris is import-ant for my inquiry because it gave rise to a new anonymous form of social intercourse—one that established an interstitial but real public sphere of civic equality. The ever-widening influence of the "empire of fashion," as we have seen, made it difficult to discern the exact social standing of those who occupied the public space even of the regulated Jardin des Tuileries. In this sense, the promenade at the Jardin, one of the key public activities of the age, became increasingly anonymous—everyone consented tacitly to the copresence of people whose real statuses were uncertain but who

were treated as abstract equals within the limited context of the Jardin. A
different pattern of anonymous copresence developed on the boulevards
and at the Palais-Royal, where the space of the promenade was unfenced
and therefore open to all. The explosion of commercialized leisure that
characterized these spaces was premised on an indiscriminate mixing of
social categories, which was necessary to amass theatrical audiences and
collections of café patrons and shoppers in sufficient numbers to make
the spaces commercially profitable. As it turned out, the undisguised
social mixing in these spaces produced a combination of liveliness and
splendor that actually increased their attractiveness, both for elites and
for common people.

In short, Parisians became accustomed to sharing public space on an
anonymous basis with persons of diverse social status. The lofty nobles
sitting at a table under the trees on the boulevard might be a table away
from a party of master artisans dressed in their finery. The former, of
course, probably arrived in a gorgeous lacquered coach, while the latter
had to walk out from their crowded neighborhood in the center of the
city. They were, that is, far from being equals and had no illusions about
this fact. But as customers at the café listening to a strolling ballad singer,
watching the performers cavort on a neighboring outdoor stage, or simply
taking in the colorful parade of fellow strollers, they were—by unspoken
convention—unconcerned about the precise social identity of those sitting at the neighboring table, so long as all were decked out with the appropriate generally available commodities: decent suits and dresses and
up-to-date wigs, hats, canes, and umbrellas. Indeed, both for the artisans
and for the nobles, it was largely this temporary suspension of the for-
malities of rank and punctilio, made possible by a commodified abstraction from their statuses, that made the boulevards and the Palais-Royal
so particularly enjoyable.

In this mixed commercial space, a de facto civil equality had been established, one that, for the limited purpose of recreation, abstracted individuals out of their everyday social roles and made them coparticipants
in a common anonymous public space—so long as they could afford the
price of the café's fare, owned the accoutrements of elementary fashionable appearance, and could enact the phrases and gestures of basic politeness. This was, of course, a highly specific form of civil equality, one
that did not imply any generalized equality either of means or of personal honor. But such a suspension of rank and such a mutually accepted
co-occupation of a common public space would have been impossible—
indeed, unthinkable—a century earlier. In this limited sphere of urban
recreation, interstitial capitalist development—of a fashion industry and

of new forms of commercial recreation—had conspired to turn the Parisian promenade into a kind of experiential objective correlative of the notions of social and political equality being developed by the philosophes. In this way, the experience of *civil* equality in Parisian strollers' and consumers' everyday recreational experience might be said to have silently prepared people for the perilous leap into the more generalized *civic* equality that became the law of the nation in the first years of the French Revolution.

II

The Philosophes and the Career Open to Talent

The Philosophe Career and the Impossible Example of Voltaire

There is little doubt that the ideas inspiring the revolutionaries to establish a regime of civic equality were brought to prominence in eighteenth-century France by a group of Paris-based intellectuals generally known as the philosophes. *Philosophe* is simply French for "philosopher." But in the eighteenth century, its plural came to designate a particular group of intellectuals—not all of whom would fit our definition of philosopher—who developed an intellectual program profoundly at odds with the doctrines that were embraced by religious and secular authorities and enforced with varying degrees of zeal. The philosophes did not work out an explicit political program centered on civic equality. Their movement was diffuse and multiple and not primarily focused on questions of political philosophy. The great exception was Rousseau, who, as we shall see, had a highly ambiguous relation to the philosophe movement and whose complicated identification with his native Genevan republic gave his political reflections a very different referent from those of native French philosophes.

It could be argued that the political thrust of the philosophe movement was expressed as much in its epistemology as in explicit political theory. The movement took root in an "absolute" monarchy where a king ruled by divine right and relied heavily on the authority of the Catholic Church. The philosophes rejected this appeal to religious authority and adopted a skeptical and empiricist epistemological stance, one that understood knowledge as based on the evidence of the senses, fortified by rational argument. This position was largely inspired by the great English thinkers of the seventeenth century, above all Francis Bacon, Isaac Newton, and John Locke. The philosophes embraced an ethic of free inquiry, philosophical skepticism, epistemological modesty, the pursuit of scientific reason, and individual freedom. Their politics was defined more by their opposition to what they regarded as the "fanaticism" of the French

Catholic Church and the tendencies toward "despotism" in the French state than by any positive political theories. Their insistence on deriving their conclusions in all areas of thought from their own reasoned inquiry rather than from established authority made them seem politically subversive even when their inquiries had no direct bearing on politics. Diderot spent several months in a royal prison as a consequence of his epistemological writings, and Voltaire avoided prison only by fleeing Paris when his book praising English empiricist knowledge was condemned. The state and church actually had good reason to distrust and fear the philosophes. If the authority of ideas is derived from independent thinking based on the evidence of the senses, then it is only the quality of the reasoning rather than the person's office or rank that deserves respect and affirmation. The philosophes' epistemology in this sense implied a kind of civic equality among thinkers and their ideas.

The philosophes pursued not only the development of rationally and empirically derived knowledge but the diffusion of such knowledge to all who could appreciate it. They wished to spread what they called "Lumières"—usually rendered in English as "Enlightenment." Their writings were meant to explore the most challenging intellectual issues of their day but also to inform and enlighten the general reading public—in France, but not only in France, since the Enlightenment was a pan-European movement. Their inquiries included the era's entire intellectual world.

No project better represents the ambitions of this intellectual movement than the *Encyclopédie ou dictionnaire raisonné des sciences, des arts et des métiers* (Encyclopedia or Rational Dictionary of the Sciences, Arts, and Trades), which was launched by the philosophes Denis Diderot and Jean le Rond d'Alembert in 1751—but not completed until 1772, when the last volumes of plates illustrating the mechanical arts were finally published. The *Encyclopédie* eventually included seventeen volumes of text (ranging from 871 to 1,098 pages of folio text each) and eleven volumes of plates illustrating everything from geometry, geology, and anatomy through music, sculpture, and architecture, to agriculture, commerce, and a vast range of arts and trades, which Diderot radically reconceptualized as applied sciences. The ambition of the *Encyclopédie* was to make the most up-to-date expert knowledge available to anyone capable of reading French. Because French was the generally accepted international language of diplomacy, science, and the arts in the eighteenth century, this linguistic limitation was less constraining than we might imagine.

The *Encyclopédie*, like the Enlightenment itself, was a collective product. Its title page indicated that it was coauthored "by a society of men of letters" and "put in order and published" by Denis Diderot and Jean le Rond d'Alembert. The articles were authored by scores of writers, generally treating their specialties. The *Encyclopédie* was, in the end, a great success, both as a commercial publishing venture and as an intellectual project. But its successes were hard won. Publication was interrupted by the French royal state, which feared the effects of its intellectual radicalism and skepticism on public opinion. D'Alembert abandoned the project after its initial suspension and many others withdrew their collaboration out of caution. Diderot had to struggle mightily, with the aid of a sadly reduced group of collaborators, to bring it to completion.

The saga of the *Encyclopédie*, which will be covered in chapter 7, indicates that the Enlightenment hardly swept all before it. Yet Enlightenment ideas progressed enormously in the eighteenth century. The Royal Academy of Sciences and the Académie Française—the pinnacles of intellectual distinction in old regime France—were both dominated by philosophes by the 1780s. The cream of the French philosophes gained great international prestige. Voltaire, Diderot, and d'Alembert corresponded with and were welcomed to the courts of crowned heads of Europe. And by the final decades of the old regime, many top administrators of the French state had themselves been converted to Enlightenment ideas.

Much has been written about the philosophes and the Enlightenment and I will not summarize this vast literature. Instead, I examine the social lives of some representative figures of the movement. In the previous chapters, I have recounted collective experiences in the rising commercial society. In this part of the book, I examine the lives of particular individuals who grappled with the contradictory demands of a well-established hierarchical society and an emerging ethic of civic equality based on commercial exchange. One of the most striking characteristics of the philosophes as a group is that few of them hailed from the elites of French society. Alexis de Tocqueville noted that in eighteenth-century France "men of letters" (i.e., the philosophes) actually became "the principal political actors of their time" even though they "possessed neither social eminence, nor honors, nor wealth, nor responsibilities, nor power" ([1856] 2004, 170–71). Tocqueville exaggerated a little. A few sword nobles were prominent philosophes, of whom the mathematician and philosopher Condorcet, a marquis, was most famous. Some robe nobles, particularly those in the royal administration, patronized the philosophes, and Turgot, who eventually served as controller general, was an important intellectual figure. The abbé Condillac, the most influential French epistemologist of the century, was from a noble family. There were also sons of wealthy bourgeois, of whom Voltaire was the most prominent, and a few wealthy financiers, like Helvétius. But most philosophes came from distinctly modest backgrounds—they were sons of provincial lawyers, merchants, artisans, shopkeepers, or minor officials who lacked family wealth and had to make their way on their own.

By the 1730s, a career as a Parisian man of letters beckoned as a possible path to prominence in French society that would otherwise have been unthinkable for such men. It is remarkable that in this profoundly hierarchical society, several artisans' and shopkeepers' sons, who in Loyseau's terms were born "vile and abject," could become celebrated members of the nation's intellectual elite, becoming, if we believe Tocqueville, the most important political actors of their time (Loyseau 1987, 30). Here was a striking, indeed, almost shocking example of what came to be called "the career open to talent," an upwardly mobile trajectory that made these men of letters natural supporters of the notion of civic equality.

My strategy in this section of the book is to focus on the experiences of three men who rose from humble backgrounds to become influential philosophes: Denis Diderot, the chief editor of the *Encyclopédie*, who was the son of a moderately prosperous cutler from Langres, a small town in Champagne; the abbé André Morellet, the son of a paper retailer from Lyon; and Jean-Jacques Rousseau, the son of a watchmaker from Geneva. I choose these three not because I regard them as most representative but because their lives have been exceptionally well documented. Morellet wrote a detailed personal memoir about his experiences, Rousseau authored his famous *Confessions*, and Diderot's life has been traced in exceptionally fine biographies by Arthur Wilson and Jacques Proust (Morellet 2010; Rousseau 1973; Wilson 1972; Proust [1962] 1995). In my biographical sketches, I focus especially on a question seldom seriously examined in writings about the philosophes: how they gained enough money to support their literary and intellectual activities. As we shall see, their financial strategies combined, in fascinatingly different ways and in different proportions, commercial publishing and patronage.[1]

These three are particularly interesting because their life experiences embodied the career open to talent in a period when that phenomenon was still a rarity—indeed, an affront to the official values of an insistently hierarchical society. Rising to prominence required them to rely—to varying degrees and in varying ways—on the standard tactics for navigating eighteenth-century French social life: exhibiting deference and seeking

1. A similar story could be told of Marmontel, a literary figure who was a companion of the philosophes and became the permanent secretary of the Académie-Française. He was a tailor's son from the tiny town of Bort in the Limousin (Marmontel 1992).

patronage. This can be illustrated by one of the central institutions in the lives of the philosophes: the frequent dinners and suppers that, since the nineteenth century, have retrospectively become known as *salons* (Lilti 2005). Salons were generally held in noble urban houses (*hôtels particuliers*) and included fellow nobles of both sexes along with men of letters, whose brilliant conversation enhanced the prestige of one's salon. A number of the most famous salons were organized and led by women.[2] The salons revolved around dinners (afternoon meals) or suppers (late-evening meals), but the proceedings lasted for several hours. There were extended conversations, often moderated by the women who hosted many of the salons, touching a range of topics—from the latest gossip, to recent theatrical or musical performances or art exhibitions, to questions of philosophy, morality, or science. Many salons were graced by musical performances. Writers would recite their latest poems or read from their latest texts. Throughout, the salons were punctuated by sallies of wit and eloquence, both from the philosophes and from the assembled aristocrats.

The salons were crucial for philosophes' careers. Young intellectuals would be introduced to a salon by friends or acquaintances who had already become regulars. Young men of letters on the make would meet other philosophes but also wealthy nobles, financiers, and government ministers whose patronage could enhance their careers. Moreover, the usually generous and delicious meals provided at the salons were a major economic boon to impoverished young writers. A philosophe well established on the salon circuit rarely ate at home. François Marmontel remarked that when the success of his first tragedy at the Comédie-Française made him a sought-after guest at dinners all across Paris, he was "freed of worries about the expenses of my table" and no longer needed to share living space with roommates to make ends meet (1992, 178). Both directly (free dinners) and indirectly (introductions to potential benefactors), entering the salon circuit was a key step in sustaining and advancing one's career as a man of letters.

The philosophes certainly recognized that they possessed intellectual and literary gifts superior to most of those whose patronage they sought but whose social superiority they had no choice but to recognize and accept. Indeed, the young philosophe was often in awe of the impeccable manners of his aristocratic hosts and fellow guests. The dissonance that resulted from their simultaneous superiority and inferiority made men of letters keenly aware of their contradictory place in Parisian society. It also made attractive to them values that underlay the notion of civic equality:

2. For an argument about the importance of these salonières, see Goodman (1994).

judgment based on rational argument rather than custom and on performance rather than status; a distrust of tradition, pomp, and authority; a willingness to engage in free and open-ended speculation and experiment; and a strongly empirical and antimetaphysical bent. These values were affirmed in their published work and guided their conversations in the salons that played such a prominent part in their daily lives.

If the philosophes' experience of simultaneous intellectual superiority and social inferiority was conducive to notions of civic equality on their part, something comparable might be said of their social superiors. To attract a Diderot, a Rousseau, or a Morellet to one's weekly dinner increased one's prestige among the fellow aristocrats who graced these dinners. The aristocrats who vied with one another to attract these famous men to their salons and who interacted with them on a daily or weekly basis in the conversations that made the Parisian salons famous were surely aware of the intellectual superiority—indeed, the brilliance—of these philosophes whose obscure birth officially placed them among the vile. A Parisian aristocrat who had listened to Morellet's brilliant satirical arguments against the assumptions of royal commercial policy or heard Diderot's speculations about the mental functioning of the deaf and the blind would have to question his or her assumptions about the fundamental superiority of nobles over commoners. Most surely continued to believe that their superior birth entitled them to respect and deference. Yet their experience in the salons must have made them aware that men with common and even lowly origins could in certain respects be their superiors. While their participation in salons may or may not have made them believers in civic equality, they realized that talent and even wisdom and virtue were not an exclusive possession of their class.

This world of aristocratic salons infiltrated by brilliant philosophes was far from the only field of activity of the men of letters. It was writing and publishing tracts, novels, stories, scientific works, plays, histories, poems, essays, and philosophical treatises that made them men of letters. This field of activity was governed by quite different norms and strategies than that of the salons. If success in the salons required a delicate mix of deference and self-promotion, the world of publication was a straightforwardly commercial affair. Publishing was a venture governed by the usual rules of commerce, which meant that authors' works found their way into print only if the publishers believed the works would sell. Eighteenth-century publishers were hard-nosed businessmen, and it was they, rather than the authors, who stood to prosper in the book trade. Authors gained no royalties from their works. Instead, they sold their manuscripts to the publishers. Even if their books became commercial successes, they gained only the price the publishers initially paid—although, of course, an author who had written a profitable book might be able to make money from later editions and would be in a better bargaining position the next time he offered a manuscript. Living entirely by the pen was a difficult affair in eighteenth-century France, as we shall see in the cases of our three philosophes.[3] Yet this barely profitable commercial venture of publishing was essential to the career of a man of letters: a well-received book would mean more invitations to salons and more opportunities for the positions, pensions, and sinecures that were the most reliable path to a comfortable life. The career of the philosophe for those who lacked family wealth—most men of letters—required a complex and exquisite balancing of commerce with deference and patronage.

The category of men of letters long predated the eighteenth century; as we have seen, Loyseau, writing in 1610, placed men of letters at the top of the hierarchy of commoners. The church, which needed a supply of competent priests and theologians, had long provided an education (in theology, philosophy, rhetoric, Latin, and Greek) to candidates for the priesthood. In the sixteenth and seventeenth centuries, under the impetus of the Counter-Reformation, various religious orders, most prominently the Jesuits, formed schools offering rigorous education that were also open to young men not preparing for careers in the church, nobles and commoners alike. By the eighteenth century, such schools—collèges, as they were called—existed in virtually every French province. Their graduates could pursue various professions: the traditional noble profession of the military; law, which could lead either to legal practice or to careers in the royal administration; the clergy, of course, typically leading to bishoprics for nobles and to less elevated ecclesiastical functions for commoners. Those from modest backgrounds could become priests but could also enter commerce, become tutors to sons of the wealthy, or become clerks or secretaries in governmental or private service. Nearly all the impecunious young men who became philosophes in the eighteenth century gained their educations in these church-sponsored schools and began their careers as tutors, translators, or hired pens.

The Impossible Career of Voltaire

The figure of the philosophe emerged as a possible model for learned young men in the middle years of the eighteenth century. The philosophe was a man of learning, talent, and accomplishment, to be sure, but was

3. See also (Darnton 1982, 1–40).

also expected to be an indomitable seeker after truth and a dedicated pub-
licist of the truths he had discovered. The emergence of the philosophe
so defined is inseparable from the career of one particularly creative man
of letters: Voltaire.[4] Although before his time there were men of letters
who were darlings of the salons, none had Voltaire's panache, daring, pro-
grammatic vision, wide audience, or influence on ambitious young men.
His example was inescapable. But if Voltaire made the career of man of
letters attractive, his position in the intellectual and social world was also
utterly unique. Inspiring as his example was, no later philosophe could
actually follow his path. Because he was extraordinarily wealthy, he could
repeatedly thumb his nose at the state authorities. He spent most of his
career living in splendor at a great distance from Paris, mounting audacious challenges to the status quo that would have been far too dangerous
for less wealthy philosophes—dependent, as they were, on the salons and
on the business and patronage opportunities of the Parisian milieu. Employing his malicious wit, boundless energy, and prodigious correspondence, Voltaire managed to maintain intellectual primacy among the Parisian philosophes from his comfortable exile. His audacious intellectual
model was an inspiration to the younger philosophes. But their relative
poverty meant that they would have to find their own way.

    Born François-Marie Arouet in 1694, Voltaire was the son of a rich Pa-
risian notary whose thirst for upward mobility was revealed by his purchase of an office in the Cour des comptes (Pomeau 1985, 17–30). The future Voltaire was educated at the Parisian Jesuit collège Louis le Grand,
which, according to his biographer René Pomeau, "served as preparatory
seminary for future high officials of the monarchy" (1985, 37). His father
wanted him to become a lawyer, the typical path to such a career, but
François-Marie, although briefly forced to study law, wished to be a poet.
His biting wit and talent as a versifier made him welcome at salons and
noble houses but got him into trouble. Suspected of writing a verse de-
faming Philippe d'Orléans, the regent of France during the minority of
Louis XV, he was banished from Paris in 1716. Allowed back, he continued writing verses aimed at the regent and was imprisoned in the Bastille for eleven months in 1717 (Pomeau 1985, 99–109). It was in prison
that he composed his first play, *Oedipe*, which became a smash hit at the
Comédie-Française a few months after his release. This secured his reputation as an author. As Pomeau puts it, "no longer a petty composer
of scandalous rhymes," he became "the great poet that France had been

---

4. The literature on Voltaire is staggeringly vast. I have primarily relied on biographies by Pomeau (1985), Vaillot (1988), and Pearson (2005).

longing for since the deaths of Corneille and Racine" (130). It was then that François Arouet adopted the nom de plume Voltaire (116).

Although he was well paid for *Oedipe* (3,000 livres plus a gold medal worth another 675), this could hardly support his extravagant lifestyle. Voltaire's father died in 1721, leaving him the sizable fortune of 152,934 livres. However, the elder Arouet distrusted his son and forbade him access to these funds until his thirty-fifth birthday, some eight years in the future. But Voltaire had already launched a series of successful speculative investments—taking advantage of his fame and his high society contacts (Pomeau 1985, 142–50). It was not the direct yield of his authorship but the profits of such investments, together with the inheritance finally gained in 1730, that made him a wealthy man. By the end of 1730, his fortune exceeded a million livres, riches comparable to those of a wealthy nobleman. As Voltaire later put it, "I have seen so many poor and despised men of letters that I concluded long ago not to increase their number" (Pomeau 1985, 261).

Voltaire, at this stage of his life, was a poet and dramatist. In 1724, he published the first version of an epic poem, *La Ligue ou Henri le Grand*, better known by its later title the *La Henriade*. This was a celebration of the virtues and triumphs of Henri IV, the first king of the Bourbon dynasty. Voltaire hoped this work would gain him a position at the royal court. But his disputatious character ruined this prospect and accidentally launched him in a sharply new direction. One evening in 1726, Voltaire traded insults with the chevalier de Rohan-Chabot at the Opera. Rohan-Chabot was a dissolute character but a member of one of the wealthiest and most powerful noble families in France. As a punishment for his impertinence, Rohan-Chabot had four thugs ambush and thrash Voltaire in the street a few days later. When, recovering from this beating, Voltaire threatened to challenge the chevalier to a duel—a presumptuous action for a commoner—he was judged rebellious and locked up in the Bastille again. Two weeks later, he was permitted to leave his confinement but on the condition that he exile himself to England (Pomeau 1985, 203–9).

Arriving in London in May 1726, Voltaire took up intensive study of the English language. Soon short of cash, he made a brief surreptitious trip to Paris to retrieve more significant sums. He rented a small apartment in London so he could attend the theater, where he first encountered Shakespeare's plays (Pomeau 1985, 212–23). He spent most of the following fall as a guest of Lord Bolingbroke, whom he had befriended in Paris a few years earlier. There he met and traded ideas with Alexander Pope, John Gay, Jonathan Swift, and other intellectuals. It was in England that Voltaire published the definitive luxury edition of his *Henriade,* which he dedicated to the British queen Caroline (230–32, 250). He finally was allowed to return to France in 1728.

This English interlude changed Voltaire profoundly. He became essentially bilingual and increasingly bicultural as well. He was impressed by English ways and thought. At Bolingbroke's suggestion, he had read Locke's *Essay Concerning Human Understanding* in French translation as early as 1724, before his English sojourn. But until this fateful voyage, Voltaire had remained a purely literary figure, essentially ignorant of modern philosophy—having never read Descartes, Leibnitz, or Spinoza (Pomeau 1985, 162, 195–96). It was the shock of exile that made Voltaire a philosophe as well as a literary author. This change of interests can be seen in his *Letters Concerning the English Nation,* written and published in English in 1733 and republished in French as *Lettres philosophiques.* This work viewed the English in a favorable light, an attitude bound to be suspect to French authorities, who regarded England as their country's great enemy. It was Voltaire's first significant work in prose. He treated a range of topics in a distinctive spare, conversational, and sardonic prose style: the various English religious sects; English government institutions; English commerce; such philosophical worthies as Bacon, Locke, and Newton; English poets and dramatists; and English nobles who supported letters and were sometimes men of letters themselves.

Voltaire began, disarmingly, with four chapters on the Quakers, whose beliefs he claimed to find heretical and confounding but whom he in fact portrayed as morally righteous for their lack of hierarchy, their informality, their plain speech, and their pacific ways. His praise of William Penn's government of Pennsylvania was a veiled criticism of hierarchical French manners and government: "This was a novel spectacle: a sovereign who called others 'thou' and 'thee,' to whom one could speak with his hat on his head, a government without priests, a people without weapons, citizens all equal before the law, and neighbors devoid of envy" (Voltaire 1907, 13). Voltaire also praised the English respect for commerce, "which has enriched the citizens of England" and "contributed to their freedom." He commended English aristocrats for being unashamed to participate in commerce and concluded his brief chapter on commerce with the statement "I, however, do not know which is the more useful to the State: a nobleman in a powdered wig who knows exactly when the king arises and when he retires, and who gives himself airs of greatness while he plays the slave in the antechamber of a minister; or a merchant who enriches his country, who sends orders from his counting house to Surat and Cairo, and contributes to the well-being of the world" (31–33). Voltaire also

praised English philosophers, especially Bacon, who championed exper-
imental philosophy; Locke, who "demonstrated that all our ideas come
to us through the senses"; and Newton, who, by shunning metaphysics
and working only from measurable physical facts and mathematically de-
monstrable truths, discovered the actual "system of the world" and the
true nature of light. Although praising Descartes, Voltaire argued that his
"metaphysical" thought had been surpassed by the more modest and empirical English geniuses (37–67).

In the French edition of this book about the English, Voltaire appended a long disputation against Pascal's famous *Pensées* (1760). Pascal
was a French Jansenist philosopher and theologian, a member of that dis-
senting but at the time well-established sect of French Catholics whose
beliefs were in many respects closer to those of Calvin than to the dominant doctrines of the Catholic Church. The Jansenists regarded human-
kind as utterly weak and corrupt and figured God as a distant and unap-
proachable figure who doled out grace according to his own inscrutable
will. Pascal preached a rigorous obedience to religious dictates. Voltaire
revolted against this profoundly pessimistic view of the human condition and what he regarded as Pascal's utterly metaphysical—and hence
both fanatical and fantastical—mode of reasoning. He spelled out this
argument in detail in what was by far the longest chapter in an otherwise concise book (Voltaire 1907, 101–22). Considering that the Parlement of Paris, the high court charged with policing French morals, was
filled with Jansenist judges, adding this provocative chapter to an already
suspiciously freethinking book was an inflammatory move.

In May 1734, a few days after the publication of the French edition of
Lettres philosophiques in Paris, an arrest warrant was issued against Voltaire. The book was officially condemned by the Parlement of Paris and
consigned to flames by the executioner. Then traveling in Burgundy, Voltaire escaped arrest. He fled to the remote chateau of his current lover,
Mme Du Châtelet, at Cirey in Champagne, where he was not further
troubled by the authorities. But the warrant meant that he was, for the
moment, definitively exiled from Paris. It is ironic that this consummate
Parisian, the toast of the city's salons, who was destined to become the
generally recognized head of the "party" of the Parisian philosophes,
spent the vast majority of his adult life outside his native city, in Cirey, in
London, in Brussels, in Holland, in Berlin, in Geneva, and eventually in
his own chateau in Ferney, located in France but on the Genevan border.

Voltaire's liaison with Mme Du Châtelet had an importance beyond
the refuge she offered in Cirey. Gabrielle-Emilie Le Tonnelier de Breteuil,
Marquise du Châtelet, was that rarity in the eighteenth century, a famous

woman of science (Ehrman 1986; Zinsser 2006; Zinsser and Hayes 2006; Hagengruber 2011). The student and sometime lover of the renowned physicist Pierre Louis Maupertuis, she published *Institutions de physique*, a discussion of contemporary scientific ideas, in 1740 (Du Châtelet 1740). She also made the definitive French translation of Newton's *Principia*, completed in 1749 shortly before her death but published only in 1759 (Du Châtelet 1759). During their years together at Cirey, Voltaire undertook a serious study of science and mathematics. Using his abundant funds, Voltaire rebuilt a wing of Mme du Châtelet's chateau, setting up a laboratory where they could replicate Newton's famous experiments in optics (Vaillot 1988, 81). The most important of Voltaire's scientific publications was *Éléments de Newton*, a study of Newton's theories that hastened the eventual acceptance of Newton in France—long delayed by the nearly universal Cartesianism of French scientists in the early eighteenth century (Voltaire 1738).

Voltaire's relationship with Mme Du Châtelet was not smooth. Both had occasional lovers on the side. She sometimes stayed in Paris, where Voltaire was initially forbidden. Meanwhile, in 1740, Voltaire made a long voyage to Berlin to visit the newly crowned King Fredrick II of Prussia, with whom he had already corresponded extensively. Thanks to lobbying by the well-placed Mme Du Châtelet, Voltaire was finally allowed to come back to Paris and Versailles in 1745. Momentarily enjoying the king's favor, in that year he was named royal historiographer and was elected to the Académie Française—an honor previously denied because of his disfavor with the court (Pearson 2005, 182–89). Meanwhile, Voltaire began a sexual affair with his widowed niece, Mme Denis. Disaster struck, however, from the other side of the by now frayed relationship. In 1748, Mme Du Châtelet fell in love with the noble military officer Jean-François de Saint-Lambert. She quickly became pregnant by him but died of puerperal fever in 1749 after giving birth to a daughter, who also failed to survive.

After Emilie's death, Voltaire initially returned to Paris and to Mme Denis, but his grief for Mme Du Châtelet and his declining favor at court soon sent him back to Berlin, where Fredrick beckoned. Arriving in 1750, he was feted, made a royal chamberlain, and awarded a stipend by the Prussian crown. He also found good intellectual company—Fredrick had lured many men of letters to his Berlin Academy. Voltaire spent two highly productive years in Berlin, where he wrote his historical study *Le Siècle de Louis XIV*; *Micromégas*, the first of his philosophical tales; and several articles for the newly launched *Encyclopédie*. But his disputatious nature again got the better of him: he wrote a satirical attack on Maupertuis, his former rival for the affections of Mme Du Châtelet, whom Fredrick had named head of the Prussian Royal Academy. This led to a break with Fredrick and Voltaire's departure in March of 1753 (Pearson 2005, 216–31).

Voltaire's affiliation with Fredrick had destroyed his welcome in Paris, so his break with the Prussian king left him with no obvious place of residence. Eventually, he and Mme Denis found lodging in Geneva, but there too Voltaire's opinions, particularly his increasingly fierce satires against Christianity and his devotion to the theater—frowned upon by the dour Calvinists dominating the city's government—eventually eroded his welcome. In 1758, he found the perfect solution, buying an extensive estate in Ferney in the French territory of Gex that directly abutted the Genevan border. Here he would be free of the meddlesome Genevans but could step across the border into Geneva should the French authorities threaten (Pearson 2005, 263–65). By this time, Voltaire's investments had made him extremely wealthy, in spite of sometimes extravagant expenses (Pearson 2005, 254). In his new estate at Ferney, he essentially made himself the lord of a small independent duchy, where he and Mme Denis could live as they wished and welcome an unending stream of guests. Voltaire took advantage of this territorial impunity to write and publish whatever he wished. Now in his sixties, exceedingly rich, and no longer concerned about losing favor at Versailles, he launched the most radical period of his career that associated with his famous rallying cry against the despotism of church and state: "*écrasez l'infâme!*" (crush the vile thing). His novella *Candide*, published in 1758, was denounced by the Parlement of Paris as contrary to religion and good morals but sold by the thousands of copies in several languages (Pearson 2005, 268). His *Dictionnaire philosophique portative* mercilessly debunked the Christian religion (Voltaire 1764). And his defense of the Protestant Calas and Servin families from persecution by the French state made him a hero of humanitarianism and a dangerous enemy of the Catholic Church. He became not only a revered playwright, a champion of the new science and philosophy, and a sardonic critic of Christian orthodoxy but a feared scourge of the injustices of church and state.

From his perch in Ferney, he established himself as the supreme judge of taste and morals and, in spite of his absence from Paris, as the leader—from his safe bastion—of the philosophe movement. Arthur Wilson, Diderot's biographer, remarked of Voltaire that "living practically in exile, two hundred and fifty miles from Paris in space and a fortnight in time, his problem was to manage by some feat of intellectual prestidigitation to seem to be leading Parisian public opinion while in reality following it. For twenty-five years he performed this sort of Indian rope trick" (1972, 214). The rope trick was accomplished in part by his prolific publications but also by a prodigious correspondence. The endless stream of letters going out from Ferney circulated widely in the Parisian salons; Voltaire was kept informed of the latest happenings in Paris by return mail. When Voltaire finally returned to Paris in 1778, still in possession of his faculties at age eighty-four but destined to die in the city of his birth a few months later, he was generally hailed as a genius and a hero. By then, the philosophes had won the high ground of moral and intellectual debate. But none of his followers in the philosophe movement had the tremendous advantage of his wealth or the physical distance from Paris that enabled him to thumb his nose at both church and state with impunity. His example was an inspiration to many, but for the rank and file of financially needy Parisian philosophes, pursuing enlightenment was a far more delicate and difficult game.

Denis Diderot

LIVING BY THE PEN

Denis Diderot was the only philosophe who rivaled Voltaire's range and influence. No one, however, could match Voltaire's cutting wit and literary panache. Diderot wrote a number of remarkable imaginative works of fiction, but fearing repression by the state and church, he left most of these unpublished during his lifetime. His great monument was the twenty-eight volumes of the *Encyclopédie*, of which he wrote an astounding proportion of the articles, on subjects of every description. But Diderot lacked the advantages of wealth and connections that enabled Voltaire to live luxuriously and to triumph repeatedly in spite of numerous run-ins with the authorities. Diderot's finances were a constant struggle—until, in 1765, when he was fifty-two, Catherine the Great of Russia patronized him by buying his library. This, together with a small inheritance from his father and sundry investments, yielded an annual income of around 6,500 livres—a decent bourgeois living finally achieved as he approached old age, but hardly magnificent (Wilson 1972, 513–14).[1]

Born in 1713 in Langres, a town of some ten thousand souls in Champagne, Diderot was the son of a cutler who specialized in lancets, much in demand by surgeons who used them to bleed patients. The family was devout: uncles on both sides were priests, and his younger brother became one as well (11–13). Denis enrolled in the Jesuit collège in Langres at ten and was a brilliant student who considered becoming a Jesuit himself. At age sixteen, he moved to Paris to continue his studies. Little is known of his doings in Paris from age sixteen to twenty-nine. He was awarded a master of arts by the Sorbonne in 1732 at the age of nineteen, but by then he had lost his taste for religion. Apprenticed briefly to a Parisian lawyer, he spent too little time studying law and too much perfecting his Latin, Greek, English, Italian, and mathematics. At this point, his father, dis-

---

1. Hereafter, citations to Wilson will appear in the text in parentheses.

gusted by his son's impracticality, cut off funding, and Diderot was forced to live by his wits: tutoring, writing sermons for hire, and translating from English for publishers (17–30). According to Jacques Proust, he earned three hundred livres in 1743 for his translation of Temple Stanyon's *The Grecian History*. It appears that he also received occasional sums from his father (Proust [1962] 1995, 90–91). This was a hardscrabble existence but acceptable for a single young man with a passion for learning.

Diderot's life and finances took a new turn in 1743 when he fell in love with Anne-Toinette Champion and married her, against his father's will. She and her mother worked in lace and linen, but at Diderot's insistence, she ceased working after marriage (42–45). A daughter born nine months after their marriage died six months later (54). This marriage, commenced in passion, became a burden for Diderot. He and his wife quarreled constantly, and Diderot took up with a series of mistresses; one of those women, Sophie Volland, whom Diderot got to know in the mid-1750s, was the true love of his life.[2] But he continued to live with his wife and to support her, however meagerly—mainly, in the early years, by translating. A son born in 1746 lived for only four years. A second son, born in 1750, failed to survive his first year (119). In 1753, a second daughter, Marie-Angelique Diderot, was born (286). She survived to adulthood and was greatly cherished by her father. She was, one might say, the one happy result of his marriage. Diderot's family obligations made his experience quite different from those of the other philosophes whose careers we shall be following. Most philosophes from mediocre backgrounds—and even those few who were wealthy like Voltaire—avoided marriage. Indeed, a remarkable number were abbés—members of the clergy and perforce unmarried, generally without benefices and forced to live by their wits like their lay associates. To mention only a few of the most prominent, there were the abbés Morellet, Raynal, Condillac, Mably, Prades, Bon, Prestré, Yvon, Gua de Malves, and Coyer. A sense of incompatibility between the life of the mind and the married state seems to have carried over from the days when learning was limited to the clerical estate.

Diderot was unusual among impecunious philosophes in his unwillingness to seek the protection of patrons. No other major philosophe was so dependent on commercial publication. He lived by his pen, until—most of his great work already accomplished—Catherine bought his li-

2. As Wilson points out (228–31), Diderot's letters to Sophie Volland are among the most valuable sources on his life and experiences. Diderot's relationship with Volland lasted until her death in 1784, a few months before his.

brary. As a consequence, he remained in relative penury but preserved his liberty to study and write as he pleased, something seemingly necessary to this utterly independent-minded and daring thinker. Nearly all of Diderot's commercial income came from the *Encyclopédie* project. His first association with the *Encyclopédie* dated from 1746, when he was thirty-three. The original idea had been to translate into French Ephraim Chambers' *Cyclopædia: or, An Universal Dictionary of Arts and Sciences*. Initially, the editor was to be the mathematician abbé Jean-Paul Gua de Malves, who was associated in this project with the mathematician and physicist Jean le Rond d'Alembert. Diderot came on board in 1746, in part, no doubt, because of his ability to translate from English. Gua abandoned the project in 1747, and the publishers made a new contract with Diderot and d'Alembert as coeditors to produce not a translation but an entirely new and far more comprehensive work. Diderot was to receive 7,200 livres over the next three and a half years, 1,200 in a lump sum at the outset and monthly payments of 144 livres thereafter. D'Alembert, who was to be responsible for the scientific articles, received 2,400 livres. The disproportion between their responsibilities is evident in this difference in payment. In August 1748, the editors and publishers were granted a royal privilege—as we have seen, a requirement for legal publication in old regime France. Thus the thirty-six-year-old Diderot and his thirty-two-year-old coeditor launched the most ambitious publishing project of the century (73–82).

The payments for the *Encyclopédie* improved the finances of the Diderot household, which moved to a larger apartment in the Latin Quarter. But this income was hardly sufficient, and Diderot supplemented it between 1746 and 1749 by publishing four other works, all anonymous. The first was *Pensées philosophiques*, which earned a condemnation by the Parlement of Paris for its skepticism about religion; the second, published in 1748, was a scurrilous novel called *Les bijoux indiscrets* (The Indiscreet Jewels), for which he received 1,200 livres from the publisher (Proust [1962] 1995, 93). In the same year, he published a compendium of essays on mathematical questions and the following year (anonymously) *Lettre sur les aveugles à l'usage de ceux qui voient* (Letter on the Blind, for the Benefit of Those Who See). The *Lettres sur les aveugles* was one of Diderot's most interesting and original philosophical works. It used the experience of those deprived of sight—how their lack of visual stimulation produced hypersensitivity of senses of touch and sound—to explore sense perception's shaping of our knowledge of the world. It applied to the blind John Locke's notion that our mind can know only what sense perception fur-

nishes it. Diderot's consideration of the case of the sightless made especially radical the ultimate relativity of truth. This freewheeling book included speculations that seemed to bring into question the existence of
God as the ultimate source of knowledge (96–101).

The taint of atheism got Diderot into serious trouble, together with
the suspicion that he had also written *Les bijoux indiscrets* and a previous
philosophical text entitled *La promenade du sceptique* (The Promenade of
a Skeptic). As Voltaire had discovered before Diderot, it was works that
cast doubt on verities of the Christian faith that were most dangerous in
the eyes of the state. On July 24, 1749, Diderot was arrested and imprisoned in the Chateau de Vincennes, on the eastern outskirts of Paris. He
denied writing these works, but the Paris police interrogated Durand, his
publisher, who admitted that Diderot was indeed the author. However,
Durand was also a member of the consortium of publishers who hired Diderot to edit the *Encyclopédie*. The consortium made a formal plea to the
authorities on Diderot's behalf, declaring that "the detention of M. Diderot" threatened to "bring about our ruin." He was, they claimed, "the only
man of letters we know of capable of so vast an enterprise" (105). After
three weeks of imprisonment and interrogation, Diderot confessed and
vowed never again to print work containing such excesses. He was then
allowed to leave his cell and to do editorial work on the *Encyclopédie*, but
he remained confined to the chateau's grounds (104–10). Eventually he
promised his captors to "do nothing in the future that might be contrary
in the slightest respect to religion and good morals" (112) and was freed,
after more than three months of confinement (116).

This experience of imprisonment made Diderot more cautious. He
did publish his *Lettre sur les sourds et muets à l'usage de ceux qui entendent
et qui parlent* (Letter on the Deaf and Dumb for the Use of Those Who
Hear and Speak), which was a companion piece to his letter on the blind,
but only after obtaining a tacit permission. But many of the imaginative
works for which he is now best known—for example, *D'Alembert's Dream*,
The Nun, *Jacques the Fatalist*, and *Rameau's Nephew*—were published only
posthumously. He feared that their publication would send him back to
prison and make impossible the completion of the *Encyclopédie*. Unlike
the wealthy Voltaire, secure in his estate at Ferney, Diderot had to behave
with a prudence that deprived his contemporaries of some of his most
provocative writings.

For the next quarter century, Diderot persevered doggedly, pour-
ing his immense talent into the grand project of the *Encyclopédie*. The
first two volumes appeared in 1751, the third in 1753, and then one a year
through 1757. This brought the project through the letter G. The success

of the early volumes enabled Diderot to obtain, in 1754, a more generous arrangement with the publishers: he was to receive twenty-five hundred livres upon the publication of each of the volumes, which were to
appear annually. He was also granted ownership of the books furnished
to him for his editorial work, the value of which probably amounted to
something like five hundred livres a year. And he was promised a payment of twenty thousand livres upon completion of the final volume.
Proust estimates that between 1754 and 1757, Diderot's annual income
probably reached about thirty-five hundred livres, enough for his family
to move to a larger apartment once again. This income was hardly handsome, but it at least elevated the Diderots from poverty (Proust [1962]
1995, 98).

The list of authors published in the *Encyclopédie* in these early years
was impressive. Besides Diderot and d'Alembert, many top men of letters
contributed articles, including philosophes like Voltaire, Montesquieu,
Turgot, and Quesnay and scientists like Daubenton and Buffon. Rousseau wrote on music, Morellet on religion, and Marmontel on literature.
These triumphant years of the *Encyclopédie* in the 1750s marked the ascension of the philosophe movement to the center of French intellectual
life. Besides his editorial work, Diderot wrote an astounding number of
articles himself on an extraordinarily wide range of topics. In particular,
he prepared articles on the mechanical arts, which constituted one of the
most remarkable features of the *Encyclopédie*. To include the mechanical
arts in an encyclopedia was to treat them no differently than such matters as poetry, theology, physics, philosophy, or natural history. In the article "Arts" in volume 1, Diderot—himself an artisan's son, it should be
remembered—extolled the value of the mechanical arts, vowing to raise
them "from the debasement where prejudice has held them for so long"
(Diderot and d'Alembert 1751, 1:171). The mechanical arts, he argued, were
in fact practical applications of science, even if, all too often, the artisans
themselves were ignorant of the scientific principles behind their practices. To write adequately about mechanical arts, Diderot noted, the man
of letters had to be well versed in natural history, chemistry, mechanics,
geometry, and physics. Armed with this knowledge, he had to visit the
workshops and interview the artisans: "He will grasp the whole nature
of a process, no motion of the hand will escape him, for he will easily
distinguish a meaningless gesture from an essential precaution" (Diderot
and d'Alembert 1755, 5:647). By essentially following this procedure, Diderot produced detailed analytical descriptions of many trades practiced
in France. These were eventually supplemented, between 1762 and 1772,
by detailed illustrations. Diderot's attention to the mechanical arts and

their disdained practitioners was a powerful assertion of the equal dignity of all occupations.[3]

If the mechanical arts were a chief focus of Diderot's efforts in the early 1750s, he also wrote on dozens of other topics. His subjects ranged, in volume 1 alone, from "Acrimonie" (Acrimony), "Amour" (Love), "Anagramme" (Anagram), and "Bonheur" (Happiness); to "Açores" (Azores), "Afrique" (Africa), and "Bedouins"; to "Anarchie" and "Bible."[4] In the first few volumes, most of the philosophical and theological topics were written by a team of enlightened clerics: the abbé Yvon, who wrote "Âme" (Soul), "Aristotelisme" (Aristotelianism), and "Athées" (Atheists); the abbé Mallet, who wrote "Abstinence" and "Absolution"; the abbé Pestré, who wrote "Baconisme" and "Cartésianisme"; and the abbé Prades, who wrote "Certitude." But this collaboration was brought to an unfortunate end when the abbé Prades was engulfed in a major scandal. In 1752, his doctoral thesis at the Sorbonne was censured as contrary to doctrine on the grounds that it contained sacrilegious ideas—for example, the common philosophe notion that the senses are the source of our ideas. He was forced to flee to Holland and eventually found refuge with Fredrick of Prussia. The ensuing scandal also cast doubt on the abbés Yvon, Mallet, and Pestré, who had to cease their collaboration with the *Encyclopédie*—although the abbé Morellet, who had befriended the abbé Prades during his studies at the Sorbonne, stepped in to contribute such articles as "Fatalité" (Inevitability) and "Foi" (Faith) in volumes 6 (1756) and 7 (1757). After the loss of this team of clerical collaborators, Diderot shifted his own emphasis from the mechanical arts, where he recruited various experts to write articles, and turned increasingly to philosophical, political, and even theological topics. Thus he authored the entries on "Consolation," "Corruption Publique" (Public Corruption), "Cyniques" (Cynics), "Droit Naturel" (Natural Law), "Eclecticisme," and "Epicurisme" in volumes 4 and 5, published in 1754 and 1755. Such topics remained among Diderot's specialties right through to the final volumes, with such articles as "Ressurection," "Scepticisme," and "Théosophes."

The abbé Prades affair began a period of worsening relations between the *Encyclopédie* and its conservative critics in the state and church. In 1752, further publication of *Encyclopédie* volumes was initially forbidden,

3. The *Encyclopédie* remains a precious record of eighteenth-century industrial processes, frequently used by historians of work, technology, and the life of common people.

4. A list of the articles attributable to Diderot is available in Proust (1996, 538). The online ARTFL Encyclopédie Project indicates the authors of all articles for which the author can be identified: http://encyclopedie.uchicago.edu/node/176.

but Malesherbes, the friend of the philosophes who oversaw the book trade for the royal government, granted a "tacit permission" that enabled publication to go forward. The volumes continued to appear on a yearly basis through 1757, when volume 7 was published. But at this point, the publication of further volumes was suspended by the state. The reasons for suppressing publication were multiple. The Seven Years' War, which pitted France and Austria against England and Prussia, was raging, and the French were not faring well. The philosophes, who had expressed much sympathy for English ideas and institutions, were regarded with suspicion by conservatives at the court and in the Parlement of Paris. Moreover, many philosophes, including Diderot and d'Alembert, had previously corresponded with and expressed admiration for the philosophe prince Fredrick the Great, now France's enemy. In this heated climate of wartime suspicion, there was an attempted assassination of Louis XV in December 1757, which provoked a great conservative panic and an accusation that the *Encyclopédie* propagated irreligion and hence rebellion. In this atmosphere and in the wake of the suppression of publication of further volumes, d'Alembert was so discouraged that he resigned as coeditor, never to return.

Making things worse, in 1758, Helvétius, a wealthy financier who hosted a philosophe salon regularly attended by Diderot, d'Alembert, and other prominent philosophes, published an openly atheist tract called *De l'Esprit* (On the Mind). This book was denounced in 1759 by the Parlement of Paris as part of an organized project "to propagate materialism, to destroy religion, to inspire a spirit of independence and to nourish the corruption of morals." Helvétius's book, it declared, was simply an abridgment of the arguments of "the Encyclopedical Dictionary . . . which according to its true purpose should have been the book of all knowledge and has become instead the book of all error."[5] A few months later, the *Encyclopédie* was "suppressed in its entirety" by a royal decree (336). The project seemed dead.

The publishers of the *Encyclopédie*, however, did not accept this conclusion. They had a small fortune tied up in the promised volumes and, supported by the stalwart Diderot, decided to carry forward their work, assuming that at some point the ban would be lifted. But the cast of authors was sadly diminished by the government's repressive action: Voltaire, Rousseau, Turgot, Quesnay, Morellet, Marmontel, and many others ceased their collaboration. Diderot continued his work as editor and kept writing articles. The Chevalier de Jaucourt, a widely educated sword

5. Citied in Wilson (1972, 333).

noble with a medical degree from Leiden, became Diderot's most trusted and diligent associate, writing thousands of mainly shorter articles on the widest variety of subjects. Hence the work of editing went forward behind closed doors, and the pages of the volumes were printed in secret and set aside for the moment when they could be bound and delivered to customers. This strained the finances of the publishers, who had to pay their printers without a corresponding stream of revenues. The Chevalier de Jaucourt, in addition to his heroic duties as writer and editor, lent the publishers twelve thousand livres in 1761. In that same year, the cash-strapped publishers protected their cash flow by converting thirty thousand livres they owed to Diderot into an annuity at 5 percent per year (435). Only in 1766 did the state lift the ban, enabling the accumulated volumes to be delivered (503). The volumes of illustrations, the production of which began during this fraught period, were delivered to customers between 1766 and 1772.

Thus in 1772, at the age of fifty-nine, Diderot's work on the *Encyclopédie* was finally complete. The immense task had dominated his existence since he first signed on as a young man of thirty-three. It had also provided the great bulk of his income, an income that rose slowly over time. The 1760s were difficult, since the publishers were gaining no income. However, Diderot's father died in 1759 and left him a decent inheritance, and the annuity created for him by the publishers in 1761 produced an additional income of fifteen hundred livres per annum. Wilson estimates that Diderot's annual income in the early 1760s was about forty-five hundred livres—a decent sum, but not enough to provide his beloved daughter with a suitable dowry. It was only when Catherine the Great purchased his library in 1765 that his income rose above what Turgot had declared a "comfortable" revenue for a Parisian—six thousand livres a year (Proust [1962] 1995, 98). Catherine offered him fifteen thousand livres for the library—which he had accumulated largely as gifts from the publishers to enable him to carry out his editorial work. She also granted him continued use of the books until his death and paid him a stipend of a thousand livres a year to act as the library's curator. In 1766, she paid him the first fifty years of his stipend, some fifty thousand livres, in advance—a sum that would yield an annual income of twenty-five hundred livres. This was yet another beneficence, since she surely did not imagine that Diderot would live to the age of 106. From this point forward, according to Wilson, Diderot's income from his combined investments amounted to about sixty-five hundred livres a year (514). He had achieved the income of a prosperous Parisian bourgeois. But with this new prosperity came the dependence on a patron that he had hitherto avoided.

As the end of the *Encyclopédie* came in sight, Diderot complained in a letter to Sophie Volland that the task had "consumed a life that I could have rendered more useful and more glorious"—noting, however, that he had no choice because he had a wife and daughter to support (Proust [1962] 1995, 115). Diderot had become particularly embittered when he learned that Le Breton, the publisher with whom he was working after 1759, had secretly purged the later volumes of some of their more daring passages in order to escape condemnation by the state's censors. According to Diderot, this "treason" mutilated his work and that of his collaborators (471–79). But Diderot's gloomy reflection about misspending his life and talents was hardly justified. By undertaking and carrying to completion the most famous literary and intellectual project of the European Enlightenment, his work on the *Encyclopédie* had certainly covered him in glory. Yet in spite of his accomplishments and his Europe-wide fame, Diderot was never elected to the Académie Française, although many scribblers of far less talent were: his reputation as an atheist absolutely barred the way.

In spite of Diderot's steadfast devotion to the *Encyclopédie*, he also worked on other projects. Between 1756 and 1759, Diderot turned his hand to theater. He completed his first play, *Le fils naturel* (The Illegitimate Son) in 1757, although it was not performed by the Comédie-Française until 1771; *Le père de famille* (Father of the Family) was completed in 1759 and performed two years later. Neither was a box office success. However, Diderot immediately published both dramas and accompanied the texts with what turned out to be epoch-making critical commentaries on the theater. The published versions, with the commentaries, were republished repeatedly, eventually in virtually all major European languages. Diderot criticized existing French theater for its unrealistic and stilted quality. Plays were written in poetry rather than prose; the stories were borrowed from the distant past and focused only on the doings of the great; the acting required more declamation than feeling; the actors barely moved; the stage was cluttered with seats for privileged customers; and the sets were poorly designed. Diderot argued for a *drame bourgeois*, a bourgeois drama that would treat the lives and moral dilemmas of ordinary men and women—bringing a kind of dramatic civic equality to the stage. He also insisted that the stage sets should be realistic and striking, that actors should move freely around a stage cleared of spectators, and that speech should be natural and demonstrate emotions realistically. Thus Diderot, who showed little talent as a dramatist, became the most important drama theorist of the century, with an immense impact on the dramatic arts all over Europe (1, 260–74, 321–22).

During this same period, Diderot also became a strikingly original critic of visual arts. A close friend of his, Melchior Grimm, was the editor of a handwritten chronicle of Parisian society and intellectual life known as the *Corréspondance littéraire*, which was sent to its distinguished foreign subscribers (including several crowned heads) in diplomatic pouches. During an absence from Paris in 1759, Grimm engaged the ever-impecunious Diderot to write a critique of that year's biennial art salon at the Louvre. Diderot's critique was so brilliant and so well received by Grimm's readers that thereafter the job fell to him whenever he was in Paris, right up to 1781, two years before his death. Diderot became a truly original critic of the arts (367–71).

But after the catastrophe of 1758–59, Diderot published virtually nothing other than the *Encyclopédie*. He continued to write prolifically. His most significant published writing from this period—aside from the *Encyclopédie*—was his voluminous contribution to *L'Histoire des deux Indes* (History of the Two Indies), but this was anonymous, since the publication was officially the work of his good friend, the abbé Raynal (1780). Many of the works for which he is now best known were put away in a drawer, to be published only after his death. This was true of his remarkable fictions and dialogues, all of which would surely have been troubled by the censors for their materialism or their shocking sexual content—including *La religieuse* (The Nun), *Supplément au voyage de Bougainville* (Supplement to Bougainville's Voyage), *La rève de d'Alembert* (D'Alembert's Dream), *Le neveu de Rameau* (Rameau's Nephew), and *Jâcques le fataliste* (Jacques the Fatalist).[6] But he also declined to publish his *Apologie pour l'abbé Galiani*, a refutation the abbé Morellet's critique of Galiani's *Dialogue sur le commerce des bleds* (Dialogue on the Grain Trade).[7] As Wilson remarks, "The real Diderot, the Diderot that the present generation . . . has come to esteem and admire, revealed himself in these unpublished masterpieces" (345). Disgusted by censorship and what he regarded as the small-mindedness of his own time, Diderot wrote what he wished, hoping, as Wilson remarks, for the positive judgment of posterity (714–17).

Diderot's reputation in his own time rested not only on his publications but also on his abilities as a raconteur and conversationalist. The abbé Morellet first encountered Diderot around 1750 in the rooms of the abbé Prades—whom he had befriended while studying at the Sorbonne.

6. These books are available in various editions, both in French and in English translations.

7. Available in Diderot (1995).

After Prades was forced to flee as a consequence of his notorious thesis, Morellet continued to meet Diderot, but in secret so as to avoid the scandal of an abbé befriending a well-known atheist. For Morellet, it was unquestionably worth the risk. He wrote in his memoirs, "The conversation of Diderot, an extraordinary a man . . . had great power and great charm; his discussion was animated by a perfect good faith, subtle without obscurity, varied in its forms, brilliant in imagination, rich in ideas that elevated those of others. . . . I have experienced few pleasures of the spirit superior to these." Although Morellet was and remained a deist who resisted Diderot's atheism, he notes, "There never was a man easier to live with or more indulgent than Diderot: he bestowed his own intelligence onto others. His wish was to make proselytes, not precisely to atheism, but to philosophy and reason" (2010, 65). Marmontel's remarks about Diderot confirm this picture: "With his calm and persuasive eloquence, his face shining with the fire of inspiration, Diderot spread his enlightenment into all minds, his warmth into all souls. Those who have only known Diderot through his writings didn't know him at all" (2010, 417).

Although the *Encyclopédie* imposed monumental demands on his time, Diderot was an intensely sociable man who relished good conversation. He made frequent visits to the Café de la Régence in the Palais-Royal to watch chess matches and encounter conversational partners. It was there that Diderot set his famous fictional conversation with Rameau's nephew. Rousseau, who formed an intense (but ill-fated) friendship with Diderot in 1742, remarks that in the 1740s, he, Diderot, and the philosophe abbé de Condillac met for dinner and conversation every week at a hotel in the Palais-Royal. Diderot, Rousseau added, never missed one of these dinners, in spite of his reputation for habitually failing to show up for other engagements (Rousseau 1973, 246).

Diderot, like most of the philosophes, also spent many evenings at salons. Although Diderot was rare among philosophes for living by his pen, many of his dinners—although not those of his wife and daughter—were supplied by the wealthy nobles and financiers who hosted salons. It was also in part through salons that he made the acquaintance of other men of letters and of influential nobles and government officials. Wilson notes that when Diderot was imprisoned at the Chateau de Vincennes in 1749, he mentioned to his captors various people who he felt would vouch for his character, including the literary stars and darlings of the salons Voltaire and Fontenelle, the famous scientists Buffon and Daubenton, the financier Helvétius, and the noble lady Mme du Deffand. The latter two presided over famous salons, and the others Diderot most likely got to know at one salon or another (111).

Diderot was also a frequent participant in the salons of Madame Geoffrin, Julie de Lespinasse, and Mme Necker. He was a particularly assiduous guest at the Sunday and Thursday dinners of the Baron d'Holbach and the Tuesday dinners of Helvétius—the two most radically philosophe salons of the era. D'Holbach, a wealthy German baron, and Helvétius, an even wealthier tax farmer, shared Diderot's atheism and materialism, although their salons included many with different opinions. Both published books denounced by the authorities as materialist and counter to religion—although their wealth and connections kept them from Diderot's or Voltaire's fate of spending time in Vincennes or the Bastille (Helvétius 1758; Holbach 1770). The salons attended by Diderot were meeting places for philosophes but also for sympathetic or curious nobles and royal officials and for intellectually adventurous foreigners visiting or stationed in Paris. Writing about d'Holbach's salon, the abbé Morellet lists, among others, David Hume, John Wilkes, Laurence Sterne, the abbé Galiani, Cesare Beccaria, Lord Shelburne, David Garrick, Benjamin Franklin, and Joseph Priestly (2010, 147–48). Diderot's fame as a conversationalist was, consequently, not limited to France.

Although Diderot avoided patronage as a means of making a living—until the sale of his library to Catherine—he made use of the connections forged at salons to recruit nobles and state officers as authors of articles for the *Encyclopédie*. Proust points out that over a quarter of the known authors of articles in the *Encyclopédie* were employed in "the state apparatus," virtually all of them robe nobles (1995, 27). Proust also notes that Diderot made use of his friend Buffon, the famous naturalist who was the author of several articles in the *Encyclopédie* but was also well connected at the court, to gain state positions or advantages for various friends and allies—indeed, in one case for his younger brother the abbé Diderot (1995, 24–25). And he made multiple efforts to convince various officials to find a position for his son-in-law. These were unsuccessful, but the son-in-law nevertheless developed a successful career in the iron industry (613–14, 655–56, 677–78, 682). Diderot's desire for complete intellectual liberty led him to avoid the entanglements of patronage and deference as much as possible, entanglements that most impecunious men of letters sought avidly as the only available path to a decent income. Yet even Diderot played the game of influence to win advantages for his friends and kinsmen and to recruit authors for his life's great project—quite apart from accepting hundreds of free dinners. In the profoundly hierarchical society of the French old regime, to refuse to play the game of patronage altogether would have been nearly impossible.

Diderot's relationship with Catherine the Great must have confirmed his views about the dangers of patronage. Catherine's gesture was exceptionally generous and, on the surface, required nothing of Diderot. But it soon became clear that Catherine wanted something in exchange for her generosity: she expected the reluctant Diderot to visit her court in Saint Petersburg. Finally, in 1773, about a half year after his daughter's marriage, Diderot finally took the plunge. He was a reluctant traveler: prior to his trip to Russia, he had seen only Langres, Paris, and the countryside around the capital where his friends had country estates. It was only in Holland, after the initial leg of his voyage to Saint Petersburg, that he first saw, and was enchanted by, the sea (619). He spent a few months in Holland on his way to Saint Petersburg visiting his old friend Dmitri Galitzin in the Russian embassy in The Hague. Holland he found extremely congenial. Leaving that nation on his return to Paris from Russia, Diderot called it "the country of liberty" and remarked that "one of the things throughout all of Holland that continually and deliciously affects one is that one never encounters there either the sight of abject poverty or the spectacle of tyranny" (652).

After an exhausting journey via Dresden and Leipzig, Diderot finally arrived in Saint Petersburg in October 1773, at the age of sixty. There he was welcomed into the Russian Academy and treated as a great celebrity. He had no interest in court life, but he soon had daily appointments with Catherine to engage in lengthy discussions ranging over literary, political, legal, and economic questions. He tried to persuade this exceptionally intelligent and well-read but despotic monarch to embrace more liberal ways—to establish universal public education, to reform the laws, to free the economy, to base government employment on merit, and so on (632–35). Catherine was not converted to his ideas. She later related that had she followed Diderot's advice, "every institution in my empire would have been overturned . . . for the purpose of substituting some impracticable theories" (640). Diderot returned to Paris via Holland the following spring, having seen little of Russia and having had negligible influence on Catherine but having fulfilled his onerous obligation to his benefactor.[8]

This arduous journey seems to have affected Diderot's health. Upon his return, he was seen less at salons and seemed to have aged markedly—he was sixty-one by then, elderly by the standards of the time. He nevertheless continued to write: much of his work for *L'Histoire des deux Indes* was composed in these later years, as was his *Réfutation de l'ouvrage d'Helvétius intitulé L'Homme* (Refutation of the Work by Helvétius Entitled Man). He also composed two works intended for Catherine of Russia, *Observa-*

8. On Diderot's visit to Russia, see Zaretsky (2019).

tions sur le Nakaz, a lengthy critical commentary on the law code she had decreed, and *Plan d'une université pour le gouvernement de Russie* (Plan of a University for the Government of Russia).[9] He also wrote two books that were actually published, both reflections on the ancient Roman philosopher Seneca—a philosophical witness of despotism who was forced to commit suicide by the corrupt emperor Nero (Diderot 1779, 1782).

During this final period, Diderot turned his attention primarily to questions of politics, broadly conceived. In Russia, he had encountered an exceptionally intelligent ruler who nevertheless presided over a despotic political regime; in Holland, he had seen a country much more liberal in its laws and customs than France. These surely stirred his interest in government and political philosophy. These were also years of intense political conflicts in France, which saw a particularly repressive regime headed by the chancellor Maupeou replaced, in 1774, upon the death of Louis XV and the accession of Louis XVI, by an all-too-brief liberal experiment headed by the philosophe Controller General Turgot.

Diderot's commentary on the Nakaz, originally intended for the eyes of Catherine but not sent to her until after his death, dissected and criticized the extensive and—in Diderot's eyes—despotic law code she had decreed (650–52). And he responded to that same monarch's request for ideas for a reform of Russian education with a lengthy outline of a comprehensive state-run system that would provide education to the entire population (something no European state had yet achieved), fill teaching positions by open competition, and establish advanced training in faculties of arts, medicine, law, and theology. Such a system, which would have codified a career open to talent in Europe's most backward country and have made Russia's education system the envy of Europe, was, of course, entirely utopian (674–76). These works on Russia long lay dormant in the Russian archives. His contributions to *L'Histoire des deux Indes* were published, but not under his own name. In the many pages he wrote, Diderot openly expressed his deep humanitarianism, deploring the horrors visited on natives of the Americas by the Spaniards and other Europeans and denouncing Europeans for their enslavement of Africans.

Diderot never developed a systematic political theory, but the writings of the late years provide a consistent political outlook. He assumed a social contract view of the political world, with personal liberty and property as natural rights. He was no republican, but he believed that the authority of monarchs arose from the consent of the people and should

---

9. These works, as well as a selection of Diderot's contributions to Raynal (1780), are available in Diderot (1995).

be limited by the laws. He hated religious fanaticism and despotism and lauded freedom of thought and humanitarianism. He espoused a fundamental equality of rights and opportunities but assumed that differences in wealth and status were inevitable. And he believed that thanks to the spread of enlightenment, human society was progressing toward these goals. As we shall see, many of these themes were destined to be prominent in the legislation of the early phase of the French Revolution. This was not because the revolutionaries learned them from Diderot's political writings, which long remained unknown. Rather, the political ideas that Diderot arrived at in the 1770s partook of and reflected the increasingly dominant ideas of the philosophe movement as a whole—a movement in which Diderot's *Encyclopédie*, not to mention his conversation, had played a foundational role.

The Abbé Morellet

BETWEEN PUBLISHING AND PATRONAGE

The abbé André Morellet constructed a career as a man of letters that was in one respect the opposite of Diderot's: he made his way in the world above all by means of patronage. Like Diderot, he grew up in a modest family: his father was a paper retailer in Lyon, and André was the eldest of fourteen children. As Morellet put it in his memoirs, his father's "trade, limited like his capital, hardly afforded him the means to give his children the long and costly education that could form a man of letters" (2010, 44).[1] Morellet found his way forward through the church, which provided him an excellent education but no career. Although he duly entered the priesthood, he had no religious vocation, never preached a sermon, and held no church office, until, on the eve of the Revolution, he was awarded a rich benefice as a reward for his services to the state as an advisor and polemicist for liberal causes—a benefice snatched away shortly afterward by the Revolution's confiscation of church property.

Robert Darnton, in his justly famous essay on "The High Enlightenment and the Low-Life of Literature," uses Jean-Baptiste-Antoine Suard, a stalwart of the salons, to show how an obsequious writer of mediocre talent could use patronage to construct a career as an honored and prosperous man of letters; Suard lived well and was eventually elected to the Académie Française. Darnton remarks that Morellet "might do just as well" as an example of the cosseted philosophes of their generation who had, essentially, sold out to the old regime—this in contrast to the embittered following generation of writers who found all the good positions already occupied by these intellectual nonentities and were obliged to live by their pens in the "grub street" of scurrilous pamphleteering (Darnton

1. Subsequent citations to this work will be in parentheses in the text.

1982, 3).[2] I think Morellet, who indeed rode his literary talents to prosperity, fame, and the Académie Française by pursuing patronage, represents his generation of philosophes much more favorably than that does Suard. Morellet's case demonstrates that it was possible to profit from patronage and nevertheless remain a committed philosophe—indeed, a stalwart critic of old regime institutions.

Morellet was born in 1727, fourteen years after Diderot. He pursued his education at Lyon's Jesuit college—the rough equivalent of the modern lycée or middle and high school. He complained, in his memoir written at the age of seventy, that he was "neglected by my first teachers, because of the mediocrity of my condition." In the early years, "I was constantly one of the last in the class and was whipped regularly every Saturday, as an example and instruction to the others." However, in his third year, "I happily found as a master a young Jesuit . . . a kind and humane man, who discovered some talent in me and who lent his hand to pull me out of the oppression in which I had previously languished." At the end of the year, he won first prizes in two subjects in a class of eighty to one hundred students. The following year, he won two prizes and an honorable mention—in spite of a rhetoric teacher who was "a Jesuit and a nobleman . . . who didn't think much of the small talents of the son of a small shopkeeper" (44–45). Decades later, at the twilight of a highly successful career, Morellet still resented the injustices visited on him by teachers who had disdained his social origin.

When André was fourteen, his family decided to invest in his further education, making use of family and patronage connections. Morellet had an uncle "who in the family was called 'the doctor,' because he read the gazette." The doctor "maintained some relations with the family of the superior of the Seminary of the Thirty-Three in Paris." By means of this connection, the doctor arranged for André to be received there "for the modest cost of three hundred francs . . . with the promise that if I showed some application and some talent, I would have a scholarship" (46). This was Morellet's first big break. He excelled at the Parisian seminary, where he found that his mediocre background had one advantage over his more privileged fellow scholars: he "had less trouble than others in submitting to the hard life led there, not having been spoiled in my father's household." Morellet's talents and hard work were soon recognized by his teachers, and he became a tutor to younger students, relieving him

---

2. Darnton later wrote a fine account of Morellet's pursuit of patronage, but one that minimizes his intellectual contributions (1995b). On Morellet, see also Gordon (1994, 177–241).

of further tuition payments. He obtained a degree of bachelor in theology, "in a manner that was called distinguished in the narrow sphere of the schools" (46–47).

After this success, Morellet wished to continue his studies at the Sorbonne, the pinnacle of ecclesiastical education in France. Such a pursuit was beyond the means of his father, but Morellet convinced a wealthy cousin, whose recently deceased father had risen from cabin boy to captain of a vessel of the French East India Company and had left him a fortune, to give him the thousand livres he needed (47). "To enter the Sorbonne, one had to submit to examinations, give a good account of one's conduct and morals, and for those, like me, who came from obscure families, show some hope of merit and success." Morellet was accepted and lived in the buildings of the Sorbonne, with some ten to twelve other students and thirty professors and doctors of the Sorbonne. They had at their disposal a church, a garden, heated rooms, a rich library, and a prepared dinner every evening (49).

His fellow students included some young nobles who were "destined by the old order of things to occupy the highest ranks of the clergy" and who might well, he remarks, have been able to help him attain in the future "the small fortune that I could reasonably aspire to" (51). He specifically lists "M. Turgot," who like Morellet entered the Sorbonne in 1748; the abbé Loménie de Brienne; and the abbé Boisgelin de Cussé. All three were freethinkers, and they were indeed destined to have famous careers, Boisgelin de Cussé as bishop of Aix-en-Provence and Loménie de Brienne as a bishop, as a cardinal, and briefly as controller general on the eve of the Revolution. Morellet never gained patronage from Brienne or Boisgelin, other than invitations for lengthy visits at Brienne's magnificent chateau. Turgot, however, played a crucial role in advancing his career. Destined for the clerical order by his father but lacking a religious calling, Turgot left the Sorbonne upon his father's death in 1750 before completing his studies. He then pursued a brilliant career in the royal administration, leading to an ill-fated term as controller general.[3]

Morellet treasured the years spent at the Sorbonne, where he "was called only 'le bon Morellet'" (the good Morellet). He earned this nickname even though he was then "as I have never ceased to be, violent in my [intellectual] disputes, but without my antagonist ever reproaching

---

3. It is a telling indication of the pervasiveness of hierarchy in eighteenth-century France that Morellet always refers to his friend and age-mate Turgot as "M. Turgot," using the abbreviation for the honorific "Monsieur." He never uses an "M." before the names of Diderot, d'Alembert, Marmontel, Rousseau, and their like.

me for even the least insult. My heat was only for my opinion, and never against my adversary" (57). Although he necessarily studied theology and church doctrine, Morellet and his friends had secular opinions and were steeped in Enlightenment philosophy: "I lived in the library. I knew no one but my confreres. I never went to the theater, because I lacked money. . . . I devoured books: Locke, Bayle, Le Clerc, Voltaire, Buffon . . . Clarke, Leibnitz, Spinoza . . . and because several of my confreres brought the same ardor to their studies that I did, our discussions were new and powerful means of instruction" (58). Morellet and his friends deviated from church doctrine by favoring tolerance for all religions: "civic toler-ance of all peaceful sects, allowing them to engage in worship publicly, even admitting them to state and civil employments—in a word the es-tablishment of no difference between a Jansenist, a Lutheran, a Calvinist, even a Jew, and a Catholic, for all purely civil duties, obligations, burdens, and effects." Here Morellet's views clearly foreshadowed the Revolution's embrace of civic equality. He claims that when such opinions appeared in their theses, their professors disapproved of the opinions but caused them no scandal (68–69). These seemed golden years to the seventy-year-old Morellet looking back on his life: "I spent in the Sorbonne, in these sweet illusions, nearly five years, always reading, always disputing, always poor, and always content" (57–58).

Eventually, Morellet took the examination for his *licence* in theology—for which all that reading and discussion of such secular authors as Locke, Voltaire, Buffon, Leibnitz, and Spinoza were surely of limited use. Morel-let remembered ranking fourteenth or fifteenth in a class of some 120 can-didates for the licence. But he added, "I can believe that there were not really fifteen of my confreres who were better than I; but I was obscure, I had no protectors; and I was very content with my lot" (58). However, finishing his licence meant expulsion from paradise. Too poor to pursue a doctorate, he had to "think about opening a road toward the small for-tune to which I aspired, which then consisted simply in having enough to stay alive." As was true for so many well-educated abbés with no reli-gious vocation, "making myself into a parish priest was . . . impossible for me to accept" (60). Nor did he imagine himself ready to make a living as a man of letters. But he found a position as the tutor for the son of a nobleman: the abbé de la Galazière, a youth several years younger than Morellet who was studying at the Collège du Plessis in Paris and prepar-ing for what would surely be a successful career in the church. This posi-tion netted Morellet a yearly salary of a thousand livres with lodging and nourishment at the collège (62).

Morellet lived in reasonable comfort as a tutor. He developed a good relationship with the young man and remained in the Latin Quarter where he could visit his former Sorbonne friends during his free time. He had sufficient leisure to learn Italian and English, "to read good books, and to accustom myself to writing" (64). He saw Turgot and the abbés de Brienne, Prades, and Bon regularly. He also, as we have seen, developed a friendship with d'Alembert and Diderot, having met the latter on a visit to the abbé Prades: "One can imagine how much my youthful nature was flattered by this commerce with men of letters who had begun to make a name in the world. I took in their opinions, but not with the docility of a novice in relation to superiors. I debated their opinions and they did not disdain mine. I had no conversation with them that failed to raise within me a new ardor for knowledge" (70). As previously noted, Diderot commissioned several encyclopedia articles from Morellet, mainly on religious subjects. These were among his first published writings.

It was during his years as a tutor that Morellet developed an interest in what would become his specialty: political economy. Morellet notes that "although metaphysical questions, which had nourished my youth, continued to occupy much of my thinking, I was imperceptibly led to more solid studies, no less abstract for those who wish to plumb their depths, and more useful to mankind when one succeeds in reaching the goal" (72). The key moment of this transition to political economy was brokered by Turgot, who, unlike Morellet, was wealthy and well connected and was working toward a career in royal administration (71). In 1755, Turgot introduced Morellet to Jacques-Claude-Marie Vincent de Gournay, an *intendant de commerce*, a high official in the state's principal economic policy office. Gournay brought to this position an interest in English political-economic writings and a distaste for the highly regulated economic policies established by Colbert in the seventeenth century and still dominant in the French administration. Gournay, whose work and influence will be discussed in chapter 12 of this book, established a celebrated salon devoted to the study of political economy: what has generally come to be known as "the Gournay circle." Gournay recruited several young and eager men of letters who quickly produced a torrent of innovative books and pamphlets on economic topics (Charles 2011). Turgot and several other members of the royal administration were regular participants, including Daniel Trudaine, the director of the Bureau of Commerce, effectively France's minister of economic affairs.

The abbé Morellet was one of the ambitious young members of the Gournay circle who published a tract on economic matters. As mentioned in chapter 4, since the 1720s, there had been an ordinance forbidding the manufacture, the sale, or even the wearing of printed cotton cloth in

France. The ordinance had been established at the behest of the French silk and woolen industries, which feared competition from the increasingly popular inexpensive and brightly colored printed Indian cloths. Daniel Trudaine opposed this ordinance but could not do so publicly, since he was expected to support the government's policies. Therefore, he recruited Morellet to write an anonymous pamphlet criticizing it. Morellet responded with a brilliant tract that ridiculed the prohibition, arguing that the ban held back French industry and commerce and violated "each person's natural right to dress according to his fancy and as cheaply as possible" (1758, 54). The pamphlet appears to have been effective: a few months after its publication, the government, headed by the Controller General Silhouette, himself a member of the Gournay circle, granted the freedom to manufacture printed cottons. Within a decade, the French cotton-printing industry was flourishing and was one of the few industries to compete successfully with its English rivals (Chapman and Chassagne 1981). In his *Mémoires*, Morellet remarks that this change in policy "was in large part the fruit of my work" (77).

If this may be an exaggeration, it is certainly true that Trudaine was pleased with Morellet's effort. Thereafter, Morellet became Trudaine's hired pen, entrusted with writing critical pamphlets on various issues of economic and administrative policy and also with preparing administrative memoirs. Morellet was not given a salaried position in the Bureau of Commerce; he was more valuable as a formally independent man of letters publishing his opinions about contemporary issues at commercial presses. Over time, Morellet received from Trudaine and from Trudaine de Montigny, his son and successor in office, various substantial "gratifications" (monetary gifts) and annuities.

Morellet's patronage link with the Trudaines was, typically for such arrangements, both advantageous and constraining. Morellet was never asked by the Trudaines to write anything that was counter to his own beliefs. Indeed, he and the Trudaines shared a very similar outlook. Daniel Trudaine was one of the most convinced reformers in the royal administration and certainly one of the most efficacious.[4] Trudaine de Montigny sustained these efforts when he succeeded to his father's position after the latter's death in 1769. Like many other royal officials, the Trudaines found the arguments of the political economists highly convincing. The enviable economic successes of England and the Netherlands, which both had much freer economies than France, offered persuasive examples. Moreover, the assumptions at the heart of political economy fit well with a ra-

---

4. Trudaine's career will be discussed in chapter 13.

tionalizing administrative logic. Like political economists, administrators tended to evaluate citizens (the word *citizen* was increasingly in circulation in both philosophe and administrative circles) more in terms of their contribution to public welfare and to the taxes they paid than in terms of their place in a hierarchy of privilege and preference. The Trudaines' arrangement with Morellet was, hence, mutually advantageous. Morellet gained a good income, published books and pamphlets that burnished his reputation, and acquired a highly placed protector. He presumably also gained some income when he sold his manuscripts to the publishers, but this paled in comparison to the income that flowed directly or indirectly from the Trudaines. The relationship was also valuable to the Trudaines, who gained an apparently independent collaborator using his access to commercial publishing to propagate arguments, theories, and perspectives on public affairs that, if sufficiently compelling, might smooth the way to desirable legal and administrative reforms.

It is important to recognize that a well-developed commercial publishing industry was a sine qua non for a patronage relationship of the kind forged between Morellet and the Trudaines. Morellet claims to have made next to nothing from the sales of his books, but his lucrative patronage relationship would have been unthinkable in the absence of a flourishing book market. It was the existence of commercial publication and of the thousands of readers who bought books that undergirded the philosophes' novel role. The conception of the philosophe as a free and independent-minded intellectual whose writings might inform the public and policy makers alike was a product of the emerging commercial society of eighteenth-century Europe. It was the well-established role of the philosophe that made a writer like Morellet, who was in fact dependent on a royal official, appear, both in the eyes of the public and in his own eyes, as a fully independent and hence believable philosophical critic of the administration. Here, as so often in old regime France, the strategies of both patron and client braided together the logics of the market with the benefits of deference and patronage.

Morellet's arrangement with the Trudaines was the foundation of his successful career, but it was also constraining. Although Morellet cared deeply about public policy and was happy to engage in intellectual combat for causes he regarded as just and rational, his time was not entirely at his disposal. This especially became a problem later in his career, when he had determined to write a dictionary of commerce. This work, which was to be Morellet's magnum opus, was to be an alphabetical encyclopedic dictionary in five folio volumes, with the entries divided into three categories: "commercial geography," "objects and materials of commerce," and "the theory of commerce and its operations." Morellet published a lengthy prospectus for his dictionary in 1769, and his publisher began to accept subscriptions (Morellet 1769c). Trudaine arranged for Morellet to receive an annual indemnity of four thousand livres to support the project. Two-thirds of this total, Morellet tells us, was spent on office expenses, including the salaries of two highly skilled assistants.

Morellet had a bad conscience about not completing his dictionary, which he finally abandoned after twenty years of work because the French Revolution made further progress impossible. As he confessed in his memoir, "I do not dissimulate that the abandonment of this enterprise . . . is the great fault of my literary life." He points out, however, that he faced "many unexpected obstacles" (185). Of these, the greatest was his obligations to his benefactors. During the time he was working on the dictionary, a number of "questions of administration arose," and not only the Trudaines but various other high government officials asked him to provide writings of various sorts. Controller General Maynon d'Invault requested two tracts against the French East India Company; Trudaine de Montigny, backed up by the duc de Choiseul, Louis XV's very influential foreign minister, requested a work in favor of freedom of the grain trade; Trudaine requested a tract against the rogue pamphleteer Linguet; Sartine and Lenoir, successive prefects of police of Paris, asked for memoirs about the Parisian food supply; and finally his old friend and benefactor Turgot, when he became controller general in 1774, asked Morellet for numerous memoirs on administrative matters (191–92).[5] "In short," Morellet wrote in his memoirs, "a great part of my life, which I would have liked to devote to this work [the dictionary], was stolen from me, by the ministers themselves, or at least was employed for their benefit" (193).

Morellet's experience makes clear the double-edged character intrinsic to even the most benign of patron-client relations. Morellet's connections to the Trudaines, brokered by Turgot and Gournay, enabled this son of a poor paper retailer to live in comfort in the capital, to be acquainted with some of the most powerful men in the royal administration, to have enough leisure to pursue a life of learning, and to have a palpable influence, by means of his writings, on some of the great economic and political issues of his time. But this entailed appropriate gratitude and deference to his patrons and meant that he had to be ready to drop whatever he was doing to compose the latest necessary polemic or administrative brief. Only in his *Mémoires*, written after his patrons had all died (and

---

5. Four of these works were published: Morellet (1769b, 1769c, 1744, 1775b).

not to be published until after his own death) could Morellet express the frustration and resentment that gave a faintly melancholy tinge to his remarkably successful life.

In spite of the occasionally onerous yoke that his position as a client of powerful patrons placed upon his neck, Morellet's life was unquestionably rich and rewarding—financially as well as intellectually. Upon leaving the Sorbonne, his goal had been simply "having enough to stay alive" and continuing his pursuit of letters (60). The position he gained as a tutor fulfilled this desire. He had time for intellectual pursuits, made a trip to Italy with his young abbé, and managed to integrate himself into the capital's social life of letters through acquaintances with d'Alembert and Diderot and especially, thanks to Turgot, his participation in the Gournay circle. When the abbé de la Galazière moved on to the Sorbonne in 1759 and no longer required a tutor, the young man's father granted Morellet a pension of one hundred pistoles (one thousand livres) per year (109). This seems to have been the first of many pensions Morellet was destined to accumulate. However, one presumes that Trudaine must have paid him something for writing his tract on the printed-cotton question, and Morellet notes that during his Italian trip with the abbé Galazière, he carried out tasks there for Trudaine. He collected and translated from the Italian "memoires about public economy" and collected samples of woolen and cotton cloths imported to Italy from England. These were to be used as "objects of imitation by our French manufactures" (106). This work was surely remunerated.

Morellet's *Mémoires* only occasionally indicates how he accumulated the wealth that, by the mid-1770s, seems to have afforded him an annual income of some seven or eight thousand livres—well above the threshold of the six thousand that Turgot claimed was necessary for a comfortable bourgeois lifestyle. By 1776, when he was fifty-three, Morellet had pensions that paid him seven thousand a year. He also had his annual four-thousand-livre payment for his work on the *Dictionnaire du commerce*, over a thousand of which he seems to have taken as a personal salary. In addition, he remarks, "I gained from time to time something from my little literary works" (235). Morellet's income from this source must have paled by comparison with his accumulating pensions. And the pensions continued to accumulate in later years. In 1777, he inherited a *rente viagère* (life annuity) worth 1,275 livres a year upon the death of Mme Geoffrin, who had long welcomed Morellet into her famous salon. In 1783, Lord Shelburne, an English diplomat who had befriended Morellet and had sponsored his extended trip to England in 1772, convinced Vergennes, the French foreign minister, to award Morellet a pension of four thousand livres a year. The reason for this largesse was that Shelburne had been inspired by his conversations with Morellet to include provisions for free trade in the treaty he had just negotiated with France at the end of the American Revolutionary War. Finally, in 1788, Morellet gained a lucrative church benefice worth fifteen thousand to sixteen thousand livres in rentes (presumably in tithes), the succession to which Turgot had granted him during his period as controller general (1774–76) (310–11). Thus Morellet was able to claim that in 1788, his income was "nearly thirty thousand livres in rentes, in benefice, and in pensions" (246). This sum would have been envied by many a nobleman.[6] In short, this son of a modest paper seller had become a wealthy man. The accumulation of wealth, however, was not destined to last: everything but his rente viagère from Mme Geoffrin was wiped out by the reforms of the Revolution, which confiscated the lands of the church and abolished all crown pensions. Morellet scraped through the most difficult years of the Revolution on this modest pension alone.

In short, Morellet's life as a famous man of letters was supported almost entirely by patronage. But if the patron-client ties with the Trudaines, Turgot, and other royal administrators were constraining, they did not reach deeply into his personal life: so long as he treated his administrative patrons with appropriate deference and carried out his assigned literary tasks—which Morellet did with personal conviction—he was free to spend his time as he wished. Morellet was a consummate man of the salons. Beginning with the Gournay circle in 1755, Morellet eventually became a regular guest at literary dinners and suppers of various descriptions. Indeed, his extensive remarks about salons in his *Mémoires* have served as a major source for scholars studying the subject (Goodman 1994; Lilti 2005).

Morellet was introduced to Madame Geoffrin by Trudaine de Montigny in 1759. He became a regular at her famous dinners from then to the time of her death in 1777. She organized one dinner on Sunday that centered on artists and another on Wednesdays for men of letters. The Wednesday dinner included, among others, d'Alembert, Helvétius, the baron d'Holbach, the abbés Galiani and Raynal, Marmontel, Thomas, Mademoiselle Lespinasse, and others—not to mention a constant stream of distinguished visiting foreigners. Mme Geoffrin directed the conversations ably, keeping them lively but generally steering them away from

6. One way of evaluating the worth of this income is to calculate the amount of investment funds needed to produce 30,000 livres at 5 percent a year: 600,000 livres. This would have been a considerable fortune for a nobleman in eighteenth-century France.

criticism of the government or the church.[7] But upon leaving the dinners, the philosophes in attendance often repaired to the nearby Jardin des Tuileries, where, as Morellet puts it, they would meet up with other friends and "criticize (*fronder*) the government and philosophize at our ease . . . abandoning ourselves to a conversation as animated and free as the air we breathed" (110).

In 1760, a year after his introduction to Mme Geoffrin's salon, Morellet experienced a setback: he suddenly found himself imprisoned in the Bastille. He had written a brief *libelle*, a satirical critique of a comedy entitled *Les Philosophes*, which was playing at the Comédie-Française. This play had raised his ire and that of his friends by mercilessly ridiculing the encyclopedists and philosophes. After showing his libelle to d'Alembert and Turgot, who found it "splendid," he had it printed by an old friend in Lyon. When the copies arrived in Paris, Morellet distributed them to peddlers. "It was read everywhere; in the Tuileries and at the Palais Royal one could see groups of readers laughing uproariously." Morellet also "read it in a few houses. . . . Everywhere I heard it called excellent" (114–15). But his satire made fun of Mme de Rebecq, a royal princess who was dying of tuberculosis and who loathed the philosophes and their doctrines. She had attended the opening night of the play and had welcomed its author to her box to congratulate him. When she learned of Morellet's libelle, she demanded that the author be punished. If it could be dangerous to criticize the royal administration and more dangerous to publish works regarded as blasphemous, it was foolhardy to satirize members of the royal family. Morellet, revealed as the author by one of the peddlers, was duly locked up in the Bastille for two months (115–16).

The sojourn in the Bastille actually enhanced his career as a man of letters. He was well fed and well treated. Malesherbes, who had gotten to know Morellet at the Gournay circle, sent him books, and Morellet used his solitude to read constantly. During his two months of confinement, he read, in English, Hume's four-volume *History of England* and his *Philosophical Essays*, all of Tacitus in Latin, and some twenty-four novels from the Bastille's library. He drafted a treatise on the freedom of the press, never published, but that, he says, proved useful in later publications (117–19).[8] Meanwhile, he consoled himself that his imprisonment might advance his "literary glory": men of letters would appreciate his entering

---

7. After her death, Morellet wrote an *éloge* in her praise (1777). The *éloge* (a eulogy) was an extended obituary of the deceased and was a common eighteenth-century literary form.

8. Presumably the later publication was Morellet (1775).

the fray on their behalf, and "men of the world, who like satire, would welcome me more than ever" (120). These thoughts were not disappointed: "I found a doubling of friendship in M. Turgot, M. Trudaine de Montigny, Diderot, d'Alembert. . . . Many houses, those of the baron d'Holbach, of Helvétius, of Mme de Boufflers, of Mme Necker, were opened to me with ease." And Trudaine treated him indulgently, judging that "when he was truly attempting to attain the public welfare I would be as good as ever to employ for the various labors" required (140).

Of the salons that he frequented, Morellet particularly valued that of the baron d'Holbach. The baron's salon assembled "the leading French men of letters: Diderot, J.-J. Rousseau, Helvétius, . . . Suard, Marmontel, Saint-Lambert, La Condamine, le chevalier de Chastellux, etc. The baron himself was one of the best educated men of his time, knowing several European languages . . . having an excellent and copious library, a rich collection of drawings . . . excellent paintings, a cabinet of natural history." The baron's salon also attracted "all the foreigners of merit who came to Paris." D'Holbach hosted two dinners a week, one on Sunday, the other on Thursday. The society there "was so truly engaging that having arrived at two o'clock . . . nearly all of us were still there at seven or eight in the evening" (147–48). The conversations were wide ranging, and "there were no bold questions of politics and religion that were not set forth and argued, for and against, nearly always with much subtlety and depth." This included the "absolute atheism" embraced by "Diderot . . . and the good baron himself," argued with "a persuasion, a good faith, and an edifying probity, even for those among us who, like me, did not believe in their teachings." The good number of "theists" present "defended themselves vigorously, but all the while loving our atheists who were such good company" (149). Morellet quotes as an example the abbé Galiani, the secretary of the ambassador of Naples: "Messieurs les philosophes, you are going too fast. I begin by telling you that if I were pope I would send you to the Inquisition, and if I were the king of France, to the Bastille, but since I have the good fortune to be neither the one nor the other, I will come back to dine with you this coming Thursday and you will listen to me just as I have had the patience to listen to you" (150).

Helvétius's salon, according to Morellet, "brought together more or less the same persons as that of the baron d'Holbach, on different days; but the conversation was less good and less sustained." Neither Mme d'Holbach nor Mme Helvétius had much interest in philosophy, but Mme d'Holbach sat in her corner without talking, while Mme Helvétius, "beautiful, with an original mind and a piquant nature . . . disrupted the philosophical discussions." Moreover, Helvétius himself was less engaged in the conversations than was the baron. But if Morellet did not appreciate Mme Helvétius as a participant in the intellectual discussions of the salon, he was deeply attached to her in other ways. He was introduced to her by Turgot, who had been her close friend in their youth. She and Morellet became very intimate: "In the following spring she brought me to her country house in Lunigny and from there, in the month of August, to her country house in Voré. In Paris, her house became mine; rarely did a day pass without my seeing her; all my evenings were devoted to her and often in the morning we would ride horses together in the bois de Boulogne. When she was at one of her country houses without me, or when I left Paris for a trip, we maintained an active and singular correspondence. . . . I can say that there are few examples of a liaison as close, as sweet, and as durable as that which attached me to her, a liaison that was sustained from 1760 to 1791," when they were torn apart by the French Revolution. Mme Helvétius, as seems clear from Morellet's account, was the love of this secular abbé's life (153–54).

Morellet was, by the early 1760s, a regular participant in three salons that met, between them, four times a week: that of Mme Geoffrin on Wednesdays, of Helvétius on Tuesdays, and of d'Holbach on Sundays and Thursdays—with occasional visits to that of Mme de Boufflers and others. In the mid-1760s, Morellet, Marmontel, and the abbé Raynal were approached by Mme Necker, who wished to establish a salon of her own. She was the wife of a wealthy Swiss banker who later served, twice, as controller general. She chose Friday for her dinner in order not to conflict with those of Geoffrin, d'Holbach, or Helvétius. In addition to Morellet, Marmontel, and Raynal, Mme Necker's dinner attracted Grimm, Thomas, the chevalier de Chastellux, and others. M. Necker sometimes attended but said little. The conversation, according to Morellet, was good, especially on literary subjects, but was "constrained by the severity of Mme Necker," whose Protestant scruples forbade discussions that broached religion (163–64).

Finally, Morellet also established a salon of his own. In the mid-1760s, he had moved to a spacious apartment on the stylish rue Saint-Honoré overlooking the Jardin des Tuileries (237, 242). He had a "society of women and of men of letters" that assembled for lunch (not for "*diner*" but for "*déjeuner*") and conversation on Sundays. It was devoted largely to conversations about literature and art and often included musical performances (241–42). His own salon seems to have constituted a more aesthetic counterpoint to the intensely philosophical discussions at the salons of d'Holbach and Helvétius.

Morellet was a supremely sociable man. By the mid-1760s, he regularly attended salons of the baron d'Holbach, Helvétius, Mme Geoffrin, and Mme Necker. These filled every afternoon except Monday. He also paid calls on other salons. Attendance at any of these salons except his own was of course optional rather than compulsory, but to judge from his own account, he must have attended frequently. His evenings, he tells us, were devoted to Mme Helvétius. In the summers, he seems to have spent much time at her country houses but also made visits "to M. Trudaine, to Brienne, etc." (256). Yet Morellet always found time to write. Speaking specifically of his experiences at Brienne's opulent chateau, he notes, "In the midst of these dissipations and parties . . . I never lost from view the principal object of my studies and works, on which I busied myself with a great assiduity. I retired early in the evenings and I worked for half of the day without leaving my room, abstaining from lunches in society, promenades, hunting parties and other distractions" (255–56). Morellet's mornings were probably devoted to writing and study in Paris as well as in the countryside.

Morellet was a prolific author—and was sufficiently respected to be elected to the Académie Française in 1785. According to my count, the catalog of the Bibliothèque Nationale de France lists forty-nine distinct titles. Some of these works are very brief, and a surprising number come from the years after 1789, when he wrote several pamphlets and was eventually forced to live by his pen. But there were numerous works in the pre-revolutionary years. The Bibliothèque Nationale de France also lists, by my count, twelve translations by Morellet, most of them from English— mainly novels translated to replenish his purse after the French Revolution confiscated his fortune. Morellet also translated works from Italian, including, in 1766, Cesare Beccaria's *Essay on Crimes and Punishments*— one of the most celebrated works of the international Enlightenment (Beccaria 1766). Although this work sold well, Morellet writes that it "gained me almost nothing, given the great cleverness of the publishers and the great ineptitude of men of letters . . . in matters of interest" (171). The English novels he translated in the 1790s were surely more remunerative. In 1786, he published a translation of Thomas Jefferson's *Observations on Virginia*, but he claimed that it was only the publishers who made any money from it (275). He also translated Adam Smith's *Wealth of Nations* shortly after its publication in 1776. This translation, however, was never published because one abbé Blavet beat him to the punch. This he regarded as a loss for French understanding of political economy. "My translation," he wrote in his *Mémoires*, "is carefully done, and everything that is at all abstract in Smith's theory, unintelligible in Blavet, who is ignorant in these matters, can be read in mine with great utility" (237).

Virtually all of Morellet's unpublished administrative memoirs, and most of his published books—as opposed to reprinted speeches, *éloges*, brief controversial pamphlets, and the like—treated some aspect of political economy. Like his tract against the prohibition of calicoes, these works argued for freeing manufacturers, peasants, and merchants from constraints on their enterprise. He wrote an unpublished memoir for Trudaine against the system of tariffs restricting commerce between regions of France, three criticisms of the monopoly held by the French East India Company, and two works in favor of freeing the trade in grain (Morellet 1769b, 1769c, 1787, 1774, 1775a). The red thread that runs through Morellet's economic writing is that the system of privileges and restrictions governing so much French economic life should give way to a system of equal access to markets for all citizens. This was, of course, a central feature of eighteenth-century arguments for civic equality, one that was embraced by important figures in the royal bureaucracy well before the Revolution. It therefore should not be surprising that he enthusiastically welcomed Adam Smith's seminal work and went to the trouble— unrewarded in the end—of carefully translating that very long and, in its day, difficult and abstract book.

The work that I believe best represents both the abbé Morellet's ideas and his situation as a writer and intellectual is his *Réflexions sur les avantages de la liberté d'écrire et d'imprimer sur les matières de l'administration* (Reflections on the Advantages of the Freedom to Write and to Publish on Matters of Administration), published in 1775. In spite of its ponderous title, this was a radical document and a spirited attack on a long-standing principle of royal government—that the affairs of the crown were to be regarded as "the king's secret" and therefore were not to be criticized by his subjects. This was a principle honored as much in the breach as in the observance in the eighteenth century. But in 1764, Controller General L'Averdy, who had made the controversial decision to abolish laws restricting the trade in grain and presumably was worried about an outpouring of hostile pamphlets, had Louis XV issue a decree that, in the words of Morellet, "forbade the printing or sale of all writings, works, or projects concerning the reform or the administration of finance."[9] Morellet enthusiastically favored free trade in grain, but he was outraged that this desired reform was accompanied by a prohibition on precisely the kind of writings to which he had dedicated his career—writings of the sort that had, moreover, helped pave the way for the policy of free trade in grain. He quickly drew up a defense of the utility of publications on what

---

9. The quotation is from the title page of the book.

he called "the political economy of interior administration" (1775c, 3). Prudently, he showed his manuscript to Trudaine, who, Morellet tells us, approved of it. But he could not obtain permission to publish it—until 1774, when Louis XVI had succeeded Louis XV and had named Morellet's friend and benefactor Turgot as controller general (158).

In this work, Morellet argues that "ignorance of the true principles of administration" keeps societies from attaining prosperity. Such principles are the goal of "that most important science called political economy," but in the current state of knowledge, the key terms of political economy, such as "commerce, riches, circulation, credit, luxury, liberty, property, etc.," are uncertain and disputed (1775c, 3–5). Moreover, erroneous political-economic notions are currently in circulation. Examples are the claim that "the acquisition of gold and silver" is the most important source of wealth; the claim that societies have departed too far from nature and consequently should give up "the arts that embellish life" and should establish laws that would deprive individuals of the "properties whose possession was the very object of the formation of societies";[10] and the claim that economic life should be devoted to "the increase of political power" and the pursuit of war (1775c, 5–7). Discovering "the true principles of political economy" is difficult, Morellet asserts, both because political economy is a new science and because the matters it considers are complicated. Political-economic questions, he points out, affect "all parts of a political society [*corps politique*]," and a "law that appears useful relative to one matter" may be "harmful to another." Hence even "the most accurate mind will be unable to arrive at the truth on its own." It is, Morellet claims, printed works that most effectively offer otherwise isolated minds the necessary help (1775c, 8–9).

Morellet judges that political economy had made remarkable progress in France, thanks largely to "works written and published at the solicitation" of M. de Gournay (1775c, 10). The principle of liberty of commerce had gained increasing acceptance, but many questions, including how to prevent "the monstrous inequality of property and wealth," could not simply be deduced from the principle of liberty of commerce. Such problems could only be solved when "an analytic knowledge of the entire organization of society and a complete theory of political economy" had become available. There was a "system of the social world to be discovered" by political economy, Morellet suggested, parallel to "the physical world that was discovered by Copernicus and Newton" (1775c, 13–14). He noted

10. This was a reference to Rousseau and those who had been influenced by his first two discourses (1751, 1755).

that political economists were reproached for being *hommes à systems,* or system builders. While enemies of the philosophes used this term as an insult, Morellet countered that systematic thought—"organized ideas, settled principles, and consequences drawn from these principles"—was precisely what was needed to clarify the consequences of government policies (1775c, 43). A well-developed "abstract science of political economy" would make it possible to "calculate the obstacles" standing in the way of good policies and make it possible to "discover the means of surmounting them" (1775c, 47).

But establishing correct principles of political economy depends on free publication. If writings on these subjects take the form of memoirs intended only for the eyes of administrators, they will lack published works' great advantage: that only published arguments are subjected to public critique and judgment. Here Morellet's account of public critique bears the marks of the specifically face-to-face public sphere that he experienced in the Parisian salons. It is, he claimed, above all the discussion of works by "learned persons" (*gens instruits*) that assures the advance of knowledge. In these discussions, "one examines, one attacks, one defends, and one sees enlightenment born from the shock of ideas and opinions." Conversation "gives birth to ideas that one would not acquire in several years of work. . . . The way another sees the object that occupies you . . . makes you see it from different angles. The difficulties raised make you realize the weakness of your opinion, or if you can resolve them, give it a new degree of solidity" (1775c, 24–25). Untrammeled publication of works on political economy and administration, combined with the discussion that ensues, would ensure the advancement of knowledge, the enlightenment of public opinion, and the improvement of government policies.

Some features of Morellet's argument would strike the modern reader as utopian. He imagined that public opinion, once it is "instructed by writings and by discussion," would become a "faithful guardian" of the truths that have emerged from publication and critical discussion. Once "a nation is instructed about its true interests," Morellet asserted, public opinion would have a powerfully stabilizing influence on government policy. Ministers may continue to come and go, but "the stability of public opinion and the instruction extended to all orders of citizens" would guarantee the permanence of enlightened economic policies (1775c, 19). This trust in the stability and wisdom of public opinion, which was widely shared by intellectuals and political commentators in the later decades of the old regime, may have been utopian (Baker 1990, 167–99). But this utopia arose from the concrete experiences of men like Morellet, who had risen from utter obscurity to positions of influence on the basis of their intelligence and their ability as writers and conversationalists, who had witnessed "philosophic" ideas initially nurtured in salons embraced by powerful government ministers, and who had, in fact, through their published work and critical discussion, done much not only to influence public opinion but to launch the very notion of public opinion as a regulative political principle. In exalting public opinion as the arbiter and beacon of public policy, Morellet and his friends were projecting into the future an idealized vision of their own experience as Parisian philosophes.

Morellet's *Réflections sur les avantages de la liberté d'écrire* can be read as an argument for the sort of civic equality and individual freedom that was eventually enacted by the French revolutionaries. The eleventh clause of the Declaration of the Rights of Man and Citizen would proclaim that "free communication of ideas and opinions is one of the most precious rights of man. Every citizen may therefore speak, write, or print freely." The abbé Morellet's account makes clear that he and his fellow philosophes managed, under the old regime, to speak and write with an essentially unlimited freedom. Actual publication was more complicated: Morellet's book was itself published only a decade after it was written, when a friendly and particularly liberal ministry was in power. Yet there was no shortage of critical or subversive books circulating in France. Publication was, in the end, a commercial affair; if a publisher believed a book had a market, it would find its way into print and be made available for sale— if often printed abroad or clandestinely.

A burgeoning commerce in books, both licit and illicit, was a condition of possibility for the career of the philosophe. The Parisian salons that nourished Morellet's intellectual life were at once a forum for the critical discussion of new printed works and a proving ground for ideas that would find their way into print. Books were also central to a man of letters' economic strategies. Although the author's revenue from printed work was rarely lucrative, sales of books to publishers were one source of earnings. As we have seen, Diderot, who was a sort of limiting case, received almost all his meager income over the first thirty years of his career from his work on the *Encyclopédie*. For Morellet, by contrast, revenue from publishing made only a small contribution; the great bulk of his considerable income was attributable to patronage. But the patronage was also completely dependent on commercial publishing: he was rewarded by his reforming administrator patrons with pensions and rentes because he dependably wrote and had published powerful and apparently independent tracts in favor of the policies they wished to institute. Morellet, to judge from his memoirs and from his *Réflections sur les avantages de la liberté d'écrire*, did not see himself as the hired pen that, formally speaking, he was but as a free and independent philosopher cum political economist writing on issues of policy and administration in his own voice and by his own volition. He seems to have viewed his sizable income not as accumulated patronage but as a just reward for his zealous and publicly valuable work as a critical intellectual. In this sense, Morellet lived, and lived happily, what we might call the real contradiction that constituted the social position of the eighteenth-century French philosophe.

Jean-Jacques Rousseau

SELF-DECEIVED CLIENTAGE

The life of Jean-Jacques Rousseau is far better known than that of Diderot or Morellet, thanks to his widely read *Confessions* (1973).[1] Rousseau's *Confessions* are quite different from Morellet's *Mémoires*. They begin with these extravagant words: "I undertake an enterprise that has no example and will have no imitator. I wish to show to my fellow men a man in all the truth of nature; that man will be me" (34). Rousseau intended to recount the history not only of his actions and thoughts but also of his moral and emotional life: his desires, fantasies, obsessions, passions, and shameful deeds. I will not dwell on his emotional and moral life, which has been analyzed at length elsewhere, although Rousseau's exceptionally passionate and self-contradictory temperament was, as we shall see, intimately connected to his career as an antiphilosophe philosophe (Starobinski 1971, 1988). Happily for my purposes, the *Confessions* also provide ample material on the practical side of his career as a man of letters.

Rousseau, the son of a watchmaker in the Calvinist city of Geneva, Switzerland, was born one year earlier than Diderot, in 1712. His mother died a few days after giving birth to Jean-Jacques. He was raised in early childhood primarily by his father. A brother, who was seven years his senior, became "libertine" at an early age and ran away from home, never to return. Jean-Jacques learned to read by the age of five or six. He recounts that he and his father had read together all the novels his mother had left them and then progressed to more serious books, including works by Molière, Bossuet, La Bruyère, and Fontenelle. His favorite author was Plutarch, who "formed this free and republican spirit, this indomitable and proud character . . . which has tormented me for all of my life"

---

1. Citations to this work will be in parentheses in the text. Translations are mine. I have also used the three-volume biography of Rousseau by Maurice Cranston (1982, 1991, 1997).

(36–38). In Rousseau's tenth year, his father had an altercation with another Genevan citizen and was forced into exile in Nyons, in a neighboring canton. Jean-Jacques was sent to live with a Protestant pastor for schooling, along with his cousin, the son of his mother's brother (41–42). At thirteen, he was apprenticed to a clerk of the court; finding the work insupportable, he became an engraver's apprentice (62). At sixteen, he and his friends returned to Geneva late after a daylong country ramble and found the gates closed. Knowing he would be thrashed by his master for staying out late and unhappy with his life and the trade he was learning, Rousseau decided to flee (75–78).

The following day, Rousseau presented himself to a priest in a town just across the border in Savoy. This priest, who specialized in converting Genevan heretics, directed him to "a good and charitable woman," one Madame de Warens, who lived in Annecy, some twenty-five kilometers to the south (82). Rather than the elderly woman he had expected, Rousseau discovered that Madame de Warens was a charming noblewoman of twenty-nine, originally from the Swiss canton of Vaud. She had abandoned her Protestant husband, fled to the kingdom of Savoy, embraced Catholicism, and placed herself under the protection of King Victor-Amadeus, who awarded her a modest pension (84–85). Rousseau was immediately stunned by her beauty and kindness: "Madame de Warens inspired in me, from the first interview, the first word, the first sight, not only the liveliest attachment but a perfect confidence that has never left me. . . . My heart was nourished by an entirely new sentiment that occupied my whole being" (87–88). He nevertheless had no choice but to leave Annecy a few days later with the blessings of Madame de Warens, traveling to Turin, the capital of the Kingdom of Savoy, where he entered a hospice for catechumens, there to undertake his conversion to Catholicism (90).

Here began a picaresque two-year period of Rousseau's life. He hated the hospice and had no taste for the religious teachings. But after two months, he abjured Calvinism, was baptized, was absolved by an inquisitor of the crime of heresy, and was put into the street with a paltry twenty livres. He found work in a printing shop presided over by a beautiful young woman but was turned out when her husband returned from a long voyage. He then became a servant to a noblewoman dying of breast cancer. After her death, the nephew who succeeded her found him a position as a servant in a count's household. But when a friend showed up and suggested a trip back over the Alps, Rousseau couldn't resist—hoping for a reunion with Madame de Warens (96–146).

When the eighteen-year-old Rousseau returned to Annecy in 1729,

Madame de Warens took him into her household. From this time forward, she called him *Petit* (little one), and he called her *Maman* (Mama)
(147–50). Rousseau assisted Madame de Warens in her occupation of
growing and preparing medicinal herbs and advanced his stunted education by reading from her library (154–56). Thinking that the priesthood
might be a proper occupation for Rousseau, Maman sent him to Annecy's
seminary, but he returned when his instructors found him unfit for the
religious life (163–68). He then began to study music, initially with the
music master at Annecy Cathedral (168–81). Returning to Annecy after
a brief voyage to Lyon, Rousseau found that Madame de Warens had left
for an extended trip to Paris (179). Her chambermaid, a woman a few
years Rousseau's senior, determined in the absence of her mistress to return to her native Fribourg, in Switzerland. Rousseau, at wits' end, agreed
to accompany her (193).

This trip, undertaken in the autumn of 1730, began a year of vagabond-
age through Switzerland. Soon destitute, he began earning a paltry living
in Lausanne and Neuchatel teaching music, which he understood poorly:
"I gradually learned music while teaching it" (205). The following spring,
he took up with a Greek Orthodox priest from Jerusalem who was attempting to collect funds for a restoration of the Saint Sepulchre Church.
After several weeks, Rousseau abandoned his priest in the canton of Solo-
turn and worked briefly for the French ambassador there. Eventually he
left for Paris on foot to take up a position as tutor to the son a friend of the
ambassador—and in search of Madame de Warens. When the promised
position was not forthcoming, the ambassador's mother took him under
her wing and attempted to find Madame de Warens—learning that she
had recently left Paris. Rousseau then returned on foot to Annecy. Stopping in Lyon, he learned that Madame de Warens had moved to Chambéry, some thirty-five kilometers south of Annecy.[2]

When, in 1731, he arrived at his patron's house in Chambéry, she welcomed him and quickly obtained a position for him working on Savoy's
land survey (229). At first this employment suited him—he was ready for
a more tranquil life—and he quickly learned the necessary mathematics.
But after eight months, he found the work dull and returned to teaching
music, mainly to young women (235, 243–45). On his return to Madame
de Warens in Chambéry, he learned that her gardener, who had taught
himself botany and assisted her in the preparation of herbal medicines,
was also sharing her bed (233). After Rousseau began teaching music,

2. This paragraph is a vastly simplified version of the account Rousseau relates in book
four of the *Confessions* (1973, 193–228).

Madame de Warens decided that "to save me from the perils of youth, it was time to treat me as a man"—that is, to have sexual relations with him as well. He reports that he was ambivalent but eventually accepted her proposal. "Was I happy?" he asked. "No, I tasted the pleasure. But I know not what invincible sadness poisoned the charm. It was as though I had committed an incest" (255). This feeling is hardly surprising, considering that Rousseau was a motherless child, that he was totally dependent on Madame de Warens, loved her dearly, and called her "Maman." Rousseau reports that this change resulted in a stable ménage à trois, suiting all parties (261). But then the gardener fell ill with a "pleurisy" that killed him (265). This was a disaster for the household, because the gardener had effectively managed Madame de Warens' economic affairs, and Rousseau—young, dependent, and inexperienced—had neither the authority nor the good sense to restrain her follies (266–67).

Over the next three years, from 1732 to 1735, Rousseau lived with Madame de Warens but traveled frequently around the region, mainly to Lyon, Nyon, and Geneva, pursuing "music, medicinal powders, projects, voyages, floating incessantly from one thing to another, attempting to settle on something without knowing what" (280). In spite of his sexual relations with Mme de Warens, his "tender mother" and "a dear friend," he was "devoured" by a need for the love of a proper mistress—and at the same time, "tormented by the bad state of the affairs of my poor Maman" (281). Eventually he fell "truly ill." Saved by the "incredible efforts" of Madame de Warens, he remained weak and sickly for months (284). In the summer of 1736, they moved to a house in the countryside, called "Les Charmettes," for his convalescence (287).

"Here," Rousseau declares, "began the short happiness of my life . . . the peaceful but brief moments that give me the right to say that I have lived" (288). "This time when I lived in retreat and was always sick was the time of my life when I was least idle and least bored" (300). He established a daily routine: he woke before dawn, took a morning walk, and then shared a breakfast of café au lait with Maman, a late sleeper. He then began his studies, moving from philosophical works ("Locke, Malebranche, Leibnitz, Descartes"), to mathematics and Latin, which were less to his liking than philosophy. In the afternoon, he would do light gardening, have dinner, and then go on to reading subjects that required less effort, such as history and geography (301–4). It was, thus, only at the age of twenty-four that he began serious studies.

If Rousseau's intellect profited from this period at Les Charmettes, his health remained doubtful. In 1737, he took a voyage to Montpellier to consult with the professors of its famous medical faculty. During the trip, he had a torrid week-long affair with a fellow voyager, one Mme de Lanarge. He remarked, "I owe to Mme de Lanarge that I will not die without having known pleasure. . . . Proud of being a man . . . I gave myself over to my senses with joy, with confidence" (321). The medical treatment, however, did him little good. Upon his return to Chambéry, he found that Maman had taken on a new protégé who had also become her lover—a young, vigorous, and hardworking but noisy and stupid fellow. Although Maman offered him the continuation of his sexual rights, Rousseau now renounced her favors. He nevertheless remained in the household and returned assiduously to his studies (330–35).

In 1740, Rousseau left Chambéry for Lyon, where thanks to Madame de Warens's connections, he worked as a tutor for the sons of M. de Mably, a wealthy nobleman who was the *grand prévot* of the city (336–38). After a year, Rousseau decided that he lacked the patience for this position and returned to Chambéry—but soon realized that he could never again be happy there. Moreover, Madame de Warens's financial affairs had gone from bad to worse: "I envisaged nothing but ruin and disasters" for his dear Maman. Thus finally, at the age of thirty, he understood that he would have to make his own way in the world but had no clear path. "I did not feel myself sufficiently learned, nor did I believe I had enough wit to shine in the republic of letters and make my fortune by this means" (340–41). He had, however, continued to study music and had devised a novel numerical form of musical notation that he fancied would revolutionize the field. Hence he decided to go to Paris and present this scheme to the Royal Academy of Sciences (342).

Thus Rousseau arrived in Paris in 1742, well read but with no formal education and little experience of the literary world. His life had been picaresque and his sentimental education downright bizarre. He had, up to this point, been utterly dependent on the patronage of Madame de Warens, except during his extensive wanderings during the years 1728 through 1731. On his way to Paris, he called on M. de Mably, whose house he had left on good terms, and made a very fortunate connection with his former employer's younger brother, the abbé Mably, who was three years Rousseau's senior. Rousseau had already met the abbé Condillac, the youngest brother (two years his junior). Both Mably and Condillac, who became famous philosophes in their own right, had been educated in Parisian seminaries and were assimilated into the capital's intellectual life. The abbé Mably supplied Rousseau with letters of introduction, including to the aging literary giant Fontenelle, and recommended a hotel near the Sorbonne where he and his brother had lived (350). Mably also connected Rousseau with the secretary of the academy of inscriptions, who introduced him to Réaumur, a distinguished member of the Academy of Sciences, who in turn arranged for Rousseau to present his memoir on musical notation before the academicians (353–54). For an utter nobody from the provinces, Rousseau arrived in Paris with surprisingly good connections.

The commissioners who examined Rousseau's project decided that it was without merit (356). Rousseau managed to publish a defense of his system, entitled *Dissertation sur la musique modern* (Dissertation on Modern Music) in January 1743. The book sold poorly, and Rousseau made nothing from its publication. Thus "I found myself on the streets of Paris, where one cannot live on nothing" (357–58). Yet he somehow managed. He continued to visit the abbé Mably and Fontenelle and established a close friendship with Diderot.[3] He mentions that he learned chess, which he played in a café "on the afternoons when I didn't go to the theater" (358). Rousseau does not tell us how he afforded the expenses of theaters and cafés; clearly he was not destitute. A friend he met in a café, the Père Castel, suggested that he should particularly seek out women as patrons. "One can do nothing in Paris except by means of women. They are like the curves to which sages are the asymptotes; the sages approach ever closer but never touch" (360). Castel introduced him to M. Dupin, a wealthy farmer-general whose wife was devoted to music. The main fruit of this connection was that Rousseau became a close friend of Mme Dupin's son-in-law, M. de Francueil, who was also musically inclined (362–64).

Meanwhile, another feminine contact bore promising fruit. The Marquise de Broglie, another acquaintance of the Père Castel, suggested Rousseau as the secretary to the comte de Montagu, the French ambassador to Venice. Rousseau took up the position, but the ambassador, unfortunately, proved to be incompetent. Rousseau traveled to Venice, where, according to his account, he did virtually all the ambassadorial work. Finally, after a year of frustration, he resigned in disgust. To return to Paris, he had to borrow money from Venetian friends and colleagues in other embassies. Eventually the ambassador was recalled and put out to pasture, and Rousseau was repaid by the royal government for his expenses. But this simply enabled him to repay his loans, so he gained nothing for his troubles. Meanwhile, his lady patron rejected him, believing that a

3. Although Rousseau's friendship with Diderot was extremely close in his early Paris years, Diderot appears sparingly in the *Confessions*. This was probably a consequence of their later quarrels and eventual enmity.

secretary could not be in the right in a dispute with a noble ambassador.[4] This experience, Rousseau remarks, soured him on "our stupid (*sottes*) civil institutions . . . which only add the sanction of public authority to the oppression of the weak and the iniquity of the strong" (403). It also convinced him of "the inconvenience of dependence. . . . I resolved to no longer attach myself to anyone but to remain in independence by making use of my own talents" (406). Thus in 1745, renouncing the pursuit of patronage and wealth, he moved back to the Hotel Saint-Quentin, where rent was cheap.

There he encountered Thérèse Levasseur, the daughter of the hotel's new housekeeper, and began an affair with her: "I was at first seeking only an amusement. I saw that I had done something more and that I had given myself a companion. . . . I found in Thérèse the supplement I needed" (408). Rousseau affirms that he "told her in advance that I would neither abandon her nor marry her" (407)—although he did in fact marry her in 1768, when they were on the run from the French authorities. Thérèse, who seems to have had limited intelligence, was a singular companion for a man of letters. She could never learn to read, knew "not a single number," and was thus unable to count money or tell time. But according to Rousseau, "This person who is so limited, so stupid, if you wish, gives excellent counsel in difficult occasions" (409). Thérèse was to be Rousseau's companion to the end of his days. She bore him five children, all of whom were consigned to the *enfants trouvés* (the municipal orphanage) to be raised as orphans—a practice that caused Rousseau much public shame when it was revealed two decades later (422–23).

His chief project at this point was an opera, *Les Muses Galantes*, which he had conceived a few years earlier. It was finally performed at the opera in 1747, without much success. Rousseau's flagging finances were helped in 1747 by the death of his father, who left him a small inheritance (415–16). He also was offered a position by M. de Francueil and Mme Dupin, both of whom were working on books, as their joint secretary. This position was hardly lucrative, with a salary of eight hundred to nine hundred livres a year (421). However, it put him in touch with a future patron, Mme d'Épinay, who was carrying on an affair with Francueil (424). Meanwhile, Rousseau renewed his relations with men of letters, particularly his friendships with Diderot and Condillac. It was Rousseau who introduced Condillac to Diderot, who in turn convinced Durand, the publisher of the *Encyclopédie*, to publish Condillac's famous first book,

---

4. This paragraph summarizes a long account on pages 368–403.

the *Essai sur l'origine des connaissances humaines* (Essay on the Origin of Human Knowledge) in 1746. Rousseau, Diderot, and Condillac began to meet weekly for dinner and conversation at an inn near the Palais-Royal. In 1749, Rousseau met Melchior Grimm, who became a fast friend but later was to become one of his principal enemies (432). Rousseau also met Diderot's coeditor, d'Alembert, who signed him up to write several articles on music for the *Encyclopédie* (425–26).

It was in the summer of 1749 that Diderot was imprisoned in the Chateau de Vincennes. When Diderot was allowed to use the garden of the chateau and receive visitors there, Rousseau paid regular calls. On the way to one visit, he picked up a copy of the *Mercure de France* and, perusing it while walking, came upon the announcement of a prize offered by the Academy of Dijon on the subject of whether "the progress of the arts and sciences has contributed to the refinement or the corruption of morals." Upon reading this notice, he reports, "I saw another universe, and I became another man." Arriving at Vincennes, "I was in an agitation that was almost a delirium." Diderot encouraged him to "give wings to my ideas and compete for the prize. I did so, and from that instant, I was lost. All the rest of my life and of my misfortunes were the inevitable effect of this moment of madness" (430–31). Rousseau argued, in what has been generally dubbed his "first discourse," that the progress of the arts and sciences had corrupted rather than refined morals. He thereby set himself against the consensus of the philosophes, generally firm believers in progress. Although he admits that "of all the works that have come from my pen, it is the weakest in reasoning and the least harmonious" (431), it nevertheless won the Academy of Dijon's competition and established Rousseau's reputation as a serious and original thinker (Rousseau 1751; 1964, 3:3–110).

Meanwhile, M. de Francueil and Mme Dupin decided to increase his payment to twelve hundred livres, which enabled him to rent an apartment in their neighborhood on the right bank, which he occupied with Thérèse and her mother for the next seven years (432). In 1750, Rousseau learned that he had been awarded the prize by the Dijon academy. This news "reawakened" the ideas that had inspired his first discourse and "animated them with a new force" (235). He also, however, had developed a serious urinary disorder and, imagining that he would not live long, decided to "pass in independence and poverty the little time that remained of my life" and to "apply all the force of my soul to break the shackles of opinion . . . without concern for the judgment of men" (442–43). Believing that he no longer needed to think about the future, he renounced the pursuit of a lucrative position as a cashier in the financial administration proposed to him by Francueil (440–41). Recognizing, however, that he needed some means of remuneration, he decided to take up copying music by the page, believing that by this means, he could "gain my daily bread without personal subjection." He also decided to radically reform his wardrobe. "I renounced gold trim and white stockings, I wore only a round wig, I put away my sword and sold my watch, saying to myself with an incredible joy, 'Thank heavens, I will no longer need to know what time it is'" (444).

But Rousseau found this reformed mode of life difficult to realize. His bad health limited his work time. He also had no choice but to spend hours on literary work. There were the articles he had promised to the *Encyclopédie* as well as responses to attacks on his discourse, which scandalized many readers—although it charmed others. Meanwhile, his literary success meant that he received invitations he was unable to turn down. "The success of my first writings had made me à la mode. . . . My room never emptied of people who, under various pretexts, came to take my time. Women employed a thousand ruses to invite me for dinner. . . . I realized then that it is not always as easy as one imagines to be poor and independent. I wished to live by my trade, but the public would not allow it" (448–49). Among the invitations he could not turn down was to the Baron d'Holbach's salon, where Diderot had introduced him (453). In short, despite his high-minded plan, Rousseau found himself unable to live by copying music, unable to retire from polite society, and unable to renounce the patronage of the wealthy.

Torn between his vow and the demands of Parisian society, Rousseau accepted a sojourn at the country house of a music-loving distant relative who had made money in the jewelry business and had retired to Passy, near Paris. (This, of course, was another example of accepting patronage.) During his stay, Rousseau began composing a new opera, which became *Le dévin du village* (The Village Soothsayer) (454–57). The opera, even more spectacularly than his first discourse, pulled him into a maelstrom of patronage and dependence. His friend and patron Duclos, a prominent man of letters and a member of the Académie Française, arranged for a private performance, which was attended by M. de Cury, the intendant of the Menu Plaisirs, the office that organized ceremonies, plays, and concerts for the royal court. Cury was enchanted and arranged for the opera to be performed before the king at the Fontainbleau palace in October 1752. Rousseau was present in a prominent box at the theater—dressed in his everyday clothes, unshaven, wearing his poorly groomed wig, and surrounded by gentlemen and ladies of the court whose dress he characterized as "excessively ornamented" (460). The performance, he related, was poorly acted but well sung and played, calling forth tears from its distinguished audience and its author alike. Afterward, Cury informed Rousseau that the king wished to present him with a pension and asked him to appear at eleven the next morning at the chateau (461–62).

Rousseau spent the following night in agony. He was terrified that he would make a fool of himself before Louis XV and Madame de Pompadour and would be unable to show himself grateful for the honor to be bestowed without "abandoning the severe air and tone" he had so self-consciously embraced. He finally decided not to expose himself to this danger: "I would lose, to be sure, the pension that was being offered . . . but I would also exempt myself from the yoke it would impose upon me. Farewell to the truth, to liberty, to courage. How would I dare to speak thereafter of independence and disinterestedness?" Rousseau sneaked off to Paris as soon morning came. His departure, he tells us, "was much talked about and was generally condemned" (463). This decision prompted his first serious dispute with Diderot, who pulled him aside two days later when he was about to go to supper with Mme d'Épinay—one of those many women who insisted that he dine with her. Diderot argued that Rousseau had been selfish in shunning the king's patronage, especially because it would deprive his companion Thérèse and her mother of a better life.

Rousseau's relations with his once intimate friends were strained by his increasing discontent with Paris, with the salons, and with the busy— not to say hectic—existence of the Parisian philosophes. His friends were also, no doubt, annoyed by Rousseau's claims of superior virtue and his ostentatious disdain for their way of life. The men of letters valued an intensely sociable existence featuring free-ranging argumentation spiced with wit and verbal sallies. Rousseau was uncomfortable in public argumentation, verbally slow and awkward, and increasingly sententious rather than witty. The philosophes had embraced the worldliness and social hierarchy of the salons, and most of them openly sought opportunities for patronage. Their general outlook was tolerant, progressive, skeptical, and reformist. They saw French and European societies that, for all their faults and oppressions, seemed to be steadily yielding to reason, science, and tolerance. By contrast, Rousseau, in the early 1750s, was becoming a grouchy antiphilosophe philosophe. He increasingly regarded the emerging urban and commercial society as corrupt and shallow and longed for a simpler and more upright form of life. He attempted to model his own existence on his sense of virtue—hence the reform of his wardrobe and his putative embrace of poverty and of earning his bread as a simple music copyist. Yet Rousseau, as much as any philosophe, remained dependent on the generous patronage of the rich and privileged. That he nonetheless claimed a uniquely virtuous independence understandingly made this self-proclaimed moralist seem hypocritical to his philosophe friends. Rousseau's break with them was driven in part by his increasingly paranoid outlook—his tendency to see plots and conspiracies as the source of his difficulties. But the break was also based on a growing clash between his and their moral visions and ways of life.

Rousseau's friendship with Diderot, which was particularly deep, took some time to unravel. The initial quarrel took place in 1752, but the definitive break occurred only five years later. The divergence of Rousseau's thinking and mode of life from that of Diderot and his friends progressed steadily. Rousseau ceased attending d'Holbach's salon in 1753, and his friendship with Grimm frayed. Rousseau claimed—implausibly, in my opinion—that his quarrels with his friends arose from their jealousy: "They couldn't pardon my having composed an opera, nor the brilliant success of this work, because none of them would have been able to follow the same career, nor to aspire to the same honors" (471). *Le Dévin du Village* was indeed played successfully at the Paris Opera and made him a sizable amount of money. In all, he received a gift of twenty-four hundred livres from the king; twelve hundred from Mme de Pompadour, at whose chateau it was played; another twelve hundred from the Paris Opera; and five hundred from one Pissot—in short, a total of fifty-three hundred livres. This work, "which cost me only five or six weeks of labor, brought me nearly as much money . . . as was later brought to me by my *Emile*, which had cost me twenty years of meditation and three years of labor" (470). For the time being, his worries about finances were allayed.

In 1753, shortly after the success of his opera, Rousseau learned that the Academy of Dijon had announced a new essay prize, this time on the question of the origin of inequality among men. He immediately decided to enter. "In order to meditate at my ease upon this great subject, I took a trip of seven or eight days to Saint-Germain," the site of an extensive forest not far from Paris. There he took long walks in the woods. "Surrounded by the forest, I sought and found the image of primitive times, whose history I proudly traced. I took a heavy hand to the petty lies of men; I dared to strip bare their nature, to follow the progress of time and of the things that had disfigured them. Comparing man as he had made himself to natural man, I showed him that his supposed perfection was the true source of his misery" (472). These reflections formed the basis of Rousseau's "second discourse": his *Discours sur les origines de l'inégalité parmi les hommes* (*Discourse on the Origins of Inequality among Men*). Rousseau remarks that this work "was more to the taste of Diderot than all my other writings" and that it was also the work "for which his counsels were most useful to me" (473). He and Diderot, despite their differences, were still friends.

In 1754, fleeing Parisian society, Rousseau made a trip to Geneva via Chambéry, where he found Madame de Warens impoverished and diminished. He proposed bringing her to Paris to live with him and Thérèse, but she declined. It was in Chambéry that Rousseau finished and dated his discourse on inequality. He then proceeded to Geneva, where he officially reconverted to Calvinism and restored his Genevan citizenship. Indeed, he determined to take up residence in Geneva with Thérèse and to exercise fully his citizen rights (475–78). He signed his discourse "Jean-Jacques Rousseau, Citizen of Geneva" and included a long dedication to the Genevan Republic. The cool reception of his discourse by Geneva's governing council, however, caused Rousseau, by this time back in Paris, to rethink his plans for repatriation.

Shortly before his departure for Geneva, he had been visiting Mme d'Épinay's chateau a few miles to the north of Paris in Eaubonne when they happened upon a "very dilapidated little cottage called the Hermitage" on her property at the edge of the Montmorency forest. Rousseau declared in transport, "Ah! Madame, what a delicious habitation! Here is a refuge made for me!" Upon his return from Geneva, he found that Mme d'Épinay had, to his amazement, remodeled it for him. "Here is your refuge, my bear. You have chosen it; I offer it in friendship. I hope it will banish your cruel idea of parting from me!" (481). Rousseau decided to accept this offer and take up residence in the Hermitage with Thérèse and her mother. Upon his return from Geneva, he also resumed his visits to d'Holbach's salon, his resolve softened by the death of Mme d'Holbach. But when the assembled philosophes heard of his decision to leave Paris and take up residence in the Hermitage, "sarcasms fell upon me like hail." His friends swore that he would be unable to do without the amusements of the city for longer than two weeks (483). This unpleasant reception marked his final break with the world of salons.

It was April 1756 when Rousseau left Paris for the Hermitage—not to live in the capital again until 1770 (489). He remarks that he had "not a penny of rente" but that he still had two thousand livres in proceeds from his opera, that his writings yielded him something, that his work as a copyist was far from lucrative but sure, and that, moreover, his small household could live cheaply, especially now that he had "given up the most expensive needs, those dependent on opinion"—that is, his fancy clothes and wigs, his sword, and his watch. He boasts that he would not stoop to writing for money: "I sensed that to write in order to have bread would soon have stifled my genius and killed my talent . . . nothing vigor-

ous, nothing great can come from an entirely venal pen. . . . It is too difficult to think nobly when one thinks only to live." The paradox, he notes,
was that "my trade could nourish me if my books failed to sell" and that
his liberation from writing for money "is precisely what made them sell"
(488–89).

Rousseau's reflections here are not entirely lucid. First, if his copying
work made him almost nothing when living in the heart of Paris, how
could it possibly sustain him living in isolation several miles from the
city where his musician and composer customers worked and resided?
Here and elsewhere, one senses that the copy work was crucial to his
self-image but never made a serious contribution to his income. Moreover, Rousseau fails to mention in this evaluation of his economic condition that he benefited from rent-free housing thanks to his patron, Mme
d'Épinay. On the same page where he boasts of his financial independence and lack of venal motives, he states, "I found it delicious to be the
guest of my friend in a house of my choice, which she had built expressly
for me" (489). Throughout his years in this region north of Paris, Rousseau was in fact profoundly dependent on patrons for his subsistence. But
he strictly avoided the language of patronage and deference, sustaining
his self-image as virtuously independent by casting these relations purely
as a matter of friendship.

Rousseau declared that at the Hermitage, he was able to lead precisely
the life he wanted. He could devote his morning to copying music "and
my afternoon to promenades, equipped with my little white notebook
and my pencil—because, never being able to write except in the open
air, I was not tempted to change my method. . . . The forest of Montmorency, which was practically at my doorstep, would henceforth be my
workroom" (490). "Here I was, at last in a dwelling of my own, in an
agreeable and solitary refuge, able to let my days slip by in that independent, equable, and peaceable life for which I felt myself born" (500). Yet
here, in the midst of this apparent freedom, Rousseau soon realized that
he was obliged to pay frequent calls on Mme d'Épinay—at her discre-
tion. "I realized that I had encumbered myself with a chain whose weight
only friendship prevented me from feeling. . . . I was never sure that I
could dispose of myself for a single day. This flaw greatly lessened the
pleasure that I previously experienced in going to see her. I found that
the liberty she had promised me was granted only on the condition that
I never make use of it. I had to submit to this yoke; I did so, even fairly
voluntarily, for one who is such a great enemy of dependence" (498). In
short, his vaunted independence was deeply compromised precisely by
the bonds of patronage.

Moreover, Rousseau was unable to leave behind his acute sense of persecution, nor was he able to find true happiness. He was tortured by the belief that Diderot and Grimm had conspired to "detach" from him the goodwill of Thérèse and her mother, with the consequence that he began to "feel myself nearly isolated." Mme Levasseur was proving extremely difficult, and Thérèse was caught between Rousseau and her mother (506–7, 510). Thus "in the midst of the situation I had most desired, unable to experience a pure pleasure, I returned in flights of fantasy to the serene days of my youth. . . . Ah! This was by no means les Charmettes! . . . Devoured by the need to love, without ever having been able truly to satisfy this longing, I saw myself reaching the gates of old age and dying without ever having lived" (515). The impossibility of experiencing love with "real persons cast me into the land of chimeras, and finding nothing in existence that was equal to my delirium, I nourished it in an ideal world, which my creative imagination had soon peopled with beings more in accord with my heart" (517). It was in this state of delirium that Rousseau invented the characters of his sentimental novel *Julie ou la nouvelle Héloïse*. He fantasized the characters, placed them on the shores of Lake Geneva, and imagined their sentiments. After several weeks of this fantasy, he began to write letters that the characters might have exchanged, letters that were initially "spare, without responses or links." Eventually he joined these assorted letters into an emerging narrative (520–21). He notes that he was chagrined by the fact that he had previously preached "austere maxims" and had pronounced "mordant invectives against the effeminate books that breathe love and languor," but he could not prevent himself from writing his own supremely sentimental novel (525).

In the midst of this fevered condition in the autumn of 1756 and the spring of 1757, he was paid several visits by Mme d'Houdetot, the sister-in-law of Mme d'Épinay. She was married to a count but was the lover of the soldier and man of letters Jean-François de Saint-Lambert, a recent acquaintance of Rousseau whom we have previously encountered as the lover of Voltaire's ill-fated mistress, Mme du Châtelet. Rousseau fell hopelessly in love with Mme d'Houdetot during their promenades in the forest: "I was drunk on love without object. . . . I came to see my Julie in Mme d'Houdetot, and soon I saw only Mme d'Houdetot, but dressed up with all the perfections with which I had just embellished the idol of my heart." When he confessed his love, Mme d'Houdetot replied with "generosity and prudence," declaring that his supposed love was a "folly" of which she intended to cure him (531–32). Their promenades, however, continued, and they exchanged many sentimental letters. But never, Rousseau tells us in his *Confessions,* "in the midst of this dangerous intoxication," did she "forget herself even for a moment" (535). This folly was, not surprisingly, eventually destructive of Rousseau's position. Mme d'Épinay, Mme d'Houdetot's husband, and eventually Saint-Lambert learned of Rousseau's actions; Mme d'Houdetot's indulgent feelings for Rousseau eventually cooled, and she demanded that he return her letters (557).

Thus began a period of spiraling crisis in Rousseau's rustic paradise. His former intimate friend Grimm had become Mme d'Épinay's lover and now treated him with utter disdain. Diderot's *Le fils naturel* had just appeared in print, with a line in the accompanying discourse that Rousseau, not unreasonably, saw as aimed at him: "Only the bad man lives alone." This led to a further deterioration in his relations with his once dearest friend (550–55). Then the indulgence of Mme d'Épinay dwindled, essentially ceasing when Rousseau declined her request that he accompany her on a trip to Lyon to consult with Dr. Tronchin, a well-known physician whom Rousseau knew from his days in that city (279). Such a request on her part was based on the tacit bargain of patronage relations—that the patronized owed deference and loyalty to the patron. Once he had excused himself from the trip, Rousseau, in spite of his illusions of perfect independence, found himself in an untenable situation.

Recognizing that he was no longer welcome, he moved out of the Hermitage in December of 1757—to take refuge in another isolated cottage a few miles away in Montmorency. This dwelling was offered to him by one M. Mathias, a member of the entourage of the prince de Conti—a prince of the blood (a close relative of the king) who was an admirer of Rousseau's writings (582–86). At Montmorency, Rousseau paid a nominal rent, and Mathias made no significant demands on his time, which made his situation there quite different from that at the Hermitage. Rousseau declares that he was "disgusted with my protector friends, who wished absolutely to dispose of my destiny and to subject me to their supposed benefits in spite of myself. I had resolved to limit myself henceforth to relations of simple benevolence, which, without hampering liberty, constitute the pleasure of life, and which are founded on a basis of equality." Such relations would enable him to "taste the sweetness of liberty without suffering dependence." But although Rousseau lists a dozen or so friends with whom he sustained these "relations of simple benevolence," he was nevertheless miserable, constantly ill and tortured by his belief that Grimm, Diderot, and d'Holbach were animating an "obscure and profound system" against him and his reputation (589). He was roused from his depression when he read d'Alembert's article on "Geneva" in volume 7 of the *Encyclopédie.* D'Alembert remarked in this article that the austere city would benefit from the opening of a theater, whose "performances would form the taste of the citizens and would give them a fineness of tact, a delicacy of sentiment, which is very difficult to acquire without the help of theatrical performances." Rousseau was infuriated by this suggestion and answered with a defense of Genevan moral austerity and a critique of the theater and actors as fateful sources of moral corruption—this in spite of the fact that he was himself the author of two operas. He wrote his critical *Lettre à d'Alembert sur les spectacles* in three weeks' time and had it published by his usual publisher, Rey, in Amsterdam (593). The preface of this work also contained a coded repudiation of Diderot, who, as we have seen, was an advocate of the theater as a moralizing influence. This public repudiation marked the final breaking point of the by now fatally strained friendship.

At this point, Rousseau avers, he had decided to expeditiously complete his literary efforts and retire to a simple country life: "I was determined . . . to renounce totally grand society, the composition of books, any literary commerce, and to shut myself off for the rest of my days in the narrow and peaceable sphere for which I felt myself to have been born" (617). He complained with uncharacteristic lucidity of his plight as an impecunious man of letters dependent on patronage. He notes that he had been thoroughly disgusted with men of letters as a class and had realized that "it was impossible to follow this career without having relations with them." This was what had led him to the Hermitage and then to Montmorency. But he found that he was

> hardly less disgusted with men of the world and in general with the mixed life that I had recently led, half by myself and half in societies for which I was not at all suited. I felt that . . . every unequal association is disadvantageous to the weaker party. Living with opulent people . . . I was obliged to imitate them in many things and in many expenses that were nothing to them but were no less ruinous for me than they were indispensable. Another man is served by his lackey . . . but I, alone, with no servant, was at the mercy of those of the household, whose good graces it was necessary to capture in order to avoid suffering. (614)

This required offering generous gratuities for their services. He complains that the good intentions of his benefactors often had economically negative effects. "If a woman wrote to me at the Hermitage from Paris . . . regretting the four sols [a fifth of a livre] that the post would have charged me for delivery, she would send it with one of her men, who would arrive dripping with sweat, and to whom I would give a dinner and an *écu* [three livres] that he had certainly well earned" (615). Thus Rousseau had found not only that his time was not at his own disposal when he lived at the behest of the great but that the economic advantages of his free rent were compromised by numerous incidental expenses of living among the opulent.

His *Lettre à d'Alembert* and his nearly completed *Julie*, he felt, would improve his finances. He expected that they would gain him some three thousand livres. He expected *Émile*, his seminovelistic treatise on education, to double this sum. He would then put about six thousand livres into a lifetime annuity, which, "combined with my copying, would enable me to subsist without writing any more." There was another project on which he had been working for years, what he called *Les institutions politiques*; of this, he planned to publish only *Le contrat social* and burn the rest. Soon he would be able to retire to a truly independent and simple rural existence and leave the troubled world of literature and of society behind him forever (617).

But by the summer of 1758, he found himself swept into another patronage relationship, this time with M. le Duc de Luxembourg (who was also a maréchal, a top-ranking general) and his wife, the duchesse. They were an elderly noble couple just one rank below the princes of the blood in the French aristocratic hierarchy. They summered in Montmorency and offered Rousseau lodging in the "petit chateau" on the grounds of their estate, which, in spite of his many vows to simplify his life, he quickly accepted. Seduced once again by an imagined perfect independence, "I was in a terrestrial paradise; I lived there with utter innocence and felt complete happiness" (623). Yet he felt the obligations of patronage: M. and Mme de Luxembourg treated him with such kindness that "I could do no less than respond by seeing them assiduously." He spent mornings with Mme de Luxembourg, dined with them, and then took a walk with M. de Luxembourg. "Seeing myself feted, spoiled by persons of such consideration, I ignored all limits and felt for them a friendship that one is only permitted to have with one's equals. . . . I assumed a complete familiarity in my manners, whereas they never let go of the politeness and formality to which they were accustomed" (623). In spite of this difference in styles of sociability, he developed a genuine friendship with M. de Luxembourg. Although he was never entirely at ease with Mme de Luxembourg, he made up for this by reading to her from the manuscript of his as-yet-unpublished *Julie*, which pleased her greatly; the next summer, he read to her from *Émile*, which "did not succeed as well" (624,

637). Nevertheless, Rousseau's relationship with the Luxembourgs continued until 1762, when the condemnation of his newly published *Émile* and a consequent warrant for his arrest sent him in flight to Switzerland.

For all of Rousseau's fantasies, upsets, illnesses, quarrels, and sense of persecution by his former friends, this six-year period of residence in Eaubonne and in Montmorency, lasting from 1756 through 1762, was a time of impressive literary and intellectual production. *Julie ou la nouvelle Héloïse* was initially published in 1761, by Rey, the Dutch publisher who had already published his second discourse and his *Lettre à d'Alembert*. *Julie* took Paris—and eventually Europe—by storm; it was Rousseau's best-selling publication. Then in the following year, *Le contrat social* was published by Rey and *Émile* by Rey and Néaulme in Holland, with a French publication of *Émile* also planned. Neither of these books, which have been much appreciated by posterity, sold well when first released. They were published at a time when, as we saw in chapter 7, the French state was in the midst of a crackdown against books and ideas it regarded as subversive—among others, the *Encyclopédie*, which remained suspended until 1766.

Malesherbes, the official censor who was a friend of the philosophes, including Rousseau, was nevertheless constrained to ban the sale of both books in France. It was more the religious than the political implications of the books that got them in trouble: *Le contrat social* dismissed the utility of Christianity as an effective civil religion and *Émile* included the "Profession of Faith of a Savoyard Vicar," which denied revelation and embraced deism. The fact that *Émile* was to be published in Paris as well as in Amsterdam put Rousseau at grave risk. On June 9, 1762, the Parlement of Paris condemned the book and ordered the arrest of its author, who escaped in a cabriolet furnished by M. de Luxembourg. Copies of the book were officially burned two days later.[5]

This incident proved a dire turning point in Rousseau's life: he was to spend most of the next two decades as a fugitive in Switzerland from 1762 to 1766, in England in 1766 and 1767, moving from place to place in France from 1767 to 1769, and finally returning to Paris in 1770, where he lived until 1778, the year of his death. He spent his final few weeks as the guest on the estate of a marquis in Ermenonville, to the north of Paris, not far from Montmorency. These were years of some agony for Rousseau, who became increasingly convinced that others, including those

---

5. Rousseau's account in *Les confessions* (680–97) tells us more about Rousseau's thoughts than about the details of his legal trouble. There is a clear narrative of these events in Cranston (1997, 348–62).

who attempted to help him, were conspiring against him. His reputation was besmirched when Voltaire, in 1764, revealed that Rousseau, the great moralist and theorist of education, had abandoned his own five children as newborn infants on the porch of the *enfants trouvés* orphanage. After being driven out of Switzerland because of his unorthodox religious beliefs, he took refuge, at the urging of Parisian friends, in England, where the philosopher David Hume welcomed him. But within a few months, he turned on Hume, whom he accused of conspiring against him, and returned to France, where he led a wandering life until his return to Paris in 1770 at the age of fifty-eight. His dispute with Hume cost him many admirers in Parisian society. But at the same time, his *Julie* and *Émile*, in particular, won him many readers and admirers—indeed, there grew a sort of cult of Rousseau.[6] Although Rousseau had claimed he intended to abandon the literary life, he continued to write and publish right up to his death in 1778—in part, no doubt, to produce income, but also, one suspects, because he had, in spite of himself, become too passionate and devoted a writer to give it up. In the years after the publication of *Le contrat social* and *Émile*, he wrote his *Confessions*, finished in 1770 but published posthumously; *Letters from the Mountain*, a lengthy polemic about the constitution of Geneva; a *Dictionary of Music*; the *Project of a Constitution for Corsica* and *Considerations on the Government of Poland*; and two more personal works, *Rousseau juge de Jean-Jacques* (Rousseau the Judge of Jean-Jacques) and *Les rêveries du promeneur solitaire* (Reveries of a Solitary Walker)—not to mention works on botany, which became a major preoccupations in his old age.[7] With the exception of the *Confessions*, none of these works attained the power of those written in his prime years, from 1755 to 1762—that is, his *Discours sur les origines de l'inégalité parmi les hommes; Julie ou la nouvelle Héloïse, Le contrat social,* and *Émile, ou de l'éducation.*

Rousseau was a contradictory man who led a contradictory life. Unlike Voltaire, Diderot, or Morellet, he did not benefit from the well-ordered educational system of the French Catholic Church. Indeed, as we have seen, it was only at age twenty-four that he began serious studies, and he was essentially self-taught. Abandoned by his father at age eleven, his adolescent years were chaotic and were anchored only by his quasi-incestuous relationship with the mercurial Madame de Warens. That Rousseau in his

---

6. On the cult of Rousseau, see Darnton (1984) and Lilti (2017).

7. On this final period of Rousseau's life, only the first few years of which are covered by his *Confessions*, see Cranston (1982). All of Rousseau's works are available in Rousseau (1964).

adult years was difficult, unconventional, socially maladroit, hypochon-driacal, prone to fantasy, and paranoid is hardly surprising. But that he be-came one of the greatest philosophers of his era seems utterly astounding for someone whose early life was so chaotic and unpromising. Rousseau was a singular character and an utterly original thinker. But although he attempted to present himself in his *Confessions* as an intrepid and coura-geous individualist who made his way through sheer inspiration and ge-nius and against all the institutional constraints and social conventions of his day, he was nevertheless as deeply enmeshed as any of his erstwhile philosophe friends in both the hierarchical patronage-based social prac-tices of old regime France and the exploitative but expansive literary mar-ketplace.

Indeed, although Rousseau imagined himself as uniquely indepen-dent and proclaimed his disdain of hierarchy and patronage, he was in fact at least as dependent on the patronage of the wealthy, well born, and well connected as Morellet—and much more so than Diderot, who had made his devil's bargain with the literary marketplace rather than with pa-trons. The difference was that the others were clearheaded about the na-ture of their bonds of dependence, whereas Rousseau tended to imagine his relations of dependence as arising from mutual and equal friendships that just happened to cross status boundaries. There was something pro-foundly adolescent about Rousseau's assertions of virile independence and rigorous morality at the same time that—in his late forties and early fifties—he indulged in extravagant fantasies of a perfect love while pas-sively accepting, as a kind of beloved but unruly child, the indulgent but constraining patronage of his wealthy benefactors.

Meanwhile, Rousseau broke definitively with his philosophe friends and with the lively salon life they had constructed. The salons themselves, as I have emphasized, were deeply structured by patronage. They were held in the homes of the wealthy, where socially inferior guests like Dide-rot, Morellet, and Rousseau accepted the lavish hospitality of their hosts without being able to return it in kind—and where they made connec-tions with patrons who could aid their ascent. But the salons in general, and most particularly the philosophe salons of d'Holbach and Helvétius, also developed an ethic of situational equality in the free-form discus-sions that were the heart of their proceedings. In these discussions, what mattered was the quality of the arguments, or the ingeniousness of the literary offerings, or the brilliance of the satirical sallies, not the formal status of the speaker. The discussions in the philosophe salons enacted a kind of voluntary civic equality *avant la lettre*. The salons were, hence, paradoxical institutions that both enacted and situationally suspended relations of patronage and deference.

It is telling that Rousseau never thrived in the salons, where he felt tongue-tied and slow-witted. A man capable of extraordinary eloquence, he faltered when he was not the sole center of attention but one of several speakers vying with one another in what was, for most of them, friendly—indeed, intensely enjoyable—intellectual sparring. It is hard not to see Rousseau's difficulties as a product of his extraordinarily difficult youth. He had had no sibling in his brief family experience and no school classes where pupils would vie and conspire with one another. It is striking that his adolescence, to judge from his *Confessions*, never involved a group of same-age friends. His sole highly cathected relationship was with Madame de Warens, his dear Maman, of whom he was her cherished Petit—her little one. Diderot, Condillac, and Grimm seem to have been his only intimate same-age friends, and these friendships frayed when, after writing the first discourse, Rousseau began to participate in the life of the salons. He eventually fled the quasi-competitive interactions with his peers—the other philosophes—and fashioned an exaggeratedly individualized and austere personage. He was the severe and fiercely egalitarian republican—a figure that of course reappears in his *Contrat social*. It was in this guise that he retreated to the supposedly simple life of the countryside. In his Eaubonne and Montmorency years, ironically, he developed his most intense relationships with social superiors—Mme d'Épinay, Mme d'Houdetot, and M. and Mme de Luxembourg. Indeed, in these relationships, the austere citizen was far less prominent than the brilliant and cherished man-child. One suspects that Rousseau's persistent hypochondria and his growing paranoia derived from the unresolved nature of this fluctuation between austere self-sufficiency and adolescent neediness. His was not an easy life to live.

But for all of Rousseau's mental suffering and moral inconsistency, there is no gainsaying his genius. His *Julie* was one of the great sentimental novels, his *Émile* inspired generations of educational thinkers, his *Discours sur l'origine de l'inégalité* and *Contrat social* remain fundamental texts of political theory to this day, and his rapturous evocation of feelings in these and other works constitutes the generally acknowledged starting point of French romanticism. Rousseau—miraculously, one feels—spun the pain and contradictions of his impossible life into brilliant works of philosophy and literature.

Rousseau is the only one of my three upwardly mobile philosophes for whom questions of politics were at the center of his inquiries. His political ideas were far more radical than those of the others. Rousseau's *Social Contract* was a fully worked-out statement of republicanism, one that was much cited and celebrated during the radical and republican phase of the French Revolution—that is, during the years between the imprisonment of the king and the end of the Reign of Terror. Rousseau embraced equality as a prime political value. His *Discourse on the Origins of Inequality* was an effort to explain what he regarded as the disastrous fall from natural equality that had accompanied the beginnings of civilization. And his *Social Contract* was an effort to chart a possible return not to natural equality but to a political and civic equality that was, in principle, still attainable by means of appropriate republican institutions. For Rousseau, equality went beyond the civic equality proclaimed in the Declaration of the Rights of Man and Citizen. He certainly regarded as necessary both equality before the law and the career open to talent. But he also required equality in the making of the law—that is, full political equality—and believed that great inequalities of wealth were incompatible with political virtue.

Rousseau's economic ideas were not highly developed. But it is clear that he rejected the pursuit of luxury, which he saw as corrupting the social life of contemporary Europe and especially that of the Paris he resolved to flee. He made his rejection clear, in the very years when he was completing his *Social Contract*, by his adoption of austere dress and manners, his vow to earn his keep by means of his honest trade as a music copier, and his repeated but repeatedly frustrated attempts to embrace a simpler life. Yet to judge from a fascinating passage in his *Emile*, published at the same time as the *Social Contract*, Rousseau nevertheless regarded the exchange of commodities as a foundation of society and in fact as necessary to human equality. There he stated, "No society can exist without exchange, no exchange without a common measure, and no common measure without equality. Thus all society has as its first law some conventional equality, whether of men or of things." Note that by "conventional equality," Rousseau means equality established by means of an explicit convention or agreement—indeed, by a social contract. Here Rousseau actually connects this fundamental convention of equality between persons to a convention of equality between things that are to be exchanged—that is, to commodities and to the money that serves as the general measure of their value. As he puts it a few sentences later, "Conventional equality among things prompted the invention of money, for money is only a term of comparison for the value of things of different kinds; and in this sense, money is the true bond of society" (1979,

189–90)[8] Rousseau, the radical opponent of the emerging commercial society, nevertheless posits a necessary link between the use of money as the general measure of the value of commodities and the very possibility of equality among persons in political society. This passage seems to demonstrate that for Rousseau, unquestionably the deepest political thinker of the eighteenth century and a famous critic of commercial society, the possibility of civic equality was nevertheless dependent on the existence of commodity exchange. In spite of his contempt for consumer goods, Rousseau seems to have accepted the existence of a powerful link between the presence of commercial exchange and the emergence of the possibility of civic equality.

8. I thank Keith Baker for alerting me to this passage.

III

Royal Administration and the Promise of Political Economy

Tocqueville's Challenge

ROYAL ADMINISTRATION AND THE
RISE OF CIVIC EQUALITY

The claim that the French Revolution's embrace of civic equality arose from the advancing social relations of commercial capitalism must confront a different argument that derives from Alexis de Tocqueville's classic *The Old Regime and the French Revolution*.[1] Tocqueville agrees with my contention that the key goal and achievement of the French Revolution was the establishment of what I am calling civic equality: "What was the true objective of the Revolution? . . . [T]he abolition of those political institutions . . . ordinarily designated as feudal, in order to substitute for them a social and political order more uniform and simpler, with equality of conditions as its basis" (68–69). Tocqueville argues that the Revolution's drive toward equality was, paradoxically, not a sharp break from the old regime, as the revolutionaries themselves imagined, but a fulfillment of the old regime state's dominant tendency. According to Tocqueville's account, over the centuries leading up to the Revolution, the monarchical government had steadily centralized political power in its own hands, depriving corporate bodies, provinces, and chartered cities of their autonomy and stripping the nobility of its former political functions. By the eighteenth century, these old political institutions were moribund, and the administrative apparatus was "very centralized, very powerful, and prodigiously active" (41). Although the nobility still retained its honorific prerogatives and pecuniary privileges, its former autonomous role in governing local and provincial institutions had been slowly but effectively usurped by royal administrators. By the later eighteenth century, according to Tocqueville, nobles and commoners were equally prostrate before the administrative dictates of the royal council.

---

1. English translations are Tocqueville (1998, 2011). My citations, hereafter in parentheses in the text, are to the Pléiade edition (Tocqueville [1856] 2004). The translation is mine.

Tocqueville particularly emphasized the role of the intendants of the various provinces in monopolizing the political powers once exercised by the nobility. These officials, first introduced by Louis XIII in the 1630s and greatly strengthened by Louis XIV in the later seventeenth century, were appointed by the royal council and served at its pleasure. The intendants were recruited not from the high nobility but from the milieu of robe nobles who staffed the royal administration, often from families recently elevated from the bourgeoisie. Yet they exercised a kind of despotic authority on behalf of the king, allocating taxes, directing public works, overseeing local affairs, and reporting regularly to the royal council. The "governors" of the provinces, generally great nobles, predated the intendants and retained their offices in the eighteenth century but were, by then, essentially powerless. "The intendant possesses the entire reality of government. . . . He is at the same time administrator and judge. The intendant corresponds with all the ministers; he is the sole agent, in the province, of the entire will of the government" (82–83). The intendants were the eyes and ears of the king and his council and an extension of the royal will.

One consequence of this centralized and bureaucratic form of government was that the once highly distinctive provinces, subjected to the same forms of administration, became more alike. Likewise, "within each province men of different classes, at least all of those above the populace, became more and more similar." As the nobles lost their habit of rule, they became hardly distinguishable from the bourgeoisie in their tastes and ideas: "The bourgeois was just as enlightened as the noble. . . . For the one and for the other, their education had been equally theoretical and literary. And Paris, which increasingly became the sole tutor for all of France, had managed to impart a common shape and outlook to all minds. . . . At bottom, all men who ranked above the populace resembled each other; they had the same ideas, the same habits, developed the same tastes, spoke the same language" (120–21).

Nobles differed from bourgeois only because they held privileges that marked their superiority in status. As we have seen, these privileges ranged from the essentially honorific right to wear swords in public to much more lucrative privileges like access to military commissions and bishoprics and exemptions from royal taxes. These privileges, which the royal administration actually multiplied as it stripped nobles of political authority, came to seem not an appropriate reward for those who played the leading role in the government of the community but rather a set of arbitrary and unjustified advantages. According to Tocqueville, this explains why, when the royal finances fell into crisis in the late 1780s, the privileges of the aristocracy were so vehemently attacked—and so quickly extinguished—in the first months of the Revolution. The monarchy, by endeavoring to simplify and rationalize the government of French society, had purposely rendered all Frenchmen political nullities, nobles no less than commoners. By doing so, it had also inadvertently rendered all educated and reasonably prosperous Frenchmen equal in fact, thus making the privileges that distinguished the aristocracy from the rest seem intolerable. It thus unwittingly paved the way for the egalitarian revolution that swept away aristocracy and monarchy alike in 1789 and replaced them with a legally mandated civic equality.

The policies of the monarchy also enhanced the cause of civic equality because they had the unintended effect of empowering the philosophes as the political conscience of the nation and of making these outsider intellectuals, rather than the ancient aristocracy, France's leading political actors. For Tocqueville, the great fault of the royal administration was that it destroyed political liberty—understood not as a bundle of individual rights but as the right and power of citizens to participate in the government of their nation and communities. According to Tocqueville's understanding of French history, the nobility—and in a more limited way, even the bourgeoisie of France's cities—had previously possessed a significant measure of liberty in this sense.[2] For him, the most damaging effect of governmental centralization was that it deprived the king's subjects—above all the nobility—of these autonomous powers of political participation, leaving everyone equally prostrate before the royal administration. This created a society in which only members of the administration itself had any real experience of government.

It was this characteristic of old regime society that gave "men of letters" the decidedly surprising role of being the most influential political actors of their era. "How," Tocqueville asks, "did men of letters, who possessed neither social eminence, nor honors, nor wealth, nor responsibilities, nor power, become, in fact, the principal political actors of their time—indeed, the only ones, because although others exercised governmental power, they alone spoke with recognized authority?" (170–71). Tocqueville observes that eighteenth-century men of letters, whose theories of course differed considerably in detail, nevertheless "all believed

2. François Furet, one of Tocqueville's most enthusiastic modern defenders, remarked that Tocqueville's notion of the noble as the chief governor of provincial society was fallacious, based not on any genuine historical knowledge of the workings of feudal society but on the myths common to his own class of postrevolutionary nineteenth-century nobles (1978, 121–98).

that it would be advantageous to substitute simple and elementary rules, deduced from reason and natural law, for the complicated and traditional customs that governed society in their era" (170). According to Tocqueville, it was the spectacle of the many "abusive or ridiculous" privileges possessed by the nobility and the church, privileges "whose weight was increasingly felt but whose pretexts seemed increasingly implausible" that drove the philosophes toward "the idea of the natural equality of conditions" (171). In short, the centralizing policies of the royal government, by stripping ancient institutions of all real political power while multiplying the arbitrary privileges of the nobles and the clergy, had the unintended consequence of making the idea of a natural right to equality seem especially attractive.

Moreover, the conditions of life of men of letters in France made them particularly inclined to have a taste for general and abstract theories in questions of government:

> Living at an almost infinite distance from practical matters, they had no experience that might have tempered their natural ardor. Nothing alerted them to the obstacles that existing facts might pose to even the most desirable reforms; they had no conception of the perils that always accompany even the most necessary revolutions. . . . The complete absence of political liberty meant that the world of public affairs was not just poorly understood by them but entirely invisible. They not only played no role in public affairs themselves but were unable even to see what others were doing. They lacked even the superficial instruction that the spectacle of a free society and the clamor of political debate gives even to those who participate least in affairs of government. They thus became much bolder in their novelties, more enthralled with general ideas and speculative systems, more contemptuous of ancient wisdom, and more confident in their individual reason. (171)

It was, in short, the lack of political liberty in old regime France— that is, the lack of any experience of participation in the government of the community—that ultimately accounted for the abstraction that so marked the thought of the French philosophes and, consequently, also marked the reforms introduced at the beginning of the French Revolution. The nobility, which had once been a genuine aristocracy—that is, a collectivity that carried out the government by the best—was reduced by the centralizing monarchy to a mere collection of privileged subjects. Their privileges, seen not as a natural reward for services rendered to the governed but as unjust advantages, inclined the French to be particularly sympathetic to the notion of natural equality—a notion taken up and developed into systems by eighteenth-century French men of letters. The philosophes' "almost infinite distance from practical affairs" and their consequent lack of experience in political matters imparted a particularly abstract character to their theories. Thus Tocqueville's account of the old regime explains the Revolution's abstraction as much as its egalitarianism.

According to Tocqueville, the philosophes made use of the one shred of political liberty still available to Frenchmen to spread their ideas to the public at large: "We had conserved only one liberty in the ruin of all the others: we could philosophize almost without constraint about the origins of societies, about the essential nature of governments and the primordial rights of the human race" (172). In the circumstances of eighteenth-century France, this freedom to speculate (and to publish one's speculations) resulted in a generalized adoption of the philosophes' ideas. The taste for these ideas spread

> even to those whose condition would naturally keep them apart from abstract speculations. There was no taxpayer injured by the unequal division of the *taille* [that is, the exemption of nobles and clergy from taxation] who was not enthusiastic about the idea that all men should be equal; there was no smallholder whose crops were devastated by the rabbits kept by his nobleman neighbor [in order to enjoy his exclusive hunting privileges] who was unhappy to hear that all privileges without distinction were condemned by reason. Every political passion disguised itself in philosophy . . . and the writers, taking in hand the direction of opinion, found themselves for a moment in the place ordinarily occupied by heads of parties in free countries. (172)

By the eighteenth century, the place once occupied by the French nobility in the government of opinions "was now empty, and the writers could move into that space and fill it themselves." Indeed, the aristocracy, whose place was being usurped, "actually favored their enterprise." Aristocrats, not realizing the extent of their peril, regarded "doctrines that opposed their particular rights, and even their very existence as nobles . . . as ingenious jeux d'esprits [intellectual games]. They joined in gladly, in order to pass the time, playing nonchalantly with their own immunities and privileges, declaiming serenely about the absurdity of all established customs." Tocqueville observes that because France had been deprived of "the last traces of public life" for over a century, nobles had no way of realizing that their way of life was genuinely under threat: since their privileges were intact and there had been no exterior changes in the "antique edifice" of French society, they mistakenly thought that their privileged position was secure (173).

From Tocqueville's point of view, then, it would be superfluous to invoke the spread of commercial relations as a key social process underlying both the drive for civic equality in 1789 and the striking abstraction of the revolutionaries' conception of state and society. For Tocqueville, abstract and impersonal equality was produced by the long and gradual process of administrative centralization—that is, by political, not by economic, causes. By depriving even the nobility of any real participation in political affairs, the monarchy effectively evacuated all authority except that of the royal will and restricted governing power to a rationalizing royal bureaucracy. It thereby unwittingly raised the philosophes to a position of de facto political authority and made it possible for abstract theories about natural equality to become the commonplace of the political discourse of all classes, even that of the nobility. Ironically, the monarchy itself had unwittingly set French history on a course toward civic equality, a course that implied its own destruction. But the civic equality that was the secret goal of the old regime state by no means entailed political liberty in the sense of participation of citizens in self-government. The telos of Tocqueville's story is not the thrilling and raucous popular politics of the years 1789 through 1794 but the despotism of Napoleon—a chilling police state with an egalitarian civil code. It was precisely this despotism that had regained ascendance in France in Tocqueville's own era in the form of the Second Empire ruled by Napoleon III, a regime for which Tocqueville felt loathing and disgust.

Tocqueville and the Intendants

The Old Regime and the French Revolution is a brilliant book. It is written by the deepest and most prescient political thinker in nineteenth-century France, motivated by an inspiring passion for political liberty and based on painstaking (and at the time highly innovative) archival research into the modes of operation and the mental habits of the eighteenth-century royal administration. Over a century and a half since its publication in 1856, the book remains an indispensable point of reference for thinking about the old regime and the French Revolution. This is especially true since the collapse of the Marxisant interpretation of the Revolution that had dominated the middle years of the twentieth century. In the ruins of the synthetic social interpretation championed by Lefebvre or Soboul, Tocqueville's vision of the centralizing royal administration and its social, political, and ideological effects has become a leading reference point for explaining the Revolution's origins and character, a reference point currently far more convincing to most historians than the rising bourgeoisie of the Marxisant historians.[3]

Subsequent research has challenged or revised many of Tocqueville's particular arguments. For example, studies of the royal intendants inspired by Tocqueville's account have sharply revised his picture of the all-powerful administrator imposing the central administration's will on prostrate provincials. According to a survey of such works made by François-Xavier Emmanuelli, himself the author of a detailed study of the intendance of Aix-en-Provence in the eighteenth century, the intendants were not the all-powerful "representatives of a centripetal, consciously leveling state" but rather had as their ambition merely "to make sure the king was obeyed and to assure him revenues sufficient for his foreign policies and his glory" (1981, 17).[4] Tocqueville's conception of the all-powerful intendant is hardly compatible with the slender means that intendants actually had at their disposal. Their staffs and budgets were tiny by comparison with those of the nineteenth-century French prefects Tocqueville had before his eyes, and it was difficult for an intendant to live on his salary in a style sufficient to be taken seriously in local society without personal wealth. The great nobles in the vicinity could ignore many of his actions because of their influence at the royal court. His decrees were often held up indefinitely by suits contesting their legality. And the various municipalities and corporate bodies under his supervision could often simply ignore his directives—except those that concerned taxes (Emmanuelli 1981, 36–50).

It is true, as Tocqueville observed, that the intendant had a vast range of formal powers. He oversaw nearly all local affairs: taxation, municipal government, military matters, administration, judicial affairs, economic regulation, public works, and the like. However, these powers were often more formal than real. Emmanuelli argues that the intendant was less a governor of local society than a supervisor, a settler of disputes, a collector of information, and an advisor on provincial affairs to the royal council. However, Emmanuelli also remarks that the intendant's opinion was nearly always heeded by the council. Indeed, of 18,500 dossiers suggesting a decision that were sent to Versailles by La Tour, the intendant

3. This was true of Francois Furet, the leading figure of the "revisionist" school of revolutionary historiography that triumphed in the 1970s and 1980s. See especially Furet (1978). Tocqueville was also a key inspiration in the work of David Bien and his many students. A collection of Bien's essays is Blaufarb et al. (2005).

4. See also Emmanuelli (1979) and Smedley-Weil (1995).

of Aix-en-Provence, fewer than twenty were disavowed by the council (1891, 86–88). But Emmanuelli argues that the success of La Tour and other intendants depended on their skill in accommodating local powers and making themselves trusted spokesmen of provincial elites' interests. To be effective, an intendant had to know how to broker deals between the local powers and the royal council. He was not in a position to simply impose dictates, either his own or the council's, on provincial society. As William Beik put it in his study of seventeenth-century Languedoc, the intendants "worked through and not against the local system of authority, for without a network of local contacts they were helpless, and this network could only be developed by sensitivity to local interests" (1988, 49).

Emmanuelli's judgments are of course strongly influenced by the case of the intendant of Aix, who presided over Provence, in the far southeast of France. Provence was not only distant from Paris and Versailles but was also a pays d'état, with its own estates possessing significant legislative and administrative powers and its own parlement. One would naturally expect a pays d'état to have considerably more independence from Versailles than a pays d'élection and hence an intendant who would be as much a mediator as a governor. But much of what Emmanuelli argues is borne out by the case of Turgot, the intendant of Limousin from 1761 to 1774. Limousin was a pays d'élection, lacking either estates or parlement and therefore more thoroughly under the thumb of the royal administration. Turgot, whom we have encountered as the friend of the abbé Morellet, was a figure of capital importance in the history of the old regime. He was the scion of an old administrative family and a friend of the philosophes, a leading political economist, and an author of articles in Diderot's *Encyclopédie*. In 1774, after his service in Limousin, he was named controller general. He was the most ardent and determined reformer among eighteenth-century controllers general. A brilliant and energetic reforming administrator in a pays d'élection, Turgot serves as a useful counterexample to Emmanuelli's less ambitious and more conservative La Tour.

Turgot, whose experience in Limousin has been carefully studied, was clearly more than a mediator and a spokesman for local elites. He arrived in Limoges, Limousin's capital, with many reforms in mind. His most impressive achievement as intendant was a major recasting of the hated corvée, an institution that forced local peasants to build and repair roads without compensation—a reform Turgot later introduced on the national level when he became controller general. Turgot had multiple objections to the corvée. It was assessed only on those who paid the taille, a tax that exempted nobles and many bourgeois, and was thus inequitable.

It was, moreover, assessed on the peasants who happened to live adjacent to a road, even though the beneficiaries of improved roads were often located elsewhere. And it was highly inefficient. The roadwork diverted peasants from the tasks of farming, at which they were experienced and competent, and put them to work road building, for which they were untrained and that, as forced laborers, they performed grudgingly and badly. Turgot convinced local rural communities that they would be better off paying an additional tax in lieu of the corvée and have the state use the money to hire trained road builders. This administrative maneuver may well have been technically illegal, but it found favor with Turgot's administrative subjects and over time led to a major improvement in local roads, which had previously been among the worst in France. It also contributed to a rise in commercial traffic and hence to the income of this exceptionally poor province. In the case of the corvée, Turgot's initiative was sufficient to impose a very consequential reform of existing practices (Kiener and Peyronnet 1979, 153–57, 237–42).[5]

But Turgot was hardly all-powerful in Limousin. His attempts at general tax reform went nowhere; he made little progress on establishing a proper land register (*cadastre*) for the province; he was unable to found a high-quality secondary school in Limoges; he found that parish officers in local communities were not only too incompetent to carry out reforms but often illiterate and corrupt; his attempts to improve agriculture—for example, by introducing wider cultivation of potatoes—were ignored by local farmers; and so on. As was the case for La Tour in Provence, his effectiveness in accomplishing any reform, including that of the corvée, depended on his persuading local powers that reforms would be to their advantage. Over the years, he became discouraged about his lack of success. He confessed to his younger friend Pierre-Samuel Dupont de Nemours in a letter of 1771, "I am quite convinced that one can be a thousand times more useful by writing good publications than by anything one can do in a subaltern administrative position" (Kiener and Peyronnet 1979, 291). Turgot found that an intendant's powers were less than they appeared to be and certainly less than Tocqueville was to imagine. In short, modern scholarship has effectively demonstrated that Tocqueville's image of the all-powerful intendant is untenable.

5. The authors, committed to deflating the Turgot legend, claim that Pierre-Marie-Jérôme Trésaguet, Limousin's engineer for the Ponts et Chaussées (the royal civil engineering corps), was actually responsible for the success of Turgot's reforms of the corvée (237–42). It is true that Trésaguet was exceptionally talented and deserves much credit, but without Turgot's initiative and consistent effort, there would have been no reform to make a success of.

However, Tocqueville was such a scrupulous researcher and so curious about the workings of old regime institutions that his own text contains a paragraph that actually makes a version of the point that his modern scholars use to refute him. Having described the royal administration as "very powerful and prodigiously active" early in *The Old Regime and the French Revolution*, Tocqueville notes in a later chapter that "the administration, which felt itself to be of recent date and of lowly birth, was always timid in its initiatives whenever it encountered an obstacle in its path. It is a striking spectacle, when one has read the correspondence of eighteenth-century ministers and intendants, to see how this government, so invasive and so absolute as long as obedience was uncontested, was dumbfounded whenever it encountered the least resistance . . . and how it then called a halt, hesitated, negotiated, weighed opinions, and often remained far short of the natural limits of its power" (145). This passage seems surprisingly consistent with the picture presented by Emmanuelli or Kiener and Peyronnet. Tocqueville is probably right when he insinuates that the intendant, a robe noble of recent extraction and usually without great independent wealth, felt intimidated by the social prestige, wealth, and moral authority of the eminent landed nobles in their provinces. This was surely one important limit to the intendant's authority. But equally important was the sheer paucity of the intendant's administrative means. Hence he had to hesitate, negotiate, and weigh opinions even when the opposition came from lowly peasant villages or urban guildsmen. Tocqueville's assessment in this brief passage presents a more accurate picture of the real powers of the intendant than do his ringing claims earlier in the text.

Clearly Tocqueville's arguments cannot be taken as gospel. Yet it certainly is true that the royal administration was intent on centralizing authority and that it made considerable strides in doing so—rapidly and brutally under Louis XIV and Colbert in the late seventeenth century, more slowly and hesitantly but significantly over the course of the eighteenth century. The corporate and aristocratic character of old regime French society meant that there were multiple points of resistance to the administration's centralizing thrusts and that victories for the centralizing state were hard won and sometimes rolled back. Equally important, the king and his administration were in an inherently contradictory position. On the one hand, they wished to improve the power and efficiency of the royal administration by establishing uniform rules and procedures— which, as Tocqueville asserted, certainly tended to place those subject to the administration on an ever more equal footing in relation to the state.

But on the other hand, the rules and norms that gave the king his powers were fundamentally aristocratic in character. The king's authority and dignity were inherited through the male line in the same fashion as noble titles and dignities; the king, from this perspective, stood at the apex of an aristocratic order and was its supreme guarantor. To reduce all subjects to a common subjection to the administration would seem to undermine the very basis of the monarchy.

Given this contradictory position, it should be hardly surprising that the policy of the royal government in the eighteenth century was endlessly vacillating. Again and again over the course of the century, the royal council would decree centralizing and rationalizing reforms under one controller general and then fail to carry them out or annul them under the next. In my opinion, this vacillation had two related causes. One was the fundamental contradiction between the aristocratic and administrative principles that rendered the royal administration ambivalent and uncertain. The other was the sheer weight of the old corporate and aristocratic institutions, which provided multiple points of resistance to centralizing and equalizing administrative policies. This resistance could only have been overcome by a royal administration fully committed to centralizing and equalizing reforms—a commitment that because of the fundamental ambivalence of its position, no royal council could ever muster.

The royal administration's ambivalence about aristocratic and corporate versus administrative and rationalist principles and modes of government surely underlay the seemingly absurd but highly consequential tendency noted by Tocqueville for the king to multiply the honorific and pecuniary privileges of the nobles at the same time that he stripped them of governmental authority. This can be read as an attempt to dodge the royal administration's contradictory situation by affirming the very aristocratic privileges that its centralizing policies were hollowing out. The great and permanent achievement of Tocqueville's *Old Regime*, in my opinion, is that it brings clearly to the fore one side of this contradictory situation—the push for administrative centralization and rationalization. At the same time, although he recognizes in passing the monarchy's contradictory desire to sustain a society based on aristocracy and privilege, this second equally important theme is overshadowed in his account of the first. If, in the light of subsequent scholarship, Tocqueville got the balance wrong, he recognized and highlighted, as none of his contemporaries and surprisingly few of his historian successors did, the reality and the profound historical importance of the old regime monarchy's abstracting and equalizing thrust.

The Limitations of Tocqueville's Arguments

Tocqueville's account, however exaggerated and one-sided, captures brilliantly one crucial facet of the old regime's contradictory character. The royal administration really did foster a dynamic that prefigured and prepared the way for the civic equality of the French Revolution. But accepting the reality of this Tocquevillian dynamic hardly cancels out the alternative explanation for the Revolution's turn to civic equality that I have proposed—that is, the subtle but powerful abstracting and leveling effects produced by expanding commercial capitalism. After all, it is perfectly possible that there were two distinct dynamics operating in eighteenth-century France, both of which nurtured and pushed to the fore notions of civic equality. Indeed, it can be argued that these two dynamics were more intimately related than they initially appear, that there was a secret affinity between Tocqueville's proposed bureaucratic abstraction and my proposed commodifying abstraction.

To pursue this possibility, we must understand certain limitations built into the structure of Tocqueville's account. First, Tocqueville takes as given—that is to say, as needing no explanation—two key parameters on which his argument depends. The first parameter is the royal government's unremitting desire to centralize authority. Tocqueville remarked that although the royal administration manifested a powerful drive toward centralization, "nothing indicates that the government of the old regime followed a deeply meditated plan in carrying out this difficult labor. It simply yielded to the instinct that drives all governments to attempt to take charge of all affairs, an instinct that remains constant in spite of the diversity of the agents" (101–2). If all governments possess the instinct to take charge of all of a community's affairs, then the fact that the government of the French old regime worked so assiduously and tirelessly to centralize its authority is merely the local expression of a transhistorical tendency and therefore requires no explanation. But this is a highly dubious claim. History provides many examples of powerful governments both before and since the eighteenth century that have purposely left all kinds of affairs to localities or to private persons rather than attempting to impose rule from the center. The eighteenth-century French government's drive to centralize (which, it must be said, was not so all-encompassing as Tocqueville claims) therefore needs to be explained rather than assumed as natural. Later in this chapter, I shall argue that the government's drive for centralization was actually tied closely to the rising importance of commercial relations in France and in the European-dominated world.

The second doubtful assumption of Tocqueville's argument is that the availability of the concept of the natural equality of men, which became the keystone of the French Revolution's regime of civic equality, itself requires no explanation. Tocqueville claims that this concept had been in circulation for centuries but that previously it had never gained much traction. "As long ago as the Middle Ages," he claims, certain "agitators" had invoked "the general laws of human societies" and proposed reconstituting their societies in accord with "the natural rights of humanity." However, "these attempts all failed: the firebrand that enflamed Europe in the eighteenth century was easily put out in the fifteenth." He then adds, "For arguments of this sort to produce revolutions, it is necessary for certain changes already to have taken place in conditions, customs, and morals, making it possible for such arguments to penetrate the human mind" (63). The changes he has in mind, of course, are the increasing uniformity of conditions introduced by the old regime government's campaign of centralization.

I agree that changes in "conditions, customs, and morals" were absolutely necessary for egalitarian ideas to be widely adopted in the eighteenth century. But I have two disagreements with Tocqueville on this point. First, eighteenth-century notions of equality were fundamentally different from those mooted in the fifteenth century—most obviously because they were secular rather than religious in character. Medieval ideas about equality were not formulated as "general laws of human societies" or "natural rights." Such language and concepts arose only during the eighteenth-century Enlightenment. Second, I disagree about the precise nature and location of the "changes in conditions, customs and morals" that made possible the widespread adoption of ideas about natural equality. Tocqueville sees such changes as taking place exclusively in relations between the state and citizens (or subjects)—that is, as a consequence of the progressive centralization of political authority. By contrast, I think it is impossible to explain the development and widespread acceptance of notions of equality in the eighteenth century without considering transformations in economic life.

Moreover, it is notable that Tocqueville's argument about how state centralization made civic equality thinkable and desirable is almost entirely *negative* in character. He does not so much claim that the centralizing administration actively and positively created equality; rather, he claims that it rendered existing inequality less salient by depriving a superior class of one of its previous modes of superiority—the nobles' exclusive or at least privileged access to the power of governing. If the royal administration made people formally equal, this was true in a fundamentally negative sense: they were alike because they were all politically null, equally deprived of political liberty. The argument about the men of letters and their assumption of political leadership in eighteenth-century France is also essentially negative in character. They gained political authority only because those who previously held real authority, above all the nobility, lost it to the centralizing administration, becoming as null politically as commoners already were. It is only against this generalized absence of political participation and political liberty that the philosophes' exercise of the one liberty that remained available—to engage in philosophical speculation—enabled them to develop and make plausible to others their ideas about politics.

Likewise, in Tocqueville's account, the men of letters' attraction to notions of abstract and universal rights of man does not arise out of some new perception that all men are somehow equal. Nowhere does Tocqueville argue that current political or social developments in the eighteenth century actually render people more equal in some positive or forward-looking sense. Indeed, he explicitly claims that the belief in natural equality was nothing new. Tocqueville's interpretation is built on a profound and systematic pessimism and cannot account for the optimism and faith in progress of the philosophes, the revolutionaries, or many eighteenth-century administrators. All embraced, in different ways and to different extents, the natural equality of rights as a foundation of a more prosperous and more just social order. The growth of commerce certainly seems to fit better the persistently progressive outlook of the appropriate eighteenth-century actors than does negative equality based on deprivation of political liberty and resentment of unmerited privilege—the two forces that drive Tocqueville's account. Even if Tocqueville's explanations are accepted as capturing real and consequential eighteenth-century social processes and conditions—as I think they should be—an explanation of the emergence of a widely held ideal of civic equality should also the take up the question of the nature and the diffusion of commercial forms of social relations in eighteenth-century France.

In the three chapters that constitute the rest of part 3 of the book, I will argue that the powerful drive toward state centralization in old regime France was closely entwined with the monarchy's desperate search for revenues. Revenues were needed above all for war; the French monarchs ruled the largest and most militarily powerful state in Europe in this era of virtually endless interstate warfare. Especially during the long reign of Louis XIV, the self-styled "Sun King" who ruled from 1642 to 1715, the pursuit of military glory became the chief goal of the state. Louis and his ministers built a huge and formidable army and an increasingly powerful navy and mounted a campaign to establish dominance in Europe. In the end, the French managed to accumulate considerable new territory on their northeastern frontier but were for the most part held in check by the combined forces of the other European states, which pursued their own military ambitions. This avid pursuit of military glory, which continued through the eighteenth century, was phenomenally expensive. It forced the French state to increase taxes sharply and to undertake other expedients to raise money. The magnificent French monarchy was constantly in debt. The old regime French state analyzed by Tocqueville pursued a policy of relentless centralization not because it "yielded to the instinct that drives all governments to attempt to take charge of all affairs" but because it was chronically and desperately short of the funds required to sustain its military adventures.

During the seventeenth century, the search for revenues was based above all on establishing a degree of internal order and control that would allow the efficient collection of taxes. But the extraction of taxes was supplemented by various other stratagems, of which the most consequential for the history of the French state was the widespread and systematic sale of state offices, generally to merchants enriched by trade, a practice already in evidence in the sixteenth century. Here we begin to glimpse the imbrication of state building with the expansion of trade. In the eighteenth century, the state continued to harvest the wealth of merchants by selling offices. But the relationship of the state to commerce and manufacturing changed significantly in these years. The royal administration, continuing its perpetual search for revenues, became ever more interested in the active promotion of commerce and industry, which its officers believed would have the happy effect of increasing the national wealth from which taxes might be extracted. In order to nurture commerce and manufacturing, Tocqueville's active, centralizing eighteenth-century state increasingly attempted to apply to France's institutions the maxims of the emerging discourse of political economy. These reforms were generally made for highly pragmatic reasons. But the fundamental assumptions of political economy posited a society sharply at odds with the reality of eighteenth-century France. Political economy envisioned persons not as nobles, commoners, clerics, or members of various privileged corporate bodies, provinces, or guilds but rather as independent, juridically identical individuals whose fundamental motivation was not the maintenance of their honor but the maximization of their comfort and wealth. In short, the bias toward civic equality that Tocqueville rightly ascertained in the prerevolutionary French state was significantly—perhaps principally—driven by the state's avid pursuit not of power per se but of revenue, which, its agents increasingly realized, depended ultimately on the economic productivity of the French people.

The three chapters that follow sketch out the development of the French royal administration from the mid-sixteenth century to the Revolution. I track the rising salience of economic reforms in the eyes of administrators of the revenue-hungry but chronically revenue-short royal state. Their widespread embrace of the new "science" of political economy, which implicitly valorized civic equality, arose from the hope that reforms would increase the wealth on which taxation was based—thus resolving the state's fiscal problems. But they could not overcome the deep contradictions between their rationalizing administrative programs and the profound inertia of a state built on privilege and tradition.

Warfare, Taxes, and Administrative Centralization

THE DOUBLE BIND OF ROYAL FINANCE

State centralization under the old regime was a response to the expense of international warfare. The royal administrators' dominant concern from the early seventeenth century right up to 1789 was to provide the monarch with means to finance his military operations, the cost of which, everywhere in Europe, had skyrocketed since the early sixteenth century.[1] This emphasis on the spiraling cost of warfare as the driver of state centralization is hardly news to scholars of the regime administrative history. But looking more carefully at the pervasive long-term effects of the administration's unceasing pursuit of cash and credit can cast a new light on an old problem.

The Military Revolution

The changes in warfare that caused spiraling state budgets in the sixteenth and seventeenth centuries have been dubbed "the military revolution." According to Geoffrey Parker, the military revolution resulted from a bundle of interrelated changes in military strategy and technology. The most obvious was the development of guns, initially heavy cannons capable of breaching the high but not particularly thick walls of medieval fortifications. The response was the development of fortifications with protruding bastions and lower but thicker walls that could withstand cannon shot. These were first built in Italy in the early sixteenth century, where the invasion by Charles VIII of France in 1494, accompanied by some forty cannons, had proved the inadequacy of older fortifications. By the mid-sixteenth century, the new style of fortifications was gener-

---

1. For the larger European dynamic linking warfare with state building, see Tilly (1990).

alized north of the Alps as well. The consequence of the new offensive technology and the responding defensive technology was a standoff, but one that changed the nature of warfare. Increasingly, wars were decided by sieges rather than by pitched battles—requiring much longer campaigns and bigger armies (Parker 1988, 6–14). The scale of the change may be gauged by the case of the French army. Charles VIII invaded Italy in 1494 with an army of 18,000 men, huge for the time; François I had an army of 32,000 when he invaded Italy in 1525; Henri II's army numbered 40,000 at the capture of Metz in 1552. By 1630, during the Thirty Years' War, armies of major states had about 150,000 men each. Louis XIV had nearly 400,000 men in arms by the end of the seventeenth century. Over two centuries, the French army grew by a factor of about twenty; armies of other states increased more or less proportionately (Parker 1988, 24). This combination of new fortifications, new guns, and growing armies greatly multiplied the cost of warfare.

A second change in military technology and strategy also ratcheted up costs. By the early seventeenth century, musketeers were rapidly displacing archers and pikemen. The problem with the musket was that it took so long to reload—roughly two minutes. The key innovation, volley fire, was made by the Dutch in the 1590s. Their technique was to have several lines of musketeers, each of which stepped back to reload as the next stepped forward to shoot. The result was a virtually continuous line of fire. This tactic was quickly adopted by other armies, notably Gustavus Adolphus's Swedish troops in the Thirty Years' War (1618–48). The tactic of volley fire was most effective if troops were spread out over a long line rather than drawn together in massed squares like those of the pikemen dominating sixteenth-century warfare. But this required enhanced discipline and courage on the part of each individual soldier as well as careful coordination of troops across an entire battlefield—qualities that required more thorough drilling and practice. Consequently, armies could not be disbanded and reassembled at will but had to continue training in peacetime. These new techniques, adopted universally, added to costs (Parker 1988, 18–24).

The final expensive innovation in European warfare was the rising importance of sea power. This was intimately connected with the building of overseas colonial empires, an enterprise in which the French, whose overseas holdings were paltry before the last quarter of the seventeenth century, were latecomers—by comparison with the Portuguese and Spanish, whose conquests dated to the beginning of the sixteenth century, and the Dutch and English, who surpassed Spanish sea power and made major conquests in the Americas and Asia in the seventeenth century.[2] The key to success in maritime warfare was the development of maneuverable gunships capable of sustained cannon fire during extended battles and of operating on long voyages on the high seas. It was the Dutch, in the early seventeenth century, who perfected such vessels—particularly what were known as frigates. But these were soon imitated by the English and, after the mid-1660s, by the French. The fleets of the English and French had, by the late seventeenth century, battled to a three-way naval stalemate with the Dutch (Parker 1988, 90–103). The cost of outfitting these navies, with a few hundred warships apiece and immense new shipyards and military port facilities, was staggering (Felix and Tallett 2009, 156).[3] In the eighteenth century, the needs of navies continued to expand, particularly those of the English and French, whose ability to sustain military power was greater than that of the much less populous Netherlands. Fortifications, thousands of horses, muskets, cannons, huge and well-drilled armies, warships with trained sailors and gunners, all were necessary for a nation intending to become or remain a great power in the late seventeenth and eighteenth centuries. France, the most populous country in Europe (other than the poorer and less developed Russia), with its tradition of military might that extended back to the Middle Ages, rose to this costly challenge.

Financing War

The fact that the dominant task of the royal administration was financing warfare means that old regime state centralization was, from the beginning, inflected by logics of commodity exchange. What counted, in the end, was not the submission of the population to the royal will per se but the ability of the state to extract a substantial share of the nation's exchangeable economic surplus. Extracting surplus logically entailed two issues: the existence of sufficient resources that might be extracted and the state's ability to extract them.

Because the French economy in the seventeenth and eighteenth centuries was predominantly agrarian, the predominant source of extractable resources was agriculture. Most agricultural production in France and in other European nations satisfied the subsistence needs of the peasants who produced it, although a portion of the annual grain harvest—

2. On the French colonial empire, see Haudrère (1997).
3. It amounted to about a third of all military expenses in France in 1693.

something like a fifth, in a normal year—had to be saved for future planting (Pounds 1979, 182). The surplus beyond these two needs went to better-off peasants in profits, to landlords and seigneurs in rents and seigneurial dues, to the church in tithes (*dîmes*), and to the state in taxes— above all, the harvest tax known as the taille (literally, the cut), from which the nobility and clergy were exempt. There were limits on how much the state could extract without undermining the productivity of agriculture or arousing serious resistance—most obviously from the peasantry but potentially from ecclesiastics and lords, whose wealth and political power dominated their provinces and whose cooperation was essential for efficient tax collection.

If agriculture was the biggest employer of labor in the eighteenth century, trade and manufactures actually accounted for a bigger share of the French national product by the time of the Revolution (Daudin 2011, 17). Commerce and industry were taxed unevenly and in a somewhat ad hoc fashion by tariffs, tolls, the *aides* (assessed on wine and other alcoholic beverages), and general consumption taxes known as the *octroi*, which were imposed in the larger cities.[4] The most hated of French consumption taxes was the gabelle, or salt tax, which dated back to the thirteenth century. As we saw in chapter 1, the royal state created a monopoly on this necessary household item, charging consumers far more than the cost of salt's production and distribution. In the late seventeenth century, the state added to the gabelle a royal monopoly on tobacco, which became very lucrative in the eighteenth century as tobacco addiction spread. The salt and tobacco monopolies applied to all classes but were especially onerous to the poor.

The French state thus used various forms of taxation to sustain its place in seventeenth- and eighteenth-century military competition. The means of collecting the levies varied. The most administratively complicated to collect was the taille, which struck every parish in the kingdom. The taille was assessed as a portion of the agricultural product and was known as a "direct" tax. As we saw in chapter 1, France was neither legally

---

4. Taxation of consumption was far more ad hoc than in Britain. The British fiscal system was based primarily on excise taxes, levied at markets, manufactories, and retail outlets. ("To excise" is literally to cut out, making this tax linguistically—but not institutionally—parallel to the French taille.) The British excise taxes were meticulously organized and imposed on a wide range of consumer goods (Brewer 1968). According to Mathias and O'Brien (1976, 609), this tax system took about 18 to 20 percent of the British income per capita in the second half of the eighteenth century and the French 9 to 13 percent. More recently, Félix (1999, 35–46) has calculated that the French tax yield was about 20 percent higher than Mathias and O'Brien estimated, thus about 11 to 16 percent.

nor administratively unified. Thus in most of France, the determination of who was subject to the taille (*taillable*) was "personal," meaning that exemptions were granted to all the properties owned by privileged persons. In portions of the south, exemptions were "real," however, meaning that they followed the properties rather than the persons, so that a noble who owned land designated *roturier* (common) had to pay taxes on its product, and a commoner who owned "noble" land did not. Different provinces also administered the taille differently, although overseeing the collection of this tax was one of the most important functions of the intendants—who were initially introduced largely for this purpose. In the pays d'élections, generally located in the center of the country—the core of the ancient monarchy—the apportionment and collection was undertaken by royal officers known as *élus* and by the intendant and his agents. However, in the pays d'états—that is, provinces that retained their estates—the apportionment and collection of the taille was managed by officers of the estates, in coordination with the intendant.

The apportioning and collection of the taille was laborious and contentious. The royal council would set the total amount of the tax for the kingdom, which was then apportioned among the provinces and then among individual parishes—a process that often gave rise to considerable haggling at each level. Each year, one of the villagers was appointed to collect each parish's taille; this was an onerous task and was hence rotated among the substantial peasants. The proceeds of the taille were collected by receivers (*receveurs*) and their employees and eventually conveyed to the royal treasury in Versailles. Raising the taille was by far the biggest and most complex task undertaken by the civilian side of the royal state. Only the totality of supply, management, and training of the military forces was comparable in scale and complexity.

The remaining "indirect" taxes, those based not on income but on commerce and consumption, were not collected by royal agents but were farmed out to syndicates of financiers who guaranteed a certain yield to the royal treasury and then organized the collection of the taxes themselves. These syndicates were rewarded both by fees paid by the treasury—a certain percentage of the promised yield—and often by surpluses collected beyond the yield promised to the treasury, not to mention the profits that arose from holding and lending out portions of the sums collected. This arrangement was convenient for the treasury because the financiers, who were exceptionally wealthy, had sufficient credit to assure the king of funds on a regular schedule even though the actual collection of duties might vary considerably from month to month and year to year. Moreover, the financiers could also make advances to the king when his treasury was in particular need, even if sufficient receipts were not yet available. Becoming a tax farmer was the surest route to vast riches in seventeenth- and eighteenth-century France. Tax farmers were denounced by moralists and by the old nobility. However, the nobility did not disdain the possibilities of tapping into these riches by marrying their sons to financiers' daughters or investing in the financiers' lucrative enterprises.

The biggest of the indirect taxes was the infamous gabelle—the salt tax. The company of tax farmers who administered it oversaw the gathering and refining of salt from the salt beds on the coasts, the transport inland and storing of the salt, and the sale of salt to the general public. They also employed a virtual army to repress rampant salt smuggling. The management of the gabelle was a huge enterprise. As we saw in chapter 1, the salt tax could vary enormously from province to province, which explains the ubiquity of smuggling. Repressing smuggling on the borders between exempt and nonexempt territories, not to mention producing, storing, and retailing the salt, was a big job—but was lucrative both for the king and for the syndicate that carried it out.

None of these taxes fell very heavily on one important category of wealth—that accumulated by merchants. Mercantile wealth, which was far more liquid than landed wealth, had been tapped to support warfare in the Middle Ages by means of confiscations, gifts, or forced loans, sometimes negotiated in meetings of the Estates General of the realm. As costs of warfare skyrocketed in the sixteenth century, monarchs began selling offices to wealthy merchants—most importantly judicial offices but also positions as tax receivers, urban councilors, collectors of various market fees, and so on (Mousnier 1971). The sale of offices accelerated in the 1520s when Francis I was at war in Italy and desperate for cash. The king got ready cash, and the officers got a combination of a public function, *gages* (an annual payment from the royal treasury), fees paid by those who used their services, and, equally important, privileges both honorific and pecuniary. Nearly all venal offices (as they were called) conferred membership in privileged corporate bodies and exemptions from ordinary taxation. The highest offices conferred nobility on the holder and, subject to certain regulations, on his posterity. This was true, for example, of offices in the *parlements* (high courts), in the *cours des aides* (high financial courts), or as *maîtres des requêtes*, offices required of those who wished to become judges in the parlements or other courts or to join the royal council as an administrator.

Venal offices, which gave wealthy commoners access to the circle of privilege and honor, became a major income source for the state, accounting, according to one calculation, for between 25 and 40 percent of the crown's income in the 1730s—equivalent, roughly, to the income from the taille or the gabelle (Doyle 1996, 9). An office, once sold by the king to one of his subjects, could be bequeathed to the officer's heir or re-sold by the officer to another, subject to the approval of the corporate body of which the officer was a member. In 1604, a royal decree known as the *paulette* stabilized the system of venal offices by guaranteeing their transferability in return for an annual payment to the royal treasury of one-sixteenth of the office's value. The stabilizing effect of the paulette resulted in a rise in the value of offices, which thereafter became secure lineage properties legally regarded as equivalent to land (Giesey 1983, 1997).

Royal Finance and Administration from François I through Louis XIV and Colbert

These three categories of funds—direct taxes, indirect taxes, and proceeds from the sale of offices—composed the vast bulk of the crown's income. The yield of all three rose significantly between the 1520s, when the wars between François I and the Hapsburg Emperor Charles V began, and France's participation in the Thirty Years' War (1635–48). This period was marked by spiraling sales of offices and by taxes that multiplied in times of war and sometimes sparked rebellions requiring armed suppression. Nevertheless, the funds raised were often short of the needs of armies, which meant that the crown had to borrow, including from financiers and from the venal officers who were tasked with collecting taxes. The problem of servicing and repaying this inevitable debt haunted the state throughout the seventeenth and eighteenth centuries.

In the first half of the seventeenth century, one means of dealing with this problem was to repudiate debts, wholly or in part: there were royal bankruptcies in 1602, 1634, and 1648. The bankruptcy of 1634 was operated largely against the very venal officers who had been charged with the duty—and privilege—of collecting taxes. The king converted the loans owed to these officers into long-term annuities, but at about half their initial value. During the decade or so following the bankruptcy, a period when taxes roughly doubled because of French participation in the Thirty Years' War, many tax officers ceased cooperating with the crown, and some joined peasant tax revolts. It was these officers' unreliability that led to the introduction of intendants to oversee collection. But the crown sometimes enforced collection by the military, a tactic that often backfired because the troops were so destructive that the areas they occupied became too impoverished to pay (Collins 1988, 98–104).

Much of the country was already in turmoil when Louis XIII died in 1643. The years of Louis XIV's minority were chaotic, marked by the widespread rebellion known as the Fronde. At the beginning of his personal rule in 1661, the rebellions of the Fronde had been thoroughly repressed, thanks to the efforts of his first minister, Cardinal Mazarin, but the state remained deeply in debt. Louis decided to govern personally, without a chief minister. He fired and jailed the existing superintendent of finances, Nicolas Fouquet, who was accused of massive peculation, and replaced him with Jean-Baptiste Colbert under the new title controller general of finances. Colbert, who hailed from a recently ennobled mercantile family, had essentially been willed to Louis by Mazarin, whose huge personal fortune he had managed with notable success. Louis recognized that Colbert's boundless capacity for work, instinct for order, and mastery of detail could help him consolidate control over his unwieldy state. As Jacob Soll has emphasized, Colbert brought the systematic skills of accountancy to bear on the organization of royal government, making Louis XIV something of an accountant king (2009, 64).

Colbert's genius was his ability to gather, order, place into files, and make strategic use of information on all matters that concerned the administration. Louis and Colbert launched a thorough reform of nearly all aspects of government. Louis quickly asserted his authority over the rebellious parlements, many of which had joined the Fronde; removed various high-born and illustrious nobles from the royal council; reduced the powers of the military governors of the provinces, who had all too often used their effective control of armed force to resist royal power; and generally enforced strict obedience and loyalty to his royal person. To the princes of the blood and the greatest nobles of the realm, he distributed offices that brought magnificence at court but no power. The ranks of the provincial nobility were purged by a "recherche de noblesse," which required all claiming nobility to produce written proofs from their archives (Goubert 1966, 65–67). The major cities, many of which had participated in the Fronde, were reduced to obedience and their ancient walls destroyed. Paris was given a more powerful and better-organized police force. Louis XIV, with the untiring assistance of Colbert, succeeded in imposing unprecedented order on the kingdom, not by increasing the size of the royal bureaucracy so much as by reorganizing and disciplining it and employing it systematically. Goubert estimates that the entire royal administration, including "the least of the scribes and bailiffs," at less than a thousand, together with some thirty intendants and their secretaries— this to rule a country with twenty million inhabitants (70–73).

The state of finances was always a priority. As of 1661, the debts from many years of war and disorder consumed in advance the entire expected revenue from 1662 and much from 1663. The new regime set up a Chamber of Justice to track down "all the embezzlements committed since 1635" in the realm of state finance. It managed to collect some 110 million livres, the equivalent of an entire year and a half of state revenue. Colbert suppressed superfluous offices and annuities, sharply cut back the remuneration of tax farmers, increased the yield of the taille and gabelle, carefully monitored expenses of the royal household, and increased the monetary yield of royal estates. From 1662 until the outbreak of the Dutch War in 1672, royal income exceeded expenses every year, and a sizable surplus was accumulated (Goubert 1996, 118–21).

The higher tax yield was enabled largely by Colbert's rationalization and tightening of the royal administration. He assigned intendants to every province, using them not only to organize the collection of taxes but to act as gatherers of useful information of all sorts. The volume of correspondence between the provinces and the royal council—and consequently the council's knowledge of the kingdom—expanded greatly (Soll 2009, 68–80). As William Beik has demonstrated in his study of Languedoc, the royal administration under Louis XIV used this enhanced information to intervene far more effectively in provincial affairs, dampening quarrels among local elites and improving cooperation both among the elites and between elites and the central government. The crown also passed on sufficient rewards, both honorific and financial, to sustain the loyalties of local notables, whose cooperation was essential for orderly and effective government and for consistent receipt of tax revenues (Beik 1988).

Colbert recognized the growing importance of international commerce in the Europe of his day and was keenly aware of the commercial superiority of the Dutch and English. He launched colonial ventures, chartering an East and a West India Company modeled on the Dutch and English companies. He established a very effective program of naval construction of both ships and port facilities, which, by the time of his death in 1683, made the French navy a formidable rival of the English and Dutch. He viewed commerce as inseparable from international rivalries. As he saw it, possessing superior commerce and manufactures meant additional revenue for a state and also the impoverishment of rival states, which would see their own commerce decline (Goubert 1966, 121–23). Quite aware of the inferiority of French manufactures to those of the English and Dutch, Colbert attempted to improve French goods by imposing extensive regulations, enforced by a corps of state-employed inspectors with the power to punish uncompliant producers. Colbert also encouraged the recruitment of foreign workers with skills scarce in France and established subsidized manufactures of prestigious luxury goods—most famously of porcelain (Sèvres), tapestries (Gobelins), and mirrors (Saint-Gobin) (Minard 1998, 15–20).

While Colbert was reorganizing the royal administration and instituting new economic regulations, Michel Le Tellier—soon succeeded by his son the Marquis de Louvois—took the military in hand. Louvois tightened discipline, increased inspections, reorganized military ranks, and established new and better storehouses of arms, munitions, grain, and fodder. Meanwhile, the celebrated royal engineer Vauban built scores of indomitable fortresses on the frontiers. There were frequent military reviews, often carried out in the presence of the king. The morale and spirit of the troops were excellent, thanks to hundreds of young nobles eager to display their bravery. By the mid-1660s, France had built the largest and most formidable army in Europe (Goubert 1966, 110).

The Problem of the Debt

All these reforms were carried out during the period of relative peace that followed the end of the Thirty Years' War. But the point of the reforms, as Pierre Goubert insists, was to establish a fiscal basis for the glory of Louis XIV. Glory was earned by the magnificence of the royal court, by the impressive order and obedience of the population, and by patronage of the arts and luxury production. But the crowning glory could be gained only by warfare (Goubert 1966, 121). The Dutch War, begun in 1672, was the first in a succession of military struggles that brought Louis plenty of glory but that ruined French finances. After a campaign of six years that eventually included armies from England, Sweden, Spain, Prussia, and the Holy Roman Empire, the French won some glorious victories in the field and gained considerable territory—Franche-Comté and portions of Flanders—but also plunged the treasury deeply into debt. The Dutch War was followed by the fourteen-month War of the Reunions in 1683 and 1684 and by the War of the League of Augsburg from 1688 to 1697, pitting France against most of the rest of Europe—an alliance of all the German princes, England, Spain, and the Netherlands. Four years after this conflict ended—France gained Alsace in the peace treaty—the War of the Spanish Succession broke out, pitting France against Austria, Prussia, England, and the Netherlands in a conflict that lasted from 1701 to 1714. In short, France was at war for twenty-seven of the forty-two years between the beginning of the Dutch War in 1672 and the end of the War of the Spanish Succession in 1714. And this train of costly wars did not end with Louis XIV's death in 1715. There was the War of the Quadruple Alliance (1718–20), the War of the Polish Succession (1733–37), the War of the Austrian Succession (1740–48), the Seven Years' War (1756–63), and the American Revolutionary War (1778–83), which France entered against England. From the outbreak of the Dutch War right up to the French Revolution, the relentless succession of wars kept the French state constantly in debt.

After 1672, Colbert's careful strategy of trimming expenses and maximizing revenues from existing sources proved grossly insufficient. Providing funds for a king intent on the pursuit of military glory required financial improvisations. Payments to military suppliers fell into arrears, and the colonels and generals, who had purchased their commands and were expected to pay their own troops, were reimbursed only slowly by the state treasury—they were subjected, in effect, to forced loans. Loans were regularly demanded from those who handled state funds, such as tax farmers and receivers of the taille—indeed, from financiers of all sorts. The crown also revived the sale of offices. Colbert, during his first decade in office, had worked to trim back venal offices, both to decrease the drain caused by the annual payment of gages and to decrease the number of public functions whose possession was effectively alienated from the state. But once the French military machine went into operation, this policy was reversed. As had been the case under François I, Henri IV, or Louis XIII, the urgent need for funds forced the crown to create and sell new offices. The number created under Louis XIV and Louis XV did not match that of their predecessors—most relevant public functions had already been sold off. But some sales of offices proved extremely lucrative. The office of the secretary of the king, which required no work whatsoever but conferred ennoblement on the officeholder and his heirs after twenty years in service or after the secretary's death in office, sold briskly right up to the Revolution—and at staggering prices (Bien 1989, 144–86).

By the later years of Louis XIV's reign, it had become clear that the extraordinary debts built up during periods of warfare could not simply be paid off once peace was restored. Rather, an immense and ever-accumulating royal deficit became a permanent feature of the state. The great problem for the French crown in servicing this debt was the king's bad credit. Because of the monarchy's history of bankruptcies, the crown could borrow only at high interest rates—often over 10 percent. The risk of bankruptcy and the high cost of borrowing haunted the market for crown debt right through the eighteenth century: creditors' distrust was revived by partial royal bankruptcies in 1715 at the end of the War of the Spanish Succession and again in 1771 in the wake of the Seven Years' War. In order to bring down borrowing costs, the crown had to demonstrate that it was capable of raising sufficient revenues to keep its debt under control. But how could it do so when it had to pay such high rates of interest? This was a vicious circle indeed.

One means the crown used was exploiting existing venal officers. There were various means of doing so. Most blatantly, the king could simply demand that the existing officers pay more for the offices they already held or face their suppression. Alternatively, the crown could announce an increase in the number of offices attributed to a particular corps—to, say, the Parlement of Dijon or Bordeaux, or the receivers of the taille of Artois, or the grain measurers in the market at Tulle or Amiens—and put them up for sale. With rare exceptions, the already existing corps of officers, loath to see the financial value and status of their offices debased, would band together and buy up the new offices themselves, financing the purchases by either mobilizing their own private credit or using the credit of the corps itself.[5] These were, in effect, forced loans to the crown by its officers. Sometimes the king could simply indicate his need for funds to prosecute the latest war and ask the corps of officers to do their share— although of course this request was also a veiled threat. Again the officers would use their good personal and collective credit to raise the necessary funds. Lower down the social scale, similar procedures were used to shake down trade guilds, whose members also had good reason not to want the number of masters increased and had good credit as a corporate body. The king used similar means to raise funds from the estates of the various provinces or from the order of the clergy, using the good credit of the church or of the estates to raise money at a low interest rate, probably 3 or 4 percent, half or less than half the rate the crown would be charged.[6] Raising loans through these corporate bodies—officers, trade guilds, estates, and the church—became a major component of state finance, helping France to remain Europe's leading power in the late seventeenth century and to contest military preeminence in Europe and the world with England in the eighteenth century, right down to the Revolution.

The Double Bind of the Old Regime Fiscal System

With hindsight, we can see that the French fiscal system as it emerged in this era was fragile and contradictory, fatally weaker than the system

---

5. Recognized as legal persons, old regime corps could take on collective debt.

6. The classic analysis of this use of the corps of officeholders to gain state revenue is Bien (1987). On raising money through the estates, see Swann (2003, 295–329) and Potter (2000).

developed by France's English rival. But in the eighteenth century itself, this was not obvious. The English crown had an even bigger deficit, and there were many criticisms of the English fiscal system as unsustainable. Yet the French old regime was eventually brought down in 1789 by an irresolvable fiscal crisis—irresolvable, that is, within the parameters of the existing system.

The old regime fiscal system suffered from cross-cutting contradictions. On the one hand, it was evident, certainly to royal administrators, that simply raising the rate of taxation on the peasant masses who bore the greatest fiscal burden threatened to decrease agricultural productivity by impoverishing the agriculturalists, thereby undermining the tax base. The seemingly obvious solution would have been to extend existing taxes to privileged nobles, clerics, venal officers, and bourgeois, who were certainly wealthy enough to bear more taxation. But the possibility of annulling the tax privileges of these groups was ideologically fraught, politically dangerous, and financially complicated. The historian of the French tax system Joël Félix put it well: "From whichever side of the question one began, a reform of the fiscal system, because it posed the problem of privileges, threated to blow to bits the very foundations of the political, economic and social organization of the old regime" (1999, 304).

The ideological justification for exempting the clergy and nobility from the taille was as old as the taille itself. The venerable medieval formula was that the clergy offered prayers to God, nobles offered their blood to defend the realm, and commoners did their part by offering work and taxes (Duby 1978). To be *taillable* was such a long-standing mark of indignity in France that annulling the clerics' and nobles' exemptions would seem an assault on the very principle of hierarchy, a principle fundamental to the monarchical state. To be sure, those who had attained nobility through venal office hardly fit the traditional formula. But singling them out for taxation would have threatened their status as genuine nobles—a status often regarded as doubtful by the ancient nobility but that had been sanctioned by the king and become fundamental to the prestige and functioning of the royal state (Ford 1953). The high judiciary and the royal administration were operated almost exclusively by venal officeholders. Subjecting officeholders to the taille would have undermined the status of the state's chief servants and also diminished the standing of the thousands of bourgeois who had purchased lesser offices—from municipal councilors, judges, and bailiffs to measurers in the markets or local postmasters—officials who were crucial to carrying out the daily functions of government.

Annulling tax privileges would also have been politically dangerous.

The centrally directed royal state that Louis XIV and Colbert constructed and that survived in its basic lineaments up to the Revolution was so thin on the ground that its efficient functioning required the active cooperation of local elites. This cooperation was assured by the state's net redistribution of resources from the peasant masses to elites by means of offices, military commissions, pensions, gifts, and tax privileges, as well as by the prestige that came from association with a glorious monarchy (Beik 1988). Because an attack on the tax privileges of these varied elites would threaten their wealth, social standing, and pride, it would endanger the day-to-day cooperation essential to the smooth functioning of the royal state and likely create open dissension from royal policies and decrees. The memory of the Fronde made the government particularly wary of stirring up conflicts with entrenched elites. Moreover, in the context of political and military rivalries between European states, the government surely feared that large-scale resistance against royal policy might be read as a military vulnerability.

A wholesale suppression of tax privileges would also have posed serious financial difficulties. The privileged venal officers were all members of royally sanctioned corporate bodies that served indirectly as a source of low-cost credit to the crown. An attack on the tax privileges of this host of privileged corporate bodies would not only undermine the loyalty of royal officials but also drastically cut the market prices of their offices—by eliminating the valuable tax benefits that adhered to the offices and by decreasing the offices' prestige and hence their value to potential purchasers. Since the combined value of a corps' offices determined how much the king could ask of the officers and was the foundation of the corps' good credit, suppressing venal officers' tax privileges would have dried up a crucial source of state credit and plunged the crown into certain bankruptcy.

In short, the state was damned if it revoked fiscal privileges and damned if it didn't. The consequence was a stalemate: the regime of tax privileges, for all its dire effects on state revenue, lasted until 1789, when the entire old regime state was dismantled by the French Revolution and the nobility was abolished. As Gail Bossenga has shrewdly argued, this double bind, the simultaneous necessity and impossibility of adequately taxing the wealth of the richest and most privileged members of the population, was a fundamental and fateful structuring feature of the fiscal and administrative history of the old regime state (Bossenga 2005). As we shall see, a succession of controllers general and subordinate royal officials attempted various means of overcoming this contradiction. One effort was the imposition in 1695 of what was supposed to be a purely temporary direct tax—the *capitation*, or head tax—that was in principle assessed on all persons and was instituted to provide funds for continued prosecution of the War of the League of Augsburg. This effort was followed later by analogous universal taxes called the *dixième* (tenth) and *vingtième* (twentieth). These taxes by no means established equality of taxation, since the privileged had to pay only the capitation and dixième/ vingtième, whereas the unprivileged had to pay these levies on top of the taille and indirect taxes. Nevertheless, the partial success of this effort indicated that the royal state, in its desperate search for funds, was willing and able to violate the boundary of privilege by taxing the wealth of all subjects. Although these taxes became virtually permanent, officially they remained temporary administrative expedients. Indeed, their imposition stirred up a potent political backlash that significantly undermined the legitimacy of the royal government and made any plan for the total abolition of tax privileges unthinkable. The principle of universal taxation was not to be generalized until after the fall of the old regime.

Universal Taxes: The Capitation, the Dixième, and the Vingtième

The imposition of taxes on those who benefited from tax privileges was introduced by Louis XIV in 1695.[7] The outlays for the War of the League of Augsburg, then in its seventh year, had ravaged the royal budget, and a poor harvest and incipient famine had sharply reduced the product of the taille. The capitation was intended as an extraordinary tax that would last only as long as the war; it was in fact suspended at the end of hostilities in 1698. Three years later, however, the deficits the war had built up led the administration to reimpose the capitation. From then through 1789, the supposedly extraordinary capitation was collected every year. The decree announcing the new tax in 1695 explicitly invoked a principle of equal obligation to pay: "We wish that none of our subjects, whatever quality and condition they may be, Ecclesiastic, Secular or Regular, Noble, Military or other, shall be exempt from the capitation." All, "without any distinction," were to pay (41). Thus Louis XIV, the very embodiment of a hierarchical state based on distinctions and privilege, was driven by the logic of monetary need to establish a tax that made no distinctions between subjects. That the capitation was to be paid by all was an exception to the normal

---

7. On universal taxation under the old regime, the essential work is Kwass (2000). In the remainder of the chapter, page citations to Kwass are in parentheses in the text.

rule: payment of the taille, a much more burdensome tax, remained subject to the traditional exemptions. But this exceptional form of tax soon became a fundamental feature of the French fiscal system.

In 1710, during the War of the Spanish Succession and on the heels of another disastrous harvest, Louis XIV created yet another universal direct tax, to be collected on top of the taille and the capitation: the dixième, which was, in principle, to be a levy of a tenth of the income of all subjects.[8] The dixième was suspended in 1717 but was reimposed from 1733 to 1737 during the War of the Polish Succession and yet again in 1741 at the outset of the War of the Austrian Succession. This tax, slightly modified, was renamed the vingtième in 1749, which implied a decline in the rate of tax from 10 to 5 percent of income. However, kings twice doubled and then tripled the vingtième, once during the Seven Years' War and once during the American Revolutionary War. In short, for most of the eighteenth century and for nearly the entire last five decades of the old regime, not one but two "extraordinary" taxes were imposed on all subjects, privileged or not.

The imposition of universal taxes indicates that the royal administration not only was aware of the potential advantages of a regime of fiscal equality but imagined itself capable of putting it into practice. A regime of equality in taxation, it might be said, is a kind of logical consequence of a state administration with the single-minded collection of money as its prime object. From the perspective of state funding, what matters is not the status, the quality, or the occupation of persons but their ability to provide cash. The taxpayer becomes not a noble, officer, peasant, townsman, or priest, nor a Parisian, Burgundian, Norman, or Marseillais. Rather, the royal subject becomes a unit of income production capable of supporting his or her proportion of the state's needs. This abstract taxpayer-citizen was conjured into existence when the royal administration developed means of collecting the new universal taxes. Yet the monarchy continued to act as the font of honor, recognizing and enforcing privileges of all sorts and continually creating new privileged persons exempted from other taxes through the purchase of offices. In this as in other respects, the old regime monarchy was deeply contradictory, pulled in one direction by the uniformity and abstraction inherent in monetary exchange and in another by the logic of honor and hierarchy.

In addition to being assessed upon the wealth of all subjects, the universal taxes were administered differently than the taille, at least in the

8. On the initial imposition of the dixième and difficulties in collecting it, see Bonney (1993, 383–416).

pays d'élection—those provinces located in the core of the kingdom. In the case of the taille, the intendant of the province imposed a collective obligation for a tax of a certain amount upon each parish, but it was the parish assembly that had to work out the division of the tax among villagers and designate one of their number as collector. Disputes about assessments were heard by the courts. By contrast, the capitation and the dixième/vingtième were assessed not upon a corporate village but upon each subject individually. It was the intendant and the collectors under his direction who assessed each person's taxes, with disputes resolved by the intendant rather than the courts. This system was both speedier and less cumbersome than the system of the taille (48–53). As Michael Kwass puts it, in the administration of the capitation and the dixième, "royal administrators and individual universal tax payers met head on" (52).

Under the system used for the taille, the assessment of any individual's tax liability was determined by his fellow villagers, who could be expected to reach a reasonably well-informed consensus about each other's wealth. But such a system could not work when the wealth to be assessed included that of nobles, merchants, and officials. The habits of command and deference that regulated relations between noble seigneurs and peasants would make assessing taxes on the lord daunting, if not impossible. Moreover, although peasants could have comprehended and could probably have estimated the value of the lord's land, buildings, and livestock with reasonable accuracy, the other kinds of property and income typically possessed by privileged persons—offices, pensions, annuities, complex debts and credits, urban town houses, and the like—would have been beyond the ken of even the most sophisticated peasant. But agents of the intendant, educated persons backed by the authority of the state, could evaluate the holdings of privileged persons with more finesse. As Controller General Terray put it in a communication to his intendants in the early 1770s, the vingtième should be distributed "with the greatest equality possible" and therefore should be based on knowledge of "the true product of the property subject to the tax."[9] The logic of equal taxation both individualized the subjects of the king and abstracted them, for this purpose, to a monetary essence—the income generated by their property.

Making a detailed investigation of the value of everyone's property simultaneously would have been impossible for the intendant's small staff of tax collectors, but these authorities could carry out selective "verifications" of the income reported to them. Not surprisingly, the verifications

9. Kwass (87), quoting letters from 1772 and 1773.

were generally applied to wealthy persons with complex holdings and diverse sources of income—which is to say, primarily the nobility. Initially, verifications were pursued only when a taxpayer protested that his assessment was too high. But eventually the administration developed a campaign of selective verifications of very wealthy nobles whose declarations of income seemed particularly suspect. This policy was first tried in the 1750s immediately following the reintroduction of the vingtième and was revived more systematically under Terray in the early 1770s and continued by his successors, especially Jacques Necker, who was the director of finances from 1776 to 1783. The verifications could be very thorough. The provincial tax controllers and their assistants would, for example, measure the taxpayer's acreage, distinguishing land as arable, pasture, or meadow and categorizing soils as good, bad, or mediocre and calculate the land's value accordingly; they would also require the landowner to present all leases, titles, and other documentation concerning income (87–95).

By the 1780s, the administration had developed reasonably accurate knowledge of the incomes of most of the population, at least in the pays d'élections. It is therefore clear that the administration had the capacity, in principle, to impose something approaching civic equality in taxation by the last decade of the old regime. But this final step was to be taken only by the new revolutionary government in the early 1790s. There has long been a debate about whether the imposition of the capitation and the dixième/vingtième actually were seriously assessed on the nobility (Marion 1919; Behrens 1963; Anderson 1974). The painstaking research of Michael Kwass has demonstrated that nobles and other privileged persons indeed paid significant sums under the regime of universal taxation, particularly in the pays d'élections. Judging from systematically calculated evidence about Normandy in northern France, Berry in the center, and Limousin in the west, Kwass estimates that privileged landowners paid only about 1 percent of their income in capitation but that the dixième and the vingtième struck noble incomes much more forcefully, generally attaining rates between 7 and 10 percent when the vingtième was doubled and tripled in the second half of the eighteenth century (Kwass 2000, 94–95). Rates may have been somewhat higher for those who held privileged offices, who, in addition to paying the vingtième and capitation on whatever land they held, also had about 10 percent of their gages withheld by the crown. The nobles and princes who inhabited Versailles as courtiers, who frequently were granted lavish pensions and gifts by the king, had the capitation and vingtième taxes withheld from these payments and therefore paid relatively high rates (103–7). Members of the clergy were spared these taxes. This was partly but far from fully compensated for by the annual "free gift" that the king extracted from them as a substitute (110–12). In short, the capitation and especially the dixième and vingtième were something close to universal.

However, the peasantry, which had always paid the vast bulk of the taille, was taxed at substantially higher rates than those who held privileges. They paid the capitation and dixième/vingtième like everyone else but paid the taille besides—not to mention the gabelle and other indirect taxes. For most of the eighteenth century, the yield of the taille was greater than that of the universal taxes, although by the 1770s and 1780s, the yield of the vingtième had slightly surpassed that of the taille (Kwass 2000, 107). In short, the proportion of their income that peasants paid in taxes was probably at least twice that paid by the much wealthier privileged persons. As this estimate makes clear, privileges continued to be lucrative right to the end of the old regime.

Resistance to Universal Taxation

By the later decades of the old regime, the royal administration had the means to institute a regime of equality in taxation. But there was no practical possibility of actually doing so, largely because even the truncated form of equal taxation instituted by the capitation and the dixième/vingtième provoked damaging political resistance. These impositions generated plenty of complaints from individual taxpayers, who claimed that their wealth had been overstated by the fiscal officials and that they were therefore assessed an unfair tax. The intendant and his staff typically adjudicated several hundred such petitions annually in the generality of Caen in Normandy between the 1760s and the 1780s (141–46). It was not unusual for these petitions to result in at least a small decrease in the assessed tax. But if individual petitions indicated that many taxpayers were unhappy, the petitioning process did not question the new taxes' legitimacy.

There was, however, serious resistance from the provincial parlements and the Parlement of Paris. These superior courts, staffed by ennobled judiciary officers, had the right and duty of registering royal laws and edicts to make them applicable within their jurisdictions. The parlements also had the right to remonstrate with the king about laws they considered unjust or unwise. As we have seen, the parlements had proved a formidable source of resistance to royal policies in the years leading up to the Fronde. Louis XIV had suppressed the parlements' right of remonstrance, but this right was restored after his death in 1715 by the regent, the Duke of Orleans. In the second half of the eighteenth century, the parlements used remonstrances to criticize a wide range of royal policies, including the administration of universal taxes (Égret 1970; Doyle 1974; Stone 1986; Swann 1995). They did not object to the imposition of these taxes per se but rather to what they regarded as encroachments that the administration of these taxes made on traditional liberties—liberties of which they, as judges, regarded themselves as guardians.

Until the 1740s, the edicts establishing universal taxes were registered without protest. But protests began in 1749, when Controller General Machaut converted the wartime dixième, established during the War of the Austrian Succession, into a peacetime vingtième. Machaut threatened to tax the clergy directly and to revoke previous arrangements that had been made with various pays d'états. These innovations roused several provincial parlements, which not only remonstrated but refused to register the edict until directly ordered to do so by the king. There were protests once again when the vingtième was doubled at the beginning of the Seven Years' War in 1756. The Parlements of Paris, Toulouse, Aix, Bordeaux, and Rouen particularly criticized tax procedures, especially the widespread verifications of taxpayers' income. They also argued that any contestations about taxes should be judged not by the intendants but only by law courts (159–61).

The real storm of protest, however, began in 1760, when the crown decreed a tripling of the vingtième. On this occasion, various parlements not only refused to register the decrees and issued blistering remonstrances but then proceeded to publish the remonstrances, thereby making the arguments widely available. The remonstrances accused the administration of exercising arbitrary authority—indeed, despotism— and adopted a language of liberty, property, the citizen, and the nation, all of which the parlements claimed to be defending.[10] The parlement of Rouen attributed the arbitrariness of the current government to a definite agent: finance. "Finance, this worm-like eater of Citizen and State, attacked, overran, subjugated everything. Even legislation became its prey: to make laws, to revoke them; to create and to destroy, only it is consulted" (163).[11] The language here was incendiary, but the perception that financial concerns dominated royal policy was largely correct. The despotism at issue in the remonstrance was above all that of the intendants, who

10. This rhetoric echoed Montesquieu's *De l'esprit des lois* (1749) as well as the language of the dissident Jansenist movement in the French Catholic Church, which was well represented among the parlementary judges. On the latter, see Van Kley (1975).

11. The quotation is from Archives Départmentale de la Seine Maritime, 1B 278, secret register of the parlement of Rouen, May 10, 1760. The printed version was Remontrances (1960).

not only imposed taxes but carried out verifications that were veritable "inquisitions" and acted as judges of all disputes. These verifications, the parlements claimed, deprived citizens of their property and denied them their due recourse to justice via the courts. The parlements insisted that jurisdiction over tax matters should belong to the judiciary, which had always judged tax disputes with respect to the taille. Here the parlements were arguing partly to defend their own professional interests as the kingdom's supreme judicial authorities. They were also defending themselves in these remonstrances against taxes they would have to pay and against verifications that could be used to discover the extent of their own wealth.

But the political argumentation of the parlements went far beyond a defense of their own corporate interests. Indeed, rather than claim that the parlements should be the ultimate arbiters in matters of taxation, the Parlement of Rouen evoked the nation, composed of citizen property holders, whose liberty could only be secured by the restoration of provincial estates and the calling of a national Estates General. It made this argument even though the parlementaires were surely aware that the establishment of vigorous provincial estates and the Estates General would restrict their own claims to power and authority. Their argument was based on an imagined history in which the nation, represented by estates, had once freely imposed taxes upon itself. As the Parlement of Rouen put it, "As long as the meeting of Estates lasted in France, the people, in the persons of its Deputies, shared in the estimation of public needs. . . . Familiar with the nature and extent of its resources, it knew how to assess and pay its contributions. These sufficed for even extraordinary expenses without diminishing the wealth of individuals. The Government flourished as did the Citizen: the subject paid more willingly that which he paid without effort; the prince received in full what was brought to him with economy." Thus the parlement pleaded with the king, "Return to us, Sire, this precious liberty, return our Estates. You will make disappear these ruinous contestations that afflict the Citizen."[12]

As Kwass points out, the parlements, in the arguments of their remonstrances, pursued "particularistic aims through abstract principle" (170). They were arguing for a system of government in which the king would entirely withdraw his administrative apparatus of intendants, subdelegates, and collectors from the provinces. In the parlement's vision, all requests from the king and others about provincial affairs would be taken up by provincial estates representing the province's "citizens." These rep-

---

12. This account is based on Kwass (161–71). The quotations (162, 165) are taken from *Remontrances* (1760).

resentatives would, as was traditional, meet in three distinct chambers, one each for the clergy, the nobility, and the commoners. Taxes, presumably, would be collected by appointed agents of the estates, and all disputes over assessments would be considered before the courts, with the parlement, as the superior court, having final judgment should there be appeals. How such a decentralized government by provincial estates and parlements would coordinate affairs with the royal council or the Estates General of the nation remained unspecified. The parlement's language of the nation and the citizen had powerfully universalistic implications: the nation was constituted by all French subjects, and all had rights as citizens. But the liberty and the property that the parlements wished to defend were undoubtedly particularist: the traditional liberties, real and imagined, of the provinces, the nobility, the estates, and corporate bodies of all kinds; property in land, buildings, and chattel; in immovables and movables; but also property in offices, distinctions, and privileges, including the privilege of immunity from taxation. By borrowing language from republican and Enlightenment discourse, the parlements were playing a dangerous game. Their language of nation, citizen, liberty, and property, once it entered the sphere of public discourse, could be, and soon was, appropriated and turned to much more universalistic ends than the parlementaires had intended.

The disputes between king and parlement of the early 1760s resulted in forced registrations of laws, mass resignation of parlementaires that brought legal business to a halt, new royal legislation, new inflammatory published remonstrances, royal audiences with parlementaires, and new forced registrations. Public support for the parlements was widespread; taxpayers, both noble and commoner, saw the parlements as their only defense against an ever-hungry fiscal apparatus. The ruckus eventually died down when the parlements, under threat from the king, registered the royal decrees with the provision that reassessments of taxpayer wealth would cease. Moreover, the end of the Seven Years' War in 1763 brought about the cancellation of the third vingtième, which naturally cooled tempers.

But this uneasy compromise lasted only until 1771, when Controller General Terray, under pressure from the staggering war debt, operated a partial royal bankruptcy by cutting the interest payments on royal bonds and began a systematic campaign of reassessments of landowners' property. The parlements responded as usual with passionate published remonstrances. This time, however, the chancellor of France, René Nicolas Charles Augustin de Maupeou, staged a coup against the parlements. He abolished three of them, remodeled the rest, and established domesticated "superior councils" that usurped parlementary power. Terray then took advantage of the weakened condition of the cowed remaining parlements to introduce an edict prolonging the two vingtièmes and declaring that they would be levied as a strict percentage of incomes. This opened the way to extensive verifications of the tax rolls that resulted in a significant overall tax increase[13] but also led to much public discontent and renewed calls for provincial estates and the Estates General.

The Maupeou coup was partially reversed in 1774, when Louis XVI acceded to the throne and restored the parlements as a gesture of goodwill. The restored parlements, chastened by their extended exile, continued to remonstrate against taxes but with less rebellious bravura than in the 1760s. As before, the main object of the parlement's displeasure was less the level of taxation than what they regarded as the arbitrary process by which the vingtième was assessed and the fact that appeals of assessments had to be made to the very officials who had ordered them—the intendants. The program of updating the assessments by means of verifications in fact continued under Louis XVI's ministers, Turgot (1774–76) and Necker (1777–83). Necker, in particular, intensified and systematized the process of reassessment, arguing that the procedure was necessary, as he put it in a decree of 1778, in order to "establish more justice and equality in the distribution of a tax which circumstance makes necessary"— and, he went on, "to give the less wealthy and weaker taxpayers the means to make themselves heard" (207).[14] Here Necker expressed the underlying logic of the royal government's administration of the vingtième: to establish formal equality among taxpayers, regardless of their rank or privileges, to make taxes a pure function of income—and hence of ability to pay—rather than of status.

The question of taxation was to play a central role in the terminal crisis of the old regime and the early years of the Revolution. It is widely recognized that the public disputes over taxation from the 1740s through the 1770s were fundamental to the development of a political language capable of mobilizing public opinion against excessive, arbitrary, or unjust taxation. This language, with its key positive terms of liberty, citizen, and property and its negative terms of arbitrary power and despotism, was sufficiently ambiguous to be used not only in defense of traditional privileges and liberties, as the parlements intended, but to argue for a regime of civic equality. It is important to note that before 1789, equality was in

13. Kwass (90–95) demonstrates that the yield of the capitation and vingtième rose significantly in the early 1770s in the presidency of Caen in Normandy.

14. From Floquet (1843, 75–76).

fact far more likely to be invoked by administrators like Terray or Turgot than by parlementaires. Here, as Tocqueville claimed, the administrators played an important role in making a certain form of equality seem possible. However, in the months leading up to the Revolution, a language of equality was linked to reworked concepts of liberty, citizenship, and property. At this point, the entire regime of privilege that was so dear to the parlements was cast into doubt, and the administrative conceptions of equality were transmogrified. The taxpayer-citizen emerged as a foundation of the new revolutionary regime.

Political Economy

A SOLUTION TO THE DOUBLE BIND?

One notable characteristic of the French royal administration in the eighteenth century was the extent to which it generated proposals for reforms of the economy. Such reforms had various motivations—ranging from the particular interests of various industries or regions to a genuine desire to improve the lives of the poor. But nearly all economic reform projects were in part motivated by fiscal concerns. Any reform that increased the economy's productivity would mean more income and consumption to tax and, through the influence of wealth on population, an increase in the number of taxable subjects. What we would call economic growth and eighteenth-century observers called the progress of commerce would automatically alleviate the state's fiscal woes.

Efforts to improve French economic performance can be traced back to Colbert, who, as we have seen, imposed detailed regulations on certain manufactures with the explicit intent of rendering French products competitive in international markets. But if Colbert's efforts remained in some sense an inspiration to royal administrators, the reforms they introduced during the eighteenth century were increasingly non-Colbertian, even anti-Colbertian. The reformers attempted to free economic life from what they saw as excessive regulation and thereby stimulate economic growth (Minard 1998). In the 1750s, a liberal school of political economy, developed in what has been dubbed the "Gournay circle," arose from within the royal administration itself. A second influential school, "physiocracy," emerged in the late 1750s and 1760s. The modes of thinking about economic and political problems introduced by these two schools were dispersed broadly in Enlightenment political discourse and embraced by many administrators of the royal state.

From the 1740s forward, most of the controllers general of finances embraced some sort of reform agenda. This was true in varying degrees of Machault d'Arnouville, Moreau de Séchelles, Silhouette, Bertin, L'Averdy,

Maynon d'Invau, Turgot, Necker, Calonne, and Loménie de Brienne, who, between them, were in office thirty-seven of the forty-five years between 1745 and 1789. In spite of this numerical dominance, the sum of their reforms was surprisingly slight. The lack of continuity was a problem: there were fourteen controllers in the final thirty-five years of the old regime, making the average tenure only two and a half years—not long given the thickets of precedents and privileges against which reformers had to strive. Moreover, a new reform-minded controller could not always be counted on to continue the reforms his predecessor introduced, and some reformers were followed by traditionalists who reversed their schemes entirely. Yet there is no denying that the royal administration was, in the final years of the old regime, far from a bastion of conservatism. This is one of Tocqueville's lasting insights. Although they had to work within a system inherited from Louis XIV and Colbert, many members of the royal administration had, by the 1780s, adopted reformist opinions and worked, within the limits of their powers, to free the economy from inherited constraints and privileges.

This reformist bent of the administration was affected by the great outpouring of Enlightenment texts in the middle years of the century. Enlightened ideas became prominent in the public sphere and in the conversations of the Parisian salons. Royal administrators—well-educated men with considerable prestige and a bent for public service—certainly read Enlightenment literature, and many took part in salon discussions. Given their social positions, it would have been strange had they not become consumers— and sometimes advocates—of the leading cultural ideas of their age.

Vincent de Gournay: An Advocate for Liberal Political Economy within the Royal Administration

Jacques-Claude-Marie Vincent de Gournay, whom we have encountered briefly in chapter 8, became an official in the Bureau of Commerce in 1751. He was the animating center of a group of political economists who boldly advocated economic liberty. The ideas of the Gournay circle were influential both within the administration itself and in the larger sphere of public discussion. Gournay and his followers were important figures in the international discourse of political economy as well; indeed, it was Gournay who brought the famous catchphrase *laissez-faire, laissez-passez* into regular usage in economic discourse.[1]

---

1. The phrase appears nowhere in Gournay's very few published writings. But in subsequent years, when the slogan had become commonplace, other economists attributed

Jacques-Claude-Marie Vincent was born in 1712 in the Atlantic port of Saint-Malo, one of several children of a wealthy wholesale merchant. After his education at the elite College de Juilly near Paris, he was sent, at the age of seventeen, to the Spanish port of Cadiz to work in a French merchant house. There he learned the business, traveled and read widely, and accumulated a decent fortune. His business partner died childless in 1746 and bequeathed to Vincent his own considerably larger fortune, including the landed estate of Gournay—whence the name by which he is generally known.[2] On the basis of this inherited fortune, Vincent de Gournay retired from commerce, purchased an ennobling office, and entered government service in 1749. He entered the Bureau of Commerce in 1751, where he worked under Daniel Trudaine, the director of the bureau and Morellet's future patron. He was expected both to represent the interests of merchants and manufacturers in a large swath of France and to oversee the system of economic regulations in his assigned territory (Turgot 1808; Schelle 1897; Charles 2011).

But Gournay was ambivalent about these duties. From early on, impressed by the prosperity of England and the Netherlands, he had read works on commerce and economic policy in English. Finding that the Anglo-Dutch ideals of economic freedom in no way contradicted his own practical business knowledge, he became a convinced economic liberal. Hence he was critical of many regulations he was expected to enforce. He regarded most merchants and manufacturers he was supposed to represent as small-minded and wedded to privileges that restricted competition. He therefore worked to convince his administrative colleagues that the French economy's heavy burden of regulation was harmful to commerce and manufactures and should be eliminated. Economic liberty, Gournay argued in a report in 1753, spreads prosperity and therefore strengthens the state. It is "the most efficacious means of opposing the nations that are jealous of us and are rivals of our commerce" (Schelle 1897, 138).

The future reforming controller general Turgot befriended Gournay when he was assigned to accompany the older man on a tour of his administrative territory. Upon Gournay's death in 1759 at the age of forty-eight, Turgot wrote an *éloge* in his honor. He related that Gournay, throughout

---

priority of usage to him. For example, the marquis de Mirabeau, a leading physiocrat, writing in the *Éphemerides* in 1775, declared that Gournay had propounded "simple and natural truths . . . which he expressed by this single axiom . . . *laissez faire, laissez passer*. Accept, excellent Gournay, this homage to thy creative and benevolent genius!" Quoted in Schelle (1897, 217).

2. Gournay also married the widow of his partner. See the preface by Simone Meyssonnier in Child (2008, viii).

his tenure in the Bureau of Commerce, had worked patiently against considerable resistance to win his colleagues over to liberal opinions (1808,
350–54). Within the Bureau, Gournay could not put his ideas directly
into practice but succeeded in "weakening the authority" of "the old principles" (358). His dedicated espousal of economic liberty brought into
question the long-standing authority of Colbert's vision—no mean feat
in the Bureau of Commerce, which had the administrative responsibility
of managing the network of Colbertian regulations.

In spite of the slow pace of reform within the administration, Turgot saw Gournay's entry into the Bureau of Commerce as launching "an
epoch of revolution" (Turgot 1808, 328). Turgot claimed Gournay was
responsible for "this happy fermentation that has arisen over the past several years" concerning "commerce" and "political economy . . . a fermentation that burst forth two or three years after M. de Gournay became an Intendant of Commerce." This fermentation of ideas had produced "works
filled with laborious research and profound views" (355–56). If Gournay's
efforts to convince administrative colleagues were slow and painstaking,
his influence on public discussion was felt more quickly. Gournay himself
published little—he wrote almost exclusively in the form of administrative memoirs intended for the bureau. His influence was instead felt via
the circle of intellectuals attracted by his ideas and generous personality.
According to Turgot, Gournay "did not regard himself as an author. Having no sense of possession of what he had written, he abandoned his manuscripts without reserve to all those who wished to instruct themselves or
who wished to write on these matters. Most of the time he did not even
keep copies of what he had written" (361).

Gournay himself expressed some satisfaction with the advance of
the ideas he espoused. In an undated manuscript, he wrote, "If our century has some advantage over past centuries, it is without doubt a consequence of the progress made . . . by the love of the public good. Books
on commerce, on manufactures, on agriculture are read avidly. . . . One
sees lords of the first rank giving serious application to these important
issues" (Child 2008, xvii). But Gournay was prevented by his administrative superiors from contributing in his own name to the developing political economy literature. At the suggestion of Trudaine, he published,
in 1754, a French translation (Child 1754) of an English pamphlet, *Brief
Observations Concerning Trade and Interest of Money,* which had been published by the English merchant Josiah Child in 1668. Gournay intended
to include his own extensive commentary along with the translation but
was dissuaded from doing so by Controller General Machaut d'Arnouville. The manuscript of Gournay's "remarks" found its way into Gour-

nay's personal archives, to be discovered only in the 1980s; its definitive edition was published only in 2008 (Child 2008).[3]

In these "remarks," Gournay made his admiration for English practices clear. The English, he declared, had outdone France by making "affairs of commerce the principal object" of its policies (Child 2008, 233).[4] France, by contrast, had not valued commerce sufficiently. For example, by encouraging wealthy merchants to purchase ennobling offices rather than continuing their commercial careers, France had "made men imagine that it was more honorable to possess [an office] than to engage in commerce" (229). Gournay asserted that war in his century is "made above all through the opposition of the wealth of nation to nation rather than in opposing man to man." The state that has "the greatest wealth can sustain war longest [and] will be able in the end to subjugate the other" (231). The best way to make France a more formidable military and political power, hence, would be to improve its commerce.

Gournay's vision was founded no less than Colbert's on a concern for France's military power. His advocacy of commercial freedom was restricted to commerce within France; he did not advocate free trade between nations. Child's treatise had warmly supported England's Navigation Acts, which gave English ships and merchants a monopoly on trade with its colonies. Gournay regarded the Navigation Acts as a foundation of English maritime trade's remarkable flourishing and believed that a similar navigation act would expand France's wealth, its merchant marine, and its military strength, just as it had for England (141, 270, 277, 307).

But Gournay argued that the regulation of commerce within France needed reform. France had relied too much on expanding state finance at the expense of ordinary people: "The state will only find a true natural resource in the prosperity of the multitude, because only then will the collection of taxes and the imposition of loans become easy" (236). He lauded commerce as the prime "source of augmentation of the king's revenues" (322). But improving the lot of ordinary people and thereby the revenues of the king would require extensive reforms. Among the most important were bringing down the interest rate, something first achieved by the Dutch and then copied by the English (162); encouraging immigration from other countries and naturalization of foreigners living in France (178–79); lifting the guilds' restrictions on new masterships (179); and

3. The manuscripts of Gournay's remarks were discovered by Tsuda (1983).

4. In the rest of this section of the chapter, notes to this work will be in parentheses in the text.

loosening Colbert's regulation of the textile industries. "Today we are the sole commercial nation in the universe that still believes that trades must be disciplined with an iron rod. . . . The fines pronounced by our regulations make the profession of manufacturer the most miserable that exists in our society, because the simple exercise of his profession exposes him to penalties" (193).

Changes on the scale Gournay recommended in his unpublished "Remarks" would have required a huge and controversial effort on the part of the royal administration. It is hence not surprising that Machaut d'Arnouville forbade the publication of his views. But Gournay found other means to get his opinions out. Members of his circle published many books, and Gournay himself, as we shall see, seems to have been the ghostwriter of one of the most influential of them.

The Gournay Circle

Gournay's circle was a salon that focused on questions of political economy. It united distinguished members of the royal administration, several experienced writers, and a number of young men in their twenties, like the abbé Morellet, who hoped to make their way as men of letters. This mixture turned out to be extraordinarily fertile. In the years between 1753 and 1758, the ideas discussed in the Gournay circle entered massively into print. No fewer than thirty books by circle members were published over these six years: some, if we are to believe Turgot's *éloge*, based significantly on Gournay's administrative memoirs. This outpouring of books played a crucial role in launching political economy as a major literary genre in eighteenth-century France, a phenomenon that dates precisely from the 1750s. There turned out to be an extremely lively market for books on economic questions (Shovlin 2006).

In addition to these writers, the Gournay circle included important administrators, including three who served at some point as reform-minded controllers general. In addition to Turgot, then at the beginning of his career, were two older men: Machaut d'Arnouville, born in 1701, who was controller general from 1745 to 1754, and Étienne de Silhouette, born in 1709, who served a half year in 1759. Daniel Trudaine, who attended regularly, was the head of the Bureau of Commerce and the director of the Corps des ponts et chausées, the French national highway bureau. Trudaine's son, Trudaine de Montigny, who inherited his father's positions after his death, was also a habitué of the circle. Finally, the circle included the great liberal magistrate Malesherbes, whom we have encountered in chapter 3. Malesherbes, a friend of the philosophes, was the president of

the Cour des aides, the kingdom's highest financial court, while simultaneously serving as the director of the book trade. As the royal censor, he
eased the publication of works by members of the Gournay circle, some
of which could have been seen as contravening the "royal secret"—the
traditional prohibition against public discussion of the affairs of the king's
government.

The works published by members of the Gournay circle spanned several genres: rather traditional works on agricultural methods or on the
products of various industries (Carlier 1755; Duhamel de Monceau 1753),
histories or descriptions of the commercial practices of different countries (Butel-Dumont 1755; Forbonnais 1758; Carlier 1753), and treatises or
commentaries on questions of economic policy, directed explicitly or implicitly at the policies of the French state (Hébert 1753; O'Heguerty 1757;
Clicquot de Blervache 1755; Morellet 1758). There were also translations,
all but one from English (Forbonnais 1753; Plumard de Danguel 1754;
Le Blanc 1754; Tucker 1755). However, as Loïc Charles (2011, 82) points
out, two of these supposed translations, by Plumard de Danguel and Le
Blanc, were actually original works posing as translations, and most of the
remainder included long introductions or extensive notes by the translators. The Gournay circle also appeared in the periodical press. The *Journal de l'Oeconomie*, a periodical apparently founded under the patronage of the royal administration in 1751 and edited from the beginning by
Georges-Marie Butel-Dumont, suddenly changed its editorial line in 1754
from a journal supporting government regulation and including many de-
scriptive articles about agricultural methods, geography, and manufactures to being a consistent mouthpiece for economic liberalism. Butel-
Dumont's entry into the Gournay circle was obviously an essential factor
in this shift, but it is also likely that opinions were changing in the governing circles that patronized the journal (Orain 2013, 565–83).

The most prolific author affiliated with the Gournay circle was François
Véron Duverger de Forbonnais, the son of a wealthy woolen cloth merchant from Le Mans (Meyssonnier 1989, 211). Forbonnais authored seven
of the thirty books published by members of the Gournay circle between
1753 and 1758—and one of these (1756) contained five memoirs that could
easily have been published as separate volumes. Forbonnais's career in political economy began with twelve articles on economic subjects that appeared in volumes 3, 4, and 5 of the *Encyclopédie* in 1753 and 1754.[5] In 1754,

---

5. These were "Chambre des Assurances," "Change," "Charte-partie," "Colonie,"
"Commerce," "Communauté," "Compagnie de Commerce," and "Concurrance" in vol.
3; "Contrebande," "Crédit," and "Culture des Terres" in vol. 4; and "Espèces" in vol. 5.

most of these were integrated into his two-volume *Élemens du commerce* (1754), a book that was republished several times and that, according to Simone Meyssonnier, "instructed neophytes in economic matters right up to 1796" (1989, 241).[6] In the *Élemens*, Forbonnais argued that commerce was not merely an object of practical significance but something like the underlying bond of society itself. Indeed, commerce was a gift of the "Supreme Being" who "wished to place men into mutual dependence by means of the variety he scattered forth on the earth. The Supreme Being formed these links in order to make peoples conserve peace among themselves, love one another, and unite in the tribute of their praise" (Forbonnais 1754, 1–2). Most of Forbonnais's *Élemens* treated practical problems of contemporary commerce, including agriculture, manufactures, liberal arts, fishing, navigation, colonies, insurance, and *change*— this final term covering protobanking activity, mainly the negotiation of commercial paper. Like Gournay, he urged his contemporaries to follow the English model (52) by encouraging free competition—"the soul" and "the most active principle" of commerce (91)—but maintaining tariffs against the goods of competitors.

The Abbé Coyer and La noblesse commerçante

Forbonnais, in the *Élemens*, adopted a stance of patient explanation of general principles rather than engaging in direct critique—even though the principles he propounded were sometimes at variance with contemporary French practices. But many publications by members of the Gournay circle were more openly critical of existing policies. The most spectacular example was the abbé Coyer's tract *La noblesse commerçante* (The Commercial Nobility), which argued that in order to catch up with its commercial and military rival England, France should encourage nobles to become merchants, ending the ancient rule that a noble who engaged in commerce automatically lost his noble status through "derogation." In his tract, Coyer avowed respect for the traditional military vocation of the nobility but argued that the career of the merchant was equally honorable and at least as useful to the nation. Hence there was no reason to deny the possibility of commerce to nobles (Coyer 1756a).[7]

Not only would the opening of mercantile occupations to the nobility benefit the nation's commerce by increasing the number of merchants;

6. The republications were in 1754, 1755, 1766, and 1795.
7. In this section, citations to this work will be in parentheses in the text.

it would also be useful to noble families and especially to younger sons of nobles. "Rather than remaining in a life of idleness, dependent and ill at ease in the charge of their older brothers," they could "enrich themselves while increasing the public fortune" (5). Likewise, desperately poor nobles reduced to plowing their own fields like peasants would be far more prosperous in a mercantile career. "Would it be better for this gentleman to remain trapped in the mud of his small fief, mired in enforced bachelorhood, with his sword rendered useless?" (19). Nobles now consigned to idleness or poverty could contribute to the wealth of the nobility as a class and to that of the nation as a whole, strengthening the merchant marine, enriching France's American colonies, contributing to the general prosperity, replenishing their own families, and breeding more potential military men than the nobles currently produced.

But along with edifying arguments of this sort, Coyer's tract also operates at a more emotional level, slipping in snide denunciations of the nobility's pretensions and insinuating that they are callous, lazy, violent, licentious, and haughty. It may have been these secondary moral denunciations that raised such a violent response from certain noble readers—but that also raised the ardor of his defenders. Coyer, the son of a merchant draper from the Franche-Comté and a petit abbé (a cleric without a benefice) who served as a tutor in a noble household, expressed resentments against the nobility that were surely felt by many commoners. Here are some examples: If the noble's sense of honor is sufficient to keep him from "committing crimes punishable by the scaffold, it doesn't prevent him from adopting all the vices that can deaden him to his misfortunes and distract him from his boredom. These are vices that loosen the bonds of society" (34). Disappointed younger sons of nobles who have prepared for an unrealizable military career lament that "we have learned very young to swear, to quarrel, to insult everything that is not noble, to handle arms, to shoot at our neighbors' hunting guards, to devastate the fields, to maim our peasants, to confound right with force. We have fashioned for ourselves souls of tigers; we are entirely educated for war" (12). "It is bad enough . . . that the military portion of the nobility should be struck with torpor as soon as the enemy has disappeared. But must even those nobles who don't fight consume their days in continual lethargy?" (35). "Isn't asking to live without working a continuous theft against the Nation?" (34). Nobles are the least fertile class in the country because their "libertinage leaves no place for the pleasures of innocence. Sterile courtesans have taken the place of fertile wives; and the wives avenge themselves on their husbands, without giving them families" (49).

La noblesse commerçante's bold argument and its insinuations that nobles were hardly noble in their mores helped touch off one of the eighteenth century's major literary and political controversies (Smith 2005, 104–42; Shovlin 2006, 58–65). The most famous denunciation of Coyer was *La noblesse militaire*, written by a military nobleman, the Chevalier d'Arcq (Sainte-Foy 1756). But there were numerous publications both denouncing and praising Coyer's position, including one defending Coyer by the ubiquitous Forbonnais (1756). Coyer himself responded to d'Arcq and to other critics in a two-volume work considerably longer than the original tract (1756). Works contributing to the dispute continued to appear as late as 1760 (D'Autrèpe 1760).

La noblesse commerçante was clearly an effective work of polemic but was thin and inconsistent as a work in the "science of commerce" as understood by the Gournay circle. For example, while Coyer claims, as one might expect, that mercantile activity fructifies a nation's agriculture, he elsewhere contradicts this by asserting that "it is not interior commerce that enriches a state. It only establishes a circulation of wealth, without increasing its mass; it is only exterior commerce to which this great work is reserved" (40, 61). Coyer's command of economic argument was distinctly superficial. But by questioning in print the common-sense notion that trade was intrinsically demeaning and implying that the contributions of merchants were as praiseworthy as those of military nobles, Coyer's proposal and the ensuing public melee put the issue of civic equality onto the eighteenth-century French political agenda.

The Abbé Morellet and the Prohibition of Calicoes

Another publication that attracted considerable attention was written by the abbé Morellet. Described briefly in chapter 8, this tract made a blisteringly effective argument against the edicts prohibiting the manufacture or sale in France of calicoes.[8] The series of edicts prohibiting calicoes were enacted at the behest of guilds representing the silk and woolen industries, which feared competition. Morellet's argument was based on the premises of the emerging liberal political economy (1758).[9] Indeed, his arguments were remarkably similar to those elaborated systematically by

---

8. The French term for such textiles was *toiles peintes* (painted cloths) or simply *indiennes* (Indians).

9. In the remainder of this section, citations to this work will be in parentheses in the text. On the history of the restrictive legislation, see Gottman (2016) and Chapman and Chassagne (1981, 104–8).

Adam Smith two decades later. First, commerce is governed by the taste of consumers, and these tastes cannot be legislated. Morellet quotes Sir Josiah Child's dictum that "commerce . . . is founded as much on fantasies as on needs" (44). It is "the empire of fashion" combined with the "inexpensiveness" of calicoes that makes people desire this type of cloth (42). Second, people are motivated by their private interests: "We should not expect from men more virtue than they possess. Even the most honest merchant works first of all for his own interest and prefers it to the public welfare. Laws should take men as they are" (47). Third, paradoxically, the pursuit of private interest through commerce actually leads to public well-being. We should "expect the general good to arise from the efforts that men make to gain their own welfare" (47).

The laws banning calicoes, Morellet points out, were a complete failure: "The use of calicoes has been very common in France for twenty years." Over this period, "smuggling has occurred constantly and across all the boundaries of the Kingdom" (27). "There is much to be gained by taking calicoes from Geneva and Savoy, from England and Holland, and introducing them into France. A plowman who gains at best twelve sols a day is continually tempted to engage in smuggling, which gains him six livres and more" (33). (There are twenty sols in a livre; Morellet asserts that a day of smuggling would net the equivalent of ten days at the plow.) Even the woolen and silk manufacturers who have argued for prohibition agree that "unless the wearing and use of calicoes is prohibited, it will be impossible to stop their introduction" into the country (33). But such a prohibition, Morellet argues, could only work if it were enforced on the rich. And "no one will seize a Duchess in her carriage or the wife of a General Farmer." And even if the wearing of calicoes could be prevented outdoors, "we shall never keep them from using calicoes in their *déshabillé*, or from using them as upholstery in their apartments. . . . I would not be astonished to see Ministers deliberating on the matter I am treating here in an apartment furnished with Persian or English fabrics" (39).

Since it is impossible to seize the clothing and furniture of "persons of a certain status" (50), the law could only be enforced "on common citizens, on bourgeois, on artisans, and on the rest of the people. But . . . this distinction would be odious, and should never happen in a well-governed state" (52). Indeed, such a procedure would be a violation "of the civil liberty of the greatest part of the Nation. This civil liberty, the free and tranquil possession of what is called one's home (*le chez soi*), is respected even by the harshest governments" (52). Here Morellet argues implicitly that enforcing the ban would be impossible without descending into outright despotism. But the natural rights that must not be violated in a well-governed state go beyond a right to privacy in one's home. To prohibit the wearing of calicoes would be "an infringement of each person's natural right to dress according to his fancy and as cheaply as possible" (54). Imposing regulations on calicoes is, therefore, not only foolish but a violation of natural rights. Here Morellet goes beyond the observation that people's tastes are whimsical and therefore incapable in practice of being dictated by the state; he claims a natural right for consumers to follow their tastes and fantasies. His argument implies that every legitimate government has an obligation to guarantee a right of free consumption. Morellet follows considerations of taste and political economy deeply into the question of political rights.

Having demolished the practical and moral arguments for banning calicoes, Morellet argues that doing so is economically foolish as well. The French, he claims, are perfectly capable of making calicoes. Although they may not be able to match the beauty of the Indian cloths, they can make them as well as the English, Dutch, and Swiss, whose productions are currently smuggled into France in great quantities. Indeed, given the French reputation for fashionable goods, there is reason to imagine that French calico producers will be exporting goods "as soon as we begin to make them; our designs on cotton cloth will tempt foreigners, just as they tempt them today on silks" (60–63). Morellet's prediction was borne out in practice. A French cotton-printing industry sprang into being immediately after the ban on import and manufacture was lifted in 1759, and the industry grew explosively. By 1785, cotton printing was one of the few branches of manufactures in which the French actually outproduced the English (Chapman and Chassagne 1981, 8).

Morellet's tract was argued brilliantly in a lively, satirical, and aggressive style. It effectively shredded the claims of those who supported the calico ban and surely helped speed the ban's definitive demise the following year, when Controller General Silhouette, himself a habitué of the Gournay circle, allowed the importation and manufacture of calicoes. Morellet was a master polemicist, able not only to make this law appear ridiculous but also to introduce arguments with political implications reaching far beyond the calico question. His polemic about this particular matter of economic policy succeeded in positing as natural laws both the sanctity of the citizen against searches for outlawed goods and the right of every person to buy and use whatever goods might suit their fancy. In this tract, Morellet put into circulation a radical statement of the fundamental rights of the citizen and of the sovereign consumer, sacred rights that should be upheld even against the king.

Clicquot de Blervache (and Vincent de Gournay) on Guilds and the Regulation of Manufactures

Another publication arising out of the Gournay circle was Clicquot de Blervache's *Considérations sur le commerce* (Considerations on Commerce, 1758).[10] The scope of the attack in this book was much broader than in Morellet's; it challenged the entire Colbertian system of regulation and the very existence of the guilds that governed manufacture and commerce in most cities. The tract is especially interesting because there is reason to believe it was essentially coauthored by Gournay himself, although Gournay's participation was never avowed. The initial version of this tract was submitted to a prize competition set by the Academy of Amiens for essays on the following question: "In what ways do guilds pose obstacles to work and industry? What advantages would the state gain from their suppression? What would be the best means of doing so? Has the assistance that guilds have provided to the kingdom been helpful or harmful?" (23). It is notable that the question does not ask *whether* guilds pose obstacles to industry but assumes that they do. Gournay's biographer, Gustave Schelle, suggests that this is because Gournay himself probably had a hand in proposing the topic for the competition (Schelle 1897, 126). Gournay had been a member of the Academy of Amiens since 1755 (Charles 2011, 80). Moreover, according to Schelle (1897, 126), Gournay was effectively the coauthor of the winning entry, which was officially submitted by a M. de L'Isle—who didn't exist.[11] The tract was later attributed to Simon Clicquot de Blervache, who presumably participated in writing it, although probably in conjunction with Gournay.

Schelle presents no real evidence for his insinuation that Gournay helped set the question for the competition—although the question's presumption that guilds were harmful and should be abolished is highly suspicious. Questions posed by provincial academies for prize contests rarely took sides quite so obviously.[12] Schelle's claim that Gournay was

10. In the rest of this section, citations to this work will appear in parentheses in the text.

11. The version submitted to the academy was De Lille (1758). According to Schelle, De L'Isle was "an invented name" (1897, 131).

12. For example, the question posed by the Dijon Academy that provoked Jean-Jacques Rousseau's shocking first discourse was "Has the reestablishment of the sciences and arts contributed to the purification or the corruption of morals?" (1751, 1). The Academy of Dijon was undoubtedly surprised by Rousseau's negative response, but such an answer was not ruled out by the question's phrasing.

effectively a coauthor of the tract seems likely. Gournay could not have openly published a book like *Considérations sur le commerce* without provoking retribution—since its argument vilified the entire range of regulations that it was his official duty to administer. The book's attribution to a fictitious author only deepens one's suspicions. The assumption that Gournay had a hand in the book's composition was shared by an eighteenth-century observer. As Schelle points out (1897, 126), Samuel Du Pont de Nemours wrote in the physiocrat journal *Les éphémérides du citoyen* in 1769 that the tract "was composed by M. de L'Isle, under the eyes and the counsel of the illustrious M. de Gournay."

There is also textual evidence of Gournay's participation. Schelle devotes an entire chapter of his biography to a particularly harsh administrative memoir that Gournay addressed to the various guilds of Lyon involved in silk manufacture. (Lyon was part of Gournay's administrative territory as an intendant of commerce.) This memoir excoriated the Lyonnais guilds for the excessive length of their apprenticeships, the steep payments required of journeymen who wished to become masters, the exclusion from mastership of journeymen who were not natives of the city, and the like (Schelle 1897, 101–11).[13] *Considérations sur le commerce* denounces precisely these practices as evidence that guilds pose an obstacle to industry, using the same arguments. *Considérations* does not cite the Lyonnais silk industry, but it details the practices of the tailors' guild of Lyon as examples of the deleterious practices of guilds in general (137–44). Moreover, when *Considérations* denounces the vast debts incurred by guilds, it is the debts of the guilds of Lyon that are specifically cited (125–26).[14] This focus on detailed evidence about the guilds of Lyon suggests that, at the very least, Gournay must have turned over a copy of his memoir to Clicquot for his reference when the latter was composing *Considérations*. It is not likely that an aspiring young man of letters like Clicquot could have learned figures about the debts of Lyonnais guilds except through Gournay: such figures were state and guild secrets in eighteenth-century France.

The authors of *Considérations* condemn the guilds as an impediment to the progress of commerce and manufactures. Guild masters, they as-

13. This text, "Mémoire sur les manufactures de Lyon, par Monsieur Vincent de Gournay," is reprinted in Charles et al. (2011, 333–43).

14. There is textual evidence that Gournay was acutely aware of this problem. In his administrative memoir on the Lyonnais silk industry, he noted that when "in need," the state "asked for big sums which it authorized [the guilds] to borrow" and that in return for this financial assistance, the guilds received the right to enact further restrictions (Charles et al. 2011, 334).

sert, enact regulations that enrich themselves but impoverish the nation. It is in the interest of the masters to "restrict the privilege of exercising a profession to the smallest number of hands; [the interest] of the State, on the contrary, is . . . to procure the means of nourishing by daily occupation as many men as possible" (20). The guilds' restrictions are of several kinds: limiting the number of apprentices, making apprenticeships unreasonably long, and charging high mastership fees for those who are not sons of masters and exorbitant fees for those who are not natives of the city. By these means, the lucky few who are "authorized by the law, make of it a rampart against the industry of those who wish to share with them the profits of the Arts and Commerce. . . . The profits held in the hands of privileged men shelter them from competition; this advantage renders them negligent and lazy, which would never happen if they were not masters capable of limiting the number sharing their privilege. . . . Hence, far from tending to propagate commerce, guilds always tend toward monopoly" (33, 35).

The authors point out that in rival states, especially England, guilds had lost their sway. Industry had left London, where guilds still existed, for "Manchester, Leeds, Halifax, Birmingham, etc.," where they did not. It is of the nature of commerce that it flees "the nuisances in which guilds enchain industry. . . . It necessarily takes refuge in the places where it will be most free" (44). It is a mistake, the authors argue, to imagine that guild regulations are the only way to govern commerce, which can be guided more efficiently and effectively by the preferences of consumers. The buyer should have "the freedom to compare, and to do business with the person who sells his work at the lowest price. The worker, instructed by the preference that is shown to another, will drop his pretensions and be contented with a more modest gain. This is the effect of competition, the most extensive and fertile principle of commerce" (48). The authors add that "low prices are the most formidable arm we can use to combat the efforts of rival countries; the consumer cannot resist this attraction." The right policy would be "to lift all the obstacles that oppose the fertile principle" of competition. By establishing guilds, France has instead "made such obstacles all the greater, making the obstacles respectable and giving them the seal of authority" (54–55). Guilds, the standard institution for regulating commerce in French cities, should be abolished. Free competition, so successful in England, should henceforth govern commerce and industry in France as well.

Considérations also condemns the entire network of regulations of the textile industry that the state, since the time of Colbert, had enforced by means of a corps of inspectors. This "immense compendium of regulations," the authors argue, should give way to the principle of commercial liberty (55). One fundamental flaw of the highly detailed and specific regulations of the textile industry was that they "gratuitously supposed" that "the manufacturer and the merchant had no other goal than to deceive, no other interest than to be swindlers" (59). The "entire function" of the regulations was "to give rules for the quality of a given work and to impose penalties and fines against those who contravened them" (60). Rather than assuming such a jaundiced view, "the principles of our laws should be sought in the very nature of commerce," of which "the soul, the base, and the most active agent" is "good faith" (61–62). "How can commerce subsist without credit, credit without confidence, confidence without good faith? What at all times is the condition of a man who engages in commerce? It is this: he is the possessor of a good which is not in his hands, of a good that circulates in those of his correspondents" (62).

Success in commerce is gained not by cheating but by "the uninterrupted continuity of modest and legitimate gains within the bounds of honesty." Because the merchant or manufacturer cannot find commercial partners if he lacks a reputation for honesty, "it is certain that the very desire for gain . . . forces him not to defraud. This curb is all the more powerful because it arises from the nature of personal interest and will always be called forth by competition" (62–63). If a few merchants or manufacturers succumb to the temptation to cheat, they "will be punished sufficiently for their bad faith by the lack of confidence and of credit" that results from their bad behavior. "One cannot deceive with impunity for long. The legislator should therefore regard these occasional frauds as an affair between particular parties who have an interest in not allowing themselves to be deceived" (63–64).

The second great fault of the Colbertian system of regulation is that defining legal goods by statute misunderstands the nature of consumption. "Are these goods not meant to satisfy, indeed to tempt, the taste of the consumer? But is this taste invariable? Does it not, on the contrary, depend on the most arbitrary things in the world . . . caprice and fantasy? If these are the two springs . . . that move the entire machine of commerce, there must not be fixed and immutable laws that restrict its agility" (68). The authors speculate that if Colbert could "witness the current state of our commerce," he would approve of abandoning statutory regulations. "He would think that now, when manufacturers are educated, emulation is animated, and industry is active, it is no longer a regulation that must be followed, but the law of competition and consumption" (74). The consumer's "personal utility, which never shuts its eyes to its real interests, will guide the consumer to the object that enables a rapid and simple purchase—without any assistance from officials" (78). If every producer knew that other producers were as free as he is, "he would have no other resource for attracting the preference of consumers than to find in his economy and his industry the means to perfect his work at the lowest possible price" (81).

The third disadvantage of the system of regulation is that it discourages invention. "Our rivals constantly gain preference over us by means of an almost inexhaustible fertility of invention" (83). But the French, saddled by regulations, were discouraged from making inventions of their own. And if they did invent something new, France's rivals would "imitate us immediately and share the fruits of our discoveries. If they invent, we cannot imitate them" (88). The regime of regulation represses the creativity of France's workers and manufacturers. They are held back by a corps of inspectors, who, "entrenched in the inflexibility of their regulations, capture industry, discourage efforts, cut the wings of genius" (90).

What, then, should be done? The authors recommended that the regulative regime should be scrapped and the corps of inspectors dissolved. Likewise, guilds should be abolished. Both regulations and guilds are "contrary to the principles avowed by all nations that have best understood the most powerful springs of commerce. . . . We should (1) render commerce prosperous, free, and necessary, (2) make it attractive for other nations to trade with us, and (3) multiply . . . the number of people engaged in commerce" (104).

The system of regulations and the corps of inspectors could, in principle, be abolished by decree. But the authors note that the case is more complicated. By a circuitous route, the state has forced the guilds deeply into debt. Under Louis XIV, the state's funds had been "exhausted by unfortunate wars" that "caused a fall in the state's credit." One way the crown got around this problem was "to make use of the credit of the guilds" (122–23). The state, cynically, attempted to suppress guilds and sell off their functions to newly created venal officers. Unlike the crown, the guilds had good credit, which enabled them to borrow money to buy up all the offices collectively so that they could continue as before—but now burdened with significant debts (124). The authors remark that "the loans of the city of Lyon have been evaluated at nearly a million (livres); those of the city of Paris must be at least triple this figure. . . . This is an immense capital that has been weighing down industry for over fifty years." Moreover, "during this time the sum of the interest payments has exceeded those of the initial capital" (126). It is therefore impossible simply to dissolve the guilds, since this would either cancel the outstanding debt or require the state to assume the debt itself—hardly practicable given the pressing weight of the kingdom's existing obligations.

The authors argue that the best solution to this problem would be to raise taxes on the idle rich, particularly on rentiers: "A state that wishes to grow by means of commerce should as much as possible cause its impositions to fall upon those who live at ease on revenue gained from sums they have lent out. The legislator of a commercial nation must differentiate between a capital that derives from industry and the product of indolence that arises from simple loan contracts." Capital invested in loans, the authors claim, "can only be taken from the nation; it can only enrich one subject at the expense of another." But capital invested in commerce "makes foreigners our tributaries and augments the capital of the state." The more the latter form of capital expands, "the more the number of industrious men will increase." Moreover, if rentier capital is limited, then "possessors of rents will be forced to work," and "the number of idle citizens will be diminished" (151–52).

If, as I suggest, we read *Considérations sur le commerce* as a statement of Gournay's convictions, its arguments are shockingly radical. *Considérations* denounces both the details and the raison d'être of the Colbertian regime of regulation, argues for a suppression of the inspectorate and the trade guilds, reveals how the royal state has forced the guilds to take on immense debts, and suggests a radically redistributive means of paying these debts down. One can certainly see why Gournay would not avow authorship of this tract. However, it is telling that such a work could have been published and widely circulated in spite of royal censorship. Yet more remarkable is that a mere six years later, its avowed author, Clicquot de Blervache, was named one of the inspectors general of manufactures, the very body condemned by his tract.[15] It is clear that the royal state itself became increasingly open to Gournay's liberal ideas.

The writings of members of the Gournay circle launched a period of intensive discussion of political economy that lasted right up to the French Revolution. The urgency and ubiquity of this discussion can be measured by the weight of political-economic works in the productions of the French book trade. We have noted that between 1750 and 1789, more books on political economy were published in France than novels (Shovlin 2006). The Gournay circle, by publishing thirty books in six years, certainly did much to launch this craze for political economy, which, of course, also affected the discussions in Paris's salons. But the

15. In addition, Louis-Paul Abeille, himself a member of the Gournay circle, was also named an inspector general in the same year; Minard (1988, 500).

role of the Gournay circle per se dissipated quickly after its leader's death in 1759. Gournay was not a prophet with disciples but rather a mentor whose generous and magnetic personality inspired a wide circle of ambitious writers. After his death, the productivity of his erstwhile emulators declined sharply, the notable exceptions being Forbonnais, whose productivity also slowed; Morellet, who continued to write on economic topics into the nineteenth century; and Turgot, who published his remarkable *Réflexions sur la formation et la distribution des richesses* in the physiocrat journal *Les éphémérides du citoyen* in 1769–70 and who also, in his administrative career as the intendant of the Limousin and as controller general of France, produced numerous administrative memos as well as the texts of edicts enacting far-reaching economic reforms (Forbonnais 1761, 1768; Morellet 1769b, 1769c, 1774, 1775c; Turgot 1788). But by the end of the 1750s, political-economic writings of many different types were being produced in abundance. There were, for example, major debates and discussions in the last four decades of the old regime about the grain trade, agronomy, international trade, colonies, and the question of luxury (Perrot 1991; Meyssonnier 1989; Larrère 1992; Shovlin 2006; Cheney 2010). French political economy, thanks in large part to the Gournay circle, had become part of the intellectual furniture of the age.

The Physiocrats

The best known of all eighteenth-century French schools of political economy was a group known as the physiocrats, who rose to prominence in the 1760s (Vardi 2012; Fox-Genovese 1976; Weulersse 1910, 1959, 1985). In their own time, the physiocrats were more often called simply *les économistes*.[16] The physiocrats, like the Gournay circle, emerged out of the salon of their intellectual leader, François Quesnay. The court physician of Louis XV's official mistress, Madame de Pompadour, Quesnay had quarters in the royal palace in Versailles. He had previously published several works on medicine but came to public notice for his economic ideas when he penned articles on "Farmers" and "Grains" in the *Encyclopédie* in 1756 and 1757. Over the course of the 1760s, he wrote several more influential texts and accumulated a corps of disciples, most prominently Victor Riquetti, the Marquis de Mirabeau (1759–60, 1763, 1769, 1776); Pierre-Samuel Dupont de Nemours (1767, 1768, 1796); Pierre-Paul Le Mercier de la Rivière (1767, 1770, 1792); and Guillaume-François Le Trosne. The

---

16. The term *economist*, which has become the general term for those who study production and exchange, was initially used specifically to designate the physiocrats.

only figure who overlapped significantly between the Gournay circle and Quesnay's salon was Turgot, who, although influenced by Quesnay's ideas, was too independent-minded to become a disciple.

Quesnay and the physiocrats agreed with Gournay that the Colbertian regulatory regime was harmful and that the proper policy for all branches of economic activity was laissez-faire—that agriculture, trade, and manufactures should be regulated only by free markets and individual initiative. But in other respects, Quesnay's and Gournay's ideas and intellectual styles diverged sharply. One of Quesnay's key doctrines was that all economic growth derived from agriculture and that trade and manufacturing, although important to the functioning of the economy, were "sterile." By contrast, as we have seen, writers from the Gournay circle recognized the importance of agriculture but saw "commerce" as the key agent of economic advance. Moreover, whereas Gournay was noted for his tolerance and open-mindedness, Quesnay was a dogmatist. He regarded his doctrines as self-evident truths and developed his own elaborate terminology. If the members of Gournay's circle went their own various ways after their leader's death, Quesnay's followers were true disciples, proud to adhere to the very letter of the master's theories even after his death in 1774. They were also talented publicists, who managed to develop the master's ideas in an accessible form and to keep them in circulation; Quesnay's own writings, by contrast, were recondite and difficult. The "economists" or "physiocrats" were often ridiculed by others as a sect and were mocked for their use of Quesnay's arcane vocabulary. But they were nevertheless read, discussed, and taken seriously right down to the end of the old regime, including within the royal administration.

The physiocrats, Quesnay included, regarded the science he had discovered as a body of "physical laws relative to society," on a par with those governing the natural world (Dupont de Nemours 1768, 8). Indeed, the term *physiocracy* literally means "the rule of nature." Society was itself a natural phenomenon, created by God and subject to laws as unerring and eternal as those that govern the course of the planets. The very existence of human society was based on the fertility of the soil, which naturally reproduced the food and raw materials necessary to life. The spontaneous productions of the soil, however, were insufficient to support large populations without dedicated work—that is, without agriculture, which was the original and most important activity of human societies. If agriculture was the source of all wealth, industry and commerce were sterile. In manufacturing and trade, in the words of Le Mercier de la Rivière, agricultural goods have "done nothing but change [their] form, without gaining anything from this change" (167).

This claim of the absolute primacy of agriculture might seem peculiar in the mid-eighteenth century, at a moment when commerce and manufacturing were expanding with unprecedented vigor. But Quesnay's investigation of the economic logic of agricultural production was extraordinarily acute. Some of the most brilliant later economic thinkers, including Karl Marx ([1867] 1977, 937–38), recognized Quesnay as a crucial source of some of their own theories. In particular, according to Joseph Schumpeter, Quesnay "laid the foundations" for the theory of capital, clarifying, as no previous economic thinker had, that successful functioning of the economy depended on setting aside a portion of previously produced wealth—capital, or what Quesnay called "advances"—to make possible continued, increasing levels of production (Schumpeter 1974, 235). Quesnay's vehicle for examining the role of "advances" in agricultural production was what he called the *Tableau économique*. The meaning of *tableau*, in French, is both "table" (as in a statistical table) and "picture." The *Tableau économique* had something of each. It was an annotated diagram indicating the flow of wealth in the yearly cycle of agricultural production. Quesnay regarded the *Tableau* as the key device for communicating his doctrines to others, but it was devilishly difficult to decipher. His ideas, however, were cogent and were eventually explained satisfactorily in prose by his acolytes.

The dynamics of agricultural capital were explained, for example, by Dupont de Nemours in his *De l'origine et des progrès d'une science nouvelle* (On the Origin and the Progress of a New Science): "Because the spontaneous productions of the land and the waters are not sufficient to provide subsistence for a numerous population . . . nature has prescribed to men agriculture, the art of multiplying productions." But agriculture "can only be established by means of preparatory labors and *avances foncières*" (Dupont de Nemours 1768, 18–19).[17] The *avances foncières* consist of the expenses of labor and materials necessary to prepare and maintain fields for agriculture, such as clearing, draining, manuring, and fencing; these must be supplemented by *avances primitives* (prior advances) for the tools, animals, buildings, and the like that are necessary for sustaining cultivation (22). The combination of *avances foncières* and *avances primitives* constitutes what we might call agriculture's capital expenses. The agricultural proprietor must also undertake *"dépenses annuelles* (annual expenses) required for the wages and the upkeep of all the men and all the

---

17. In the rest of this chapter, citations to this work will be in parentheses in the text. *Foncière* is an adjective referring to landed property; an *impôt foncière*, for example, is a tax on landed property.

animals whose labor contributes to the exploitation of the land" (22–23). Such expenses are deducted from the value of the harvest and should, in principle, include funds set aside annually to make up for the occasional "great accidents" that beset agriculture, such as frost, hail, disease, or floods. The *avances foncières* and *primitives*, combined with the *dépenses annuelles*, constitute the *reprises des Cultivateurs* (probably best translated as the cultivator's costs). Anything produced beyond these costs constitutes the *produit net*, the net product or profit, which belongs to the proprietor of the land (24).

The produit net of all agricultural proprietors, summed up across an entire nation in a given year, represents the net annual gain in a nation's wealth. Increasing agricultural profits, however, benefit not only the proprietors but the entire nation. The proprietor, of course, has an incentive to increase his produit net, by increasing his capital investments (his *avances*), in order to improve his land's yield. "The more agriculture is expanded and perfected, the more it renews the annual production of consumables," which will increase the general welfare and lead to a rising population. "It is thus that the prosperity of all humanity is attached to the greatest possible *produit net*, and hence to the best possible situation for proprietors of the land." What assures the highest possible produit net is free competition, both between proprietors and among those who do the work, since this will ensure maximum efficiency. "There must be the greatest possible liberty in the employment of all properties, whether personal, mobile, or landed, and the greatest possible security in the possession of that which one acquires by the use of these properties" (26–27).

Physiocratic theory thus had a clear conception of the role of capital expenses in sustaining production of profit as the necessary means for accumulating capital and therefore as the key driver of economic growth. Quesnay also pioneered the application of mathematical calculation as a means of understanding economic life. Schumpeter regarded Quesnay's *tableau économique* as the first instance of econometrics, at once a foreshadowing of the work of Walras on equilibrium and Leontief on national accounts (Schumpeter 1994, 23–24). Yet for all its theoretical brilliance and its foreshadowing of later developments in economic theory, physiocracy was in other respects strangely archaic. It ruled out of court any consideration of the dynamics of trade and manufacture—by far the most progressive sectors of the eighteenth-century French and European economies—in explaining economic growth. Instead, it sketched out a kind of agrarian utopia, one based not on the small peasant proprietors who were in fact the dominant players in the actual French agrarian economy but rather on enterprising large-scale farmers who leased land from enlightened landlords. In one of his first published works on economic questions, the article on "Fermiers" in volume 6 of the *Encyclopédie*, Quesnay declared that the key to improving agriculture was the capitalist farmer who was not himself a landowner but rented a sizable holding from a landlord and applied the most up-to-date techniques to its cultivation. This meant using horses rather than oxen for traction, increasing the herds of cattle and sheep, adopting new crop rotations and irrigation techniques, and so on. The role of the proprietors was to provide investment funds to improve the productivity of the land, not to undertake the hands-on management of production. This might be characterized as an idealized version of the pattern that had developed in England since the sixteenth century. But unlike the economic thinkers associated with the Gournay circle, Quesnay and his followers did not avow reference to the English model. They claimed to have deduced their physical science of society de novo from supposedly self-evident God-given first principles.

Physiocratic theory exalted the role of great landed proprietors—which, in the conditions of the old regime, meant in practice the nobles and the clergy—as the sole accumulators of the net product. However, the political theory they deduced from their first principles deprived nobles, clergy, and commoners alike of any political power. The king alone should exercise what they called "tutelary authority" (*l'autorité tutélaire*) over society. The king, far from being arbitrary, would rule by means of a "legal despotism" (*déspotisme légale*). He would, that is, be the guarantor and the administrator of the natural laws of the economy; the landowners would simply benefit from this enlightened form of rule by raking in ever more net product and reinvesting it in agriculture, thereby spreading wealth through the entire nation. Indeed, the king himself was hardly a political figure in the physiocrats' scheme; he would simply administer the two simple laws that God and nature had decreed: "the conservation of the right of property and the liberty that is inseparable from it." The king's decrees "should be only acts specifying these essential laws of the social order." The physiocratic utopia, like so many utopias before it, would have no place for politics (30).

This hypermonarchical physiocratic political theory was tightly joined to their theory of taxation. Taxes serve "as conservators of property. They are the great link, the federative knot . . . of society" (39). The laws of nature, physiocrats claimed, dictated that taxes necessary for adequate functioning of the state should be taken solely from the net product of agriculture—that is, from the landowners' profits. The purpose of taxation is "to furnish the recurrent expenses" of the state. It "therefore can only be taken from recurrent wealth . . . the net product of agriculture"

(41, 43). Any other taxes would limit "the liberty of human labor," diminish harvests, and harm humanity (42, 45). Taxes are not an attack on property but "a use" of humanity's "right of property." Taxes assessed on the net product "cost nothing to anyone, are not paid by anyone, and take away no property whatsoever" (60–61). They are, as it were, paid by nature's bounty alone.

A tax so conceived would perfectly align the interests of the king with that of the nation (61). If, on the other hand, the governing authority were democratic, aristocratic, or an elective monarchy, the interests of those exercising the sovereignty would diverge from those of the nation because the rulers would be tempted to shape laws to benefit disproportionately themselves or their heirs. But a hereditary monarch's interests never diverge from those of the nation. His interest and that of his progeny are for taxes to be high enough to ensure the proper functioning of the laws that nature dictates but that nevertheless enable as much of the net product as possible to be plowed back into agriculture to assure future wealth both for himself, through taxes, and for the nation (64–69).

The physiocratic system was arcane, complicated, and based on chains of deductive logic. It was therefore hardly likely to be adopted in its entirety by any administrator or monarch—who had to deal with the actual complexity of government, the political pressures infesting the court, the contingencies of war and peace, and the vested interests of privileged bodies of all kinds. But some of the practical proposals deduced from this system were attractive to progressively minded administrators. The simplicity of a single tax on the net product of landed proprietors, unencumbered by aristocratic privilege, would have obvious advantages over the French state's complex maze of taxation, with its universally recognized fault of overburdening the peasantry. The notion that instituting laissez-faire would result in a rapid increase in national wealth, an idea shared by the physiocrats and political economists of the Gournay circle, was surely intriguing. The concept of the king and his administration governing the nation quasi-automatically as a "legal despot" must also have had its attractions. Finally, although the physiocrats hardly trumpeted this feature of their thinking, it was fundamentally hostile to pecuniary privileges of all kinds—positing instead a body of apolitical citizens devoted to exercising their rights to property and to the free employment of their labor. Some of these attractions were surely present in the mind of Turgot, who had attended Quesnay's salon and was broadly sympathetic to physiocratic theory, when he acquired a position of political power.

Navigating the Double Bind

EFFORTS AT REFORM

The proliferation of political-economic writings in the years following 1750 supplied potential reforming administrators with a wide range of ideas and suggestions. Putting these ideas into practice was an entirely different matter. In this chapter, I will chronicle attempts at reform carried out by royal administrators. I begin with the most famous case, the brief "philosophe" ministry of Turgot from 1774 to 1776, and then consider the ministry of Jacques Necker, who between 1776 and 1781 pursued reforms of a very different sort. I follow the discussions of these two ill-fated ministries with accounts of three more targeted reform efforts undertaken at a lower level in the state's administrative apparatus. My goal is to indicate both the breadth of reformist sympathies in the royal administration and the formidable difficulties the reformers faced. What I have called the old regime's double bind was an immense obstacle: the state's finances had to be improved, but the accumulation of privileges and fiscal work-arounds inherited by the royal administration blocked most paths to improvement. As we shall see, strenuous reform efforts were undertaken, aimed both at unleashing the nation's productive capacity and at rationalizing its financial structures, but most were ultimately undone. A careful examination of such efforts, both grand and more targeted, will illuminate both the range and ambition of the reform efforts and the tenacity of the jerry-built system in place. In the end, fundamental reform was blocked. The double bind was only to be overcome by a revolution.

Turgot's Ministry

On March 9, 1774, Louis XV died of smallpox at the age of sixty-five after a reign of fifty-nine years. He was succeeded by his grandson Louis XVI, age twenty. A few months later, on August 24, Louis XVI named Turgot as his controller general.[1] Turgot was a friend of the philosophes, a major political-economic thinker, a former member of the Gournay circle, and a sometime participant in Quesnay's salon. He had served effectively as the intendant of Limoges, instituting a successful reform of the corvée and greatly improving the region's previously wretched roads. His appointment raised great hopes among the philosophes and economic liberals. At last, one of their own had attained the kingdom's most powerful administrative position. The abbé Morellet and the philosophe Condorcet were friends and advisors, and Turgot's personal secretary was Dupont de Nemours. The moment for a thorough reform of the royal administration seemed to be at hand.

Turgot introduced fundamental reforms on several fronts. His approach to specifically financial problems was cautious; he believed that taxes on the common people, particularly the peasantry, were already too high. His main financial effort was to pare back expenses carefully to better balance them with income. He rejected making war on England when the North American colonies revolted in 1776 on the grounds that the debt burden was already too great. France entered the war only after Turgot's dismissal later that year. Turgot's major initiatives were aimed less at financial problems than at restructuring the French economy. He hoped to solve the monarchy's perennial fiscal problems by increasing the kingdom's wealth and hence its taxable income. At the very beginning of his term in office, he introduced free trade in grain everywhere in the kingdom except Paris, where, prudently, controls remained in place. In the spring of 1776, he introduced two additional far-reaching reforms— abolishing trade guilds and abolishing the corvée as a means of constructing roads. These reforms raised storms of resistance, eventually costing Turgot support from both common people and elites, certainly contributing to his fall from office in May 1776.

Freeing the grain trade had become a notable cause for both liberals of the Gournay circle and the physiocrats. They criticized long-standing royal policy, which set price caps, banned sales of grain outside regulated markets, limited movement of grain from region to region, and prohibited its export. These measures were intended to protect the populace against surges in bread prices when harvests were poor. Physiocrats and liberals argued that the fundamental problem of grain supply was insufficient production and that freeing trade would raise prices, in part by opening up an export market, thereby incentivizing farmers to invest more and increase yields. Under a regime of free trade, it was claimed, when harvests were

---

1. On Turgot's ministry, see Dakin (1939), Faure (1967), and Poirier (1999).

poor, farmers in regions with excess production would sell to consumers in regions with production deficits (and hence high prices), thereby alleviating shortages. The free play of supply and demand would enhance the interests of both producers and consumers of this most important of commodities while also improving the overall economy (Kaplan 1976). Although arguments in favor of freeing the grain trade had dominated political-economic discussions of the past two decades, they were still controversial. A widely circulated dissent published by the abbé Galiani (1770) argued that grain, because it supplied bread to the people, could not be treated like other commodities and that its supply should be assured by the state. Moreover, the notion that the king should guarantee the grain supply was deeply embedded in popular culture.

Turgot's decree freeing the grain was poorly timed. The harvest of 1774 was meager, which meant that prices would rise and that poor people in cities and countryside alike would be hungry and agitated until the next good harvest. In the spring of 1775, the rural areas surrounding Paris were wracked by a series of grain riots, which came to be known as the "Flour War." Turgot acted quickly to repress the disorders, mobilizing the army for that purpose, hanging two supposed leaders, and then declaring an amnesty (Bouton 1993; Poirier 1999, 232–42). But his popularity was gravely affected by these events; the public, unsurprisingly (if incorrectly), blamed the high prices on his new policy. This emboldened those in the court and administration who distrusted his reformist goals.

Turgot, nevertheless, continued to roll out reforms. He pared back the number of privileged treasurers who handled the royal finances and had notoriously profited by lending out the funds they held. He replaced the concessionaires who handled the postal service with a state *régie* (agency) and instituted vastly improved coach services from Paris to all the major cities and to the major frontier crossings. The most significant of the reform projects, which became known as the "Six Edicts," were not introduced until March 12, 1776. Of these, the most consequential and controversial were the fifth, which abolished the corvée throughout the country, and the sixth, which abolished the trade guilds. Both were resisted strenuously by the Parlement of Paris, which published blistering remonstrances against the decrees before being forced by the king to accept them. The arguments for and against these decrees indicate clearly the stakes, real and imagined, that were involved in any fundamental reform of old regime institutions.

Turgot's edicts were framed by a discourse of rationality and natural rights. Concerning the abolition of the guilds, Turgot wrote a memorandum to the king saying, "I regard, Sire, the destruction of the guilds and the total abolition of the constraints that these establishments impose upon the industry of the poor and laborious portion of your subjects as one of the greatest benefits that could be accorded to your peoples; it is, after the liberty of commerce in grains, one of the greatest steps that the administration could take toward the amelioration, or rather the regeneration, of the Kingdom" (Schelle 1923, 5:159). The king's edict abolishing the guilds, written, of course, by Turgot, could be seen as carrying out the program originally stated two decades earlier in the pamphlet by Clicquot de Blervache and Gournay. The edict began,

> We owe our subjects the full and entire enjoyment of their rights. We owe this protection above all to that class of men who, having no property other than their labor and their industry, have all the more need and right to employ to their full extent the only resources they have for their subsistence. We have viewed with sorrow the multiple infringements that our institutions have made upon these natural and common rights; institutions that are, to be sure, ancient, but that neither time, nor opinion, nor even actions emanating from Royal authority that seem to have consecrated them, have been able to legitimate. (Flammermont 1898, 239)[2]

Indeed, "God . . . has made of the right to work the property of all men, and this property is the first, the most sacred, and the most imprescriptible of all" (242).

Yet this right had been abridged:

> In nearly all the cities of our Kingdom, the exercise of the different arts and trades is concentrated in the hands of a small number of masters banded together in communities, who alone, to the exclusion of all other citizens, produce or sell the objects of the particular commerce over which they have exclusive privileges. . . . The effects of these establishments are, with regard to the State, a significant diminution of industrious labors; with regard to a numerous portion of our subjects, a loss of wages and means of subsistence; and with regard to inhabitants of cities in general, subjection to . . . an effective monopoly. (241)

Historically, "these abuses have been introduced by degrees. They were originally the work of particular interests, which established them against

---

2. In the remainder of this section, citations to this work will be in parentheses in the text.

the public. But after a long interval of time, the authorities, in part surprised, in part seduced by an appearance of utility, have given them a sort of sanction." The state, once it had recognized the guilds, constrained them to contribute to its financial needs: "It was, no doubt, the attraction of this means of finance that prolonged illusions concerning the immense prejudice that the existence of guilds causes to industry and the infringement it causes to natural rights" (242).

Recognizing the error of the previous policy, the king decreed that henceforth

> it will be free to all persons, of whatever quality and condition they may be, indeed to all foreigners, even if they have not obtained from us letters of naturalization, to embrace and exercise throughout our Kingdom, and notably in our good city of Paris, whatever commerce and whatever profession of arts and trades seems good to them. To this effect, we . . . extinguish and suppress all corps and communities of merchants and artisans, as well as masterships and guilds. We abrogate all privileges, statutes, and regulations given to these corps and communities so that our subjects cannot be troubled in the exercise of their commerce and professions for any cause or any pretext whatsoever. (248)

The effect of this edict on the guilds was immediate and electric. The guilds, led by the wealthy and prestigious Six Corps of Paris, quickly drew up memoirs attacking the proposed edict, which threatened to deprive guild masters of privileges they regarded as secure rights and to strip them of authority over their journeymen and apprentices.[3] The Six Corps lamented that the edict would condemn them "to wander in an immense void, confounded in a crowd of intriguers and usurers, servile and dishonorable men." Nearly all the guilds' memoirs claimed that the result of the edict would be social anarchy—"social confusion," "the confusion and mixture of orders," and "the most horrible chaos." By destroying the authority of the guild masters, it would bring about "the ruin of subordination," "a pernicious spirit of independence," and "the insubordination of inferior agents." Urban society would, in effect, be turned upside down.[4]

The Parlement of Paris also opposed the abolition of guilds in formal remonstrances, which stressed that the abolition would result in insubor-

---

3. The merchants that make up the Six Corps were the drapers, grocers, mercers, furriers, stockingers, and goldsmiths.

4. The quotations from guild memoirs are taken from Kaplan (2001, 84–87). On the theme of the abolition of guilds as turning society upside down, see Kaplan (1986).

dination and chaos in the trades and in the kingdom's cities. But the parlement framed its arguments in the traditional juridical language of royally sanctioned corporate organization and hierarchical order, a language we have explored in chapter 1 through a discussion of Loyseau. Indeed, referring to him as "one of our most enlightened authors," the parlement quoted Loyseau in their remonstrance against the abolition of the corvée: "If persons were not distinguished according to Estate, there would be nothing but disorder and confusion. Because we cannot live together in equality of condition, it is necessary that some command and others obey" (287).[5] The guilds, the parlement affirmed, are only one of a whole series of "corporations" that make up society, whose existence has arisen from the nature of society itself. "From the greatest of all, which are empires, down to the least, which are families, men have always united to protect themselves, always commanded by superiors or watched over by parents" (309).[6] This surveillance "reinforces a general calm in the interior" of all these corporations. "It is a chain of which all the links are joined to the first chain, the authority of the Throne, and which it is dangerous to break" (309).

The parlement was also worried about the maintenance of public order. The abolition of the guilds by destroying the hierarchical ordering within the world of work would gravely threaten the security of the kingdom's cities:

> There are above all classes over which the police must unite all its vigilance. The rich ... are interested in good order. But in protecting the poor, the police must watch closely over their conduct; the poor stand only to gain from troubles. ... Fruitful surveillance can be maintained only when one can command. But what will be the authority of the masters when their workers, always independent, always free to deliver themselves to another, can easily escape from their workshops? An apprentice, barely initiated into the first principles of his art ... will take up work on his own account. Who will follow him in the details of his domestic life and who will answer for him to the police?

Such reflections, the parlement adds, "become terrifying when applied to these beings born for the trouble of societies, whose passions, less controlled by education, will join to their brute natural energy the activity

---

5. The Loyseau quotation is (1987, 14).

6. In French, *parents* may mean either "parents" or "relatives." Thus being watched over by *parents* would include surveillance by relatives other than one's mother and father.

they acquire amidst the license of cities. What mode of policing could have been gentler than that of the guilds? The workers were inspected by their masters, the masters by the officers they had chosen: a correspondence of interest united them to one another" (310).

The parlement warns that without the guilds, trade itself will be devastated. "Commerce, already too disdained, will decline more and more; honest families will flee" from trade. "False gold will be mixed with true; cloths will have neither the width nor the quality required, without inspectors who verify and surveillants who examine. . . . What state will survive in such anarchy?" Such a regime will be particularly dangerous in Paris, "where the details are lost in the immensity, where the citizen lives unknown in his own home, whereas in most provincial cities the common relations between inhabitants naturally establish a mutual surveillance" (312–19).

The parlement also denied Turgot's assertion that French manufactures were currently losing ground to their rivals; indeed, they assert, it was precisely Colbert's system of regulations that had raised French manufactures to a position of superiority over its rivals. Ending regulations will destroy French superiority: "Must we not fear that a rapid decadence will extend equally to all trades? The foreigner, tricked by flawed merchandise, repelled by imperfect work, will take to other countries the tributes he used to bring to us" (315–16). The remonstrance ended with a plea to the king:

> Your Majesty will conclude from all these reflections that this law, dangerous in its execution, would tend to substitute confusion for good order; that for an active and vigilant policing it would substitute a policing . . . powerless in its means; that it would deprive the existing masters of privileges that they have acquired on the faith of the most venerable laws; that by isolating citizens it will awaken personal interests but weaken the general interest; that it will expose the capital to the most distressing disorders and will expose commerce to unending troubles; that fraud, bad faith, cupidity, and imperfect workmanship will introduce distrust among your subjects and sooner or later repel the preferences of foreigners. (319)

The controller general and the parlements clearly were at loggerheads about the abolition of guilds. The differences were not about policy details but about contrasting overall visions of the state and society. Turgot embraced a language of natural rights that attacked privilege and the power of corporate bodies and argued that all citizens had an equal right to employ their labor as they saw fit. The parlement embraced a vision of the state as a great corporation formed by countless subordinate corporations in which privilege and hierarchy alone could guarantee order and public safety. In this standoff, the king, for the time being, sided with his controller general.

The Corvées

The edict abolishing corvées raised constitutional issues akin to those raised by the abolition of the guilds. Turgot, fresh from his experience in the Limousin, was keenly aware that corvées were a much-hated imposition on the peasantry. Under the regime of the corvée, when new roads were constructed or old ones needed improvement or repair, peasants in the parish where the work was to be done were simply drafted by the local authorities and required to do the road work, thus pulling them away from the fields and forcing them to work without pay. The result was disgruntled peasants and mediocre road construction. The edict suppressing the corvée established a system similar to what Turgot had introduced during his intendancy in Limoges: road construction would be performed by private contractors and paid for by taxes raised in the parish where the work was being done. But this reform of the corvée was different in two important respects. First, it was a nationwide policy officially decreed by the king, not a cobbled-together solution arranged by an enterprising intendant. And second, the taxes to support the roadwork were now to be paid by all residents of the parish, including nobles and others who were exempt from the taille. As the decree put it, "The work heretofore done by corvées . . . will, in the future, be done by means of a contribution by all those proprietors . . . who are subject to the vingtièmes, among whom the allocation will be made in proportion to their contribution to the rolls of this tax" (Schelle 1923, 5:211). As we have seen, the nobles were required to pay the vingtième. This occasional road-construction tax was now to be added to the payments of the vingtième, with noble landowners, who were the nation's wealthiest persons, subject to the largest assessments.

The decree abolishing the corvée, like that abolishing guilds, was subjected to blistering remonstrances by the Parlement of Paris before the king enforced its acceptance. As was true of its argument against the abolition of guilds, the remonstrance against the abolition of the corvée raised a stirring defense of the traditional understanding of state and society. The parlement's argument, although occasionally employing terms borrowed from eighteenth-century enlightened discourse, was built on a fundamentally archaic rhetoric about the ancient constitution of the kingdom. The bulk of the parlement's remonstrance focused not on the question of road building and its organization but on a single issue, the breaching of the nobles' tax privilege, a privilege that, according to the parlement, derived from the fundamental principles of social order. The vehemence of the argument in this remonstrance may have arisen in part from the fact the privileges being revoked in this edict directly touched the parlementaires' interests: as nobles, they were exempt from the taille.

The parlement began with a declaration of principle: "Justice, Sire, is the first duty of kings. . . . The first rule of justice is to conserve to each that which belongs to him. This is the fundamental rule of natural law, of the law of nations and of civil government, a rule that consists not solely in maintaining the rights of property, but also in conserving those rights attached to persons, which derive from prerogatives born with the state." The parlement warns that "systems with an appearance of humanity and good intentions that tend . . . to establish an equality of duties between men and to destroy these necessary distinctions, would quickly lead to disorder, the inevitable consequence of absolute equality, and would produce the overthrow of civil society, whose harmony can only be maintained by that gradation of powers, of authorities, of preeminences, and of distinctions that keep everyone in his place and guarantee all ranks from confusion." This order, the parlement added, arises "not only from the principles of all good government: its source derives from divine institution." After this statement of principle, the parlement warned the king the dire effects of imposing a new tax on the nobles: "What then are not the dangers of a project produced by an inadmissible system of equality, the first effect of which is to confound all the orders of the State by imposing upon them the uniform yoke of this territorial tax?" (Flammermont 1898, 278–79).

The parlement then delved into the corvée's history, which, it claimed, derived from the initial conquest of the Gauls by the Franks: "The corvée was owed to the Franks by their men, but . . . the Franks were also required to make their men serve on diverse works useful to the king and the State, such as the communications necessary to royal officers sent to oversee the administration of the provinces." The corvée, hence, was part of the original constitution of the state. When, centuries later, the serfs "obtained emancipation," they "became free but common (*roturier*) citizens, still subject to the corvée (*corvéeable*). To abolish the corvée would therefore violate the ancient constitution of the realm" (Flammermont 1898, 281–83). Maintaining the traditional distinctions between clergy, nobles, and commoners was absolutely essential to the welfare of the state; "this distinction . . . derives from the origin of the Nation; it is born with our mores, it is the precious chain that links the Sovereign with his subjects." According to this "antique rule of the duties and obligations of your subjects," the clergy is to devote itself to religion and to relief of the poor; "the Noble devotes his blood to the defense of the State and assists the Sovereign with its counsel"; and "the lowest class of the Nation, which cannot render such distinguished services to the state, serves by paying taxes and engaging in industrious bodily labor" (Flammermont 1898, 287). This formula, a cliché since the eleventh century, remained, in the eyes of the parlement, the appropriate rule for the present (Duby 1978).

This remonstrance had little to say about the specifics of the decree banning the corvées. Rather, the parlement denounced the institution of a new tax payable by nobles as an assault on the very principles of the state. It utilized the clichés about France's ancient constitution, going back to the supposed institutions imposed on the Gauls by the Franks, to justify privileges in the present. It equated hierarchy with order, claimed this order was a product of both God's will and France's immutable constitution, and predicted that any legislation infringing noble privileges would destroy the state. Besides the archaism redolent of Loyseau's treatise of 1610, there is more than a whiff of panic in the parlement's reaction. As we shall see, however, they were right to regard this new tax as the beginning of an assault on the hierarchical social order itself.

Opposition to imposing the road-construction tax on the nobility had also arisen within the royal administration itself. Even before the decree's official publication, the proposal had been criticized at length by Miromésnil, the administration's top judicial official. Turgot had answered his critique point by point. This exchange, intended for the eyes of the king, revealed both the essence of the traditionalist opposition to the decree and the forthright radicalism of Turgot, a radicalism far more explicit than he avowed in public statements. Miromésnil declared, "It could be dangerous to destroy absolutely all the privileges. . . . I cannot fail to say that in France the privilege of the nobility should be respected, and that I believe it to be in the interest of the king to maintain it" (Schelle 1923, 5:182). To this Turgot responded with a detailed rebuttal, arguing not so much for the wisdom of this particular tax as against the principle of noble privileges in general.

Turgot responded that Miromésnil "seems to adopt the principle that, according to the constitution of the State, the nobility must be exempt from all taxes. He seems even to believe that this is a universal prejudice, dangerous to upset." Turgot claimed, on the contrary, that this idea was generally regarded "as a superannuated pretension abandoned by all enlightened men, even within the order of the nobility." It would be thought "a paradox by the largest part of the nation, whose interests it wounds. Commoners certainly make up the greatest number, and we are no longer in a time when their voices are not counted." Turgot then stated a more general and philosophical argument in favor of taxing the nobility:

> We should discuss the proposition in itself. If it is envisaged from the point of view of natural law and the general principles of the constitution of societies it presents the most marked injustice. What is a tax? Is it a charge imposed upon the weak by force. . . . This is hardly the idea one has of a paternal government, founded on a national constitution according to which the monarch has been elevated above all others to assure the happiness of all; in which the government is made the depository of public power in order to maintain the properties of each . . . by means of justice and in order to defend them against exterior military attacks. The expenses of government having as their object the interest of all, all must contribute; and the more one enjoys the advantages of society, the more one should regard oneself as honored to share in the expenses. It is difficult, from this point of view, for the pecuniary privileges of the nobility to appear as just. (Schelle 1923, 5:182–83)

Following this implicit enunciation of social contract political theory, according to which the monarch was not chosen by divine right but by the consent of the nation, Turgot went on to spell out the practical evils that spring from the nobles' tax exemptions: "It is because we have been unable to make the nobles or the clergy pay that we have had to force their tenants and even their miserable sharecroppers to pay in their stead. As a consequence, we see perpetuated all the evils arising from the allocation of the *taille* and from the form of its collection, although everyone knows their sad effects. It is in order to pass over the privileged that we have multiplied taxes on consumption and that we have established a tobacco monopoly, so harmful because of the enormous amount they cost the people." These taxes on consumption are all the more harmful because they "have called into existence new armies both of smugglers and of agents [of the tax farmers], both lost to useful labor, occupied in destroying one another by the murders and tortures occasioned on one side by the attractions of fraud, and on the other by the necessity of repressing it" (Schelle 1923, 5:184). Finally he declared, "What an administration, that would make the poor bear all the public expenses in order to exempt the rich!" (Schelle 1923, 5:189).

Turgot assures Miromésnil that he does not plan to do away with all noble privileges. He asks,

> Does it follow that we should destroy all privileges? No: I know as well as everyone else that one must not always do the best possible thing; and that, if one should not renounce correcting bit by bit the defects of an ancient constitution, one must work to that end only slowly, to the extent that public opinion and the course of events renders such changes possible. It would be absurd to wish to make the nobles and the clergy pay the taille, because prejudices have attached . . . an idea of vileness to this tax. . . . We must allow the privilege of the nobles with respect to the taille to subsist as an established rule that would be unwise to change; but we must not be dupes, nor should we regard it as something just in itself, even less as something useful. (Schelle 1923, 5:185)

One suspects that Miromésnil was not reassured by this supposed disavowal, which made it clear that Turgot regarded the abolition of all noble tax privileges as "the best possible thing," an action to be avoided only because of current prejudices.

This internal administrative document, intended only for the eyes of the king, makes clear Turgot's profoundly radical intentions. The major reforms he introduced, all of which were revoked once he fell from office, were bold in the context of the old regime. The freeing of the grain trade turned its back on centuries of precedent, the abolition of the guilds foresaw a thorough rearrangement of the rules of work and commerce in the urban crafts, and the abolition of the corvée would at once free the peasants from a major burden and establish a precedent for a piecemeal rolling back of noble tax privileges. In this confidential memo, Turgot set forth his true convictions, with radical implications far beyond the specifics of these decrees. He invoked the sanction of public opinion; asserted that the views of the commoners, who made up the greatest number of the population, should be consulted in making policy; implied that the French state was to be subject to natural law and that its monarchical constitution arose from a social contract; and made it clear that the nobility's fiscal privileges were harmful, based on force and prejudice, and should eventually be erased. Already in 1776, Turgot was espousing many of the principles of civic equality that were adopted by the National Assembly in 1789. The Parlement of Paris was not wrong to detect in Turgot's decrees a profound hostility to what it regarded as the principles of the French monarchy's ancient constitution.

The radical cast of Turgot's political and administrative visions are set forth more comprehensively in a remarkable document known as the *Memoir on Municipalities*. The memoir was prepared for Turgot upon his accession to the controller generalship by his assistant and confidant, Pierre-Samuel Dupont de Nemours, whom we have met as a physiocrat in chapter 12. This memoir was apparently intended for eventual presentation to Louis XVI but had not been shown to the king when Turgot was dismissed in 1776. I think it best to regard it not as a policy document to be presented to the king in its existing form but as a somewhat utopian statement of the ideal toward which Turgot—and Dupont—believed reform should tend. It is important to realize that the memoir was written not by Turgot himself but by Dupont, a physiocrat whose cast of mind was certainly more utopian and dogmatic than Turgot's. Dupont kept possession of the memoir after Turgot's fall and made it public only in 1787, during the crisis leading to the French Revolution, when reform proposals of every stripe were being circulated.[7]

The memoir proposed a radical transformation of the kingdom's governing structures. According to Dupont/Turgot, the kingdom of France as it existed in 1774 entirely lacked an organized constitution. What the Parlement of Paris regarded as the ancient constitution of the realm was to the memoir "a society composed of different orders badly united, and of a people among whose members there are but very few social ties. . . . It follows that there exists a perpetual war of claims and counter-claims which reason and mutual understanding have never regulated, in which Your Majesty is obliged . . . to decree on everything, in most cases by particular acts of will." If, by contrast, "the various parts composing your realm had a regular organization . . . you could govern like God by general laws" (Schelle 1922, 4:576). There is certainly a hint here of the "legal despotism" of the physiocrats. The reforms proposed in the memoir intended to establish for the first time a formal constitution for the state—one that would radically transform the nature of government and enhance the efficacy of the king, or perhaps one should say of the administration.

The memoir called for the establishment of a nested system of representative assemblies at the parish, regional, provincial, and national levels. The parish assemblies would be empowered to allocate taxes among the taxpayers and to direct local public works and poor relief; the higher assemblies, composed by delegates from lower ones, would oversee the distribution of taxes and funds between the subordinate administrative

7. See "Mémoire sur les municipalités" in Schelle (1922, 4:568–628). For interpretations of the memoir, see Baker (1975, 1978) and Sewell (1980, 127–33).

units. The parish assemblies would represent all landowners in France, nobles and commoners alike, making no distinction of status. Citizens would be allocated votes according solely to the value of the landed property they owned. Petty proprietors would receive fractional votes, middling proprietors full votes, and the wealthy multiple votes, all in proportion to the value of their holdings. To exercise the votes they had coming, individuals would have to declare openly their property's value; hence the claim for votes in the assembly would simultaneously be a declaration of liability for taxes. This system would achieve automatically the most vexing task of the administrator—equitably allocating taxes—and would wipe out the exemption from the taille of nobles, clerics, and many wealthy bourgeois. At the same time, it would pool the opinions of citizen proprietors about the needs of their communities, scientifically weighting them by the citizens' real proprietary stake in society, enabling the parish assemblies to handle such local administrative details as the division of the tax burden and the appropriate allocation of funds to public works while enabling the royal government to devote itself to "the general considerations of wise legislation" (Schelle 1922, 4:576).

This scheme proposed not only a thorough transformation of royal taxation but a complete reorganization of the state. It would apply to all provinces of France, breaking down distinctions between pays d'état and pays d'élection, between the provinces subject to the gabelle and the *provinces réputées étrangères*. French territory itself would be made uniform, subject to identical regulations. The plan would, as the memoir claimed, endow France with a constitution, establishing it for the first time as a unified, rationally organized nation-state. The memoir, as Keith Baker has remarked, "implied the reconstitution of the monarchy on the basis of civic equality." It would have created "a legal system in which individual subjects were equally protected under the law." It thus prefigured much of what was eventually put into place by the revolutionaries in 1789; it even explicitly invoked the universal rights of man (Baker 1978, 296).

But as Tocqueville pointed out in his own brief comment on the memoir, the assemblies would be concerned "only with administration and never with government"; they "would have advice to give rather than a will to express" ([1856] 2004, 175). The *Memoir on Municipalities*, for all its radicalism, embodied a purely administrative vision of the political order, one to be based on a rationalistic scheme of automatic self-administration that would establish civic equality and impose uniform procedures for all of France. But it would keep all political power in the hands of the royal council. As Tocqueville pointed out, the scheme was utterly utopian. Any governmental restructuring that so fundamentally revised existing social, political, and administrative order and at the same time formed assemblies of the population empowered to discuss public issues would inevitably have led not to calm and automatic self-administration but to extensive political tumult, perhaps even revolution (175). Had the king ever been shown the memoir, he would probably have cashiered Turgot even sooner than he did.

Tocqueville was fascinated by the *Memoir on Municipalities* because it seemed to exemplify perfectly the telos of the royal administration: a regime with full civic equality but no political freedom. I see it as representing an extreme version of the abstract, equalizing, rationalistic, centralizing side of the royal government's contradictory tendencies. It was a remarkably pure expression of a centralizing bureaucratic rationality that had penetrated the royal administration, one profoundly at odds with the preservation of a corporate and aristocratic society. The memoir illuminates the goal envisioned by the old regime's most radical administrative reformer. It also indicates that the Parlement of Paris was by no means paranoid to see Turgot, from its point of view, as a dangerous innovator prepared to dismantle the old regime state and society in its entirety. But it is wrong to see the *Memoir on Municipalities* as the telos of the royal administration because the administration had no single telos; it was driven by conflicting goals and visions, by what I have called its double bind. It was a system profoundly structured by privilege that was dependent on a wide range of privileged agents to successfully perform its most important task—providing the king with adequate financial means. But it could not expect to do so over the long run without eliminating the privileged orders' tax exemptions and freeing industry and trade from the privileges of the various provinces and of trade guilds. The royal administration was caught in a contradiction and therefore vacillated: between different approaches to reform and between reform and reaction.

The Six Edicts were both the high point of Turgot's ministry and a major cause of his undoing. Turgot's influence over Louis XVI was sufficient to obtain a *lit de justice*, a special session in which the king imposes his will on the parlement, forcing the parlement to register the Six Edicts in April 1776. But the combination of displeasure with Turgot among courtiers and conservative administrators and Turgot's opposition to joining the American Revolutionary War in support of the colonies led to his fall from office in the following month. During a very brief term in office, Turgot's successor, Ogier de Clugny, overturned all his major reforms. In October of the same year, Ogier was himself succeeded by Jacques Necker, a Genevan banker resident in Paris who had gained a reputation as a financial wizard.

Necker's Ministry

The appointment of Necker was in some ways even more surprising than that of Turgot. Turgot was known for his liberal convictions but was otherwise a conventional choice. The scion of a distinguished robe noble family, he had worked his way up the hierarchy, serving ably both as a subordinate official at Versailles and as an intendant in the provinces. Necker, by contrast, had no experience in royal administration and was a commoner, a foreigner, and a Protestant—therefore ineligible to become a *maître des requêtes*, the venal office required of all members of the royal council. Hence Necker could not actually hold the office of controller general. He was instead named "director of finances" and Taboureau de Réaux, an elderly administrator, was officially designated controller general. It was Necker, however, who made the major decisions, and in June 1777, Taboureau de Réaux resigned in disgust from his false position. Thereafter, Necker, although still officially director of finances, became the recognized head of the government.

Necker had been campaigning for the office of controller general since 1773. His bank was one of the three biggest operating in Paris. It had profited from grain speculation immediately after the brief freeing of the domestic grain trade in 1763 and from speculation in French Canadian financial obligations at the end of the Seven Years' War in 1763. In both cases, Necker probably benefited from inside information about state policy. He became particularly famous—or notorious, depending on one's opinions—when he refloated the French East India Company in the years after the Seven Years' War, a policy that had failed by 1769 but from which Necker had nevertheless profited greatly. By 1770, his wife had launched a prestigious salon in Paris that enhanced his reputation as a man of intellectual ambition; by 1772, he officially retired from active direction of the bank (Lüthy 1961, 373–99). His *Éloge de Colbert* of 1773, awarded a prize by the Académie Française, was widely understood as a praise of his own virtues and a tacit bid for direction of the royal administration (Necker 1773). But Turgot, not Necker, became controller general upon the new king's accession to the throne in 1774. During Turgot's ministry, Necker kept himself in the public eye, publishing a critique of the freeing of the grain trade in the spring of 1775, shortly after Turgot's edict and in the midst of the Flour War (1775). When Turgot was dismissed in 1776, Necker was an obvious candidate in spite of the impediments posed by his religion and nationality. His reputation as a successful financier overwhelmed other concerns: France was, in the autumn of 1776, about to enter what was certain to be a very expensive war, and Necker was a successful banker who knew how to handle finances and float loans. As Herbert Lüthy remarks, "What was expected of him was that he should 'organize confidence,' keep the state's treasury full, be the magician of credit—and that is what he did" (1961, 419).

France did not declare war on Britain until February 1778, but by the summer of 1776 it began a clandestine campaign supplying American rebels with weapons and gunpowder and launched a crash program to build up its navy. The supplies of French arms were crucial to the survival of the American army in the war's first year. The defeat of British general Burgoyne in the Battle of Saratoga in the fall of 1777 convinced the French government that the rebellion might succeed. The French recognized the United States in February 1778, entering formal combat in March, when Britain declared war on France. The eventual victory of the Americans was greatly aided by France, particularly the French navy, which neutralized what otherwise would have been overwhelming British superiority at sea. French troops also joined the ground campaign and contributed to the victory at Yorktown, Virginia, which ended the war in 1781. Thus the French avenged their defeat in the Seven Years' War by helping strip Britain of its prized American colonies.

The American Revolutionary War, however, put tremendous strain on a French budget already staggering under debts from previous conflicts. At the beginning of the war, the additional cost was estimated at 150 million livres per year (Necker n.d., 9–10). The declaration of war necessitated the immediate establishment of a third vingtième—a 50 percent increase over the two vingtièmes already being collected (Égret 1975, 92–93). But Necker resolved not to further increase tax rates that were already universally regarded as too high; the war, consequently, had to be financed by a major increase in borrowing. Necker's genius and connections as a banker were exactly what was required. The crown's loans were typically bought by bankers or financiers and then sold to a variety of investors. Necker, himself a lion of the banking community, was particularly efficacious at getting his loans fully subscribed.

During most of the seventeenth and eighteenth centuries, the crown had borrowed from the public by means of *rentes perpetuelles* (perpetual annuities), which meant that in exchange for a large sum of cash, the crown would pay the lender (or rentier) an annual sum equal to 5 percent of the total principal—indefinitely, so that the rente could be passed on to the rentier's heirs. But the crown's promises of payments had been abused often, most recently in the wake of the Seven Years' War, by delaying payments, cutting the interest rate, or arbitrarily decreasing the capital on which the rente was to be paid. Investors lost interest in rentes perpetuelles by the late 1760s, as had the bankers who bought and retailed them. Crown borrowing thereafter, particularly under Necker, mainly took the form of lottery loans and *rentes viagères* (life annuities). Lottery loans were unlike lotteries in our day because everyone who paid something in got a financial return. But the loans were structured so that those who drew lucky numbers would get huge returns on investment while the rest would get a lower rate than that available on other rentes (Krukeberg 2014, 44). Lottery loans were taken up by a wide range of people, many of them small investors. Necker himself commented that adding an element of lottery to loans "spreads, without inconveniencing anyone, the pleasure of anticipation." The element of chance attracted additional funds "because everyone experiences, through the effects of imagination, the potential benefits of fortune" (Necker 1785, 3:206). During his ministry, Necker launched successful lottery loans totaling eighty-five million livres. But the most important form of loan during Necker's time in office was the rente viagère, which brought in over 280 million during the American Revolutionary War (Égret 1975, 96).

The administration had good reasons for favoring the rente viagère, which, unlike the rente perpetuelle, was amortized upon the death of the person on whose *tête et vie* (head and life) it was based. This meant, however, that the annual interest payment owed by the state, usually 8 to 10 percent, was higher than that on rentes perpetuelles. The initial idea was that investors could gain a reliable source of income for the rest of their lives by converting a sizable portion of their fortune into an annual rente. However, one also could establish a rente viagère on two lives—say the lives of oneself and one's wife, son, or daughter. By the time of Necker's administration, various combinations and speculations had become possible. Because rentes viagères were often offered at the same rate regardless of age, the rente was often placed on the head of a young person, often a child relative. Indeed, there was no obligation to establish the rente on the life of a relative; one could choose any child (Lüthy 1961, 470–78). This means of prolonging the life of rentes viagères beyond the death of the person who initially established them rendered them increasingly expensive for the state, but this was not clearly realized until some years later.

The main disadvantage of these rentes from the point of view of the rentier (or lender) was that they could not be sold to others on an open market. But Necker's fellow Genevan bankers found a way around this problem. Beginning in 1758, they would take out loans "on the heads and lives of thirty demoiselles of Geneva" and sell shares of these loans to their customers. The banker himself would buy thirty separate contracts, each on the life of a carefully chosen healthy seven-year-old girl from a good family in Geneva and turn these thirty separate contracts into a single mass of annual payments. The banker then sold negotiable shares of this mass of rentes to buyers. The demoiselles of Geneva in fact turned out to be long-lived. Geneva had a healthy climate, was a leader in medical science, and had such good civic records that it was possible to pick girls from particularly long-lived families. According to Herbert Lüthy's calculations, the average age at death of the demoiselles in these late eighteenth-century pools was sixty-three—a remarkable figure for this period (1961, 279–81). In the late eighteenth century, these rentes became "a great article of exportation for the Genevans, equal to watches and jewelry" (280). Many in France, Switzerland, and elsewhere in Europe bought rentes viagères of this sort—including persons of relatively limited means. "In a manner almost too symbolic," Lüthy says, the practice of marketing these rentes viagères seems to mark "the passage from a form of personal economy to a pure mobile capitalism" (279). Necker's massive recourse to borrowing kept the state afloat during the very expensive American Revolutionary War. His loans were fully subscribed, largely because the bankers who retailed rentes viagères had confidence in their fellow Genevan.

When he entered office, Necker was not regarded as a reformer. He had written a book condemning the freeing of the grain trade, which was the *nec plus ultra* of political-economic reform in France in this era. In a three-volume work written after his fall from office, Necker presented himself explicitly as an opponent of reforms in Turgot's vein. Indeed, he criticized "the economists"—here he surely meant to include Turgot—for their proposal that the vast array of existing taxes should be replaced by a single tax on agricultural revenues. There is in general, he wrote, "a great vice in the abstractions of political economy." The political economists thought only about the benefits their policies could be expected to have in a distant future: "If the duration of a single generation is insufficient for the execution of their ideas, they . . . embrace the entirety of posterity in their projects. . . . They apply to men, whose lives are but an instant, calculations that apply only to an indefinite future." According to Necker, "plans for administration should be . . . aligned with our lifespans and our moral affections, which constitute the essential portion of happiness or misery. Then we will not sacrifice the present to the future in our projects" (1785, 1:97–99).

Necker also noted that sweeping reforms had generally not succeeded. He pointed out that the edicts establishing a national land survey in 1763 and abolishing the corvées in 1775, "even though both were registered with great solemnity . . . have been formally abandoned." Such laws not only attract conscious resistance but suffer from flagging energy on the part of administrators once the zeal for reform has encountered the complexity of the changes necessary to carry them out. Moreover, reforms made by one minister are not always pursued by his successor: "Finally, one cannot really expect that the Sovereign will hold to the laws of political economy with that vigor of sentiment that is born from conviction. After all, the utility of such laws is, for a long time, only a kind of abstraction, whereas resistance and rumors cause a very real fatigue" (1785, 1:184–85). Here Necker, however gently, faults the inconstancy and lack of vision of France's eighteenth-century kings as well as the court intrigue and rumors that make consistency in policy impossible to sustain.

If Necker criticized the political economists' systemic economic and social reforms, he nevertheless undertook significant reforms of the financial institutions he oversaw. We have seen that he instituted a thoroughgoing process of "verifications" to assure the fair distribution of the vingtième—which, after its tripling at the French declaration of war against the English, had become a significant burden on the wealth of otherwise tax-exempt nobles (Kwass 2000, 94–95). But he also introduced important reforms in the financial institutions themselves. The finances of the eighteenth-century French state, as John Bosher points out, were managed not by a public royal treasury but by consortiums of financiers who profited mightily from the state's business (1970, 6). The direct taxes (the taille, capitation, and vingtième) were paid not to the state but to "receivers" in each province. Receivers were venal officers who took a cut of the taxes and who could also make use of the tax fund they were holding in their private businesses (Bosher 1970, 9–11). Indirect taxes were leased out to consortiums of tax farmers who undertook the labor-intensive task of collecting them. These consortiums were essentially private enterprises, and they made big profits working on behalf of the state. The best organized were the General Farms, which collected the taxes on salt and tobacco as well as the *aides* (a range of levies including internal customs tolls and taxes on food and other consumer goods). Every six years, the General Farms negotiated a new lease with the royal administration. The general farm employed some fifteen thousand guards and twenty thousand clerks, accountants, cashiers, and inspectors (Bosher 1970, 74–76). It advanced to the crown half the amount it was to collect over its six-year contract, paying an installment of the total at the beginning of each year. Most of the remaining revenues it owed to the state it did not turn over to the crown but paid out itself on the crown's behalf—for example, to owners of state rentes (Bosher 1970, 93).

When the various taxes were delivered to Versailles, they went not to a central treasury but to consortiums of "treasurers," venal officers who actually made the state's payments but who were essentially private financiers. They took a cut for their services and also speculated with the funds they were holding on the state's behalf. In addition to making various scheduled payments, the treasurers often loaned money to the crown for emergency expenses—seemingly charging the crown for the use of its own money (Bosher 1970, 92). As with the guilds and various bodies of venal officeholders, the king relied on the treasurers' good credit to get access to money at rates below what he could himself obtain on the loan market.

This pattern of state finance had important flaws. Necker's predecessors Terray and Turgot had suppressed a number of these financial offices to save money directly and to simplify the accounts and make central oversight more effective (Bosher 1970, 160). Necker pushed these reforms much further, suppressing the offices of receivers and accountants of the royal domains and forests, reducing a corps of 481 venal officers to a single crown-controlled bureau (*régie*) of eighteen men with subsidiary employees to do the actual collection. In 1780, he took the collection of the *aides* away from the General Farms, joining it with the collection of the royal domains and forests, forming a *régie générale* to perform both functions. While these reforms saved money, their greatest significance was increasing crown control by turning functions formerly carried out by venal officers to state employees. Necker also suppressed all forty-eight offices of the receivers general of finance, who collected the taille, capitation, and vingtième, establishing a single treasury that could be directly overseen by the administration. This eliminated the receivers' ability to engage in private business with government funds (Bosher 1970, 158–61). By the time of his dismissal in 1781, Necker "had taken great strides in the direction of a truly public system of public finance. . . . All this showed a policy of developing a bureaucracy . . . as an alternative to the private management of government funds by venal accountants" (Bosher 1970, 164–64).

Necker also accomplished a more spectacular innovation in the sphere of state finance: he made an accounting of the state's budget available to the public in the form of a *Compte rendu au roi* (Report to the King). The *Compte rendu* was officially addressed to the king but actually intended for the general public of French citizens; its preface stated that the publication of the state's accounts "could have the greatest influence upon public confidence" (1781, 2). This was a startling innovation because the crown's finances were traditionally considered to be a royal secret. This notion had already been contested in the public sphere, notably in the tract by the abbé Morellet discussed in chapter 8 (1775c). But not until 1781, at Necker's hand, were the state's accounts made accessible to the public.

This rather dry compilation of figures was avidly taken up by the French reading public: the *Compte rendu* became one of the century's best sellers (Shovlin 2006, 2). The public was greedy for authentic information about budgetary mechanisms and the financial condition of the state. Necker argued that publication of the state's finances should become a regular affair—an "institution," as he put it. This would have a strongly positive effect on the state's finances: knowing that the French finances were in balance would increase the state's credit, making investors more willing to loan to the crown and at lower interest rates. According to Necker, making the accounts available to the public would render the French as confident about their government's finances as the English were about theirs. One cause of England's "great credit" is "the public notoriety to which the statement of its finances is subjected. Every year this statement is presented to the Parliament and then printed; and all the lenders hence are made regularly aware of the relation maintained between revenues and expenses. They are not troubled by suspicions and chimerical fears that result from obscurity. In France, we have constantly made the state of our finances a mystery" (1781, 2–4). Necker presented his *Compte rendu* as a means of instilling confidence in the soundness of the French budget among the broad public of potential investors.

It was above all the publication of the *Compte rendu* that made Necker the most popular of all eighteenth-century finance ministers among ordinary French men and women. Here was a minister willing to break with state secrecy, who believed it important to inform the public at large about the state's financial affairs and to submit himself and his policies to an effective vote of confidence in the tribunal of public opinion. But Necker's popularity in public opinion was not sufficient to overcome the machinations at court and in the administration. Indeed, his audacity in publishing "the royal secret" intensified opposition to Necker. Many courtiers were dismayed by Necker's reforms: the financiers who had been displaced were influential in the court, where they commonly invited nobles to join in investments that would earn easy money. This helped sustain the favor of courtiers, whose influence on policy weighed heavily in royal politics. Besides, suppression of venal offices posed a potential threat to all officeholders, who were a fundamental integument of the ancien régime French state. Necker's reforms and publication of the *Compte rendu* set off a reaction against him, and he was dismissed by Louis XVI in May 1781, only a few months after the *Compte rendu* appeared. Necker's successors undid most of his reforms, restoring the power of the venal financiers. As had been the case with his archrival Turgot, reforms that struck at privileges could not be sustained. Public management of French finances and public discussion of the budget would be achieved only after the Revolution.

Necker retired to Geneva but continued to court French public opinion, publishing a rosy three-volume account of his ministry's policies. In *De l'administration des finances de la France* (On the Administration of French Finances), Necker made much of relations between the minister and the public. "Since the progress of enlightenment has brought men who are governed closer to those who govern, ministers have become actors in the theater of the world . . . whose conduct is severely observed." A minister can "persuade, fortify moral ideas, excite imaginations, [and] tie together opinions and sentiments with bonds of confidence." In England, he continued, orators in the House of Commons are recognized by the public; in despotisms, the minister cares only about the prince's opinion; but in France, "where, because of the happy mixture of liberty, sensibility, and enlightenment, and because of the memory of so many ills due to the administration of finances, the good minister can enjoy at every moment the fruit of his work" (1785, 1:v–viii). Necker was once again launching a campaign for office as the chief minister, this time appealing directly to public opinion. In the end, this campaign was successful. In August of 1788, in the midst of the crisis that led to the Revolution, Louis XVI turned in desperation to Necker, who regained office to great popular acclaim. Thus Necker became the last finance minister of the old regime.

In his *Compte rendu* and in *De l'administration*, Necker claimed that the ordinary budget showed a surplus during his ministry—except for the extraordinary war expenses, which were covered by borrowing, receipts were somewhat greater than expenses. In fact, the immense borrowing had burdened the budget with new expenses. In 1786, Controller General Calonne announced to the king that the state was teetering on the brink of bankruptcy, touching off the financial and political crisis that led to the Revolution. French finances had been in crisis on several occasions over the past two centuries, most recently at the end of the Seven Years' War in 1763. On these occasions, the state had declared limited bankruptcies of one kind or another—usually by reducing or delaying interest payments on debts or by canceling debts outright, often supplemented by shaking down financiers who were major crown creditors. But during the agonizing crisis that lasted from 1786 to 1789, the king and his ministers, including Necker when he was recalled in 1788, absolutely rejected the possibility of even a partial bankruptcy. Here we discover an important effect of

Necker's massive turn to loans marketed to an ever-broader public: the state was now heavily dependent on the confidence of a wide array of ordinary investors. Even the hint of a bankruptcy would drive down the market value of the negotiable portion of the state's debt and immediately dry up the market for new loans, thus greatly worsening the state's financial position rather than improving it. Thus in yet another way, a certain civic equality had found its way into the actions of the royal administration: it now depended, as never before, on the good opinion of a wide range of anonymous investors.

Three Sustained Efforts at Reform

Not all efforts at economic and fiscal reform were tied up with the fates of particular ministers. There were also reform efforts that lasted through a succession of ministries. Some attained impressive results; others were consistently frustrated. The notion that the royal administration should concern itself with the state of the economy could be traced back to Colbert, who introduced a new framework of regulations combined with subsidies that was intended to improve the quality of French manufactures and make them capable of withstanding competition from the Netherlands and England. But over the course of the eighteenth century, ideas about the relationship of the state and the economy changed. Colbert's relatively static, zero-sum, hierarchical view of economic life increasingly gave way to a vision of ever-changing consumption patterns, steady advances in technique, and rising wealth—all enlivened by free commercial exchange. Colbert's regime of economic regulation and management could not, in the end, stand up against the expansive commercial capitalism of the eighteenth century. But the institutional structure of the state that Colbert established remained largely intact until the Revolution. In this section of the chapter, we will see how an essentially Colbertian administrative corps attempted to reform French institutions from within to make them more consonant with the emerging commercial capitalist economy.

THE SINGLE DUTY PROJECT

The first case study examines an attempt to complete a reform Colbert himself began: replacing tolls assessed on goods transported by road or river within the kingdom by a uniform tariff barrier at the nation's frontiers. The tolls, most of them originally imposed by local territorial lords in the Middle Ages, were converted to indirect state taxes. Because they were an important element of the royal fiscal system, they were difficult to eliminate. Colbert managed to cancel tolls within a large region surrounding Paris, creating what was known as the Five Great Farms. This "customs union" composed the entire northern half of France except Flanders, Artois, Alsace, Lorraine, and the Franche-Comté along the eastern frontier and Brittany and the Vendée in the far west. Outside this area, however, and between the Five Great Farms and the remaining provinces, tolls on interregional commerce remained in place, and tariffs imposed on foreign goods were not uniform. The completion of this reform of internal tolls was avidly pursued—but never achieved—by eighteenth-century royal administrators. These unsuccessful attempts, elegantly analyzed by John Bosher, illustrate the difficulty of achieving economic reforms in the eighteenth century (1964).

The duties that remained after Colbert's partial reform could add 15 or 20 percent to the price of certain French-made goods sold in France. Indeed, foreign goods sometimes paid lower duties than domestic goods transported from another province. The need for reform was evident, but the path forward was perilous. When changes in economic policy are proposed, then and now, some groups stand to be harmed by the new policy even if the net overall benefit is clear. Reforms of the internal duties were often opposed by mercantile interests in provinces outside the Five General Farms, especially in the *provinces réputées étrangères*. Under the existing system, merchants in these areas were subject only to very low duties when trading with foreign countries; a single duty system threatened to disrupt their established commercial relations.

Powerful financial interests also stood in the way. Since 1668, the crown had leased the collection of all the indirect taxes to the financial syndicate known as the General Farms. The farmers paid a lump sum to the crown for the right to collect the taxes for the entire period of their six-year lease. Thus the perpetually impecunious monarch could immediately access great sums of money to pay for past, present, or future wars without waiting for the taxes to trickle in. It was evident that eliminating internal tolls would, by encouraging commerce and industry, increase the taxable product over the long run, but this reform threatened the short-run interests of the tax farmers and hence their willingness to extend credit. In this case, as in many others, the interest of the crown as a debtor conflicted with its interest as a generator of revenue.

During the regency that followed the death of Louis XIV in 1715, the Council of Commerce, a body established to represent the interests of merchants and manufacturers within the administration, took up the idea of reform. Michel Amelot, who became the head of the council in 1716, gained support for this scheme from the regent Philippe d'Orléans and his chief minister, the infamous John Law. Law was a Scotsman who attempted to introduce monetary and financial reforms similar to those made in England after the Glorious Revolution of 1688, but he was driven from office in 1720 when his scheme for a national bank and a paper currency blew up in a spectacular bubble (Faure 1977; Murphy 1997; Kaiser 1991; Shovlin 2016). Considerable progress toward reform of duties had been made in negotiations between the various interested parties between 1716 and 1720. But Law's successor, de la Houssaye, showed no interest in the reform, so the effort languished once Law fell from office (Bosher 1964, 37–44).

However, Lallemant de Betz, one of the General Farmers, undertook a long-term project of research on the foreign and domestic trade of France, based on the farm's archives. By 1738, he had drawn up a plan to replace the internal and external duties with a tariff, collected at the frontiers, that would be revenue neutral for both the farm and the state. The plan won the support of the General Farmers who, wagering that reform was inevitable, decided it should be done under their auspices. This plan hence sidestepped one of the likely sources of opposition, but it foundered in the early 1740s in face of opposition from the *provinces réputées étrangères* (Bosher 1964, 44–52).

A new effort was launched when Henri Bertin, a member of the Gournay circle, served as controller general from 1759 to 1763. He established a committee, composed principally of royal officials but including one farmer, to prepare a new plan. The peripheral provinces complained as usual, but the main problem was a worry that revenue would drop during the period of transition between systems. Considered in the later years of the Seven Years' War, which put the budget under tremendous stress, the mere possibility of lost revenue meant that this reform was shelved. But unlike previous plans, this one became publicly known—which meant that it could serve as the basis of future attempts, once the budget was brought under control (Bosher 1964, 53–94).

Bosher observes that by the time Jacques Necker began his first term as controller general in 1777, the royal administration's thinking had shifted to favor the long-term economic policy advantages of a single duty system over the question of immediate revenue (Bosher 1964, 103). By 1778, Necker had set Guillaume-François Mahay de Comeré to work on the problem. Within a few years, he produced a systematic plan that was introduced to the Assembly of Notables called by Necker's successor Calonne to address the financial emergency facing the crown in 1786. Comeré's plan would have eliminated the internal tolls but also suppressed the gabelle, which threatened the existence of the General Farms. The General Farms' opposition helped delay action on the proposal (Bosher 1964, 116–17). Comeré's single duty project was therefore caught up in the political crisis leading to the Revolution, and action was postponed until the impending meeting of the Estates General in 1789. It was taken up and passed only after the French Revolution had occurred. The very same Comeré, assisted by many of his clerks, prepared the legislation that was eventually passed by the National Assembly in November 1790, finally establishing a French national customs union (Bosher 1964, 148–56). Thus a reform that Colbert initiated in the 1660s, that several generations of royal officials knew would contribute to the nation's prosperity, that would make the nation's fiscal system more uniform and rational, and that had been proposed again and again during the eighteenth century, could only be enacted when the Revolution eliminated the contradictions of the old regime fiscal system and established a regime of generalized civic and fiscal equality. This story perfectly illustrates the difficulty reforming economic and fiscal policies in the decades leading up to the Revolution.

CORPS DES PONTS ET CHAUSSÉES

Daniel-Charles Trudaine, the abbé Morellet's benefactor and Vincent de Gournay's superior in the Bureau of Commerce, was one of the old regime monarchy's most effective administrators. Trudaine had a typical early administrative career. Born in 1703 in Paris, the son of a royal official, he became a *maître des requêtes*, served as the intendant of Auvergne from 1730 to 1734, and became a councilor of state in Versailles. In 1743, Controller General Orry, dissatisfied with the state of France's roads, named Trudaine to oversee the Corps des ponts et chaussées (the Corps of Bridges and Roads)—which was utterly transformed under his guidance. In 1749, Trudaine was also named the director of commerce, the administration's chief officer for economic affairs. Trudaine thereafter oversaw the corps of inspectors of manufactures, the officials who enforced Colbert's regulations concerning the manufacture of cloth. In 1751, as we have seen, Vincent de Gournay became an intendant of commerce, serving directly under Trudaine. Trudaine, as his sole biographer remarks, was at once Gournay's "chief from the administrative point of view and his disciple with respect to ideas" (Andrieux 1923, 32).[8] Trudaine was a regular in Gournay's circle, where his already liberal inclinations were forti-

---

8. This forty-eight-page doctoral thesis in law at the University of Lyon is, as far as I have been able to determine, the only extant biographical work on Trudaine.

fied. He eventually hired two other members of the Gournay circle, Louis Abeille and Simon Clicquot de Blervache, as inspectors of manufactures and did his best to transform the mission of the corps more or less in harmony with Gournay's ideas. Trudaine was recognized as an administrator of great devotion and talent; he more than once turned down offers to serve as controller general in order to continue his work on France's bridges, roads, and manufactures. Considering the progress he made in these areas and the inability of controllers general to introduce reform schemes that could last, this seems to have been a wise choice.

The Corps des ponts et chaussées was founded by Colbert but was not a well-organized administrative body: the engineers who composed it were relatively autonomous operators who often gained positions through patronage and whose training was haphazard. Trudaine, who had improved roads in Auvergne while an intendant there, recognized that endowing France with good roads and bridges could contribute importantly to the kingdom's welfare. He made the Corps des ponts et chaussées his life's work, remaining at its head from 1743 until his death in 1769, when he was succeeded by his son Philibert Trudaine de Montigny.[9] When the younger Trudaine died in 1777, his successor, Jean-François Tolozan, essentially continued the Trudaines' policies.

The desire to improve roads had several sources, including a wish for more rapid administrative communication between Paris and the provinces and for easier movement of military supplies. But much of the motivation was economic. A better road system would mean better and more reliable transportation of goods and a speeding up of the circulation of capital and market information. Improving the Corps des ponts et chaussées was thus a reform of precisely the sort political economists favored. Its success, however, depended on the very illiberal corvée for road work, which had been made obligatory throughout the kingdom in 1738. This was "the precondition for all operations because it procured for the engineers of the ponts et chausées the enormous, if not very efficacious, manpower they needed" (Arbellot 1973, 766). Indeed, Trudaine de Montigny, like his father a devoted member of the Gournay circle, was highly ambivalent about Turgot's abolition of the corvée in 1776 because he feared the new regulations would stall progress on the roads (Picon 1992, 50).

Central control over construction and maintenance of roads and bridges required both accurate knowledge of the existing infrastructure and plans for improvements. In 1744, Trudaine created a centralized draft-

---

9. On Trudaine's career, besides Andrieux (1923), see Petot (1958), Picon (1992), and Arbellot (1973).

ing bureau (*bureau des dessinateurs*), located in Paris, to provide accurate maps of the entire French road system. This bureau was at the origin of the famous École des ponts et chaussées, which today remains a prestigious engineering school. In 1747, Trudaine selected Jean-Rodolphe Perronet to run the bureau and to oversee the training of engineers. Perronet, trained as an architect, had served as an engineer for the corps in Normandy. This proved a brilliant choice. Perronet quickly transformed the drafting bureau into a school of civil engineering, which he headed with distinction right up to the French Revolution. Dissatisfied with the engineers in place, Perronet, with Trudaine's full support, established a system of ranks within the corps, with inspectors at the top and a descending order of engineers, subinspectors, subengineers, students, and geographers—the last being draftsmen aspiring to become students. At the outset, all grades below full engineer had to work at the drafting bureau under Perronet's close supervision in order to hone their skills (Petot 1958, 141). After a few years of remedial training—combined with dismissals of the least competent—the abilities of the subinspectors and subengineers had improved enough that they no longer needed to spend time at the bureau. Instead, the bureau had effectively been transformed into a school for new engineers (Petot 1958, 148–49).

What came to be known as the École des ponts et chaussées had no professors, other than Perronet. Students took courses in architecture at the École des arts, and the more advanced students trained the beginners in the specifics of drawing accurate maps and designing roads and bridges (Picon 1992, 84–85). Thanks largely to Perronet's devotion and astounding energy, this unorthodox means of training engineers succeeded. From the 1750s to the French Revolution, the École des ponts et chaussées turned out a steady stream of well-qualified engineers—generally between fifteen and twenty per year—who continually replenished the ranks of the Corps (Picon 1992, 95). The students were carefully selected by Perronet from good families—"at least born into respectable families in the bourgeoisie," in Peronnet's words. They were expected to have a classical education and some instruction in mathematics, draftsmanship, and architecture (Picon 1992, 91). Sons of state employees were greatly overrepresented among students, accounting for nearly a third of the total, and most of the rest were sons of merchants, doctors, lawyers, building contractors, or rentiers (Picon 1992, 100).

Besides effective technical training, the school instilled a powerful esprit de corps. The students enforced a code of honor, sometimes denouncing to Perronet fellow students whose behavior they found wanting. The bonds and sense of pride formed during the school years carried over into the corps' work life. Engineers were to obey their superiors strictly, were forbidden to collude with contractors, were not to engage in public controversies, and were to reside in their districts. They could marry only with the permission of Trudaine and Perronet, which assured alliances with good families. They were to participate in the best society of their localities (Petot 1958, 172–74). The school continued to serve as a focal point for the corps in another way: it was largely Perronet's recommendation that determined salary increases or promotions from one grade to another within the corps (171). Perronet was not only the schoolmaster but also effectively cohead of the corps with Trudaine, and he kept himself informed about his many former students. A student admitted to the school was, in short, gaining admission not just to an education but to a lifelong identity with and submission to the prestigious Corps des ponts et chaussées.

However, the corps was not an entirely authoritarian affair; it also had a strong collegial side. An important institution was the monthly assembly held at Trudaine's residence in Paris. These gatherings were attended by the inspectors, who were resident in Paris and were the highest officers in the corps after Trudaine and Perronet, but also by any engineers from the provinces who happened to be in Paris at the time. Memoirs proposing new projects or discussing assorted technical and administrative problems were discussed at length. Discussions were free and frank, and the opinions expressed carried great weight in determining the corps' projects and policies. The gatherings were sociable as well as professional occasions—a moment when the elite of the corps could mingle and converse with one another and with Trudaine. The professional discussions were followed by a dinner hosted by the latter (Petot 1958, 160). The assemblies partook both of the sociability of the old regime's salons and of the high seriousness of its academies of arts and sciences.

The Corps des ponts et chaussées was a particular institution, headed for a very long time by two effective leaders and with an uncommon esprit de corps. It made remarkable improvements in the French highway system. Systematic maps of France's roads, produced by the drafting bureau, enabled engineers in Paris to envisage the system as a whole and to determine where work was most needed (Picon 1992, 45; Arbellot 1973, 775–79). Sinuous and narrow roads were broadened and straightened. Road surfaces were made more durable and repaired more quickly. Pierre-Marie-Jérôme Trésaguet, the Corps des ponts et chaussées engineer who worked with Turgot in Limousin in the 1760s, developed a system for the use of stone in road construction that the corps adopted. Trésaguet's system was essentially that subsequently attributed to the British engineer

McAdam in the early nineteenth century: the road surface was slightly convex, with a foundation of large stones, covered by smaller stones and topped with gravel—the whole nine or ten inches thick (Picon 1992, 41; Arbellot 1973, 770–71; Trésaguet 1775).

A few decades of steady and efficient work transformed the road network of France. Guy Arbellot estimates that over six thousand lieux (about twenty-four thousand miles) of new roads had been built by 1780; this was the equivalent of thirty-four roads stretching all the way from Paris in the north to Marseille on the Mediterranean coast (1973, 773). Arbellot remarks that the road system completed by the 1780s had established "the skeleton of the entire network of road communication" of France, one that "has been preserved practically intact right up to our day"—this in an article written in 1973, when the system of modern limited access *autoroutes* that would transform the French highway network was still in planning or under construction (791).

These improvements made for faster and more reliable transportation. Arbellot used *L'indicateur fidèle ou guide des voyageurs* (The Faithful Indicator or Guide for Travelers), which listed the schedules of French coach services, to calculate changes in travel times between Paris and various French cities for 1765 and 1780. The changes were substantial. For example, a trip from Paris to Strasbourg, which took eleven and a half days in 1765, took only four and a half in 1780. The trip from Paris to Toulouse declined from fifteen and a half to seven and a half, from Paris to La Rochelle from ten to five, and nearer to Paris, that from Paris to Caen from five to two days. In a few cases, good roads and fast coaches had already been in service in 1765: the trip from Paris to Lyon took five days in both 1765 and 1780 and that from Paris to Lille two days in both years (Arbellot 1973, 786–90). The improvements resulted from better roads, superior coaches, and better-organized coach services. In 1775, Turgot removed the coach services from the Ferme des Postes and created a new state-run Régie des diligences et messageries. This new state agency used fast coaches with good springs (*diligences*) and eliminated the slower *coches* and *carosses*. (The *diligences* came to be known colloquially as *Turgotines*. This was one of Turgot's reforms that was not overturned by his successors; Arbellot 1973, 189.) Relatively light and fast *diligences*, already in use on a few intercity routes in 1765, could have been employed only on the vastly improved roads constructed by the Corps des ponts et chaussées.

The Corps des ponts et chaussées was a major exception to the general run of reform efforts undertaken by the eighteenth-century royal administration. The reforms, begun in the 1740s, progressed without interruption right up to the French Revolution, endowing the country with good roads, sturdy and well-designed bridges, and a cadre of highly trained and highly disciplined civil engineers.

THE CORPS OF INSPECTORS OF MANUFACTURES

A regime of regulation of manufactures, particularly manufactures of woolen cloth, was instituted by Colbert in 1669. The regulations, briefly discussed in chapter 4, established norms for dyes, thread counts, quality of raw materials, weight, length, and breadth of various categories of cloth. These norms were to be maintained by the appropriate guilds located in French cities, but Colbert also established a corps of inspectors, employed directly by the central administration, to oversee the regulations, including in rural areas without guilds. Cloth that passed inspection was marked with a small lead seal, and substandard cloth was subject to fines and confiscations. The work of the corps was directed by the Bureau of Commerce (previously called the Council of Commerce), headed by a director of commerce—who was effectively, as Phillipe Minard puts it, "a quasi-minister of industry and commerce" (1988, 26).[10] This was the position assumed by Daniel Trudaine in 1749.

The corps of inspectors was itself closely supervised. During the first three decades of the eighteenth century, there were about forty inspectors, rising to fifty by the mid-1740s and fluctuating between fifty-five and sixty-five from the 1750s through the 1780s (66). Until 1740, most inspectors served for less than twenty years; thereafter, careers became essentially lifetime propositions—most served between twenty-one and fifty years. In 1740, a new career ladder that lasted until the end of the old regime was introduced. One began as a "student," working under a senior inspector; if judged capable, the student was promoted to subinspector and could expect eventually to rise to the rank of full inspector (69). The inspector's salary was mediocre, but the job conferred authority and prestige and was secure. From the 1740s forward, the inspector of manufactures was a kind of old regime prototype for what, in the nineteenth century, became known as the *fonctionnaire* (73–114).

Trudaine became the director of commerce in 1749. His opinions were already liberal; in the early 1730s, when serving as intendant of Auvergne, he wrote that he was "infinitely opposed to all exclusive privileges [here concerning the manufacture of cutlery] that only serve to hamper commerce and give occasion to much mischief" (Andrieux 1923, 15). These

---

10. Hereafter, citations to Minard will be in parentheses in the text.

opinions were strengthened when Vincent de Gournay became one of his chief subordinates. As noted in chapter 12, Gournay introduced ideas at odds with existing practices of the inspectors of commerce, both in official discussions concerning economic regulation and in his noted circle. This emphasis on commercial and industrial liberty rather than enforcement of the Colbertian code seems to have been reflected in Trudaine's policies.

Under Trudaine, the task of the inspectorate shifted significantly from enforcing regulations to gathering information on broader economic conditions in the districts and disseminating technical knowledge. Previously, inspectors had been assigned to specific geographical clusters of cloth manufacture, but in 1754, Trudaine reorganized the geography of inspection. He assigned one inspector (sometimes assisted by one or more subinspectors) to each of the "generalities," the administrative districts overseen by royal intendants. The inspectors were to enforce regulations but also to report regularly about conditions in all manufactures in the district (58–59). "Progressively, what was demanded of inspectors was not only figures from the bureau de marque on production and sales of specific textiles, but also estimates of the production of paper manufactures, tanneries, and manufactures of glass or pottery, and even, at the very end of the old regime, of forges and metallurgical factories" (174). In this way, the inspectors became, under Trudaine, something like agents of a ministry of commerce and industry rather than a police force.

Trudaine also eventually changed the profile of the inspectors general, the highest-ranking members of the corps. For some time, he declined to replace inspectors general who retired or resigned: having risen through the ranks, most were strongly wedded to the Colbertian task of enforcing standards of manufacture. In the 1760s, Trudaine began to place experts from outside the corps into these positions. The most important of these was Paul Abeille, a lawyer at the Parlement of Brittany and a confirmed liberal who had been a member of the Gournay circle and served as Gournay's secretary. Recruited as an inspector general in 1765, he acceded to the crucial position of secretary to the Bureau of Commerce in 1768, a post he retained after Trudaine's death in 1769 (204). In 1766, Trudaine also appointed Simon Clicquot de Blervache as an inspector general—the author, as we have seen, of a famously scathing critique of the program of regulations that inspectors of manufacture were expected to enforce. Nothing could more stunningly indicate the change in direction Trudaine was attempting to impose on the corps than his choice of Clicquot as inspector general. The physiocrat Dupont de Nemours also served for a time as in this capacity. It was Abeille, however, who had the greatest practical impact, laboring mightily in his position as secretary to rationalize the corps' information-gathering and policy-making apparatus (203–10). Trudaine also appointed as inspectors general a number of technical experts, including the famous mechanical inventor Jacques Vaucanson, several chemists and physicists, and John Holker, an exiled Englishman well versed in the new mechanical techniques of textile production (137). This new set of inspectors signaled a clear change in the corps' vocation.

Awareness of the English textile innovations was an essential motivation for the adoption of this change: French merchants, manufacturers, and bureaucrats were aware of the English technical wizardry and growing competitive advantage. The English Catholic John Holker became the most important force for promoting technical innovation within the corps of inspectors. As a young man, Holker had made a career in the Manchester textile industry, but he had been forced to flee the country because of his participation in the unsuccessful Jacobite rebellion of 1745. Settling in Rouen, where a good deal of cotton manufacture was already going on, he was noticed by the local inspector, who introduced him to Trudaine in 1751. Holker managed to recruit skilled workers from England and smuggled new machinery into France. He employed the workers and machines in a factory producing cotton velours near Rouen, which was declared a royal manufacture by Trudaine's Bureau of Commerce. Both English and French workers trained in Holker's mill went on to establish comparable enterprises elsewhere (216–17). In 1755, Holker was named an "inspector general of foreign manufactures established in France," an ad hoc position he held while continuing to direct his own enterprise, contrary to normal regulations. He passed this position on to his son Jean in 1768 (233). It was the younger Holker who introduced Hargreaves's spinning jenny into France in the 1770s and Arkwright's water frame in the following decade (217; Chassagne 1991, 181–87).

Trudaine and his successors—Trudaine de Montigny and Jean-François Tolozan—also used a long-standing Colbertian strategy to encourage manufacturing innovations. They awarded substantial subventions— amounting to some 5.5 million livres—to successful innovators and to skilled workers who emigrated from England (196–217). In short, the Bureau of Commerce devoted substantial manpower and cash to developing up-to-date technologies of production in French industries. Its consistent efforts bore a substantial responsibility for the wide-ranging industrial upsurge in France in the second half of the eighteenth century.

However, the corps of inspectors was hardly unanimous in its response to the new directions coming from above. Some of the corps' Colbertian ethos was passed on from generation to generation because training was carried out by existing senior inspectors. Promotion of "students" to sub-inspector could depend on taking up the attitudes as well as the skills of the inspectors to whom they were apprenticed. Over time most inspectors embraced their role as purveyors of technical knowledge, which was compatible with a strict adherence to the Colbertian quality standards. Indeed, it was something of a point of pride for inspectors to take on this role. But many resisted relaxation of the statutory standards.

Nevertheless, by the 1770s, the language and ideas of the political economists had become widely diffused both in the royal administration and in civil society at large. Such ideas were taken up by some merchants who chafed under the system of regulation. Thus the wholesale woolen merchants of Romans questioned the necessity of regulations in 1776, declaring that "he who produces well finds his reward in ready sales, the good price of his merchandise, and the satisfaction of his customers; he who produces badly is punished by the discredit into which he falls and the difficulty he has in selling his cloth" (269). Regulations, therefore, were quite beside the point. Or a young woolen manufacturer from Sedan whom we cited in chapter 4, engaged in a dispute with the local inspector in 1781, arguing that the producer's task was "to follow or to anticipate the tastes of consumers. Such is the goal that producers must propose to themselves." And because these tastes "vary from one instant to another . . . regulations can only . . . conform to tastes at the time of their promulgation; hence their validity can only be ephemeral" (Gayot 1998, 79, 92). On the other hand, Sedan manufacturers of the very high-quality, heavy black cloth destined mainly for export tended to support the maintenance of standards and the affixing of seals, which they felt strengthened their position as high-end producers in the international market (286–87).

The majority of the corps, according to Minard, supported continuing the regime of regulations, although with varying degrees of rigor. Others were entirely won over to the liberal ideas of the Trudaines and the political economists. One such was Jean-Marie Roland de la Platière, an inspector of manufactures in Amiens, who was fated to become minister of the interior after the Revolution. In 1785, as the author and editor of a volume of the *Encyclopédie méthodique* devoted to manufactures, arts, and trades, Roland published a memoir arguing in detail that all regulations should be suppressed (1785, 289–96). But as Minard emphasizes, rather than a sharp divide between traditionalists and liberals, there was a range of intermediate opinions. Even Roland argued that manufacturers should be required "to bring to a public depository all products of industry, in order to register their nature, type, and quantity and to give each of them a government seal," mainly because it was the key to gathering good information about industrial production (295).

In 1781, Necker circulated a modified set of regulations, urging that the regime of inspection be continued but that inspections be carried out with "prudence and circumspection" rather than with rigor. The regulations also maintained the Trudaines' strong emphasis on information gathering and the diffusion of industrial technique (330–31). By the time the old regime came to an end, the liberal reform ideas introduced by Trudaine had strongly influenced the corps of inspectors but had not entirely triumphed. In 1791, however, two years into the Revolution, the Allarde law decreed complete freedom of enterprise, abolishing the guilds and entirely sweeping away the corps of inspectors.

The Possibilities and Limits of Reform in the Old Regime

The juxtaposition of these different reform efforts inspires several observations. I shall begin with reflections focused on comparisons of specific cases of reform and move toward more general conclusions. The histories of the Corps des ponts et chaussées and the corps of inspectors of manufactures present parallels. First, they were both administered by the Bureau of Commerce under the watchful eye of Daniel Trudaine and his successors. Second, both were administrative corps with a hierarchy of grades, whose officers were assigned to "generalities," the principal administrative districts of the old regime state and thus distributed throughout France. In both cases, the supervision of the corps was entrusted to an active, talented, and long-serving official: Perronet in the case of the Corps des ponts et chaussées and Abeille in the case of the corps of inspectors of manufactures. As a consequence, the reform policies pursued by the administration were sustained for several decades. By comparison with most efforts undertaken by the controllers general, the reforms of road building and maintenance and of the inspection and promotion of manufactures were quite successful.

Yet the successes of the Corps des ponts et chaussées certainly surpassed those of the corps of inspectors of manufactures. The administration of the latter succeeded in broadening the original job description of the inspector to include diffusion of technical knowledge and the collection of wide-ranging economic information. But due to the resistance of many inspectors down to the end of the old regime, it succeeded only partially in freeing cloth manufacturing from the constraints of Colbert's inspection system. By contrast, the Corps des ponts et chaussées, reformed root and branch, quickly became highly efficacious and effectively centralized. Indeed, it actually survived the Revolution intact and continues to flourish today. The corps of inspectors of manufactures, which was eliminated definitively in 1789, never attained such a degree of unity and precision.

How can this difference be explained? One advantage of the Corps des ponts et chaussées was that its object was more clearly defined and more under its own control than that of the corps of inspectors of manufacturers. Its goal was to provide the kingdom with a good transportation infrastructure by designing, building, and maintaining roads and bridges. The work was undertaken at the expense of the state; the Corps des ponts et chaussées engineers hired, paid, and oversaw the contractors who did the work. The inspectors of manufactures, by contrast, had a more diffuse task. Even before Trudaine and his successors broadened the inspectors' duties, their task was both to enforce regulations and to gather statistics on a diverse collection of manufacturers who produced different cloths for different markets, with wide ranges of skills. When the administration attempted to soften enforcement and added new information gathering and the provision of technical advice to the inspector's tasks, what was expected of the inspector became less clearly specified. The corps of inspectors remained disciplined and competent, and it eventually embraced the new initiatives from the central administration: the inspectors' work surely contributed to the impressive growth of manufacturing in France in the final decades of the old regime. But the results of its efforts were more diffuse than the ever-accumulating stretches of good roads and sturdy bridges constructed by the Corps des ponts et chaussées.

The Corps des ponts et chaussées had another, perhaps paradoxical, advantage. Decades before Trudaine launched his reform efforts, the corps of inspectors was already an exceptionally well-organized bureaucracy, with entrenched values and an esprit de corps, and new inspectors were trained as apprentices under existing inspectors. The veteran inspectors did their best to instill in the "students" their own values, which revolved around the fastidious application of the Colbertian regulations. It consequently took some decades of effort for the reform-minded directors of commerce and their hand-chosen inspectors general to instill new mores and habits into the corps—a process still incomplete when the French Revolution suppressed the corps. By contrast, the Corps des ponts et chaussées before Trudaine and Perronet reorganized it was a haphazard affair, quite incapable of resisting the initiatives of the administration. The initial disorganization of the corps left a free field for the innovations introduced by the administration. Thus members of the older generation of engineers were either retrained and absorbed into the better-funded and tightly organized new corps within a few years or dismissed from the service. Moreover, the fact that the engineers all passed through the École des ponts et chaussées supplied them with a unique and powerful esprit de corps. Paradoxically, the superior initial organizational discipline of the corps of inspectors of manufactures limited the efficacy of administrative reforms.

The case of the remarkably successful Corps des ponts et chaussées, together with that of the perhaps lesser but real successes of the reform efforts in the inspection of manufactures, can help us understand the failure of the other reform efforts considered in this chapter. First, both cases benefited from the long tenure of capable and powerful leaders who guided the reforms. At the Corps des ponts et chaussées, the leadership of the Trudaines spanned thirty-four years (1743–77), and the career of Perronet as its cohead and director of the school spanned forty-two years (1747–89). The Trudaines served as directors of commerce and therefore heads of the corps of inspectors of manufacturers for twenty-eight years (1749 to 1777) and were succeeded by the like-minded Jean-François Tolozan. Moreover, Paul Abeille became the secretary to the Bureau of Commerce and thus effectively the chief inspector the year before the death of the elder Trudaine and remained in that post under Tolozan. Such extended periods of executive power made sustained reform much more likely to succeed. The contrast with the other reform efforts investigated in this chapter is clear. Turgot was in office for a mere two years and Necker for a little under five. Such terms were close to the norm—after the middle of the eighteenth century, no controller of finances served more than five years in succession. Such short terms in office meant that reforms enacted by one controller were unlikely to be sustained; both Turgot's reforms and Necker's were overturned by their successors. And attempts to end internal tolls were likewise bedeviled by the frequent succession of controllers. The exception was the commission headed by Comeré, which survived the fall of Necker's first ministry and whose plan was eventually adopted. But this happened only after the Revolution had cleared the ground of obstacles: eliminating the General Farms, which had resisted reform, and replacing the former provinces, with their varying statuses and modes of government, with judicially uniform "départements."

A second reason that reforms of the Corps des ponts et chaussées and the corps of inspectors of manufactures could proceed effectively was that they posed little threat to powerful entrenched interests. The reforms undertaken by the Corps des ponts et chaussées benefited virtually all interests, with the exception of the utterly disfranchised peasants who were forced to perform corvée labor—and even they benefited from the better roads they were forced to build. Something similar was true of the corps of inspectors of manufactures: the manufacturers were generally happy to learn about technical improvements and to see regulations loosened and seizures of cloth ended. Moreover, neither of these reforms in any way threatened the finances of the state—indeed, to the not inconsiderable extent that they enhanced taxable wealth, they actually improved state finances.

By contrast, the elimination of internal tolls would have harmed several entrenched interests—those of the General Farm that collected the tolls, those of the various financiers who profited from them, and those of the *provinces réputées étrangères*. Turgot's abolition of the guilds and corvée and Necker's reforms of the fiscal administration all threatened entrenched interests or were perceived as threatening powerful and well-organized groups: guildsmen, nobles, parlements, provincial estates, courtiers, and financiers. This meant that the reform efforts were immediately drawn into the politics of a system that was stacked against innovation. The only exception was the freeing of the grain trade, which was seen by the poor as harming their interests but had no obvious ill effect on more privileged classes. It is therefore revealing that it was Turgot's abolition of the guilds and the corvées, not the freeing of the grain trade, that brought him down. The political system of the old regime, with its fiscal double bind, its obstreperous parlements, and its intrigue-ridden court, managed to turn back all but highly specific and unthreatening kinds of reform—until, that is, the entire system was blown apart in the French Revolution.

But stepping back from the practical fates of the various efforts chronicled in this chapter, we should realize that even the failures attest to a rising sense of the need for reform during the eighteenth century. The belief that it was appropriate for the government to introduce schemes aimed at increasing the efficiency and productivity of the French economy was widespread among both royal administrators and the educated public. At least from the 1750s forward, reform was on the state's agenda. The nature of the efforts undertaken by the royal administration varied greatly in scope and intent—from controversial grand initiatives like the ambitious economic restructuring program rolled out by Turgot to the many relatively anonymous efforts, large and small, undertaken by royal intendants, engineers of the Corps des ponts et chaussées, and inspectors of manufactures aiming to improve markets, manufacturing techniques, or the circulation of knowledge in their districts. I have remarked that the chief goal of intendants and royal officials in the late seventeenth century had been to ensure obedience and provide the state with sufficient tax revenues; to these goals had been added, by the end of the old regime, the promotion of economic prosperity. This constituted a major reimagining of the purpose of the royal government.

This change was paralleled by a remarkable advance of political-economic discourse in civil society. The publication of Montesquieu's *The Spirit of the Laws* in 1748, the publication of the first volumes of Diderot and d'Alembert's *Encyclopédie* in 1751, the flood of publications by members of the Gournay circle in the 1750s and by the physiocrats in the 1760s—not to mention dozens and dozens of more obscure works—meant that some knowledge of political-economic argument was expected of those participating in intellectual circles. Societies of agriculture proliferated. Local academies established essay contests on political-economic topics, like those won by Jean-Jacques Rousseau or Simon Clicquot de Blervache in the 1750s. Well before the coming of the Revolution, French administrators and literate society in general were bathed in notions derived from political economy.

As we have seen, the vogue for political economy owed much to the perception that France was falling behind England in both economic and military terms. The political economy of the Gournay circle was strongly influenced by earlier English economic writings and by an admiration for English economic policies. The physiocrats, although loath to attribute any of their ideas to anything other than the genius of Quesnay, obviously admired English farming practices. Much economic reform attempted to adapt English ideas and policies to French circumstances—as a means of overcoming English geopolitical advantage. Nevertheless, by the 1760s, French political economy was essentially as highly developed as the English. As we have previously remarked, the significance of French thought in the history of political economy is marked by the fact that the term *economist* and the slogan *laissez-faire*—not to mention the concept of the *entrepreneur*—were French, not English, in origin.

But the interpenetration of political economy and the royal administration that is evident from the time of the Gournay circle forward was not simply a case of intellectual influence. Administrators were attracted to political economy because it seemed to offer the royal administration something it drastically needed: a possible way out of its fiscal and governmental double bind. They could not raise taxes on France's wealthiest citizens—the nobility—who possessed tax privileges. Yet administrators could not end tax privileges because so many of the privileged were creditors of the state, and their good credit depended on precisely on their privileges. Given this impasse, it appeared to many that the most promising way to increase the chronically inadequate tax yield would be to follow the precepts of political economy, which promised a steady increase in the economic activity and wealth on which taxes were based.

But in adopting the viewpoint of political economy, the administrators—and, for that matter, the literate public—were adopting a method of valuation of persons and activities that fundamentally contradicted the traditional foundation of the state. Rather than judging the worth of persons by their formal status as nobles, clergy, or commoners, political economy implicitly (and at times explicitly) judged worth by a person's ability or willingness to produce useful goods or services, to consume, and to invest. Monetary exchange value, not tradition, birth, nobility, or rank, became the criterion of valuation. Persons came to be regarded as having the same essential status—that of participants in the market. And in the market, positions are not permanent but provisional or temporary. They depend on what one brings for sale and the extent of demand and supply for an item—factors that inhere not in the person but in the anonymous and ever-changing balance of aggregate tastes, skills, and needs and in the never-fixed availability of alternative means of producing goods and of satisfying wants. In short, the viewpoint of political economy stands in implicit conflict with a society based on privilege, birth, and rank. By adopting an increasingly political-economic viewpoint, servants of the royal state were, usually unwittingly, positing a society based on civic equality.

The Revolution and the Advent of Civic Equality

The French Revolution established civic equality as the basis of public law and state administration. It also implicitly or explicitly adopted political-economic notions of citizens as free producers and consumers of goods. As we saw in the introduction to this book, the first article of the Declaration of the Rights of Man and the Citizen, adopted by the National Constituent Assembly in September 1789, began with a ringing statement: "All men are born and remain free and equal in rights. Social distinctions may be founded only on common utility. The goal of any political association is the conservation of the natural and inalienable rights of man. These rights are liberty, property, security, and resistance to oppression." The law, it goes on, "must be the same for all, whether it protects or punishes. All citizens being equal in its eyes, are equally admissible to all dignities, places, and public employments, according to their capacity and with no other distinctions than their virtues and their talents."

As unexceptional as these proclamations may sound in the twenty-first century, readers of this book should immediately recognize that they signified a profound transformation of old regime France, where hierarchy was pervasive and privilege a constituent principle of the social and political order. Privilege was a kind of private law that either exempted a particular category of persons from duties incumbent on others (like the nobles' and clergy's exemption from the obligation of paying the taille) or that gave its holder the right to undertake some action forbidden to the nonprivileged (like the exclusive right of nobles to become army officers or to sit in the front pews in church). These rights and exemptions were enforceable in courts of law. Legal statements by kings and parlements insisted that the unwritten French constitution was based on a hierarchy of differentiated conditions, rights, and duties dating back to the very foundation of the state. We have seen that it was by reference to such claims that the Parlement of Paris denounced as illegal Turgot's attempts to abolish the corvée in 1776. By founding the new revolutionary constitution on equal rights for all citizens and guaranteeing equal access to dignities, places, and public employments, the Constituent Assembly annihilated whole categories of rights and advantages previously taken for granted. In 1789, civic equality was a profoundly revolutionary principle.

Civic equality was a lasting foundation of the new political and legal regime. Although many of the Revolution's innovations were rolled back in subsequent years and decades, this was not true of civic equality, which was embraced by Napoleon's empire and even by the restored monarchy in 1815. The task of this chapter is to trace out the contours of the crisis of the old regime, to show how and why civic equality arose as a key feature of the new Revolutionary regime, and to consider some of the political conundrums and practical problems posed by this momentous transition.

The Prerevolution

The political crisis that eventually led to the French Revolution has come to be called the "prerevolution."[1] The crisis emerged from the long-standing financial difficulties of the state. This episode is worth considering in some detail because it demonstrates beyond a doubt the continuing power of the old regime's double bind. The prerevolution may be said to have begun in August 1786, when Charles-Alexandre de Calonne, the controller general since 1783, announced to Louis XVI that the state's budget was dangerously unbalanced. An extensive study of the notoriously opaque crown finances determined that the annual deficit was over 100 million livres, as against total receipts of some 475 million. Meanwhile, the vingtième, the special tax established to finance the American Revolutionary War, was set to expire in 1787, which would decrease revenues sharply (1–2). It was clear that drastic measures would be required to avoid bankruptcy. A partial bankruptcy like those used to resolve previous state financial crises was unthinkable now that all possible solutions to the crisis would require floating sizable loans to the investing public, which any hint of bankruptcy would render impossible. To avoid the looming catastrophe, the crown would have to cut expenses radically and increase revenues. New taxes, therefore, were inevitable.

Calonne drew up an ambitious program, borrowing ideas from reforms proposed but not enacted over the course of the eighteenth century. He wished to establish a more unified state structure, abolish inter-

---

1. Égret (1962). An English translation is Égret (1977). Over the next several pages, I cite the English translation extensively, using page numbers in parentheses in the text.

nal tolls, establish a national bank, lease out the royal domains, replace the vingtième tax with a new land tax paid by all landowners, and establish regional assemblies of proprietors that would be responsible for raising the new levies (2–3). In order to bypass the parlements, which he knew would try to block or delay these policies, Calonne convened an Assembly of Notables—composed of princes of the blood, great nobles, prelates, high-crown officials, parlementary magistrates, and urban mayors—to discuss the proposed reforms. The Assembly of Notables, divided into several sections, each headed by a prince of the blood, began work in late February 1787 (6–7).

The notables displayed less deference to the king and his first minister than expected. Calonne's most important proposal was a land tax on all holdings, making no distinction between peasants, nobility, and clergy. It would effect a massive upward readjustment of the tax burden to the previously privileged. Moreover, the taxes would be assessed by a hierarchy of assemblies like those previously suggested in Turgot's *Memoir on Municipalities*, with no distinction made between the traditional three estates. Calonne's plan was drawn up by Pierre-Samuel Dupont de Nemours, the well-known physiocrat who had prepared the *Memoir* for Turgot and was now working as Calonne's assistant (10). The proposal to create the new assemblies was opposed most bitterly by representatives of the pays d'état, who objected that their traditional provincial assemblies would be deprived of their power over tax assessment. Most bishops and nobles claimed to agree in principle that equal taxation was necessary but balked at the proposed means (14).

Calonne responded with a pamphlet appealing to the public against the notables, who he claimed were motivated by a defense of their privileges. Led by Loménie de Brienne, the archbishop of Toulouse and Sens, the notables went on the attack. On April 8, Louis XVI, fatefully prone to vacillation, asked for Calonne's resignation, and Brienne was appointed in his place (22–24). Having spearheaded the opposition to Calonne, Brienne came into office with the notables' full confidence. He recognized, however, the seriousness of the financial crisis and the need for deep reforms. He was, it will be remembered, an old friend of the abbé Morellet and an adept of political economy. But as a very wealthy and powerful bishop from a noble family, he wished to maintain the distinction of orders and the clergy's independence. By the time Brienne became controller, committees of the notables had more closely examined the state of royal finances and determined that the deficit was worse than Calonne had estimated, some 133 to 145 million livres. In response to this somber news, the king promised retrenchments in expenses and improvements in income that would amount to forty million. Making up the additional one hundred million would unquestionably require increased taxes. Yet the notables alleged that they lacked authority to decree new levies (32–33). It was now up to the king and his controller to take the necessary action. In May 1787, after four months of fruitless debate, the notables were dismissed.

Brienne and his staff made progress at reducing state expenditures, progress that was crucial when the estimated deficit for 1788 rose to over 160 million (54). They cut over seven million livres from the bloated expenditures of the royal household at Versailles, which included the royal hunt and stables (43–44). The royal administration was reorganized and made more efficient. Royal pensions and monetary gifts were pared back and the granting of new pensions curtailed (45–46). The military was reorganized and unnecessary expenditures eliminated, a saving of nearly ten million (53). In all, these reductions came to between thirty and thirty-one million livres—a significant figure and an important sign of the crown's seriousness, but one that paled against the magnitude of the deficit (54). A large revenue increase, and therefore new taxes, would clearly be needed to avoid state bankruptcy.

Brienne also launched reforms in the administration and judiciary. He consolidated the state's banking functions into a single entity, making possible reliable crown accounts based on money actually received and paid out. This procedure rendered obsolete Necker's famous but highly inaccurate *Compte rendu* of 1781, which had shown a balanced budget on the basis of estimates of receipts and expenses for an average year and failed to specify vast supposedly extraordinary expenses (62). Brienne's ministry also proposed to increase the powers of local courts and decrease those of the parlements. It granted civil status to Protestants (74–83). It put forward a plan, accepted by the notables, for local, provincial, and perhaps national assemblies that would in the future apportion taxes— although these assemblies would both hold elections and deliberate separately by order (64–70). In short, Brienne's ministry made or proposed very significant reforms.

But raising new taxes was more difficult. In July 1787, Brienne presented new tax decrees for review by what was known as the Court of Peers, essentially the Parlement of Paris plus princes of the blood and various peers of the realm (87). He began with two measures straight from Turgot's agenda: free trade in grain and abolition of the corvée. By now these reforms were generally favored by the country's elites and were easily accepted. However, the Court of Peers rejected his tax decrees, which proposed expansion of stamp taxes for legal documents and imposition of a new tax paid by all landowners regardless of rank. The Court of Peers responded with remonstrances arguing that such taxes were unconstitutional unless approved by an Estates General—a body composed of representatives of the three estates that had not met for 175 years but was theoretically regarded as having the sole power to accept new taxes. The remonstrances, printed and widely circulated in Paris, confirmed an opinion already circulating in public discourse: that the crisis should be resolved by the calling of an Estates General. The king dismissed the Court of Peers' remonstrances in a *lit de justice*, reaffirming his prerogative to administer the kingdom as he saw fit. When the parlement resisted, the king, on August 14, 1787, ordered the decrees registered as law and banished the Parlement of Paris to the provincial city of Troyes. But responding to a popular outcry supporting the parlement, Brienne withdrew the disputed decrees and instead proposed an extension of the existing vingtième tax through 1792. The still exiled parlement accepted this compromise but added that any new taxes could be approved only by an Estates General. The parlement returned to Paris to general public acclaim on September 20, 1787 (93–105).

Brienne then decided to bargain for time. He calculated that he could right the kingdom's finances in five years by continuing the third vingtième, cutting expenditures drastically, and floating new loans to the public. He promised that the Estates General would be called in 1792—believing that the crisis would then be resolved and the estates would meet in a more tranquil era (106–7). In May 1788, the crown staged a coup against the Parlement of Paris, establishing a new plenary court that would take over many of its functions (170). But in the summer of 1788, the state faced an impossible financial squeeze and responded by paying its creditors with treasury bills yielding 5 percent annually rather than cash—in other words, replacing payments with yet more loans. This was a disguised partial bankruptcy, which ended Brienne's ministry (183–84). He resigned on August 25, 1788, and was replaced by Necker, whose popularity with the public and reputation as a financial wizard made him the obvious candidate. Two years had passed since Calonne had revealed the financial crisis, and virtually nothing had been accomplished.

Toward the Estates General

Necker's return calmed financial markets and pleased the public. Necker quietly reversed most of Brienne's reforms, restoring the parlements to their full powers and entrusting a solution of the state's constitutional crisis to the forthcoming Estates General. After the activist ministries of Calonne and Brienne, Necker's was strangely passive. Calonne and Brienne were convinced reformers, and their ministries replayed at an accelerated rate the history of reform efforts over the seven decades since Louis XIV's death. Both, for example, took up key elements of Turgot's reforms. But the ecclesiastical and noble elites who dominated the Assembly of Notables refused any abrogation of their fiscal privileges and, with the backing of the parlements, insisted on the separation of orders. Either Calonne's or Brienne's reforms might well have been enacted had there been an intelligent and determined king willing to stand up against the privileged orders, but Louis XVI was no such king. The experience of the years 1786 to 1788 seemed to indicate that even under the direst conditions, reforms that both administrators and informed citizens regarded as necessary could not be passed by the regime as currently constituted. The double bind held fast. The consequence was a recourse to the Estates General, an institution that in the 1780s existed only in the abstract. To place power in the hands of an Estates General was to declare a moral bankruptcy of the political and administrative order of the old regime.

By August 1778, when Necker became controller general, it was clear that the French state's crisis was to be sorted out by an Estates General. But what this body would be and how it would be chosen was uncertain. Brienne's decree convoking the estates had granted broad press freedom so that citizens could give their advice about the composition and goals of the estates. The consequence was a proliferation of political clubs and an outpouring of pamphlets. We have seen that under old regime conditions, expression of political opinions was highly circumscribed and forced into indirect forms—patient attempts at administrative reform; parlementary remonstrances; statements of abstract political theory; arguments about political economy; published legal briefs; allusions in poetry, pornography, and fiction; and discussions in salons, learned academies, and masonic lodges. But with the calling of the Estates General, political writing and political argument became bold and open. The political nation was no longer limited to the king, the court nobility, the royal administration, and the parlements. Educated people and, increasingly, even the working population of Paris and other cities began to discuss politics openly in the nine months between the calling of the Estates General in August 1788 and its first meeting in May 1789.

The Parlement of Paris, which had won over public opinion when it called for the Estates General in 1787, forfeited its popularity when, in September 1788, it declared that the Estates General should be convened "following the form observed in 1614." In that year, the last time the estates had met, the three estates had deliberated separately, and each of the estates had had the same number of delegates. The patriot or national party, as it was coming to be called, insisted that the Third should be "doubled"— that is, should have as many delegates as the clergy and nobles combined. To this was added the demand that the delegates should meet, deliberate, and vote as a single body. These questions of the "doubling of the Third" and "deliberation in common" became central political issues of the fall of 1788 and the subject of many pamphlets. Necker, unable to convince the king to resolve this dispute in favor of the Third Estate, summoned the notables back into session in November to discuss the appropriate manner of constituting the Estates General. In these deliberations, there was general, if grudging, support for equalizing the tax burden, but doubling the Third Estate and voting by head rather than by order were soundly defeated (200). The princes who led the sections of the notables wrote a joint memoir to the king stressing the danger of doubling the Third Estate but pledging to "renounce, out of generosity, prerogatives that have a pecuniary interest, and support public taxes in the most complete equality."[2] But the parlement's declaration and the princes' memoir further enflamed public opinion in Paris and in cities all across France, where its arrogant language and its defiance of public opinion were roundly denounced (205–10). Upon the publication of the princes' memoir, government securities plunged on the stock market (211).

Necker, forced to arbitrate the question of doubling the Third Estate, managed with difficulty to obtain from the king a Solomonic statement known as the "Result of the Council of 27 December 1788," which accepted the doubling but was silent about deliberation in common. Ministerial comment on the statement indicated that common deliberation would occur where the interests of the orders were identical, which implied no joint deliberation about the status of existing privileges (202). The ministerial comment did, however, guarantee citizen participation in provincial estates and a regular periodic convening of the Estates General. It also guaranteed individual freedom and freedom of the press (213). But the Result of the Council resolved nothing. The king was feckless and incapable of thinking beyond the existing order of things, and Necker, a Swiss Protestant who by no means enjoyed the king's full confidence, made no effort to develop his own reform program. The way forward was destined to remain unclear until May, when the Estates General would meet and tackle the manifold knotty problems. The absence

2. Quoted in Égret (1977, 202).

of a coherent royal policy left the field open for public opinion, in the form of clubs, committees, and pamphlets. The most explosive issue in the months before the meeting of the Estates General was that of aristocratic privilege.

In the flurry of publication in the winter and spring of 1789, there were arguments on all sides of many issues. But the well-publicized quarrels in the parlements and the Assemblies of Notables about exemptions from taxation, the doubling of the Third Estate, and deliberation in common focused public attention less on proposals for administrative reforms than on the quarrel between commoners and the privileged. Timothy Tackett, who has written the best study of the deputies to the Estates General, points out that noble deputies, while generally recognizing that they should bear more tax burden, stoutly defended their other privileges and expressed resentment against the commoners' pretensions. Meanwhile, some future deputies from the Third Estate expressed sharp antagonism toward the nobility in their prerevolutionary pamphlets and argued for the suppression of all noble privileges (Tackett 1996, 106–19). But it was the abbé Sieyès's famous pamphlet, *What Is the Third Estate?*, that developed the most systematic and influential argument against privileges (Sieyès 1970).[3] His widely read pamphlet not only set forth an absolutely uncompromising critique of the nobility but tied that critique to a political strategy that strongly influenced deputies of the Third Estate in the summer of 1789 and foreshadowed many of the political changes of the Revolution.

What Is the Third Estate?

Emmanuel-Joseph Sieyès was yet another enlightened abbé (Brédin 1988; Sewell 1994, 8–21). Born in 1748 in Fréjus, a small town in Provence, he was the son of a minor royal official. He accepted a career in the church in spite of his lack of religious convictions because it seemed the only way to get ahead. A mediocre student of theology at the Seminary of Saint-Sulpice in Paris, Sieyès was an insatiable reader of the philosophes. Unlike most enlightened abbés, he was unsociable in the extreme: there is no evidence of his participation in salons. In spite of his prodigious philosophical reading, he published nothing before 1788.[4] He spent his prerevolu-

3. For a detailed analysis, see Sewell (1994).
4. He had prepared for publication but never published a manuscript critical of the physiocrats entitled "Lettre aux économistes sur leur système de politique et de morale." This work is available in Sieyès (1985, 25–44).

tionary career not as a man of letters but as what he called an "ecclesiastic administrator," but definitively not what he called an "ecclesiastic priest." He never served as a *curé*, heard confession, or preached a sermon (Sieyès 1795, 12–13). For a commoner's son, he succeeded well as an ecclesiastical administrator: since 1780, he had been the vicar general of the diocese of Chartres at a time when most vicars general were nobles' sons. Sieyès was roused to action by the prerevolutionary crisis. His first tract, written in the summer of 1788, had the uninspiring title *Vues sur les moyens d'exécution dont les représentants de la France pourront disposer en 1789* (Views on the Means of Action That Could Be Available to the Representatives of France in 1789; 1788b). By the time it was completed, his opinions had already been radicalized, and he quickly wrote a second pamphlet, *An Essay on Privileges* (1788a), and a third, the much more famous and influential *What Is the Third Estate?*—published in January 1789.

Unlike most pamphlets, *What Is the Third Estate?* did not begin by discussing such practical issues as the form in which the estates should meet or the reforms it should consider. Instead, it began with the more fundamental question summarized in its title. Here are the book's first lines:

The plan of this book is fairly simple. We must ask ourselves three questions.
1. What is the Third Estate? *Everything.*
2. What has it been until now in the political order? *Nothing.*
3. What does it want to be? *Something.* (Sieyès 1970, 119–20)[5]

These three questions and answers correspond to the first three chapters of the book.

The first chapter began with an assertion about social ontology, stated in the language of political economy:

What does a nation require to survive and prosper? It needs *private* activities and *public* services.
(1) Since land and water provide the basic materials for human needs, the first class . . . includes all the families connected with work on the land.
(2) . . . Goods acquire an increased value . . . through the incorporation of varying amounts of labor. In this way, human industry manages to improve the gifts of nature. . . . Such are the activities of the second class of persons. (3) Between production and consumption . . . a variety of inter-

5. In the remainder of this section, citations to this work appear in parentheses after the quotation.

mediary agents intervene, to help producers as well as consumers; these are the shopkeepers and merchants. . . . Such is the function of the third class of persons. (4) Besides these three classes of useful and industrious persons who deal with things fit to be consumed or used, society also requires a vast number of special activities and services. . . . This fourth class embraces all sorts of occupations, from the most distinguished liberal and scientific professions to the lowest of menial tasks.

Such are the labors that support society. But who performs them? The Third Estate. (21–22)

Sieyès's classification of four types of occupations introduces a conception of society utterly different from the standard three hierarchically ordered estates of the old regime. Within this radically political-economic social metaphysics, there was literally no place for the nobility.

Of course, the nobility could claim its services to society took place in the sphere of public affairs. But Sieyès attacked this argument explicitly. He asserted that nineteen out of twenty public services are performed by the Third Estate. "Only the well-paid and honorific posts are performed by the privileged order." And this, rather than a service to the public, is actually "a social crime, a veritable act of war." Because aristocrats have a monopoly on such posts, their work is badly done: "Are we unaware that any work from which free competition is excluded will be performed less well and more expensively? . . . Without [the nobility] the higher posts would be infinitely better filled. . . . If the privileged have succeeded in usurping all well-paid and honorific posts, this is both a hateful iniquity towards the generality of citizens and an act of treason to the commonwealth" (122–23). Sieyès concluded that the nobility, in spite of its claims of superiority, was actually *nothing*: "It is not a part of our society at all; it may be a burden for the nation but it cannot be part of it." The Third Estate, by contrast, is *everything*:

Who then is bold enough to maintain that the Third Estate does not contain within itself everything necessary to constitute a complete nation? It is like a strong and robust man with one arm still in chains. If the privileged order were removed, the nation would not be something less but something more. What then is the Third Estate? Everything, but an "Everything" that is fettered and oppressed. What would it be without the privileged order? It would be a free and flourishing everything. Nothing can function without the Third Estate; everything would work infinitely better without the others. (124)

What Is the Third Estate's first chapter, in short, posited the social nullity of the aristocracy. Given Sieyès's social ontology, which uses assumptions from political economy to define society as a collection of producers united by common work on nature, the nobility has no real place in it. The nobility is "foreign to the nation because of its idleness" (124–25).

The Third Estate performed the whole of society's useful work yet was regarded as "nothing"—as inferior beings unfit to participate in political society. But the crisis unfolding since 1786 had roused the Third Estate. They began to claim a right to political representation, demanding the calling of the Estates General, a doubling of the Third Estate, deliberation in common, and counting of votes by head. Sieyès argued in favor of these demands but argued that they were far too timid. The Third Estate, he remarked, "wishes to become something," but it is asking to become only "the least thing possible"—that is, to gain representation alongside the clergy and nobility in the Estates General (134). Since, in actuality, the Third Estate is everything, performing all of society's useful labor and constituting 99 percent of France's population, by rights, it alone constitutes the nation, and its representatives should constitute the nation's government.

What ought to have been done to solve the crisis of the state, Sieyès argued, would have been to call not an Estates General but a national constituent assembly competent to establish a proper constitution for France. Such a body could not be constrained by the forms of the existing political and legal regime but should be made up of representatives of the nation as it really is—"in the forty thousand parishes that embrace all the territory, all the inhabitants, and all those who pay taxes to support the common good" (187). This body should then form a constitution that would reflect the French nation's real needs and desires. But given that the archaic Estates General had been called, what strategy should the Third Estate's representatives adopt? Since the Third Estate was actually "everything," its representatives meeting in Paris in May would be "the authentic trustees of the national will" (201). Sieyès therefore suggested a strategy: "The Third should assemble separately, it will not cooperate with the nobility and the clergy nor will it vote with them, either by *order* or by *head*. . . . It is alleged that the Third Estate cannot form the *Estates General* by itself. So much the better. It will form a *National Assembly*" (197). This radical suggestion was probably not widely accepted by his readers, nor was it taken up in other pamphlets. But Sieyès opened up a strategic possibility and gave it a proper philosophical backing. The surprising thing is that something very close to this strategy was followed by the deputies of the Third Estate in the summer of 1789—at the suggestion of Sieyès himself, who served a deputy of the Third Estate for Paris.

The Estates General

Assembling an Estates General was a complex operation, especially difficult because its procedures had to be invented anew. Because the state and society had been so thoroughly transformed since 1614, the precedents from previous Estates General gave little guidance to officials in the 1780s. The process of selecting delegates was utterly different from that of the sixteenth or seventeenth century, when Third Estate delegates were generally senior members or heads of the various corps (parishes, guilds, bailiwicks, municipalities, and so forth) who could be expected to speak for their subordinates. They would draw up *cahiers de doléances* (lists of grievances) to present to the king. But it was the corps, not collections of individual citizens or taxpayers, who were represented. There was, hence, no attempt to take into account the number of persons represented by each delegate. As François Furet remarks, the consultation of 1789 was organized according to a different and essentially democratic logic. The drawing up of *cahiers* was retained, but the number of delegates from each bailiwick was proportional to its population, and delegates were chosen by the votes of all adult male taxpayers. It was the greatly expanded and improved royal administration, which now kept close track of the population, that made this new democratic form of representation possible (Furet 1987). Although the division between the clergy, the nobility, and the Third Estate was maintained in 1789, a logic of democratic proportionality governed the choice of delegates within the Third Estate and even within the clergy. In the case of the clergy, this meant a delegation made up primarily of lower clergy, not of bishops and abbots, a fact that turned out to have significant consequences.

The elections to the Estates General began in February and March 1789. For the Third Estate, elections in the parish or neighborhood would choose deputies to the bailiwick assemblies, who then chose deputies to the provincial assemblies, who chose delegates to the Estates General in Paris. On May 4, the delegates assembled in Versailles for a procession to the church of Saint-Louis, where they heard a solemn mass, and then to the chateau to pay respects to the king. The following day, they attended an opening session where, in the king's presence, they were treated to a rambling three-hour speech by Necker that contained no clear program.

On the sixth, the delegates of the three estates met separately in their respective halls in the palace.[6]

Each estate was a sizable deliberative body. There were about 250 delegates of clergy and of nobles and about 600 delegates of the Third Estate. The clergy and nobles quickly organized themselves and began verifying the delegates' credentials. The Third Estate, however, called for the joint verification of credentials as the first step toward deliberation and voting in common—that is, toward a merging of the three estates into a single body. The Third Estate's proposal to this effect was rejected by the nobility on May 6 by a vote of 188 to 46. The vote by the clergy on the same day was also negative but much closer: 133 to 114 (Tackett 1996, 129, 134). The Third Estate refused to proceed to a verification of their credentials on the grounds that only verification in common was acceptable. In mid-May, the delegation of the Third Estate from Brittany argued forcefully for declaring the assembly of the Third the National Assembly—the strategy that Sieyès had suggested—but the majority voted to attempt negotiations with the other orders (128). While the negotiations dragged out for weeks with no resolution, the delegates of the Third Estate continued to debate issues in front of a growing crowd of spectators. The public, clearly, was greatly interested in the course of events and favorably inclined toward the claims of the Third Estate.

Sieyès, elected as a delegate to the Third Estate from Paris, where the elections were held extremely late, joined the meetings in early June. On June 8, he introduced a motion to, in his words, "cut the cable": that the Third Estate should begin a roll call of deputies of all three orders, explicitly inviting the nobles and clergy to join them. The motion passed almost unanimously, and the roll call began on the twelfth. On June 17, the delegates to the Third Estate, by an overwhelming vote, declared themselves the "National Assembly" and then one by one swore an oath "in the name of God, the king, and the nation, to fulfill faithfully and zealously the functions with which I have been entrusted." They then passed unanimously a motion granting the National Assembly complete control over taxes (Tackett 1996, 146–48). The Third Estate had transformed itself into a would-be National Assembly and claimed a cosovereignty with the king. Historians generally regard the declarations of June 17 as the first act of the French Revolution.

6. There are many histories of the events of the summer of 1789. Unless I make a controversial point or quote particular passages, I will not give citations. I remain partial to George Lefebvre's (1947, 1939). I have also relied on Tacket (1996).

A few days later, on June 20, the deputies of the newly declared Assembly found their meeting hall locked and guarded by the king's soldiers. They learned that Louis XVI had decided to take the situation in hand by calling a royal session. Fearing a dissolution of the Assembly, the deputies crowded into a tennis court a few blocks away, where they swore what came to be known as the "tennis court oath," vowing to remain assembled until a constitution was framed. On the twenty-second, the Assembly found a meeting place in the Church of Saint-Louis and was joined by a majority of the clergy, led primarily by the lower or parish clergy, and a sprinkling of liberal nobles. At the royal session on the twenty-third, the king offered a set of reforms that would probably have been accepted in May, promising equality of taxation, the right the of estates to meet regularly and consent to taxes, a guarantee of individual liberty and freedom of the press, and various administrative reforms. But he insisted that the three orders deliberate separately in matters concerning noble and clerical privileges and implied that the estates would be dismissed if they failed to submit to his will. But when the Third Estate and some of the clergy remained in place at the end of the session and vowed to remain assembled, the king failed to use force to clear the hall. Indeed, on June 27, he ordered the remaining representatives of the nobles and clergy to join the National Assembly. France, it appeared, was about to become a constitutional monarchy. On July 7, the Assembly appointed a constitutional committee; on the ninth, it officially changed its name to the National Constituent Assembly, and on the eleventh the Marquis de La Fayette proposed a "Declaration of the Rights of Man and Citizen."

Revolution

In fact, the king seemed to have been planning a coup against the Assembly. He had for some time been massing royal troops in the Parisian area. On the morning of July 12, Necker was dismissed and replaced by a reactionary. It appeared that the king would use the troops to disperse the National Assembly and enforce obedience. The population of Paris had already been much politicized by the remarkable events of the summer, and its unrest was compounded by worries about high bread prices and threatened grain shortages. The Parisian people's response to the threat against the Assembly and the city was rapid. Huge crowds paraded in the streets, raided gun shops, and attacked the toll barriers where goods coming into the city were taxed. The Paris electors quickly organized an emergency civic militia to defend the city against a possible attack and to maintain order internally. But this fledgling militia was drastically short of arms and ammunition. On the morning of the fourteenth, immense crowds, led by the militia, marched to the Invalides, the military hospital and old soldier's home in western Paris, where, without a battle, they commandeered a huge cache of arms. The militia was now armed but lacked ammunition, so the crowd marched on to the Bastille, a forbidding fortress on the eastern edge of the city, where gunpowder was known to be stored. It was this search for gunpowder that led to the Bastille's fall, an event seen ever since as the key triumph of the French Revolution (Godechot 1970b; Sewell 1996).

The commander of the Bastille attempted to negotiate with emissaries of the crowd, but eventually the fortress was assailed by the militia, aided by a rebellious contingent of royal troops known as the French Guards. After a brief but bloody battle, the Bastille was liberated, the gunpowder confiscated by the rebels, and the captured defenders trooped across the city to the Hotel de Ville. There the assembled crowd killed and beheaded the Bastille's luckless commander and the *prévôt des marchands*, the chief of the former municipality, who was suspected of treachery. The city was now in the hands of the militia and the French Guards. When the Assembly, in Versailles, learned of the violence on the evening of the fourteenth, the news was initially regarded as "disastrous." According to the Assembly's minutes, the news "produced . . . the most mournful impression. All discussion ceased." The representatives believed that the events in Paris would strengthen the king's hand and undermine the Assembly (Réimpression 1958, 2:155, 188). But the consequences were precisely the opposite. The defection of the French Guards and the lack of defense of the cache of arms at the Invalides meant that the king's troops had lost control of Paris. On July 16, Louis XVI dismissed the new ministry, recalled Necker, and sent the troops surrounding Paris back to their provincial barracks. On the seventeenth, Louis came to Paris, accompanied by members of the National Assembly. There he appeared on the balcony of the Hotel de Ville and placed upon his hat the blue, white, and red rosette that had been adopted as the badge of the Parisian patriots, a gesture taken as a sign of his capitulation. Meanwhile, messages poured in from the provinces hailing the Assembly and the Parisians. The taking of the Bastille had, surprisingly, consolidated the power of the Assembly and the patriot party. It also gave birth to the very concept of revolution as it has come to be understood ever since—a forceful rising of the sovereign people that both catalyzes and legitimizes a profound transformation of the structure of the state (Sewell 1996).

Cities across the country rallied to the National Assembly and established provisional municipalities as well as militias soon known as the

National Guard. The governing structure of the old regime largely disintegrated. The intendants fled from their posts, great nobles retreated from the royal court to rural residences, and the king's government was essentially paralyzed. The National Assembly possessed no bureaucratic agents of its own and was governing by improvisation. In this atmosphere of barely managed chaos, excitement was general, tempers were short, and the future seemed profoundly open, both for good and for ill. While the Parisian populace, deputies to the Assembly, and provincial urban elites were attempting to navigate the new political situation, rumors and fears of conspiracies multiplied.

In this moment of generalized insecurity, extraordinary rumors began to trouble the countryside, leading to a mass panic of unprecedented scale, what historians later dubbed the "Great Fear" (Lefebvre 1973). The panic began independently at several different places in rural France on July 20—that is, shortly after the probably garbled news of the Parisian events must have reached the countryside. At each origin point, it was reported that troops of brigands had been seen advancing into the fields and cutting the standing grain before it could ripen. This was a kind of peasant vision of the apocalypse. The result was a rural panic that had spread over much of the French countryside by the early days of August. The bells in the steeple would be rung, and the villagers would assemble, arm themselves, and march out in pursuit of the imaginary brigands, usually sending forth a messenger to nearby villages announcing the terrifying news. Many of these villages would mobilize in turn and send out their own messengers. By this means, the panic could spread a hundred miles or more in a few days. Sometimes the peasants, once armed and mobilized, attacked the lords' chateaux and burned the charters that listed their dues and charges. Georges Lefebvre argued that this series of events persuaded the mass of the peasantry that they were threatened by a vast aristocratic plot. More recently, it has been countered that villagers sometimes turned to the local lord or magistrate to lead their militias, making the local events as much the last hurrah of the rural old regime as an antiseigneurial peasant rebellion (Ramsay 1992). In any case, from the point of view of the capital, the news was alarming: chateaux in flames, crops menaced by brigands, and armed men everywhere. It was less the peasants than the journalists and deputies in Paris and Versailles who attributed the disorders to an aristocratic plot. Legislators feared they were witnessing a general peasant rising against the feudal system that would threaten not only the lord's seigneuries but rural property in general. They feared such a rising could result in general anarchy and destroy the possibility of a peaceful constitutional revolution.

The Abolition of Privilege

A crucial consequence of the Great Fear was the famous evening session of the National Assembly on August 4. The night of August 4 might be said to mark the climax of this book's complicated story. During that session, the National Assembly took the radical and unexpected step of definitively abandoning the regime of privileges that had long defined the French state and society and replacing it with a new system based on equality before the law (Kessel 1969).[7] This extraordinary event was the result of a legislative stratagem that succeeded beyond its authors' hopes. A group of patriot legislators caucused on the evening of August 3 and developed a plan they hoped would quell the peasant disorders. They decided to propose both the end of fiscal privilege and an abolition of the peasants' feudal dues—with the latter to be bought out over time by the peasants. They recruited two liberal nobles, the duc d'Aiguillon and the vicomte de Noailles, to introduce these proposals, which met with rapturous support from the patriots but some consternation from many nobles and prelates. However, several minutes into the debate, the duc du Châtelet, one of the richest and most prestigious noble landowners, who was not involved in the legislative conspiracy and not previously identified with the patriot party, passionately denounced feudalism from the tribune and declared that he was renouncing forthwith his own feudal rights.

This extraordinary act of renunciation by a great nobleman touched off an emotion-laden cascade of further renunciations. Nobles flocked to the tribune to renounce feudal obligations, seigneurial courts, exclusive hunting rights, and the keeping of dovecotes—greeted by thunderous applause and tears of joy. Not to be outdone, clerics renounced their tithes. Venal officeholders renounced venal offices and royal pensioners their pensions. Third Estate representatives renounced the privileges of their provinces and cities. The entire Assembly was swept up in a tide of generous civic enthusiasm. The consequence was a holocaust of privileges of every description, a massive renunciation that, in principle, left standing only individual Frenchmen with their sacred and equal rights as citizens of the French nation. The emotionally charged session, which lasted nearly until dawn, changed overnight the course of French history. The night of August 4 indelibly marked the establishment of a new form of state and society. As the chevalier de Boufflers declared before the as-

---

7. An acute analysis of the social dynamics of the night of August 4 is Ermakoff (2015, 82–99). On political and constitutional consequences, see Fitzsimmons (2003).

sembly, "Let us abandon all distinctions; let us only regret that we have nothing else left to sacrifice; let us consider that henceforth the title of 'Frenchman' will be distinction enough for every generous soul" (Kessel 1969, 164). Or as the Third Estate deputy Gantheret put it in letter a few days later, "In the future, only wealth, talent, and virtue will distinguish one man from another. . . . We are a nation of brothers" (Tackett 1996, 178).

In the days following August 4, a committee of the Assembly drew up a decree specifying legally the decisions taken. This "Decree Relative to the Abolition of Privileges" was adopted on August 11. It began with a ringing phrase: "The National Assembly entirely destroys the feudal regime." This claim, however, was followed by a number of caveats. The committee distinguished feudal dues deriving from personal serfdom, which were abolished without compensation, from those not regarded as so derived, which were to remain in place until the peasants' annual payments had redeemed them. The lords' right to maintain dovecotes was abolished, as were their exclusive hunting rights. Seigneurial courts were suppressed, although they were to operate until new courts could be established. The end of feudalism was thus declared yet partially postponed. The peasants, however, generally ignored these limits, resisting efforts to collect the remaining dues and rarely making redemption payments. This was a source of considerable rural unrest for the next few years, until, in 1793, during the ascendency of the Jacobins and the Committee of Public Safety, all redemption payments were canceled (Markoff 1996).

The decree of August 11 also suppressed the church's tithes, promising to establish new means of supporting the clergy. The sale of judicial and municipal offices, which, as we have seen, had been used massively to staff the royal administration since the late sixteenth century, was abolished. Pensions would be trimmed, and in the future, the king would be allowed only a fixed pension budget. Taxes were finally made equitable: "Pecuniary privileges in matters of taxation . . . are abolished forever. Taxes will be levied on all citizens and properties in the same manner and the same form." Local privileges were abolished: "Since a national constitution and public liberty are more advantageous to the provinces than the privileges which some of them have been enjoying, and which must necessarily be sacrificed for the intimate union of all parts of the realm, it is declared that all the particular privileges of provinces, principalities, regions, cantons, towns and communities . . . are abolished forever, and will be absorbed into the law common to all Frenchmen." Civic equality was explicitly declared: "Every citizen, without distinction of birth, is eligible for all ecclesiastical, civil, and military positions and dignities, and no useful profession will imply derogation."

The decree ended with the promise that a medal would be struck and that a *Te Deum* mass would be "sung in thanksgiving, in all the parishes and churches of the realm." The assembly also proclaimed King Louis XVI as the "Restorer of French Liberty." However, a note of disquiet entered the decree. "The National Assembly," it asserted, "will wait upon the king in a body, to present his Majesty the decree which it has just passed, to pay him the homage of its most respectful gratitude, and to beseech him to permit a *Te Deum* to be chanted in his chapel, and to attend it himself." The leaders of the Assembly were uncertain of the king's true feelings about this most recent turn of events and wished to force him to indicate approbation of their deeds personally and to do so in the Assembly's presence—effectively, as it turned out, for the time being (*Archives parlementaires* 1879, 397–98, 434). But the relation of the king to the Revolution remained highly uncertain.

The Declaration of the Rights of Man and Citizen

The catharsis of the night of August 4 created a moment of unity and cleared the way for the task of writing a constitution. It also established the foundation of civic equality on which the constitution would be based. Beginning August 12, the day after the passage of the decree abolishing privileges, work on the constitution began in earnest. The first step was to draft a Declaration of the Rights of Man and Citizen, a project already announced on July 11, when Lafayette presented a brief draft to the Assembly just before the extraordinary events of July and early August.

The drafting of the Declaration of the Rights of Man and Citizen was a complicated affair that was hashed out in debates over two weeks. Drafts of several proposals were circulated and entered into the record on August 12. Among these was a "Declaration of the Rights of Man in Society" by the abbé Sieyès, who saw the rights of man as inseparable from—indeed, derived from—his economic being. Thus,

> Article 1. Man receives from nature imperious needs, together with
> means sufficient to satisfy them . . .
> Article 5. Every man is the sole proprietor of his person. He can sell
> his services, his time, but he cannot sell himself. This first property is inalienable . . .

Article 8. Every citizen is free to employ his strength, his industry, and his capital as he judges good and useful to himself. No form of work is forbidden to him. He may keep or transport as he wishes all kinds of commodities, and sell them wholesale or retail. . . . No individual, no association, may restrict, much less prevent, these operations. (*Archives parlementaires* 1879, 422)

Sieyès's declaration proposed truths of political economy as the foundation of rights in general. He embraced civic equality but emphasized natural inequality in wealth. Hence article 19, "Although men are not equal in means, that is to say in wealth, in intelligence, in strength, etc., it does not follow that they are unequal in rights. Before the law, every man is equal to every other; the law protects all without distinction." But as we see in his proposed article 17, his political-economic perspective implied limits on political as opposed to legal rights: "The law can only be the expression of the general will. Among a populous people, it must be the work of a body of representatives chosen . . . by all the citizens who have, for the public good, both an interest and a capacity" (*Archives Parlementaires* 1879, 423). This implied economic qualifications for suffrage, an opinion that, as we shall see, was widely shared.

Several other proposals were elaborated by individuals or by various "bureaus" of the assembly, apparently twenty or so.[8] Some were officially presented to the Assembly and published in the *Archives parlementaires*. There was a "Charter Containing the French Constitution in Its Fundamental Objects" by a conservative monarchist whose opinions were made clear by the dating at the beginning of the document: "the year 1789 after Jesus Christ, 1371 years after Hugues Capet, the trunk of the currently reigning august house of Bourbon."[9] He stressed duties more than rights but did proclaim civic equality: "Men, who are unequal in moral and physical means, are equal in rights in the eyes of the laws." Such an affirmation from a conservative legislator indicates that the question of civic equality was now beyond discussion. There was a lengthy proposal by Rabaut de Saint-Étienne, a leading Protestant deputy, that emphasized freedom of conscience and worship. There was a veritable treatise of fifteen double-column pages by Mounier, entitled "Considerations

---

8. The *bureaux* were subgroups of representatives in which discussions of issues could be pursued more effectively than in the huge National Assembly (Tackett 1996, 142). The estimate of twenty proposals comes from Bredin (1988, 132).

9. The statement about Hugues Capet is utterly puzzling. He was king from 987 to 996.

upon Governments and Principally upon That Which Is Appropriate to France" that included no draft declaration (*Archives parlementaires* 1879, 400–422).

Given the diversity of proposals, the Assembly on August 13 appointed a committee of five members to "receive the plans for a constitution." On the following day, the comte de Mirabeau, the committee's most prominent member, read its "project for a declaration of the rights of man in society." This proposal was criticized from all sides, among other reasons for its lack of precision. A frustrated Mirabeau suggested that a declaration should only be made once the constitution as a whole had been completed. But the Assembly had essentially promised the public it would produce a declaration forthwith. Mirabeau's draft was tabled, and a free-wheeling discussion ensued. A member of the clergy demanded a declaration of duties as well as rights. The Marquis de Lally-Tollendal suggested following the example of the English and avoiding abstract statements, stating instead specific legal rights. Eventually the Assembly agreed to choose by vote among the draft declarations on offer as the basis for an article-by-article discussion. The Assembly chose the most concise of the declarations on offer, that of the sixth bureau. Sieyès's draft gained the second most votes (*Archives parlementaires* 1879, 439–59).

Definitive debates on the declaration thus began on August 20 and proceeded methodically with little discussion of philosophical issues. The texts eventually chosen were thoroughly debated, usually stripped of unnecessary verbiage, and then accepted by large majorities. The only extensive disagreement concerned freedom of religion. Rabaut de Saint-Étienne delivered a long speech favoring complete religious freedom. This was countered by speakers insisting that the Catholic Church should be officially recognized and that allowing all religious sects would spread disorder. After two days of arguments, the Assembly opted for a lukewarm declaration of religious toleration. The final article read "No one may be disturbed because of his opinions, even in religion, provided that their expression does not trouble the public order as established by law." The article-by-article debates lasted from August 20 to August 27 (*Archives parlementaires* 1879, 462–83). The resulting declaration was remarkably direct, clear, and pithy. It proved inspiring for contemporaries in France, but not only in France. It stands today as the opening section of the constitution of the Fifth French Republic. Because it sums up admirably the principles of the French Revolution, principles that contrasted sharply with those of the old regime it replaced, it seems worth citing in full in this book:

The representatives of the French people, constituted as the National Assembly, considering that ignorance, forgetfulness, or contempt for the rights of man are the sole causes of public misfortunes and the corruption of governments, have resolved to set forth in a solemn declaration the natural, inalienable, and sacred rights of man, so that the constant presence of this declaration may ceaselessly remind all members of the social body of their rights and duties; so that the acts of the legislative power and those of the executive power may be more respected, since it will be possible at each moment to compare them against the goal of every political institution; and so that the demands of the citizen grounded henceforth on simple and incontestable principles, may always be directed to the maintenance of the constitution and to the welfare of all.

Consequently, the National Assembly recognizes and declares, in the presence and under the auspices of the Supreme Being, the following rights of man and citizen.

Article 1. Men are born and remain free and equal in rights. Social distinctions can be based only on public utility.

Article 2. The goal of every political association is the preservation of the natural and imprescriptible rights of man. These rights are liberty, property, security, and resistance to oppression.

Article 3. The principle of all sovereignty resides essentially in the nation. No body, no individual, may exercise authority that does not emanate expressly from it.

Article 4. Liberty consists in the ability to do whatever does not harm another; hence the exercise of the natural rights of each man has no limits except those which assure to other members of society the enjoyment of the same rights. These limits may be determined only by law.

Article 5. The law may rightfully forbid only actions that are harmful to society. That which is not forbidden by the law must not be hindered, and no one may be constrained to do that which it does not order.

Article 6. The law is the expression of the general will. All citizens have a right to participate personally, or by representation, in its formation. It must be the same for all, whether it protects or punishes. All citizens being equal in its eyes are equally admissible to all dignities, places, and public employments, according to their capacities, and with no other distinction than that of their virtues or their talents.

Article 7. No man may be accused, arrested, or detained except in cases determined by the law and according to the forms it has prescribed.

Article 8. The law must establish only penalties that are strictly necessary, and no one may be punished except under a law that has been established and promulgated prior to the offense and applied legally.

Article 9. Every man being presumed innocent until declared guilty, if it is deemed indispensable to arrest him, any rigor not necessary to secure his person must be severely repressed by the law.

Article 10. No one must be disturbed for his opinions, even in religion, provided that their expression does not trouble public order as established by law.

Article 11. The free communication of thoughts and opinions is one of the most precious rights of man: every citizen may therefore speak, write, and print freely, except in cases of an abuse of this liberty as determined by the law.

Article 12. The guarantee of the rights of man and citizen requires a public force: this force is therefore instituted for the advantage of all, and not for the particular benefit of those to whom it is consigned.

Article 14. All citizens have the right to state, personally or through their representatives, the necessity of the public tax, to consent to it freely, to oversee its employment, and to determine its quantity, distribution, mode of collection, and duration.

Article 15. Society has the right to hold every public agent accountable for his administration.

Article 16. Any society in which a guarantee of rights is not secured or the separation of powers is not determined has no Constitution.

Article 17. Property being an inviolable and sacred right, no one may be deprived of it unless legally stated public necessity clearly requires it, and then on condition of a just and prior indemnity.

Most of the declaration's articles were aimed in one way or another at establishing or protecting civic equality—or to put it negatively, to forbid the old regime practices that denied civic equality. The declaration is at once a death certificate for the old regime (Lefebvre 1947, 174) and a birth certificate of a new one. It outlawed practices that under the old regime had created privileges and a hierarchy of rights. The old regime state had, for example, established different judicial penalties for nobles than for commoners, given nobles exclusive access to certain public positions, or restricted access to certain occupations to those who were members of a guild. Powers and rights that previously had been regarded as inhering in the king were now proclaimed to belong to society and to the individuals who make it up. It is citizens, gathered into a society or nation, who have sovereignty, make the laws, hold public agents accountable, and determine taxes. The citizens' property is inviolable; citizens are free to hold opinions and to communicate them to others in speech or in print; actions not expressly forbidden by law would not be hindered. The society posited by the declaration is a society of rights-bearing, self-governing individuals, free to acquire property, to buy and sell, speak and publish, and determine by means of laws formulated by their representatives the regulations that govern political and social life. Although the declaration does not state political-economic first principles in the way that Sieyès's proposed declaration did, it incorporates a point of view whose development would have been impossible without the rise of political-economic thinking and the advancing commercialization of social relations that had made political economy attractive to philosophes and statesmen. It was a charter for a commercial society.

Remaking the State

The Decree Relative to the Abolition of Privileges and the Declaration of the Rights of Man and Citizen were statements of constitutional and legislative principles. They promised a profound transformation of the French state and society, but the hard work of constructing new political and legal institutions in conformity with these proclamations remained to be done. This immense task had to be carried out in a period of great uncertainty and political turmoil. A constitution had to be written. A new code of laws had to be developed. The country's local and regional administration had to be rebuilt. The relation of church to state had to be reconstructed. A new tax system had to be devised. Meanwhile, the National Assembly was constantly deflected from the process of state reconstruction by what were in effect administrative issues, often of an urgent character—maintaining a frequently troubled public order, overseeing grain shipments, resolving political disputes in the provinces, dealing with the state's always doubtful fiscal health, and so forth. The king essentially ceded administrative power to the National Assembly yet often refused his cooperation with their actions. Indeed, he refused to indicate his acceptance of the Declaration of the Rights of Man and Citizen until the October Days (October 5 and 6) when a great crowd, led by Paris market women, marched to Versailles and forced the king to accept the declaration and to return with them to Paris. There he and his entourage moved into the Tuileries Palace—effectively, from that time forward, under the watchful and suspicious eyes of the Parisian people. The Assembly followed a few days later. Never, however, did Louis XVI develop a working relationship with the Assembly. He had neither the desire nor the ability to become an effective constitutional monarch.

The relative comity among potential factions that had seen the National Assembly through the crisis of July, the night of August 4, and the devising of the Declaration of the Rights of Man and Citizen faded after October 1789. A group of Monarchiens, as they were called—largely composed of deputies from the First and Second Estates—organized itself and attempted to moderate or roll back the radical reforms that the August events had seemed to authorize. These conservative deputies were eventually matched by an organized group of more radical deputies who called themselves the "Friends of the Constitution" but were better known as the Jacobin society—named, ironically, for the former monastery that became their meeting place. The conservatives sat on the right side of the Assembly and the radicals sat on the left, giving rise to the notion of the political left and right that has lasted to this day. The development of a left-right split complicated what would in any case have been a difficult set of tasks for a collectivity that was at once a constituent assembly writing a constitution and a legislative body devising all manner of laws. Moreover, it became the de facto executive as well, given the indolence, passivity, and occasional hostility of Louis XVI. At the same time, the Assembly had to deal with the ever-restive Parisian people, whose actions and sympathies were feared by the right and the center but courted by the Jacobins.

It was in the workings of this increasingly factionalized Assembly that the legal consequences of the civic equality declared in September 1789 were worked out, sometimes limiting equality's extent and sometimes elaborating it. In the fall of 1789, conservative deputies successfully introduced into the constitution a distinction between "active" citizens—those who paid taxes above a minimal threshold—and a poorer class of "passive" citizens. Both were guaranteed equal protection of the laws, but only active citizens gained the suffrage. Eligibility to serve in legislative bodies required a yet higher tax payment. This decision was denounced by radical deputies as a violation of the declaration's promise of equality of rights. There was, however, relatively little dissent from another radical constitutional and administrative change: the abolition of the former provinces and their replacement by equally sized "departments," divided into cantons and municipalities, with each level to be governed by popular election. This immense administrative reorganization was regarded as necessary to destroy the privileges of provinces, which, as we have seen, had greatly varying rules about taxation, government, administration, and commercial affairs. The reorganization of the nation's territory obliterated what might be called spatial privileges and extended the principle of equality before the law to the details of organization of the national territory (Ozouf 1989; Margadant 1992; Sewell 2004). The assembly also began the process of producing a unified and systematic legal code. As we have seen, old regime France was subject to a variety of provincial legal regimes divided into a southern region governed by versions of Roman law and northern regions governed by versions of common law. The making of a new uniform code was devilishly complicated and required a systematic unraveling of old and deeply entrenched monarchical legal principles. Indeed, it was not until 1804, under Napoleon, that a new civil code was adopted. Doing away with the last of ancient forms of property was not entirely completed until the 1830s (Blaufarb 2016).

In the course of 1790, the left managed to obtain majorities in support of two constitutional measures that alienated many moderates and conservatives from the Revolution. The first was the outlawing of all titles of nobility. The night of August 4 had eliminated the nobility's legal privileges, but nobles had continued to use their titles and to regard themselves as having a recognized superiority of status. Some nobles took the outlawing of noble titles as a deep insult, inducing them to resign from the National Assembly and become hostile to the Revolution. The second measure was a "civil constitution of the clergy" that essentially made the clergy into public servants, reshuffled episcopal sees to make them correspond to the new departments, declared that bishops would henceforth be chosen by popular election, and imposed a solemn oath of loyalty to the constitution on all clergy. The civil constitution of the clergy—and especially the required oath, which many devout priests regarded as contrary to their oath of obedience to the pope—caused a lasting split in the clergy and eventually pushed the "nonjuring" clergy into open opposition to the new regime (Tackett 1986).

The left-right split became implacable in June 1791, when Louis XVI fled his semicaptivity in the Tuileries Palace only to be arrested in Varennes, near the country's northeastern border and forcibly returned to the capital. The National Assembly was much disturbed by this event, having by then nearly completed a constitution establishing a constitutional monarchy that reserved important powers to the king. Unwilling to start its constitutional work over, it implausibly claimed that his flight had been a kidnapping. But no one was deceived: Louis XVI was now clearly hostile to the new regime (Tackett 2003). In September 1791, the National Assembly officially proclaimed a constitution that assigned the king significant powers. Under these circumstances, the Constitution of 1791 was not destined to last.

If the role of the monarch was thenceforth in doubt, the Constitution of 1791 spelled out in its preamble the extent of the break with the principles of the old regime:

> The National Assembly, wishing to establish the French constitution on the principles it has recently recognized and declared, abolishes irrevocably the institutions that injured liberty and the equality of rights.
>
> There no longer exists nobility, nor peerage, nor hereditary distinctions, nor distinctions of orders, nor feudal regime nor patrimonial justice, nor titles of any kind, nor denominations and prerogatives that derived from them, nor any knightly order, nor any corporate bodies or decorations that require proofs of nobility or that suppose distinctions of birth, nor any other superiority than that of public officials in the exercise of their functions.
>
> There is no longer venality or heredity of any public office.
>
> There is no longer, for any part of the Nation, nor for any individual, any privilege, nor exception to the law common to all Frenchmen.
>
> There are no guilds, nor corporations of professions, arts, and crafts.
>
> The law no longer recognizes religious vows, nor any other engagement that would be contrary to the natural rights of all Frenchmen.

The Constitution of 1791, which established a limited monarchy, was short-lived. But it boldly set forth the extensive consequences of the establishment of civic equality that were to remain in place, with few exceptions, until the present day. Its preamble made clear that the old regime, with its many distinctions of legal status, had been annihilated by the Revolution.

Beyond 1791

The course of the Revolution over the next several years was tumultuous; it has been recounted in detail by generations of historians.[10] The constitution produced by the National Constituent Assembly in September 1791

10. Histories of the Revolution that I have found particularly valuable include Lefebvre (1962–64), Rudé (1959), Soboul (1959), Sydenham (1966), Furet (1978), Baker (1990), and Tackett (1990, 2015).

lasted less than a year. France went to war with the surrounding monarchical powers in 1792; the monarchy was overthrown by a popular rebellion on August 10 of that year; in September, a Republic was declared;
Louis XVI was executed in January 1793; and by then much of France was
engulfed in a civil war. An emergency government known as the Committee of Public Safety managed to win both the civil and the international
wars, but it also launched a reign of terror that decimated both its internal
enemies and many of its former political allies before being overthrown
in 1794. The moderate republic that succeeded the terror was internally
unstable but remained successful on the battlefield. It finally succumbed
in December 1799, when Napoleon Bonaparte, the most successful of the
generals, seized power in a coup. He eventually established an empire,
conquered most of Europe, and remained in power for a decade and a
half. But after a disastrous attempt to add Russia to his conquests, Napoleon was defeated and deposed, giving way in 1815 to a restoration of the
Bourbon monarchy, in the person of Louis XVIII, Louis XVI's brother.
After twenty-six years of striving, heroism, and slaughter, France was
once again ruled by a Bourbon king.

Yet much had changed—and changed permanently—between 1789
and 1815. After the taking of the Bastille, the popular classes became and
remained a force to be reckoned with in French politics. The political
fate of France was determined by popular insurrections in October 1789,
when the king was forced to accept the Declaration of the Rights of Man
and Citizen and dragged to Paris; in August 1792, when the monarchy
was overthrown and a Republic declared; in May and June 1793, when
the moderate "Girondin" faction was expelled from the legislature; and in
July 1794, when vast crowds of Parisians went into the streets to support
the overthrow of Robespierre and the Committee of Public Safety. A final rising in 1795 was put down by the army. But if insurrections might be
quashed by force, the possibility of revolutionary risings remained very
real; preventing them became and remained a constant concern of governing authorities everywhere. The revolutionary genie could not be put
back into the bottle, as the successful French revolutions of 1830 and 1848
and the unsuccessful Paris Commune of 1871 were to prove—not to mention revolutions elsewhere, from Berlin and Vienna in 1848, to Russia in
1905 and 1917, to China in 1911 and 1949, to Cuba in 1959, to the Arab
Spring in 2011.

The victories of popular insurrections in Paris in 1792 and 1793 pushed
the program of the Revolution sharply to the left in ways that challenged
the apparent consensus of September 1789. The new republican constitution adopted in 1793 had an expanded Declaration of the Rights of Man

and Citizen that included a guarantee of property rights and maintained the key provisions of the original declaration that assured equality before the law. But the new declaration was more solicitous of the rights of the popular classes. It outlawed both slavery and "domestic servitude"—the form of domestic service that placed one's will under that of the head of household. It made public assistance a right and declared that education should be available to all. It explicitly guaranteed the right of petition and made "insurrection . . . the most sacred of rights and the most indispensable of duties" whenever "the government violates the rights of the people" (Godechot 1970a, 79–83). In the heat of the fierce internal conflicts and external wars of these years, the guarantees of meticulous judicial procedures included in the declaration of 1793 were cast aside, and people were imprisoned and sometimes put to death when merely suspected of treasonous activities or thoughts. In the discourse of the radical Parisian sansculottes, who dominated the assemblies of the Parisian neighborhoods, the simple fact of wealth could make one a political suspect. Under pressure from the sansculottes, the Committee of Public Safety eventually established price controls on what they called goods of prime necessity. From the point of view of the sansculottes, the right of property was no longer absolute and measures limiting free exchange were imperative (Soboul 1959). Complaints about economic justice bubbled to the surface in the ideology of the sansculottes and confronted the emphasis on economic liberty and absolute rights of property that had pervaded the Constituent Assembly and was consecrated in its Declaration of the Rights of Man and Citizen. It was, however, only in the nineteenth century, especially after 1830, that critiques of classical political economy and the "bourgeois" regime of property became major oppositional tropes (Sewell 1980).

The regimes that followed Thermidor increasingly restricted political rights and relied on military force to protect against a resurgence of the sansculottes. But the principles of civic equality decidedly remained in place. Napoleon's regime reestablished a modified imperial monarchy, made a concordat with the church, invited nobles who had emigrated to return, and created a new imperial nobility that rewarded generals, politicians, and civil servants who had served the country well. In spite of these moves toward a revived monarchy, there was no restoration of privilege, equality before the law was strictly practiced, and careers remained decidedly open to talent. Indeed, it was under Napoleon that the unified civil law code, the famous "code Napoléon" was enacted. When Napoleon conquered new territories in the Low Countries, Germany, and Italy, the code Napoléon was imposed there as well. Napoleon, it might be said, both put the brakes on the Revolution and saved some of its most important features for the long haul.

Napoleon's empire was definitively brought to an end in 1815, thanks largely to the failure of his attempt to conquer Russia. The allied monarchs of Europe then restored the Bourbons to the throne, in the person of Louis XVIII, Louis XVI's brother. But the terms of the Restoration also marked the permanent gains of the Revolutionary era. Louis XVIII restored nobles' titles and granted them a separate legislative body, the Chambre des Pairs (Chamber of Peers), but did not reestablish their privileges. He granted a constitutional charter that made the king "the supreme head of the State" but required positive votes of both houses of a bicameral legislature to establish new laws. The charter opened by stating a series of "public rights of Frenchmen." The enumeration made clear that the civic equality established in August and September 1789 remained a fundamental right:

> Article 1. The French are equal before the law, whatever may be their titles or ranks.
>
> Article 2. They contribute equally, in proportion to their fortune, to the expenses of the State.
>
> Article 3. They are all equally admissible to civil and military employments.
>
> Article 4. Their individual liberty is equally guaranteed. No one must be pursued or arrested except in cases foreseen by the law and in the forms it prescribes.
>
> Article 5. Everyone may profess his religion with an equal liberty, and obtain for its practice the same protection.
>
> Article 9. All properties are inviolable.

There were restrictions. For example, while religious liberty was guaranteed, the Roman Catholic Church was designated the state religion. Likewise, although, as stated in article 8, "all Frenchmen have the right to publish and to have their opinions printed," this right was limited later in the article by the statement that such publications must conform "to the laws that must punish the abuses of this liberty" (Godechot 1970a, 219). As had been true under Napoleon and would remain true for most of the nineteenth century, the publication of opinions deemed subversive could be punished by fines and imprisonment.

The essentials of civic equality not only remained at the base of all French constitutions after 1789 but were deeply embedded in France's codes of law—codes that in essence have remained in place until today.

The Napoleonic code, adopted in 1804, was imposed on most of the European territories conquered by French armies and remained in place after Napoleon's defeat. This was true of Belgium, the Netherlands, Poland, and most of Western Germany, as well as Spain, Portugal, and their vast American colonies. The commercial society that steadily conquered Europe and North America in the eighteenth and nineteenth centuries, with its characteristic abstraction of social relations, eventually made civic equality a practical necessity of daily life and embedded it in both codes of law and citizens' common sense. But it was in France, in the economic, cultural, and political effervescence of the eighteenth century and the rigors of the French Revolution, that the contours of civic equality were most boldly and influentially worked out and anchored in place.

* EPILOGUE *

Civic Equality and the
Continuing History of Capitalism

In the period since the French Revolution, the limitations of civic equality have become starkly evident—but so, I shall argue, has its continuing value. During the Revolution itself, the question of how far civic equality was to extend was disputed, sometimes violently. One of the major issues leading to the insurrection that overthrew the monarchy in August 1792 was a protest against the constitution's designation of men too poor to pay significant taxes as "passive citizens"—thus denying them the right to vote or hold office. Radical women agitated for full citizen rights in 1793—but their movement was suppressed, and French women, shamefully, were denied the suffrage until 1944. Slaves in the Caribbean did not become emancipated citizens until 1794, and then only because they mounted successful insurrections against their masters—but slavery was reimposed in 1803 and maintained until 1848. In spite of the declaration's soaring rhetoric, the civic equality so solemnly proclaimed in September 1789 came, in practice, with significant limitations.

Additional limitations became clear over time. As we have seen, civic equality as understood by the revolutionaries was closely intertwined with the discourse of political economy. The revolutionary legislators imagined that freeing citizens to produce, sell, and buy as they saw fit would significantly reduce inequality. The revolutionaries suppressed the noble and clerical privileges they considered responsible for the old regime's most extreme inequities, and they systematically cleared the way for commercial enterprise by eliminating internal tolls, abolishing the guilds, and outlawing "coalitions" of workers who attempted to raise wages by organizing strikes or boycotts. Only in the course of the nineteenth century did it become clear that material inequality was proliferating anew in spite of the abolition of legal privileges. Free enterprise, it became apparent, enabled the propertied and wealthy to prosper at the expense of the poor and propertyless. That advancing capitalism produced gross inequalities among legally equal citizens became glaringly visible only when inequalities arising from archaic "feudal" privileges had been swept away.

In the wake of the Revolution of 1830, which overthrew the Bourbon dynasty and replaced it with a more liberal Orleanist monarchical regime, radical workers and some sympathetic intellectuals began to rework the revolutionary language of 1789, claiming that concentrated property ownership arising from a free-enterprise economy had actually become a new form of privilege and that some form of social ownership would be necessary to institute the equality promised but not realized by the Revolution of 1789. Early socialist doctrines, developed in the 1830s and 1840s, accused the propertied of "exploiting" propertyless workers in the same heartless way they would exploit a field or a mine. The French Revolution of 1848, which briefly established a republic with universal suffrage, was wracked with struggles between quasi-socialist advocates of what was called "the organization of labor" and defenders of property and order (Sewell 1980). From 1848 forward, in France but also elsewhere in the emerging capitalist world, advocates of social equality maintained that civic equality like that invoked in the Declaration of the Rights of Man and Citizen required expansion to encompass economic and social equality or, more radically, should be replaced by entirely new conceptions of equality and of the social order. Socialisms of several varieties, both revolutionary and evolutionary, proliferated in the later nineteenth and twentieth centuries in Europe and around the world.

The ideal of civic equality was the product of a particular moment in the history of capitalism. Since its origin, capitalism has been powerfully expansive. Originally coalescing in Europe and its overseas extensions in the sixteenth century, capitalism has increasingly consolidated its dominance over the entire world. The eighteenth century was a period of unprecedented prosperity in the northwest European core of the emerging capitalist world, which expanded its hegemony over the Atlantic, the Americas, the Indian Ocean, and South Asia. For inhabitants of France but also of other northwest European countries, both incomes and populations increased in the eighteenth century, income that could now be spent on an attractive array of new consumer goods—from Asia, from the Caribbean, from other European states, and from their own country's workshops. In the context of this eighteenth-century economic and geographical expansion, intellectuals all over Europe began to think of history as progressive, a perception that has been a distinctive characteristic of modernity (Koselleck 2002). The assumption that history is progressive has of course remained dominant up to the present—and for good historical reasons. When viewed from the very long perspective of hominid history, capitalism has effected an astoundingly rapid transformation of the human career. Since 1700, the world's human population has expanded tenfold, from about seven hundred million to some seven billion, and despite this crowding, present-day humans are much healthier, with longer life expectancies, and are taller, stronger, and vastly more literate and numerate than their eighteenth-century ancestors (Fogel 2004). Over the past three centuries, the naturalness of progress has become our common sense, even though this notion has recently been challenged by the looming prospect of catastrophic global climate change. It was in the context of the early decades of this immense progressive social transformation of human history that the French could repudiate a social order justified by an imagined ancient feudal constitution and an unchanging God-given social hierarchy and therefore dare to reconstruct their nation on the forward-looking principles of civic equality, political economy, and popular sovereignty. The transformations introduced by the French Revolution were an explicable product of this moment in the history of capitalism.

But this was only one phase in capitalism's history. Over its career of some four or five centuries, capitalism, while always characterized by the exploitation of labor and nature to produce a seemingly endless accumulation of capital and wealth, has also transformed itself, passing through quite distinct historical phases. The eighteenth-century capitalism whose social, political, and cultural ramifications are explored in this book was, as I have argued, structured above all by commercial exchange. It was in the specific context of this commercial capitalist economy that civic equality emerged as a framework for a radical restructuring of social, political, and economic life. The industrial revolution, which was consolidated only in the nineteenth century, inaugurated a second era of capitalism, one dominated by factory production, steam engines, railroads, steamships, and unprecedentedly rapid growth of cities. It was in this era, when vast urban proletarian populations were being formed, that the French Revolution's version of civic equality came to seem inadequate and was challenged by socialist alternatives.

The transformations of capitalism have of course continued, with a twentieth-century phase of growing state-centered management of the economy, eventually characterized by more or less generous social welfare schemes, and a post-1980 phase of rapid globalization of production, financialization of economic life, skyrocketing inequality, and looming environmental catastrophe. At the time of the writing of this book, in the wake of four decades of rapidly increasing economic inequality, my central argument about eighteenth-century France can appear paradoxical:

How could the advance of capitalism, which now seems utterly antithetical to social equality, make the embrace of civic equality seem a practical possibility? But we must be careful not to project present realities and values onto the past.

Capitalism, in eighteenth-century France—or for that matter in eighteenth-century Europe—was not the dominant organizing principle of the social world. This was capitalism's rosy dawn, a period when its logic of abstract relations between independent and functionally equivalent actors could serve as an attractive countermodel to the hierarchical and fixed social mores of old regime societies. It is certainly true that capitalism, even then, involved exploitative relations between those in possession of significant wealth and those who had little more than their labor power. But these unequal relations were hardly visible in comparison to the encrusted privileges and the accompanying cascade of disdain so evident in the eighteenth-century social world. Moreover, the existing social order appeared rigid, with its defenders insisting above all on its supposedly unchanging qualities, its descent from a feudal "ancient constitution," and its social and political forms sanctioned by God. In this context, the forward-looking, individualizing, abstracting, and dynamic qualities of nascent capitalism could appear liberating and indeed could be liberating. As I have argued at length in this book, those who experienced these features of capitalism, as entrepreneurs, consumers, urban strollers, readers, writers, upwardly mobile intellectuals, enlightened state officials, and even liberal-minded nobles and clerics, could accept the possibility and even the desirability of a future social world based on civic equality. When, in 1789, the old regime fell into an irremediable crisis, it was civic equality that emerged as the viable alternative.

For all of capitalism's faults in the years since 1789 and for all the inequalities and indignities that have characterized regimes purportedly based on civic equality in capitalist societies, I would argue that the civic equality ideal and the legal guarantees found in most modern constitutions continue, on balance, to be a force for good. Indeed, enhanced claims for equal treatment—for workers, for women, for religious and racial minorities, for immigrants, for the poor, for those who adopt nonconformist lifestyles—typically rely significantly on the rhetoric of civic equality and the legal rights it guarantees. Whatever changes might be required to make our societies more just, I find it hard to imagine a good society in which civic equality is not a fundamental value. Here I see a parallel with Jürgen Habermas's observations about the public sphere. He claims that in spite of the deformations that institutions of the public sphere have undergone in the years since 1800—the commercialization and trivialization of newspapers, broadcast media, and, I'm sure he would now add, the internet—the original ideal of the public sphere remains as valid today as it was in the eighteenth century (Habermas 1989). Likewise, whatever oppressions and perverse interpretations may have been propagated in its name, the ideal of civic equality retains its value as a necessary standard for a decent civil and political society. The Declaration of the Rights of Man and Citizen emerged from a particular moment in the history of modern capitalist societies, a moment now long eclipsed. Yet however paradoxically, it remains an essential ideal for politics now and into the future.

Acknowledgments

The idea for this book arose from discussions in the Social Theory Workshop at the University of Chicago. This biweekly gathering, which for twenty-six years I directed jointly with my late friend and colleague Moishe Postone, brought together faculty and graduate students to discuss one another's research and to ponder theoretically the historical dynamics of social life. Thanks above all to Moishe, the question of how commodity relations infused the social experiences and cultural forms of the modern world figured often in our free-ranging discussions. Eventually I began to suspect that the expansion of commodity relations might illuminate the origins of the French Revolution, one of the signal events in the emergence of modernity. This book, which tracks down and refines my hunch, is the product of fourteen years of research and writing. During that time I benefited from a peaceful and productive year at the National Humanities Center and from over a decade's generous support and much intellectual stimulation from the Successful Societies Program of the Canadian Institute for Advanced Research. I gained confidence that I might be on the right track from responses to presentations of my evolving ideas: at meetings of the French Historical Studies Association and the Social Science History Association, at workshops on the history of capitalism and cultural sociology at Harvard, at a history department colloquium at UCLA, and at the Social Theory Workshop itself. A few years ago, Michael Kwass generously read and critiqued the final part of the book, on the travails of the eighteenth-century royal administration. It was a particular pleasure to rely on Michael, whose teacher I had been during his graduate work at the University of Michigan but who had become the perfect expert to evaluate and correct the arguments hazarded by an aged novice in old regime history. The University of Chicago Press's readers, one of whom was Keith Baker, have given me very generous and helpful comments. My editor at the press, Priya Nelson, has ably guided me through the shoals of the publication process. My wife, fellow French historian Jan Goldstein, has combed through the entire manuscript, helping me sharpen my arguments and trim thousands of words from what remains a long book. Her love, learning, generosity, moral support, and wonderfully stimulating conversation have kept me and this project afloat over the years. I gratefully dedicate the book to her.

References

Agulhon, Maurice. 1970. *La vie sociale en Provence intérieure au lendemain de la Révolution*. Paris: Société des Études Robespierristes.

Allen, R. C., and C. O'Grada. 1988. "On the Road Again with Arthur Young: English, Irish, and French Agriculture during the Industrial Revolution." *Journal of Economic History* 48: 93–116.

Amoldi, Fils. 1761. "Lettre sur l'envoi des échantillons." *Journal de Commerce*, December 1761.

Anderson, Perry. 1974. *Lineages of the Absolutist State*. London: New Left Books.

Andrieux, Charles. 1923. *Trudaine: Sa vie, son oeuvre, ses idées*. Clermont-Ferrand: Raclot frères.

Arbellot, Guy. 1973. "La grande mutation des routes de France au milieu du XVIIIe siècle." *Annales: ESC* 28 (3): 765–91.

Archives parlementaires de 1787–1860. 1879. Vol. 8. Under the direction of M. J. Mavidal. Paris: Librairie Administrative de Paul Dupont.

Arnaud, Ambroise-Marie. 1791. *De la balance du commerce et des relations commerciales extérieures de la France dans toutes les parties du globe particulièrment à la fin du règne de Louis XIV et au moment de la revolution*. Paris: Buisson.

Austen, Ralph A. 2017. "Monsters of Postcolonial Economic Enterprise: East India Companies and Slave Plantations." *Critical Historical Studies* 4 (2): 139–78.

Bailey, Colin B., et al. 2007. *Gabriel de Saint-Aubin, 1724–1780*. Paris: Musée du Louvre, Somogy Art Publishers, and the Frick Collection.

Baker, Keith Michael. 1975. *Condorcet: From Natural Philosophy to Social Mathematics*. Chicago: University of Chicago Press.

———. 1978. "French Political Thought at the Accession of Louis XVI." *Journal of Modern History* 50: 230–79.

———. 1990. *Inventing the French Revolution: Essays on French Political Culture in the Eighteenth Century*. Cambridge: Cambridge University Press.

Ballot, Charles. (1923) 1976. *L'introduction du machinisme dans l'industrie française*. Geneva: Slatkine Reprints.

Barber, Elinor G. 1955. *The Bourgeoisie in 18th Century France*. Princeton, NJ: Princeton University Press.

Béaur, Gérard, Philippe Minard, and Alexandra Laclau, eds. 1997. *Atlas de la Révolution française*. Vol. 10, *Économie*. Paris: Editions de l'EHESS.

Beccaria, Cesare. 1766. *Traité des délits et des peines*. Translated by André Morellet. Philadelphia.

Beguillet, Edme. 1779. *Description historique de Paris et de ses plus beaux monumens*. Paris.

Behrens, C. B. A. 1963. "Nobles, Privilèges, and Taxes in France at the End of the Ancien Regime." *Economic History Review* 2 (15): 451–75.

Beik, William. 1988. *Absolutism and Society in Seventeenth-Century France: State Power and Provincial Aristocracy in Languedoc*. Cambridge: Cambridge University Press.

Berg, Maxine. 2002. "From Imitation to Invention: Creating Commodities in Eighteenth-Century Britain." *Economic History Review* 45: 1–30.

———. 2004. "In Pursuit of Luxury: Global History and British Consumer Goods in the Eighteenth Century." *Past and Present* 182: 85–142.

Berman, Marshall. 1982. *All That Is Solid Melts into Air: The Experience of Modernity*. New York: Penguin Books.

Bezucha, Robert J. 1974. *The Lyon Uprising of 1834: Social and Political Conflict in the Early July Monarchy*. Cambridge, MA: Harvard University Press.

Bien, David D. 1987. "Offices, Corps, and a System of State Credit: The Uses of Privilege under the Ancien Régime." In *The French Revolution and the Creation of Modern Political Culture*. Vol. 1, *The Political Culture of the Old Regime*, edited by Keith Michael Baker, 89–114. Oxford: Pergamon.

———. 1989. "Manufacturing Nobles: The Chancelleries in France to 1789." *Journal of Modern History* 61: 445–86.

Birn, Raymond. 1970–71. "The Profits of Ideas: Privilèges en Librarie in Eighteenth-Century France." *Eighteenth-Century Studies* 4 (2): 138–40.

Blackbourn, Robin. 1997. *The Making of New World Slavery: From the Baroque to the Modern, 1492–1800*. London: Verso.

Blaufarb, Rafe. 2016. *The Great Demarcation: The French Revolution and the Invention of Modern Property*. New York: Oxford University Press.

Blaufarb, Rafe, Michael S. Christofferson, and Darrin M. McMahon, eds. 2014. *Interpreting the Ancien Régime*. Preface by Keith Baker. Oxford: Voltaire Foundation.

Bloch, Marc. 1931. *Les caractères originaux de l'histoire rurale française*. Oslo: H. Aschehoug.

Bois, Paul. 1960. *Paysans de l'Ouest*. Le Mans: Vilaire.

Bologne, Jean-Claude. 1993. *Histoire des cafés et des cafetiers*. Paris: Larousse.

Bonney, Richard. 1993. "'Le secret de leurs familles': The Fiscal and Social Limits of Louis XIV's Dixième." *French History* 7 (4): 383–416.

Bosher, John. 1964. *The Single Duty Project: A Study of the Movement for a French Customs Union in the Eighteenth Century*. London: Athlone.

———. 1970. *French Finances 1770–1795: From Business to Bureaucracy*. Cambridge: Cambridge University Press.

Bossenga, Gail. 1991. *The Politics of Privilege: Old Regime and Revolution in Lille*. Cambridge: Cambridge University Press.

———. 2005. "Markets, the Patrimonial State, and the Origins of the French Revolution." *1650–1850: Ideas, Aesthetics, and Inquiries in the Early Modern Era* 11: 443–509.

Bourguignon, François, and Lévy-Leboyer. 1985. *L'économie française au XIXe siècle*. Paris: Économica.

Bouton, Cynthia A. 1993. *The Flour War: Gender, Class, and Community in Late Ancien Regime Society.* University Park: Pennsylvania State University Press.

Brédin, Jean-Denis. 1988. *Sieyès, clé de la révolution française.* Paris: Editions de Falois.

Breen, Timothy H. 1986. "An Empire of Goods: The Anglicization of Colonial America, 1690–1776." *Journal of British Studies* 25: 333–57.

———. 2004. *The Marketplace of Revolution: How Consumer Politics Shaped American Independence.* Oxford: Oxford University Press.

Brewer, John. 1968. *The Sinews of Power: War, Money, and the English State, 1688–1783.* New York: Knopf.

Brewer, John, and Roy Porter, eds. 1993. *Consumption and the World of Goods.* London: Routledge.

Brown, Gregory S. 2005. *A Field of Honor: Writers, Court Culture, and Public Theater in French Literary Life from Racine to the Revolution.* New York: Columbia University Press. Also available at www.gutenberg-e.org.

Burrows, Simon. 2018. *The French Book Trade in Enlightenment Europe II: Enlightenment Bestsellers.* London: Bloomsbury.

Butel, Paul. 1974. *Les négociants bordelaise, l'Europe et les îles au XVIIIe siècle.* Paris: Aubie.

Butel-Dumont, Georges-Marie. 1755. *Histoire et commerce des colonies angloises dans l'Amérique septendrionnale.* London.

———. 1758. *Histoire et commerce des Antilles angloises.* Paris.

Caraccioli, Louis Augustin. 1768. *Dictionnaire Critique, Pittoresque et Sentencieux, Propre à faire connoître les usages du Siècle, ainsi que ses bisarreries. Par l'Auteur de la Conversation avec Soi-Mêm.* Vol. 2. Lyon: Chez Benoît Duplain.

———. 1777. *Paris le modèle des nations étrangères, ou l'Europe Françoise.* Venice.

———. 1789. *Lettres d'un Indien à Paris à son ami Glazir, sur les Moeurs François, et sur les Bizarreries du tems, par l'Auteur des Lettres recréatives et morales.* Vol. 2. Amsterdam.

Carlier, Claude, abbé. 1753. *Dissertation sur l'état de commerce en France sous les rois de la première et de la seconde race.* Amiens.

———. 1755. *Memoire sur les laines.* Brussels.

Carrière, Charles. 1973. *Négociants marseillais au XVIIIe siècle.* Marseille: Institut Historique de Provence.

The Case of the Silk Weavers Humbly Offered to Both Houses of Parliament. 1713. London.

Chapman, S. D., and S. Chassagne. 1981. *European Textile Printers in the Nineteenth Century: A Study of Peel and Oberkampf.* London: Heinemann.

Charles, Loïc. 2011. "Le cercle de Gournay: Usages culturels et pratiques savants." In *Le cercle de Vincent de Gournay: Savoirs économiques et pratiques administratives en France au milieu du XVIIIe siècle,* edited by Loïc Charles, Frédéric Lefebvre, and Christine Théré, 63–88. Paris: Institut National D'Études Démographiques.

Chartier, Roger. 1991. *The Cultural Origins of the French Revolution.* Durham, NC: Duke University Press.

Chartier, Roger, Guy Chaussinand-Nogaret, Huges Neveux, Emmanuel Le Roy Ladurie, and Bernard Quilliet. 1981. *Histoire de la France urbaine.* Vol. 3, *De la Renaissance aux Révolutions.* Paris: Seuil.

Chartier, Roger, and Daniel Roche. 1984. "Les pratiques urbaines de l'imprimé." In *Histoire de l'édition française,* edited by Jean Henri Martin and Roger Chartier. Vol. 2, *Le livre triumphant, 1660–1830,* 402–29. Paris: Promodis.

Chassagne, Serge. 1979. "La diffusion rurale de l'industrie cotonnière en France, 1750–1850." *Revue du Nord* 61 (240): 97–114.

———. 1980. *Oberkampf: Un entrepreneur capitaliste au Siècle des lumières.* Paris: Aubier Montaigne.

———. 1991. *Le coton et ses patrons: France, 1760–1840.* Paris: Editions de l'École des Hautes Études en Sciences Sociales.

Cheney, Paul. 2010. *Revolutionary Commerce: Globalization and the French Monarchy.* Cambridge, MA: Harvard University Press.

———. 2017. *Cul de Sac: Patrimony, Capitalism, and Slavery in French Saint-Domingue.* Chicago: University of Chicago Press.

Child, Josiah. 1754. *Traités sur le commerce et sur les avantages qui résultent de la réduction de l'intérêst de l'argent, avec un petit traité contre l'usure, par le Chevalier Thomas Culpeper.* Amsterdam.

———. 2008. *Traités sur le commerce de Josiah Child, suivis des Remarques de Jacques Vincent de Gournay.* Edited with a preface by Simone Meyssonnier. Paris: L'Harmattan.

Clay, Lauren R. 2013. *Stagestruck: The Business of Theater in Eighteenth-Century France and Its Colonies.* Ithaca, NY: Cornell University Press.

Clicquot de Blervache, Simon. 1755. *Dissertation de l'effet que produit le taux d'interest d'argent sur le commerce et l'agriculture.* Amiens.

———. 1758. *Considérations sur le commerce, et en particulier sur les compagnies, sociétés et maîtrises.* London.

Cobban, Alfred. 1968. *The Social Interpretation of the French Revolution.* Cambridge: Cambridge University Press.

Cohen, Lisbeth. 2003. *A Consumers' Republic: The Politics of Mass Consumption in Postwar America.* New York: Vintage.

Collins, James. 1988. *The Fiscal Limits of Absolutism: Direct Taxation in Early Seventeenth-Century France.* Berkeley: University of California Press.

Coornaert, Emile. 1941. *Les corporations en France avant 1789.* Paris.

Coquery, Natacha. 2011. *Tenir boutique à Paris au XVIIIe siècle: Luxe et demi-luxe.* Paris: Éditions du comité des travaux historiques et scientifiques.

Cottereau, Alain. 1997. "The Fate of Collective Manufactures in the Industrial World: The Silk Industries of Lyons and London, 1800–1850." In *World of Possibilities: Flexibility and Mass Production in Western Industrialization,* edited by Charles F. Sabel and Jonathan Zeitlin, 75–152. Cambridge: Cambridge University Press.

Couturier, Marcel. 1969. *Recherches sur les structures sociales de Châteaudun, 1525–1789.* Paris: SEVPEN.

Coyer, Gabriel François. 1756a. *La Noblesse commerçante.* London.

———. 1756b. *Dévelopement et défense du système de La noblesse commerçante.* Amsterdam.

Crafts, Nicholas R. F. 1985. *British Economic Growth during the Industrial Revolution.* Oxford: Oxford Economic Press.

Cranston, Maurice. 1982. *Jean-Jacques: The Early Life and Work of Jean Jacques Rousseau, 1712–1754.* Chicago: University of Chicago Press.

———. 1991. *The Noble Savage: Jean-Jacques Rousseau, 1754–62.* Chicago: University of Chicago Press.

———. 1997. *The Solitary Self: Jean-Jacques Rousseau in Exile and Adversity.* Chicago: University of Chicago Press.

Crouzet, François. 1996a. "Angleterre et France au XVIIIe siècle: Analyse comparée de deux croissances économiques." *Annales: ESC* 21 (2): 323–53.

———. 1996b. "Bordeaux: An Eighteenth-Century Wirtschaftswunder?" In *Britain, France, and International Commerce: From Louis XIV to Victoria*, edited by François Crouzet, 42–57. Aldershot, UK: Variorum.

Crow, Thomas E. 1985. *Painters and Public Life in Eighteenth-Century Paris*. New Haven: Yale University Press.

Crowston, Clare. 2001. *Fabricating Women: The Seamstresses of Old Regime France, 1675–1791*. Durham, NC: Duke University Press.

———. 2013. *Credit, Fashion, Sex: Economies of Regard in Old Regime France*. Durham, NC: Duke University Press.

Dakin, Douglas. 1982. *Turgot and the Ancien Régime in France*. London: Methuen.

Darnton, Robert. 1982. "The High Enlightenment and the Low Life of Literature." In *The Literary Underground of the Old Regime*, 1–40. Cambridge, MA: Harvard University Press.

———. 1984. "Readers Respond to Rousseau: The Fabrication of Romantic Sensibility." In *The Great Cat Massacre and Other Episodes in French Cultural History*, 215–56. New York: Basic Books.

———. 1995a. *The Corpus of Clandestine Literature in France, 1769–1789*. New York: W. W. Norton.

———. 1995b. "An Exemplary Literary Career." In *André Morellet (1727–1819) in the Republic of Letters and the French Revolution*, edited by Jeffrey Merrick and Dorothy Medlin, 5–26. New York: Peter Lang.

———. 1995c. *The Forbidden Bestsellers of Pre-revolutionary France*. New York: W. W. Norton.

———. 2015. "The Demand for Literature in France, 1769–1789, and the Launching of a Digital Archive." *Journal of Modern History* 87 (3): 509–41.

Daudin, Guillaume. 2011. *Commerce et prospérité: La France au XVIIIe siècle*. Paris: Presses de l'Université Paris-Sorbonne.

D'Autrèpe. 1760. *L'arithmétique de la noblesse commerçante, ou Entretiens d'un négociant et d'un jeune gentilhomme*. Paris.

DeJean, Joan. 2005. *The Essence of Style: How the French Invented High Fashion, Fine Food, Chic Cafés, Style, Sophistication, and Glamour*. New York: Free Press.

De L'Isle, M. 1758. *Mémoire sur les corps de métiers, qui a remporté le prix, au jugement de l'Académie d'Amiens, en l'année 1757*. The Hague.

de Vries, Jan. 1984. *European Urbanization, 1500–1800*. Cambridge, MA: Harvard University Press.

———. 2008. *The Industrious Revolution: Consumer Behavior and the Household Economy, 1650 to the Present*. Cambridge: Cambridge University Press.

Deyon, Pierre. 1967. *Amiens, capitale provincial: Étude sur la société urbaine au XVIIe siècle*. Paris: Mouton.

———. 1979. "La diffusion rurale des industries textiles en Flandre française à la fin de l'ancien régime et au début du XIXe siècle." *Revue du Nord* 61 (240): 83–96.

Deyon, Pierre, and Philippe Guignet. 1980. "The Royal Manufactures and Economic and Technological Progress in France before the Industrial Revolution." *Journal of European Economic History* 9 (3): 611–32.

Deyon, Pierre, and Franklin Mendels. 1979. "La proto-industrialisation: Théorie et réalité." *Revue du Nord* 240: 9–15.

Diderot, Denis. 1765. "Mercerie." In *Encyclopédie ou dictionnaire raisonné des sciences, des arts et des métiers*, edited by Denis Diderot, 369. Vol. 10. Neuchatel: Samuel Faulche.

———. 1779. *Essai sur la vie de Sénèque.* Paris.

———. 1782. *Essai sur les règnes de Claude et Néron; et sur les moeurs et les écrits de Sénèque.* London.

———. 1995. *Oeuvres.* Vol. 3, *Politique*, edited by Laurent Versini. Paris: Robert Lafont.

Diderot, Denis, and Jean Le Rond d'Alembert, eds. 1751–72. *Encyclopédie ou dictionnaire raisonné des sciences, des arts et des métiers.* 26 vols. Paris: Neuchatel.

Doppet, Amédée. 1788. *Les numéros parisiens, ouvrage utile et necessaire aux voyageurs à Paris.* Paris: Imprimerie de la Verité.

Dornic, François. 1955. *L'Industrie textile dans le Maine et ses débouchés internationaux, 1650–1815.* Le Mans.

Doyle, William. 1974. *The Parlement of Bordeaux and the End of the Old Regime, 1771–1790.* New York: St. Martin's.

———. 1975. *Louis XV et l'opposition parlementaire, 1715–1774.* Paris: Armand Colin.

———. 1996. *Venality: The Sale of Offices in Eighteenth-Century France.* Oxford: Oxford University Press.

Dubois, Laurent. 2004. *A Colony of Citizens: Revolution and Slave Emancipation in the French Caribbean, 1789–1804.* Chapel Hill: University of North Carolina Press.

Duby, Georges. 1978. *Les trois ordres: Ou, l'imaginaire du féodalisme.* Paris: Gallimard.

Du Châtelet, Gabrielle Émilie Le Tonnelier de Breteuil, marquise. 1740. *Institutions de physique.* Paris.

———. 1759. *Principes mathématiques de la philosophie naturelle.* 2 vols. Paris.

Duhamel de Monceau, Henri-Louis. 1753. *Traité de la conservation des grains et en particulier le froment.* Paris.

Dulaure, J. A. 1787. *Nouvelle description des curiosités de Paris.* 2 vols. Paris: Lejay.

Dupâquier, Jacques, ed. 1988. *Histoire de la population française.* Vol. 2, *De la Renaissance à 1789.* Paris: Presses Universitaires de France.

Dupont de Nemours, Pierre-Samuel. 1767. *La Physiocratie ou constitution essentielle du gouvernement le plus avantageux au genre humain.* Yverdon.

———. 1768. *De l'origine et des progrès d'un science nouvelle.* London.

———. 1796. *Philosophie de l'univers.* Paris.

Edelstein, Dan. 2014. "Enlightenment Rights Talk." *Journal of Modern History* 86 (3): 530–65.

Égret, Jean. 1962. *La prérevolution française.* Paris.

———. 1970. *Louis XV et l'opposition parlementaire, 1715–1774.* Paris: Armand Colin.

———. 1975. *Necker: Ministre de Louis XVI.* Paris: Champion.

———. 1977. *The French Prerevolution, 1787–1789.* Translated by Wesley D. Camp. Introduction by J. F. Bosher. Chicago: University of Chicago Press.

Ehrman, Esther. 1986. *Mme du Châtelet.* Leamington Spa, UK: Berg.

Eisenstein, Elizabeth. 1965. "Who Intervened in 1788? A Commentary on the Coming of the French Revolution." *American Historical Review* 71 (1): 77–103.

———. 1979. *The Printing Press as an Agent of Change: Communications and Cultural Transformations in Early Modern Europe.* 2 vols. Cambridge: Cambridge University Press.

————. 1983. *The Printing Revolution in Early Modern Europe*. Cambridge: Cambridge University Press.

Emmanuelli, François-Xavier. 1974. *Pouvoir royal et vie régionale en Provence au déclin de la monarchie, psychologie, pratiques administratives, défrancisation de l'intendnance d'Aix*. 2 vols. Lille: Service de Reproduction des Thèses de l'Université.

————. 1981. *Un mythe de l'absolutisme bourbonien: L'intendance du milieu du XVIIième au XVIIIième siècle*. Aix-en-Provence: Université de Provence.

Engrand, Charles. 1979. "Concurrences et complémentarités des villes et des campagnes: Les manufactures picarde de 1780 à 1815." *Revue du Nord* 61 (240): 61–81.

Ermakoff, Ivan. 2015. "The Structure of Contingency." *American Journal of Sociology* 121 (1): 64–125.

Fairchilds, Cissie. 1993. "The Production and Marketing of Populuxe Goods in Eighteenth-Century Paris." In *Consumption and the World of Goods*, edited by John Brewer and Roy Porter, 228–48. London: Routledge.

Faure, Edgar. 1967. *La disgrâce de Turgot*. 2 vols. Lausanne: Editions Rencontre.

————. 1977. *La banqueroute de Law, 17 juillet 1720*. Paris: Gallimard.

Federici, Ferdinand. 2008. *Flagrants délits sur les Champs-Élysées: Les dossiers de police du gardien Federici, 1777–1791*. Edited by Arlette Farge. Afterword by Laurent Turcot. Paris: Le Mercure de France.

Félix, Joël. 1999. *Finances et politique au siècle des Lumières: Le ministère de L'Averdy, 1763–1768*. Paris: Comité pour l'histoire économique et financière de la France.

Félix, Joël, and Frank Tallett. 2009. "The French Experience, 1661–1815." In *The Fiscal-Military State in Eighteenth-Century Europe: Essays in Honour of P. G. M. Dickson*, edited by Christopher Storrs, 147–66. Farnham, UK: Ashgate.

Ferrières, Madeleine. 2004. *Le bien des pauvres: La consommation populaire en Avignon (1600–1800)*. Seyssel: Champ Vallon.

Fitzsimmons, Michael P. 2003. *The Night the Old Regime Ended: August 4 and the French Revolution*. University Park: Pennsylvania State University Press.

Flammermont, Jules. 1898. *Remontrances du Parlement de Paris au XVIIIe siècle*. Vol. 3, 1768–1788. Paris: Imprimerie Nationale.

Floquet, Amable. 1843. *Histoire du parlement de Normandie*. Vol. 7. Rouen.

Fogel, Robert William. 2004. *The Escape from Hunger and Premature Death, 1700–2100, Europe, America, and the Third World*. Cambridge: Cambridge University Press.

Fontaine, Laurence. 1996. *History of Pedlars in Europe*. Durham, NC: Duke University Press.

Forbonnais, François Véron Duverger de. 1753. *Considérations sur le commerce d'Espagne*. Dresden.

————. 1754. *Élemens du commerce*. Leiden.

————. 1756. *Divers mémoires, sur le commerce, recuellis du même auteur. Ce volume contient, Essai sur l'admission des navires neutres dans nos colonies. Examen des prétendus inconvéniens de la faculté de commercer en gros, sans déroger à sa noblesse. Lettre sur les bijoux d'or et d'argent. Deux mémoires sur la compagnie exclusive des glaces*. Paris.

————. 1758. *Théorie et pratique du commerce de la marine. Traduction libre sur l'espagnol de Don Geronimo de Ustariz*. Paris.

————. (1761) 1861. *Mémoire et considérations sur le commerce et les finances d'Espagne*. Amsterdam.

————. 1767. *Principes et observations économiques*. 2 vols. Amsterdam: Rey.

———. 1768. *Examen du livre intitulé Principes sur la liberté du commerce des grains.* Paris.

Ford, Franklin L. 1953. *The Robe and the Sword: The Regrouping of the French Aristocracy after Louis XIV.* Cambridge, MA: Harvard University Press.

Forty, Adrian. 1986. *Objects of Desire: Design and Society Since 1750.* London: Thames and Hudson.

Fox-Genovese, Elizabeth. 1976. *The Origins of Physiocracy: Economic Revolution and Social Order in Eighteenth-Century France.* Ithaca, NY: Cornell University Press.

Franklin, Alfred. 1893. *Le café, le thé et le chocolat.* Vol. 13 of *La vie privée d'autrefois: Arts et métiers. Modes, moeurs, usages des parisiens du XIIe au XVIIIe siècles d'après des documents originaux ou inédits,* edited by Alfred Franklin. Paris: Plon.

Furet, François. 1978. *Penser la Révolution française.* Paris: Gallimard.

———. 1981. *Interpreting the French Revolution.* Translated by Elborg Forster. Cambridge: Cambridge University Press.

———. 1987. "La monarchie et le réglement electoral de 1789." In *The French Revolution and the Creation of Modern Political Culture.* Vol. 1, *The Political Culture of the Old Regime,* edited by Keith Michael Baker, 376–81. Oxford: Pergamon.

———. 1988. *La Révolution: De Turgot à Jules Ferry.* Paris: Hachette.

———. 1992. *Revolutionary France, 1770–1880.* Translated by Antonia Nevill. Oxford: Blackwell.

Furet, François, and Mona Ozouf, eds. 1989. *A Critical Dictionary of the French Revolution.* Translated by Arthur Goldhammer. Cambridge, MA: Harvard University Press.

Galiani, Ferdinando. 1770. *Dialogues sur le commerce des blés.* London.

Garden, Maurice. 1970. *Lyon et les Lyonnais au XVIIIe siècle.* Paris: Les Belles Lettres.

Garrigus, David. 2001. "The French Slave Trade: An Overview." *William and Mary Quarterly* 58 (1): 119–38.

Garrigus, John. 2006. *Before Citizenship: Race and Citizenship in French Saint-Domingue.* New York: Palgrave Macmillan.

Gayot, Gérard. 1998. *Les draps de Sedan, 1646–1870.* Paris: EHESS.

Giesey, Ralph E. 1983. "State Building in Early Modern France: The Role of Royal Officialdom." *Journal of Modern History* 55: 191–207.

———. 1997. "Rules of Inheritance and Strategies of Mobility in Prerevolutionary France." *American Historical Review* 82: 271–89.

Godart, Justin. (1899) 1976. *L'ouvrier en soie: Monographie du tisseur lyonnais, Etude historique, économique et sociale.* Geneva: Slatkine-Megariotis Reprints.

Godechot, Jacques. 1970a. *Les constitutions de la France depuis 1789.* Paris: Garnier-Flamarion.

———. 1970b. *The Taking of the Bastille: July 14, 1789.* Translated by Jean Stewart. Preface by Charles Tilly. New York: Scribners.

Goldmann, Lucien. 1967. "La pensée des 'Lumières.'" *Annales: ESC* 22 (4): 752–79.

Goodman, Dena. 1994. *The Republic of Letters: A Cultural History of the French Enlightenment.* Ithaca, NY: Cornell University Press.

———. 2009. *Becoming a Woman in the Age of Letters.* Ithaca, NY: Cornell University Press.

Gordon, Daniel. 1994. *Citizens without Sovereignty: Equality and Sociability in French Thought, 1670–1789.* Princeton, NJ: Princeton University Press.

Gottman, Felicia. 2016. *Global Trade, Smuggling, and the Making of Economic Liberalism: Asian Textiles in France, 1680–1760.* London: Palgrave Macmillan.

Goubert, Pierre. 1960. *Beauvais et le Beauvaisis de 1600 à 1730: Contribution à l'histoire sociale de la France du XVIIe siècle.* Paris: SEVPEN.

———. 1966. *Louis XIV et vingt millions de français.* Paris: Fayard.

———. 1969. *L'ancien régime.* Vol. 1, *La Société.* Paris: Armand Colin.

Grantham, George. 1989. "Agricultural Supply during the Industrial Revolution: French Evidence and European Implications." *Journal of Economic History* 49 (1): 43–72.

———. 1991. "The Growth of Labor Productivity in the Production of Wheat in the Cinq Grosses Fermes of France, 1750–1929." In *Land, Labor, and Livestock: Historical Studies of European Agricultural Productivities,* edited by B. M. S. Campbell and M. Overton, 478–502. Manchester: Manchester University Press.

———. 1993. "Divisions of Labor: Agricultural Productivity and Occupational Specialization in Pre-industrial France." *Economic History Review* 46 (2): 478–502.

———. 1997. "Espaces privilégiés: Productivité agraire et zones d'approvisionnement des villes dans l'Europe préindustrielle." *Annales: Histoire et Sciences Sociales* 151 (2): 695–725.

Grimm, Friedrich Melchior. (1784) 1879. *Correspondence littéraire, philosophique et critique.* Vol. 11, edited by Maurice Tourneux. Paris: Garnier Frères.

Guignet, Philippe. 1977. *Mines, manufactures et ouvriers du Valenciennois.* New York: Arno.

———. 1979. "Adaptations, mutations et survivances proto-industrielles dans le textile du Cambrésis et du Valenciennois du XVIIIe siècle." *Revue du Nord* 61: 240.

Gullickson, Gay L. 1986. *Spinners and Weavers of Auffay: Rural Industry and the Sexual Division of Labor in a French Village, 1750–1850.* Cambridge: Cambridge University Press.

Habermas, Jürgen. 1965. *Strukturwandel der Öffentlichkeit: Untersuchungen zu einer Kategorie der bürgerlichen Gesellschaft.* Neuweid, Berlin: Luchterhand.

———. 1978. *L'espace publique: Archéologie de la publicité comme dimension de la société bourgeoise.* Translated by Marc B. de Launay. Paris: Payot.

———. 1989. *The Structural Transformation of the Public Sphere.* Translated by Thomas Burger with the assistance of Frederick Lawrence. Cambridge, MA: MIT Press.

Hafter, Daryl M. 1995. "Women Who Wove in the Eighteenth-Century Silk Industry of Lyon." In *European Women and Preindustrial Craft,* edited by Daryl M. Hafter, 42–64. Bloomington: Indiana University Press.

Hagengruber, Ruth, ed. 2011. *Emilie Du Châtelet between Leibnitz and Newton.* Springer.

Hamon, Maurice, and Dominique Perrin. 1993. *Au coeur du XVIIIe siècle industriel; condition oubriere et tradition villageoise à Saint-Gobain.* Paris: Éditions P. A. U.

Harvey, David. 2003. *Paris, Capital of Modernity.* London: Routledge.

Haudrère, Philippe. 1997. *L'empire des rois, 1500–1789.* Paris: Denoël.

Hauser, Arnold. 1951. *The Social History of Art.* London: Routledge.

Hébert, Claude-Jacques. 1753. *Essai sur la police générale des grains.* London.

Helvétius. 1758. *De l'esprit.* Paris: Durand.

Hesse, Carla. 1991. *Publishing and Cultural Politics in Revolutionary Paris, 1789–1810.* Berkeley: University of California Press.

Hobsbawm, E. J. 1954. "The General Crisis of the European Economy in the 17th Century." *Past and Present* 5: 33–53.

Hoffman, Philip T. 1991. "Land Rents and Agricultural Productivity: The Paris Basin, 1450–1789." *Journal of Economic History* 51 (4): 771–805.

Holbach, Paul Henri Thiry, baron d'. 1770. *Système de la nature, ou Des lois du monde physique et du monde moral*. London.

Horn, Jeff. 2012. "A Beautiful Madness: Privilege, the Machine Question and Industrial Development in Normandy in 1789." *Past and Present* 217: 149–85.

———. 2015. *Economic Development in Early Modern France: The Privilege of Liberty, 1650–1820*. Cambridge: Cambridge University Press.

Hunt, Lynn. 1984. *Politics, Culture, and Class in the French Revolution*. Berkeley: University of California Press.

———. 1992. *The Family Romance of the French Revolution*. Berkeley: University of California Press.

Isherwood, Robert M. 1986. *Farce and Fantasy: Popular Entertainment in Eighteenth-Century Paris*. New York: Oxford University Press.

Jackson, Richard A. 1984. *A History of the French Coronation from Charles V to Charles X*. Chapel Hill: University of North Carolina Press.

Jefferson, Thomas. 1786. *Observations sur la Virginie, par M. J****. Translated by André Morellet. Paris.

Johnson, Christopher H. 1995. *The Life and Death of Industrial Languedoc, 1700–1920*. New York: Oxford University Press.

Johnson, James H. 1996. *Listening in Paris: A Cultural History*. Berkeley: University of California Press.

Jones, Colin. 1996. "The Great Chain of Buying: Medical Advertisement, the Bourgeois Public Sphere and the Origins of the French Revolution." *American Historical Review* 103: 18.

Jones, Colin, and Rebecca L. Spang. 1999. "*Sans-culottes, sans café, sans tabac*: Shifting Realms of Necessity and Luxury in Eighteenth-Century France." In *Consumers and Luxury: Consumer Culture in Europe, 1650–1850*, edited by Maxine Berg and Helen Clifford, 37–62. Manchester: Manchester University Press.

Jones, Jennifer M. 1994. "Repackaging Rousseau: Femininity and Fashion in Old Regime France." *French Historical Studies* 18 (4): 939–67.

———. 2004. *Sexing La Mode: Gender, Fashion and Commercial Culture in Old Regime France*. Oxford: Berg.

Joynes, Carrol. 1987. "The Gazette de Leyde: The Opposition Press and French Politics, 1750–1757." In *Press and Politics in Pre-revolutionary France*, edited by Jack R. Censer and Jeremy D. Popkin, 133–69. Berkeley: University of California Press.

Kaiser, Thomas E. 1991. "Money, Despotism, and Public Opinion in Early Eighteenth-Century France: John Law and the Debate on Royal Credit." *Journal of Modern History* 63 (1): 1–28.

Kaplan, Steven L. 1976. *Bread, Politics and Political Economy in the Reign of Louis XV*. 2 vols. The Hague: Martinus Nijhoff.

———. 1986. "Social Classification and Representation in the Corporate World of Eighteenth-Century France: Turgot's 'Carnival.'" In *Work in France: Representations, Meaning, Organization, and Practice*, edited by Steven Laurence Kaplan and Cynthia J. Koepp, 176–228. Ithaca, NY: Cornell University Press.

———. 1988. "Les 'faux ouvriers' et le Faubourg Saint-Antoine au XVIIIe siècle." *Annales ESC* 43: 453–58.

———. 1989. "Reflections sur la police du monde du travail, 1700–1815." *Revue historique* 261: 253–88.

———. 2001. *La fin des corporations*. Translated by Béatrice Vierne. Paris: Fayard.

Kaplow, Jeffrey. 1964. *Elbeuf during the Revolutionary Period: History and Social Structure*. Baltimore: Johns Hopkins University Press.

Kessel, Patrick. 1969. *La nuit du quatre août*. Paris: Arthaud.

Kiener, Michel C., and Jean-Claude Peyronnet. 1979. *Quand Turgot régnait en limousin: Un tremplin vers le pouvoir*. Paris: Fayard.

Klein, Naomi. 2000. *No Logo: Taking Aim at the Brand Bullies*. New York: Picador.

Koselleck, Reinhart. 2002. "The Eighteenth Century as the Beginning of Modernity." In *The Practice of History: Timing History, Spacing Concepts*, translated by Todd Samuel Presner, Kerstin Behnke, and Jobs Welge, foreword by Hayden White, 154–69. Stanford: Stanford University Press.

Kriedte, Peter, Hans Medick, and Jürgen Schlumbohm. 1981. *Industrialization before Industrialization: Rural Industry in the Genesis of Capitalism*. Translated by Beate Schempp. Cambridge: Cambridge University Press.

Krukeberg, Robert. 2014. "The Royal Lottery and the Old Regime: Financial Innovation and Modern Political Culture." *French Historical Studies* 37 (1): 25–52.

Kwass, Michael. 2000. *Privilege and the Politics of Taxation in Eighteenth-Century France: Liberté, Égalité, Fiscalité*. Cambridge: Cambridge University Press.

———. 2003. "Ordering the World of Goods: Consumer Revolution and the Classification of Objects in Eighteenth-Century France." *Representations* 82: 87–116.

———. 2004. "Consumption and the World of Ideas: Consumer Revolution and the Moral Economy of the Marquis de Mirabeau." *Eighteenth-Century Studies* 37 (2): 187–213.

———. 2006. "Big Hair: A Wig History of Consumption in Eighteenth-Century France." *American Historical Review* 111: 631–59.

———. 2014. *Contraband: Louis Mandrin and the Making of a Global Underground*. Cambridge, MA: Harvard University Press.

La Bruyère, Jean de. (1687) 1916. *Les caractères*. Paris: Henri Didier.

Larrère, Catherine. 1992. *L'invention de l'économie au XVIIIe siècle: Du droit naturel à la physiocratie*. Paris: Presses Universitaires de France.

Lears, Jackson T. 1994. *Fables of Abundance: A Cultural History of Advertising in America*. New York: Basic Books.

Le Blanc, Jean-Baptiste, abbé. 1754. *Discours politiques de M. Hume, traduits de l'anglois*. Amsterdam.

Lefebvre, Georges. 1924. *Les paysans du Nord pendant la Révolution française*. Paris: F. Rieder.

———. 1939. *Quatre-vingt-neuf*. Paris: Maison du livre française.

———. 1947. *The Coming of the French Revolution*. Translated by R. R. Palmer. Princeton, NJ: Princeton University Press.

———. 1962. *The French Revolution*. Vol. 1, *From Its Origins to 1793*. Translated by Elizabeth Moss Evanson. New York: Columbia University Press.

———. 1964. *The French Revolution*. Vol. 2, *From 1793 to 1799*. Translated by John Hall Stewart and James Friguglietti. New York: Columbia University Press.

———. 1973. *The Great Fear of 1789: Rural Panic in Revolutionary France*. Translated by Joan White. Introduction by George Rudé. New York: Vintage.

Lemaire, C. (1698) 1985. *Paris ancien et nouveau*. Vol. 2. Paris.

Le Mercier de la Rivière, Pierre-Paul. 1767. *L'ordre naturel et essentiel des sociétés politiques*. London.

———. 1770. *L'intéret general de l'État, ou la liberté du commerce des blés*. Amsterdam.

———. 1792. *Heureuse Nation ou gouvernement des Féliciens*. 2 vols. Paris.

Lemire, Beverly. 1991. *Fashion's Favourite: The Cotton Trade and the Consumer in Britain, 1660–1800*. Oxford: Oxford University Press.

Léon, Pierre. (1970) 1993. "L'élan industriel et commercial." In *Histoire économique et sociale de la France*, edited by Fernand Braudel and Ernest Labrousse, 499–582. Paris: Presses Universitaires de France.

Lepetit, Bernard. 1988. *Les villes dans la France moderne, 1740–1840*. Paris: Albin Michel.

Leroudier, E. 1911. "La décadence de la Fabrique lyonnaise à la fin du 18e siècle." *Revue d'Histoire de Lyon* 10: 343–61, 415–44.

Le Roy Ladurie, Emmanuel. 1966. *Les paysans de Languedoc*. 2 vols. Paris: SEVPEN.

Le Trosne, Guillaume-François. 1777. *De l'ordre social*. Paris.

———. 1788. *De l'administration provincial et de la réforme de l'impôt*. Basel.

Lever, Evelyne. 1996. *Philippe-Égalité*. Paris: Fayard.

L'Hilberderie, Antoine-Nicolas Joubert de. 1774. *Le dessinateur pour les fabriques d'étoffes d'or, d'argent et de soie*. Paris.

Lilti, Antoine. 2005. *Le monde des salons: Sociabilité et mondainité à Paris au XVIIIe siècle*. Paris: Fayard.

———. 2017. *The Invention of Celebrity*. Cambridge, UK: Polity.

Liu, Tessie P. 1994. *The Weaver's Knot: The Contradictions of Class Struggle and Family Solidarity in Western France, 1750–1914*. Ithaca, NY: Cornell University Press.

Loyseau, Charles. 1608. *Traicté des seigneuries*. Paris.

———. 1610a. *Cinq livres du droit des offices*. Paris.

———. 1610b. *Traité des ordres et simples dignitez*. Paris.

———. 1987. "A Treatise on Orders." In *Readings in Western Civilization*, edited by John W. Boyer and Julius Kirshner. Vol. 7, edited by Keith Michael Baker, 13–31. Chicago: University of Chicago Press.

———. 1994. *A Treatise of Orders and Plain Dignities*. Edited by Howell A. Lloyd. Cambridge: Cambridge University Press.

Lüthy, Herbert. 1961. *La banque protestante en France de la révocation de l'Édit de Nantes à la Révolution*. Vol. 2, *De la banque aux finances (1730–1794)*. Paris: SEVPEN.

MacKendrick, Neil, John Brewer, and J. H. Plum. 1982. *The Birth of a Consumer Society: The Commercialization of Eighteenth-Century England*. London: Hutchinson.

Malesherbes, Chrétien-Guillaume de Lamoignon de. 1775. *Discours prononcé dans l'Académie française le 16 février 1775*. Paris.

———. 1979. *Mémoires sur la librairie et sur la liberté de la presse*. Introduction and notes by Graham E Rodmell. Chapel Hill: University of North Carolina Press.

Marczewski, Jean. 1961. "Some Aspects of the Economic Growth of France, 1660–1958." *Economic Development and Cultural Change* 9 (2): 369–86.

Margadant, Ted W. 1992. *Urban Rivalries in the French Revolution*. Princeton: Princeton University Press.

Margairaz, Dominique. 1988. *Foires et marchés dans la France préindustrielle*. Paris: EHESS.

Marion, Marcel. 1919. *Histoire financière de la France depuis 1715*. Vol. 1, *1715–1789*. Paris.

Markoff, John. 1996. *The Abolition of Feudalism: Peasants, Lords, and Legislators in the French Revolution.* University Park: Pennsylvania State University Press.

Markovich, Tihomir J. 1976a. "La croissance industrielle sous l'Ancien Régime." *Annales: ESC* 31 (3): 369–86.

———. 1976b. *Histoire des industries française.* Vol. 1, *Les industries lainières de Colbert à la Révolution.* Geneva: Droz.

Marmontel, Jean-François. 1992. *Mémoires.* Edited and introduction by Jean-Pierre Guicciardi and Gilles Thierriat. Paris: Mercure de France.

Marx, Karl. (1867) 1977. *Capital: A Critique of Political Economy.* Translated by Ben Fowkes, and introduction by Ernest Mandel. Vol. 1. New York: Vintage.

———. 1978. "Economic and Philosophical Manuscripts of 1844." In *The Marx-Engels Reader,* edited by Robert C. Tucker, 66–132. 2nd ed. New York: W. W. Norton.

———. 1993. *Gründrisse: Foundations of the Critique of Political Economy (Rough Draft).* Translated with a foreword by Martin Nicolaus. London: Penguin.

Mathias, Peter, and Patrick O'Brien. 1976. "Taxation in Britain and France, 1715–1810: A Comparison of the Social and Economic Incidence of Taxes Collected for the Central Governments." *European Journal of Economic History* 5 (3): 601–50.

Maza, Sarah. 1993. *Private Lives and Public Affairs: The Causes Célèbres of Prerevolutionary France.* Berkeley: University of California Press.

———. 2003. *The Myth of the French Bourgeoisie: An Essay on the Social Imaginary, 1750–1850.* Cambridge, MA: Harvard University Press.

Mendels, Franklin. 1972. "Proto-industrialization: The First Phase of the Industrialization Process." *Journal of Economic History* 32 (1): 241–61.

Mercier, Louis-Sebastien. 1994. *Tableau de Paris.* Vol. 2, edited by Jean-Claude Bonnet. Paris: Mercure de France.

Meyssonnier, Simone. 1989. *La balance et l'horloge: La genèse de la pensée liberale en France au XVIIIe siècle.* Paris: Les Editions de la Passion.

Miller, Lesley Ellis. 1998. "Paris-Lyon-Paris: Dialogue in the Design and Distribution of Patterned Silks in the 18th Century." In *Luxury Trades and Consumerism in Ancien Régime Paris: Studies in the History of the Skilled Workforce,* edited by Robert Fox and Anthony Turner, 139–67. Aldershot, UK: Ashgate.

Minard, Philippe. 1998. *La fortune du colbertisme: État et industrie dans la France des Lumières.* Paris: Fayard.

Mintz, Sidney W. 1985. *Sweetness and Power: The Place of Sugar in Modern History.* New York: Penguin.

Montesquieu, Charles de Secondat, baron de. 1749. *De l'esprit des lois.* Amsterdam.

Moore, Jason W. 2010a. "'Amsterdam Is Standing on Norway' Part I: The Alchemy of Capital, Empire and Nature in the Diaspora of Silver, 1545–1648." *Journal of Agrarian Change* 10 (1): 33–68.

———. 2010b. "'Amsterdam Is Standing on Norway' Part II: The Global North Atlantic in the Ecological Revolution of the Long Seventeenth Century." *Journal of Agrarian Change* 10 (2): 188–227.

Morellet, André, abbé. 1758. *Réflexions sur les advantages de la libre fabrication et de l'usage des toiles peintes en France.* Geneva.

———. 1769a. *Examen de la réponse de M. N** [Necker] au mémoire de M l'abbé Morellet, sur la Compagnie des Indes.* Paris.

———. 1769b. *Mémoire sur la situation actuelle de la Compagnie des Indes.* Paris.

———. 1769c. *Prospectus d'un nouveau dictionnaire de commerce.* Paris.

———. 1774. *Refutation de l'ouvrage qui a pour titre Dialogues sur le commerce des bleds.* London.

———. 1775a. *Analyse de l'ouvrage intitulé De la legislation et du commerce des grains.* Amsterdam.

———. 1775b. *Réflexions sur les avantages de la liberté d'écrire et d'imprimer sur les matières de l'administration.* London.

———. 1775c. *Théorie du paradox.* Amsterdam.

———. 1777. *Portrait de Mme Geoffrin.* Amsterdam.

———. 1787. *Mémoires relatifs à la discussion du privilege de la Nouvelle Compagnie des Indes.* Amsterdam.

———. 2010. *Mémoires de l'abbé Morellet de l'Académie française, sur le dix-huitième siècle et sur la Révolution.* Introduction and notes by Jean-Pierre Guicciardi. Paris: Mercure de France.

Morinau, Michel. 1970. *Les faux-semblants d'un démarrage économique: Agriculture et démographie en France au XVIIIe siècle.* Paris: Armand Colin.

Mousnier, Roland. 1971. *La vénalité des offices sous Henri IV et Louis XIII.* 2nd ed. Paris: Presses Universitaires de France.

———. 1980. *Les institutions de la France sous la monarchie absolue, 1598–1789.* Vol. 2, *Les organes de l'État et la société.* Paris: Presses Universitaires de France.

Murphy, Antoine E. 1997. *John Law: Economic Theorist and Policy Maker.* Oxford.

Necker, Jacques. 1773. *Éloge de J.-B. Colbert, discours qui a remporté le prix de l'Académie française en 1773.* Paris.

———. 1775. *Sur la legislation et le commerce des grains.* 2 vols. Paris.

———. 1781. *Compte rendu au roi.* Paris.

———. 1785. *De l'administration des finances de la France.* 3 vols. Lausanne.

———. n.d. *Sur l'administration de M. Necker par un citoyen français.* n.p.

Nemeitz, Joachim-Christophe. 1727. *Séjour de Paris, c'est à dire, instructions fidèles, pour les voyageurs de condition.* Leiden.

Nougaret, Pierre-Jean-Baptiste. 1773. *Almanach forain ou les Différens spectacles des boulevards et des foires de Paris.* Paris.

Oberkirch, Henriette-Louise d'. 1970. *Mémoires de Madame d'Oberkirch sur le cour de Louis XVI et de la société française avant 1789.* Edited and introduction by Suzanne Burkard. Paris: Mercure de France.

O'Heguerty, Pierre-André. 1757. *Remarques sur plusieurs branches de commerce de navigation.* n.p.

Olivier-Martin, François. 1938. *L'organisation corporative de la France d'ancien régime.* Paris: Sirey.

Orain, Arnaud. 2013. "*Le Journal Oeconomique,* le cercle de Gournay et le pouvoir monarchique: Quelques preuves matérielles d'un lien organique." *Dix-Huitième Siècle* 45: 565–83.

Ozouf, Mona. 1976. *La fête révolutionnaire, 1789–1799.* Paris: Gallimard.

———. 1987. "Public Opinion." In *The French Revolution and the Creation of Modern Political Culture.* Vol. 1, *The Political Culture of the Old Regime,* edited by Keith Michael Baker, 419–34. Oxford: Pergamon.

———. 1988. *Festivals and the French Revolution.* Translated by Alan Sheridan. Cambridge, MA: Harvard University Press.

———. 1989. *L'homme régénéré: Essais sur la Révolution française.* Paris: Gallimard.

Pardailhé-Galabrun, Annik. 1991. *The Birth of Intimacy: Private and Domestic Life in Early Modern Paris*. Translated by Jocelyn Phelps. Philadelphia: University of Pennsylvania Press.

Parker, Geoffrey. 1988. *The Military Revolution: Military Innovation and the Rise of the West, 1500–1800*. Cambridge: Cambridge University Press.

Pascal, Blaise. 1760. *Pensées de M. Pascal sur la religion et sur quelques autres sujets, qui ont esté trouvés aprés sa mort parmy ses papiers*. Paris.

Pearson, Roger. 2005. *Voltaire Almighty*. New York: Bloomsbury.

Perrot, Jean-Claude. 1975. *Genèse d'une ville moderne: Caen au XVIIIe siècle*. Paris: Mouton.

———. 1991. *Une histoire intellectuelle de l'économie politique, XVIIe et XVIIIe siècles*. Paris: Editions de l'École des Hautes Études en Sciences Sociales.

Petot, Jean. 1958. *Histoire de l'administration des ponts et chaussées, 1599–1815*. Paris: Marcel Rivière.

Peyssonnel, Charles de. 2007. *Petite chronique du ridicule*. Edited and annotated by Mario Pasa. Paris: Payot.

Picon, Antoine. 1992. *L'Invention de l'ingénieur moderne: L'École des Ponts et Chaussées, 1747–1851*. Paris: Presses de l'École National des Ponts et Chaussées.

Pinto, Isaac de. 1771. *Traité de la circulation du credit*. Amsterdam.

Plumard de Danguel, Louis Joseph. 1754. *Remarques sur les avantages et desavantages de la France et de la Grande Bretange et autres sources de la puissance des États. Traduis de l'anglois du chevalier John Nickolls*. Leyden.

Poirier, Jean-Pierre. 1999. *Turgot: Laissez-faire et progrès social*. Paris: Librairie Académique Perrin.

Pomeau, René. 1985. *D'Arouet à Voltaire: 1694–1734*. Vol. 1 of *Voltaire en son temps*. 5 vols., edited by René Pomeau. Oxford: Voltaire Foundation.

Poni, Carlo. 1997. "Fashion as Flexible Production: The Strategies of the Lyon Silk Merchants in the Eighteenth Century." In *World of Possibilities: Flexibility and Mass Production in Western Industrialization*, edited by Charles F. Sabel and Jonathan Zeitlin. Cambridge: Cambridge University Press.

Popkin, Jeremy D. 1987. "The *Gazette de Leyde* and French Politics under Louis XVI." In *Press and Politics in Pre-revolutionary France*, edited by Jack R. Censer and Jeremy D. Popkin, 75–132. Berkeley: University of California Press.

Postone, Moishe. 1993. *Time, Labor, and Social Domination: A Reinterpretation of Marx's Critical Theory*. Cambridge: Cambridge University Press.

Potter, Mark. 2000. "Good Offices: Intermediation by Corporate Bodies in Early Modern French Public Finance." *Journal of Economic History* 60 (3): 599–626.

Pounds, Norman J. G. 1979. *An Historical Geography of Europe*. Cambridge: Cambridge University Press.

Prévost de Saint-Lucien, Roch-Henri. 1787. *Le provincial à Paris, ou état actuel de Paris*. Vol. 3, *Le Marais*. Paris: Watin.

Proust, Jacques. (1962) 1995. *Diderot et l'Encyclopédie*. Paris: Albin Michel.

Quéniart, Jean. 1978. *Culture et société urbaine dans la France de l'Ouest au XVIIIe Siècle*. Paris: Librairie C. Klincksieck.

Ramsay, Clay. 1992. *The Ideology of the Great Fear: Rural Panic in Revolutionary France*. Baltimore: Johns Hopkins University Press.

Ravel, Jeffrey S. 1999. *The Contested Parterre: Public Theater and French Political Culture, 1680–1791*. Ithaca, NY: Cornell University Press.

Raynal, Guillaume-Thomas-François, abbé. 1780. *Histoire philosophique et politique des établissemens et du commerce des Européens dans les deux Indes.* 3rd ed. Geneva.

Reddy, William M. 1984. *The Rise of Market Culture: The Textile Trade and French Society, 1750–1900.* Cambridge: Cambridge University Press.

Remonstrances du parlement de Rouen au sujet de l'édit du mois du février dernier, &de la declaration du 3 du même mois. 1760.

Rigogne, Thierry. 2013. "Entre histoire et mythes: Le premier siècle des cafés à Paris (1660–1789)." In *Les histoires de Paris (XVIe-XVIIIe siècle),* edited by Thierry Belleguic and Laurent Turcot, 161–80. Vol. 2. Paris: Hermann.

———. 2018. "Readers and Reading in Cafés, 1660–1800." *French Historical Studies* 41 (3): 473–94.

Riquetti, Victor, Marquis de Mirabeau. 1759–60. *L'ami des hommes.* 7 vols. Paris.

———. 1763. *Philosophie rurale ou économie générale de l'agriculture.* Paris.

———. 1769. *Leçons économiques.* Amsterdam.

———. 1776. *Lettres sur la législation ou l'ordre dépravé rétablit et perpétué.* Bern.

Robinson, E. 1963. "Eighteenth-Century Commerce and Fashion: Mathew Boulton's Marketing Techniques." *Economic History Review* 16 (1): 39–60.

Roche, Daniel. 1994. *The Culture of Clothing: Dress and Fashion in the "Ancien Régime."* Translated by Jean Birrell. Cambridge: Cambridge University Press.

———. 2000. *A History of Everyday Things: The Birth of Consumption in France.* Translated by Brian Pierce. Cambridge: Cambridge University Press.

Roland de la Platière, Jean-Marie. 1785. *Encyclopédie méthodique.* Vol. 1, *Manufactures, arts et métiers.* Paris: Panckoucke.

Rosenband, Leonard N. 2000. *Papermaking in Eighteenth-Century France: Management, Labor, and Revolution at the Montgolfier Mill, 1761–1805.* Baltimore: Johns Hopkins University Press.

Rosny, Antoine-Joseph-Nicolas. 1801. *Le Péruvien à Paris.* Paris: Huguin.

Rougemont, Martine de. 1988. *La vie théâtrale en France au XVIIIe siècle.* Paris: Champion.

Rousseau, Jean-Jacques. 1751. *Discours qui a remporté le prix à l'académie de Dijon. En l'an 1750. Sur cette Question proposée par la même Académie: "Si le rétablissement des Sciences et des Arts a contribué à épurer les Moeurs." Par un Citoyen de Genève.* Geneva.

———. 1755. *Discours sur l'origine et les fondements de l'inégalité parmi les hommes.* Amsterdam.

———. 1959–69. *Oeuvres completes.* 4 vols., edited by Bernard Gagnebin and Marcel Ramond. Paris: Gallimard, Librairie de la Pléiade.

———. 1960. *Politics and the Arts: Letter to d'Alembert on the Theater.* Translated and edited by Allan Bloom. Ithaca, NY: Cornell University Press.

———. 1973. *Les confessions.* Preface by J.-B. Pontalis. Edited by Bernard Gagnebin and Marcel Raymond. Notes by Catherine Koenig. Paris: Gallimard.

———. 1979. *Emile, or On Education.* Translated with an introduction and notes by Allan Bloom. New York: Basic Books.

Rude, Fernand. 1944. *Le mouvement ouvrier à Lyon de 1827 à 1832.* Paris: Domat Montchrestien.

Sainte-Foy, Philippe-Auguste de, chevalier d'Arcq. 1756. *La noblesse militaire, opposé à la noblesse commerçante, ou, Le patriote François.* Amsterdam.

Saint-Jacob, Pierre de. 1960. *Les paysans de la Bourgogne du Nord au dernier siècle de l'Ancien Régime.* Paris: Les Belles Lettres.

Saint Léon, Étienne Martin. 1909. *Histoire des corporations de métiers, depuis leurs origins jusqu'à leur suppression en 1791*. Paris.

Sargentson, Carolyn. 1996. *Merchants and Luxury Markets: The Marchands Merciers of Eighteenth-Century Paris*. London: Victoria and Albert Museum.

———. 1998. "The Manufacture and Marketing of Luxury Goods: The Marchands Merciers of Late 17th and 18th-Century Paris." In *Luxury Trades and Consumerism in Ancien Régime Paris: Studies in the History of the Skilled Workforce*, edited by Robert Fox and Anthony Turner, 99–137. Aldershot, UK: Ashgate.

Schelle, Gustave. 1897. *Vincent de Gournay: Laissez faire, laissez passer*. Paris: Guillaumin.

———, ed. 1913–23. *Oeuvres de Turgot et documents le concernant, avec biographie et notes*. 5 vols. Paris: Librairie Felix Alcan.

Schumpeter, Joseph A. (1954) 1994. *History of Economic Analysis*. Edited from manuscript by Elizabeth Boody Schumpeter. Introduction by Mark Perlman. London: Routledge.

Sewell, William H., Jr. 1974. "État, Corps, and Ordre: Some Notes on the Social Vocabulary of the French Old Regime." In *Sozialgeschichte Heute: Festschrift für Hans Rosenberg zum 70. Geburtstag*, edited by Hans-Ulrich Wehler, 49–68. Göttigen: Vandenhoeck & Ruprecht.

———. 1980. *Work and Revolution in France: The Language of Labor from the Old Regime to 1848*. Cambridge: Cambridge University Press.

———. 1994. *A Rhetoric of Bourgeois Revolution: The Abbé Sieyès and "What Is the Third Estate?"* Durham, NC: Duke University Press.

———. 1996. "Historical Events as Transformations of Structures: Inventing Revolution at the Bastille." *Theory and Society* 25: 841–81.

———. 2004. "The French Revolution and the Emergence of the Nation Form." In *Revolutionary Currents: Transatlantic Ideology and Nationbuilding*, edited by Michael Morrison and Melinda Zook, 91–125. Lanham, MD: Rowman and Littlefield.

———. 2008. "The Temporalities of Capitalism." *Socio-economic Review* 6: 517–37.

———. 2010. "The Empire of Fashion and the Rise of Capitalism in Eighteenth-Century France." *Past and Present* 206: 83–120.

———. 2014a. "The Capitalist Epoch." *Social Science History* 38 (1): 1–11.

———. 2014b. "Connecting Capitalism to the French Revolution: The Parisian Promenade and the Origins of Civic Equality in Eighteenth-Century France." *Critical Historical Studies* 1 (1): 5–46.

Sgard, Jean. 1983. *La Presse provincial au XVIIIe siècle*. Grenoble: Centre de Recherches sur les Sensibilités, Université des Langues et Lettres de Grenoble.

Shovlin, John. 2006. *The Political Economy of Virtue: Luxury, Patriotism, and the Origins of the French Revolution*. Ithaca, NY: Cornell University Press.

———. 2016. "John Law's System and Geopolitics." *Journal of Modern History* 88 (2): 275–305.

Sieyès, Emmanuel-Joseph. 1788a. *Essai sur les privilèges*. n.p.

———. 1788b. *Vues sur les moyens d'exécution dont les représentants de la France pourront disposer en 1789*. n.p.

———. 1789. *Qu-est ce que le Thiers État?* n.p.

———. 1795. *Notice sur la vie de Sieyes: Membre de la première Assemblée Nationale et de la Convention*. Paris.

———. 1970. *Qu-est ce que le Thiers État?* Critical edition with notes and introduction by Roberto Zapperi. Geneva: Librairie Droz.

———. 1985. *Écrits politiques.* Edited by Roberto Zapperi. Paris: Edition des Archives Contemporaines.

Skocpol, Theda. 1979. *States and Social Revolutions: A Comparative Analysis of France, Russia, and China.* Cambridge: Cambridge University Press.

Smedley-Weil, Anette. 1995. *Les intendants de Louis XIV.* Paris: Fayard.

Smith, Jay. 2005. *Nobility Reimagined: The Patriotic Nation in Eighteenth-Century France.* Ithaca, NY: Cornell University Press.

Soboul, Albert. 1959. *Les Sans-culottes parisien en l'an II: Mouvement populaire et gouvernement révolutionnaire, 2 juin 1793–8 thermidor an II.* Paris: Librairie Clavreuil.

———. 1975. *The French Revolution, 1787–1799: From the Storming of the Bastille to Napoleon.* Translated by Alan Forrest and Colin Jones. New York: Vintage.

Soll, Jacob. 2009. *The Information Master: Jean-Baptiste Colbert's Secret State Intelligence System.* Ann Arbor: University of Michigan Press.

Sonenscher, Michael. 1989. *Work and Wages: Natural Law, Politics, and the Eighteenth-Century French Trades.* Cambridge: Cambridge University Press.

Spang, Rebecca L. 2000. *The Invention of the Restaurant: Paris and Modern Gastronomic Culture.* Cambridge, MA: Harvard University Press.

Starobinski, Jean. 1971. *La transparence et l'obstacle.* Paris: Gallimard.

———. 1988. *Transparency and Obstruction.* Translated by Arthur Goldhammer with an introduction by Robert Morrissy. Chicago: University of Chicago Press.

Stone, Bailey. 1986. *The French Parlements and the Crisis of the Old Regime.* Chapel Hill: University of North Carolina Press.

Styles, John. 2007. *The Dress of the People: Everyday Fashion in Eighteenth-Century England.* New Haven: Yale University Press.

Swann, Julian. 1995. *Politics and the Parlement of Paris under Louis XV.* New York: Cambridge University Press.

———. 2003. *Provincial Power and Absolute Monarchy: The Estates General of Burgundy, 1661–1790.* Cambridge: Cambridge University Press.

Tackett, Timothy. 1986. *Religion, Revolution, and Regional Culture in Eighteenth-Century France: The Ecclesiastical Oath of 1791.* Princeton, NJ: Princeton University Press.

———. 1996. *Becoming a Revolutionary: The Deputies of the French National Assembly and the Emergence of a Revolutionary Political Culture (1789–1790).* Princeton, NJ: Princeton University Press.

———. 2003. *When the King Took Flight.* Cambridge, MA: Harvard University Press.

———. 2015. *The Coming of the Terror in the French Revolution.* Cambridge, MA: Harvard University Press.

Terrier, Didier. 1996. *Les Deux ages de la proto-industrie: Les tisserands du Cambrésis et du Saint-Quentinois, 1730–1880.* Paris: EHESS.

Thé, café ou chocolat? Les boissons exotiques à Paris: Musée Cognacq-Jay, 27 mai-27 septembre 2015. 2015. Paris: Paris-Musées.

The Case of the Silk-Weavers, Humbly Offered to the Consideration of Both Houses of Parliament. 1713. London.

Thiéry, Luc-Vincent. 1784–87. *Almanach du voyageur à Paris.* Paris: Hardouin.

Thompson, J. K. J. 1982. *Clermont-de Lodève, 1633–1789: Fluctuations in the Prosperity of a Languedocian Cloth-Making Town.* Cambridge: Cambridge University Press.

Thornton, Peter. 1965. *Baroque and Rococo Silks*. New York: Taplinger.

Tilly, Charles. 1964. *The Vendée*. Cambridge, MA: Harvard University Press.

———. 1990. *Coercion, Capital, and European States, AD 990–1990*. Cambridge, MA: Basil Blackwell.

Tocqueville, Alexis de. (1856) 2004. *L'ancien régime et la Révolution*. In *Oeuvres*, introduction by François Furet and Françoise Mélonio, edited by Françoise Mélonio. Vol. 3. Paris: Librairie de la Pléiade, Gallimard.

———. 1998. *The Old Regime and the Revolution*. Edited with an introduction by François Furet and Françoise Mélonio. Translated by Alan S. Kahan. Chicago: University of Chicago Press.

———. 2011. *The Ancien Régime and the French Revolution*. Edited by Jon Elster. Translated by Arthur Goldhammer. Cambridge: Cambridge University Press.

Toutain, Jean-Claude. 1961. "Le produit de l'agriculture française de 1700 à 1958: La croissance." *Économies et Sociétés. Cahiers de l'ISEA* 115: 1–283.

———. 1987. "Le produit intérieur brut de la France de 1789 à 1982." *Économies et Sociétés. Cahiers de l'ISEA*, no. suppl. 115: 1–129.

Trésaguet, Pierre-Marie-Jérôme. 1775. *Mémoire sur la construction et l'entretien des chemins fait en rachat de corvée dans la généralité de Limoges*. Paris.

Truant, Cynthia. 1996. "La maîtrise d'une identité? Corporations féminines à Paris aux XVIIe et XVIIIe siècle." *Clio, Histoire, Femmes et Société* 3: 55–69.

Tsuda, Takumi. 1983. *Traités sur le commerce de Child avec les Remarques de Vincent de Gournay. Economic Research Series*. Tokyo: Hitosubashi University, Kinokuniya.

Tucker, Josiah. 1755. *Questions importantes sur le commerce*. Translated by Anne-Robert-Jacques Turgot. London.

Tulchin, Allan A. 2019. "Weekly Enlightenment: The *Affiches de Bordeaux*, 1758–1765." *French Historical Studies* 42 (2): 175–202.

Turcot, Laurent. 2007. *Le promeneur à Paris au XVIIIe siècle*. Preface by Arlette Farge. Paris: Gallimard.

Turgot, Anne-Robert-Jacques. 1788. *Réflexions sur la formation et la distribution des richesses*. n.p.

———. 1808. "Éloge de M. de Gournay." In *Oeuvres de Mr. Turgot, ministre d'État, précédé et accompagnées de mémoires et de notes sur sa vie, son administration et ses ouvrages*, edited with notes by Samuel Dupont de Nemours. Vol. 3, 321–75. Paris: Delance.

Turnovsky, Geoffrey. 2010. *The Literary Market: Authorship and Modernity in the Old Regime*. Philadelphia: University of Pennsylvania Press.

Vaillot, René. 1988. *Avec Madame Du Chatelet: 1734–1749*. Vol. 2 of *Voltaire et son temps*. 5 vols., edited by René Pomeau. Oxford: Voltaire Foundation.

Van Kley, Dale. 1975. *The Jansenists and the Expulsion of the Jesuits from France, 1757–1765*. New Haven: Yale University Press.

Vardi, Liana. 2012. *The Physiocrats and the World of the Enlightenment*. New York: Cambridge University Press.

Voltaire. 1733. *Letters Concerning the English Nation*. London.

———. 1734. *Lettres philosophiques*. Amsterdam.

———. 1738. *Éléments de Newton donné par M de Voltaire*. Amsterdam.

———. 1764. *Dictionnaire philosophique portative*. London.

———. 1907. *Philosophical Letters or, Letters Regarding the English Nation*. Edited by John Leigh. Translated by Prudence L. Steiner. Indianapolis: Hackett.

Weber, Caroline. 2006. *Queen of Fashion: What Marie Antoinette Wore to the Revolution.* New York: H. Holt.

Weir, David R. 1991. "Les crises économiques et les origines de la Révolution française." *Annales: ESC* 46 (4): 917–47.

Weulersse, Georges. 1910. *Le movement physiocratique en France (de 1756 à 1770).* 2 vols. Paris.

———. 1950. *La physiocratie sous les ministères de Turgot et de Necker.* Paris.

———. 1959. *La physiocratie à la fin du règne de Louis XV.* Paris.

———. 1985. *Le physiocratie à l'aube de la Révolution.* Paris.

Williams, Eric Eustace. 1994. *Capitalism and Slavery.* Chapel Hill: University of North Carolina Press.

Williams, Raymond. 1977. *Marxism and Literature.* Oxford: Oxford University Press.

Wilson, Arthur M. 1972. *Diderot.* New York: Oxford University Press.

Young, Arthur. 1792. *Travels, during the Years 1787, 1788, and 1789. Undertaken More Particularly with a View of Ascertaining the Cultivation, Wealth, Resources, and National Prosperity of the Kingdom of France.* Bury St Edmunds.

Zanon, Antonio. 1763–64. *Dell'agricoltura, dell'arti e dell commercio.* 4 vols. Venice.

Zaretsky, Robert. 2019. *Catherine and Diderot: The Empress, the Philosopher, and the Fate of the Enlightenment.* Cambridge, MA: Harvard University Press.

Zinsser, Judith. 2006. *Dame d'Esprit: A Biography of the Marquise Du Chatelet.* New York.

Zinsser, Judith, and Julie Hayes, eds. 2006. *Émilie Du Châtelet: Rewriting Enlightenment Philosophy and Science.* Oxford.

Zukin, Sharon. 1991. *Landscapes of Power: From Detroit to Disney World.* Berkeley: University of California Press.

Index

Abeille, Louis-Paul, 318, 323, 326, 328
absolutism: claims of, 151; limits of, 32–34, 236; Loyseau on, 20–21, 24; organization of, 28
abstraction: and administration, 237–38, 258–59, 305; of civic equality, 8; concrete history of, 10; in Declaration of the Rights of Man and Citizen, 8; in French Revolution according to Tocqueville, 231–32, 185; in markets, 53, 95; in political economy, 194–95, 197, 309; in public sphere, 77, 80; of social relations in capitalism, 7–8, 53–54, 69, 78, 238, 371; in thought of philosophes, 230–32, 240; in urban promenade, 146
Académie Française, 153, 162, 173, 181–82, 194, 209, 306
academies, 85, 88, 101, 270, 320, 330, 338
administration, royal: bureaucracy of, 228; careers in, 157; centralization of, 16, 28, 129, 232, 237–41, 243, 245, 251; and civic equality, 238–40, 258, 265, 331, 344; Colbert and, 253; criticism of, 129, 187, 191, 195, 199; and Enlightenment, 168; fiscal problems and, 15–16, 246, 267, 291, 306–14; fundamental ambivalence of, 236–37; limited powers of, 236; *Memoir on Municipalities* and, 303–5; Morellet and, 188, 273; Necker and, 306–14; officials of, 35, 153, 228; opposition to reform in, 293, 299–300, 312; and political economy,
13, 15, 28, 35, 196, 167–73, 286, 291; and provincial society, 261; and reform, 267–70, 294–305, 309–12, 314–31, 336; reorganization of in Revolution, 357–58; size of, 35, 250; staffed by venal officers, 266; and tax collection, 259–62; Tocqueville on, 16, 26, 228–29, 236–37, 304–5; Trudaine and, 317–28; Turgot and, 191, 294–305. *See also* intendants
agriculture: capitalism in, 8, 56–57; crops, 37–38, 46; growth of, 46, 57; labor productivity in, 45; main source of aristocracy's income, 36; in Parisian region, 46, 57; patterns of land tenure in, 36; physiocrats on, 5, 286–90; predominance of, 36; slave-based, 62; taxes on, 33, 246–48; techniques, 45–46
aides, 246, 310–11
Aiguillon, Armand, duc d', 349
almanacs, 99
Alsace, 27–28, 30, 99, 252, 315
Amelot, Michel, 315
American Revolutionary War, 2, 41, 122, 192, 253, 258, 292, 305, 307–9, 334
Amiens, 124, 279, 325
anonymity: authorial, 167, 174, 186; in cafés, 93–94; and capitalism, 8, 10, 69, 76, 86, 331; and clothing, 134; of investors, 314; in promenades, 131, 136, 146; in publics, 70–71, 73, 81, 86, 141; in restaurants, 94–95
Arbellot, Guy, 321

tobacco, 30–31, 52, 126, 246, 301, 310

Tocqueville, Alexis de: on abstractness of philosophes' ideas, 230–32; on administration's assault on political liberty, 229; on administrative centralization and Revolution's goal of equality, 16, 227–32; on despotism, 232; influence on later historians, 232–33; on intendants, 228, 235–36; limitations of his arguments, 238–40; on *Memoir on Municipalities*, 305; on philosophes, 153–54, 229–31; on similarity of nobles and bourgeois, 228, 231

tolls, 30, 246, 310, 314–17, 333, 335, 346, 365

Tolozan, Jean-François, 318, 324, 328–29

Toulouse, 35

Tourcoing, 59, 124

trades, 22

treasurers, 311

Trésaguet, Pierre-Marie-Jérôme, 320–21

Trudaine, Daniel: career of, 269, 317, 322, 328; director of Bureau of Commerce, 185, 321; director of Corps des ponts et chaussées, 272, 318–20, 327; director of inspectors of manufactures, 317, 321–26; exceptionally effective administrator, 317; Gournay's chief and disciple, 169; member of Gournay circle, 185, 272, 317, 326; as patron of Morellet, 186–89; as reformer, 186, 317, 321–26

Trudaine de Montigny, Philibert: ambivalent about Turgot's reform of the corvée, 318; director of inspectors of manufactures, 324, 326; member of Gournay circle, 272; patron of Morellet, 186–91; succeeded Daniel Trudaine as director of Bureau of Commerce, 186, 272

Turgot, Anne Robert Jacques: abolition of guilds by, 60–61, 293–98, 329; contributions to *Encyclopédie*, 169, 171; critique of privileges by, 301–2; economic writings of, 285; éloge of Gournay, 269–70, 272; embrace of so-cial contract theory, 301; freeing the grain trade, 293; friend and patron of Morellet, 183, 185, 188, 190–92; influenced by Quesnay, 286, 290; intendant in Limoges, 234–35, 298; invocation of equality by, 266; invocation of natural rights by, 193–95; member of Gournay circle, 185, 189; and *Memoir on Municipalities*, 303–5, 335; overturning of reforms of, 305, 313; reform ministry of, 16–17, 178, 196, 268, 291–305; reform of corvée, 234–35, 293, 298–302, 318, 329, 333; reorganization of coach services by, 321; service under Trudaine and Gournay, 269; at Sorbonne, 182; suppression of financial offices by, 311; verifications of tax assessments during ministry of, 265

Valenciennes, 125

venality of office. *See* office: sale of

Vendée, 36, 37

Versailles: as center of fashion, 103, 107–8, 116, 127, 133–34, 135; court of, 84, 133, 260, 328; nobles and, 29, 92; royal palace, 29, 356; as seat of administration, 34, 133–34, 247, 311; as site of Estates General, 344, 347–48

vile persons, 25

villages, 37

vineyards, 38

vingtième (tax), 257–62, 264–65, 298, 307, 310–11, 334, 336–37

Voltaire (François-Marie Arouet): attacks on despotism, 163; as author of censored books, 84; becomes philosophe, 160; career of, 15, 157–64; on commerce, 160; corresponds with royals, 153; death of, 164; and epistemology, 152, 161; exiled from Paris, 161–64; exile in England of, 159–60; in Ferney, 163; in Geneva, 162; great wealth of, 159; impossible example of, 158; imprisonment in Bastille, 158, 159; influence on philosophes, 158; as letter-writer, 74; as playwright, 88, 159–60; in Prussia, 162–63